WRITTEN IN KATAKANA, IT COMES OUT AS "VIRTUAL MEIJI" LIKE A 3-D FIGHTING GAME. HOW COOL IS THAT?!
SOUNDS MORE "RANT" THAN "RAVE," TO ME. BUT, WHATEVER.

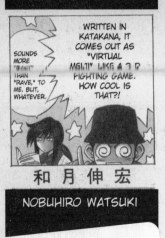

和月伸宏

NOBUHIRO WATSUKI

VIRTUAL MEIJI

WRITTEN WITH THE CHARACTER FOR "IMAGINATIVE," VIRTUAL MEIJI IN *KANJI* IS "KASŌ MEIJI"–A PHRASE FOUND IN A REVIEW OF "RUROKEN" I HAPPENED TO COME ACROSS IN A BOOKSTORE. "WHAT A GREAT TURN OF PHRASE!" I THOUGHT, IMPRESSED, AND THUS WAS FREED OF AT LEAST ONE CONCERN. A MANGA SERIES THAT DOESN'T HIT READERS OVER THE HEADS WITH MEIJI HISTORY, BUT ONE THAT'S HIGHLY ENJOYABLE... THAT ALLOWS ITS FANS TO LIVE A LITTLE OF THE MEIJI ERA EVERY TIME THEY READ IT... *THAT* IS "RUROUNI KENSHIN."

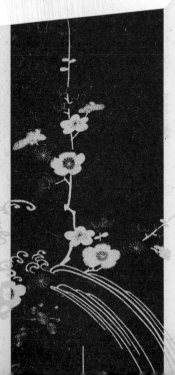

Rurouni Kenshin, which has found fans not only in Japan but around the world, first made its appearance in 1992, as an original short story in ***Weekly Shonen Jump Special***. Later rewritten and published as a regular, continuing ***Jump*** series in 1994, ***Rurouni Kenshin*** ended serialization in 1999 but continued in popularity, as evidenced by the 2000 publication of ***Yahiko no Sakabatô*** ("Yahiko's Reversed-Edge Sword") in ***Weekly Shonen Jump***. His most current work, ***Busô Renkin*** ("Armored Alchemist"), began publication in June 2003, also in ***Jump***.

RUROUNI KENSHIN
VOL. 10: MITSURUGI, MASTER AND STUDENT
The SHONEN JUMP Graphic Novel Edition

STORY AND ART BY
NOBUHIRO WATSUKI

English Adaptation/Gerard Jones
Translation/Kenichiro Yagi
Touch-Up Art & Lettering/Steve Dutro
Cover, Graphics & Layout/Sean Lee
Editor/Avery Gotoh

Supervising Editor/Kit Fox
Managing Editor/Elizabeth Kawasaki
Director of Production/Noboru Watanabe
Editorial Director/Alvin Lu
Executive Vice President & Editor in Chief/Hyoe Narita
Sr. Director of Licensing & Acquisitions/Rika Inouye
Vice President of Sales & Marketing/Liza Coppola
Vice President of Strategic Development/Yumi Hoashi
Publisher/Seiji Horibuchi

Printed in the U.S.A.

Published by VIZ, LLC
P.O. Box 77010
San Francisco, CA 94107

SHONEN JUMP Graphic Novel Edition
10 9 8 7 6 5 4 3 2 1
First printing, December 2004

www.viz.com

THE WORLD'S
MOST POPULAR MANGA

SHONEN JUMP
GRAPHIC NOVEL
www.shonenjump.com

SHONEN JUMP GRAPHIC NOVEL

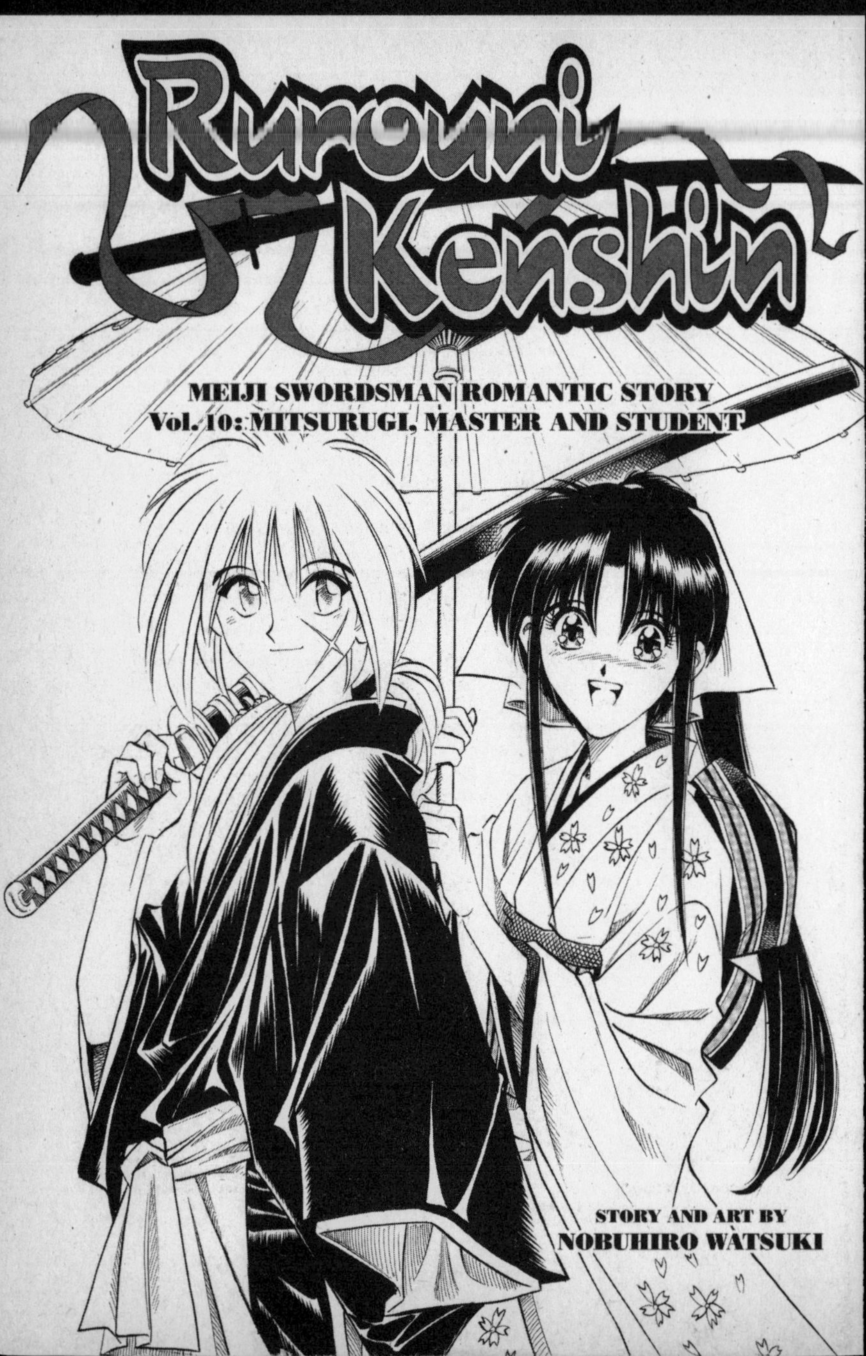
Rurouni Kenshin
MEIJI SWORDSMAN ROMANTIC STORY
Vol. 10: MITSURUGI, MASTER AND STUDENT
STORY AND ART BY
NOBUHIRO WATSUKI

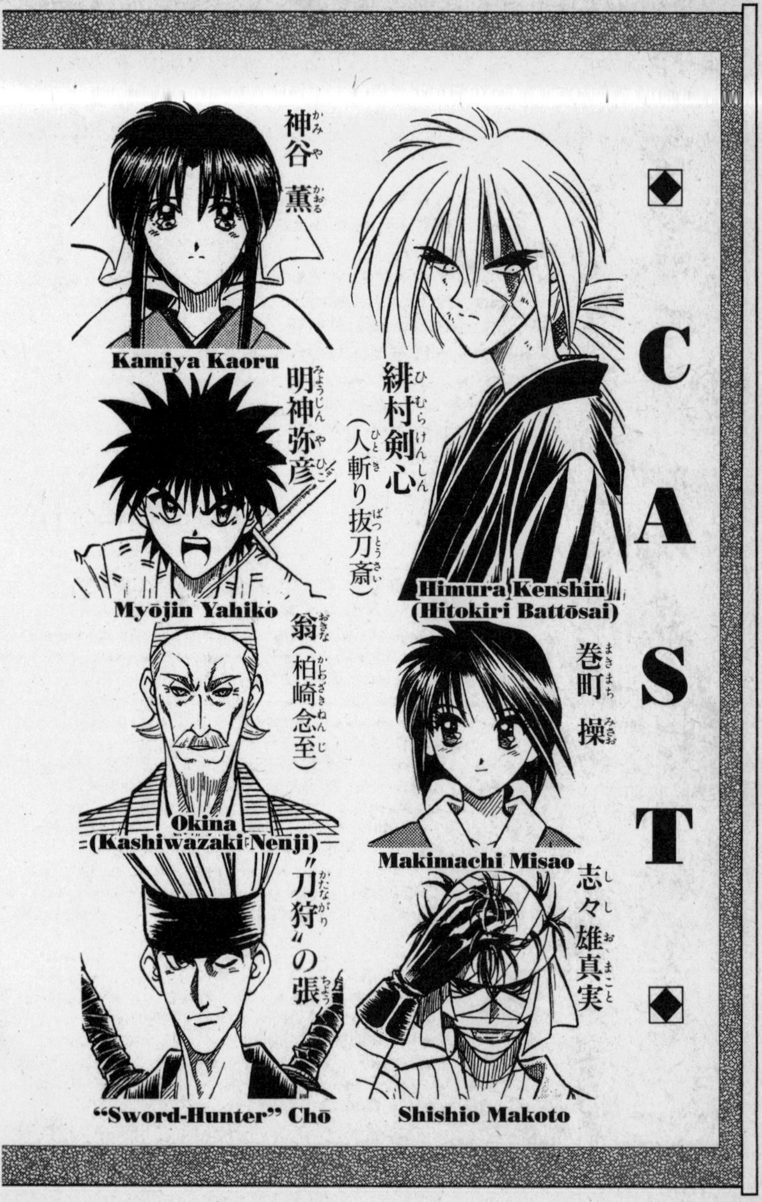
CAST
緋村剣心
（人斬り抜刀斎）
Himura Kenshin
(Hitokiri Battōsai)
神谷薫
Kamiya Kaoru
明神弥彦
Myōjin Yahiko
巻町操
Makimachi Misao
翁（柏崎念至）
Okina
(Kashiwazaki Nenji)
志々雄真実
Shishio Makoto
〝刀狩〟の張
"Sword-Hunter" Chō

Arai Seikū

新井青空

伊織

Iori

Once he was *hitokiri*, an assassin, called Battōsai. His name was legend among the pro-Imperialist or "patriot" warriors who launched the Meiji Era. Now, Himura Kenshin is *rurouni*, a wanderer, and carries a reversed-edge *sakabatō* to prohibit himself from killing.

THUS FAR

Ōkubo Toshimichi, head of the government's "Internal Affairs," tries to hire Kenshin to assassinate Shishio Makoto, the successor to "Hitokiri Battōsai." But it is Ōkubo who is assassinated, and Kenshin sets out for Kyoto to find his killers... despite the protests of Kaoru and the others. On the East Sea Road, he meets a girl named Misao and travels with her to a village occupied by Shishio's men—where he reconnects with Saitō Hajime, an intelligence agent for the police and ex-member of the Shinsengumi. There, they encounter Shishio himself, but the assassin refuses to fight Kenshin (because he is no longer *hitokiri*) and vanishes. Behind him Shishio leaves Sōjirō—the "Sword of Heaven"—to fight, and Kenshin's *sakabatō* is shattered.

Arriving in Kyoto, Kenshin asks Okina (Misao's surrogate father, and ex-Oniwabanshū) to find the sword-smith, Arai Shakkū. But Shakkū is dead, and the son who inherited his skills desires only peace and has abandoned the making of blades. Now Kenshin must search elsewhere for a new *sakabatō*, but his meeting with Shakkū's son—and the existence of Shakkū's last sword—have been found out by Shishio's men....

CONTENTS

RUROUNI KENSHIN
Meiji Swordsman Romantic Story
BOOK TEN: MITSURUGI, MASTER AND STUDENT

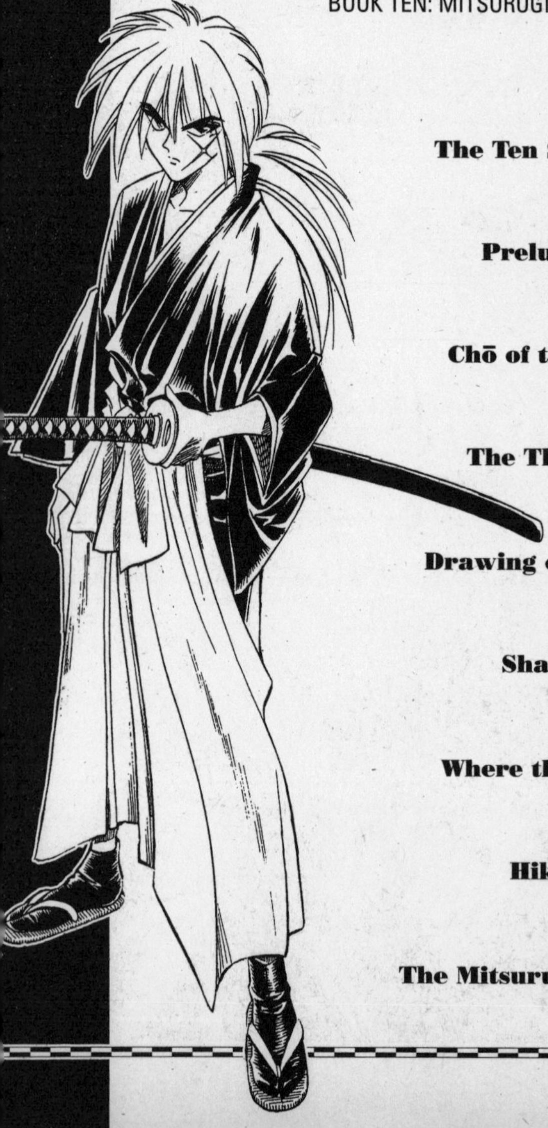

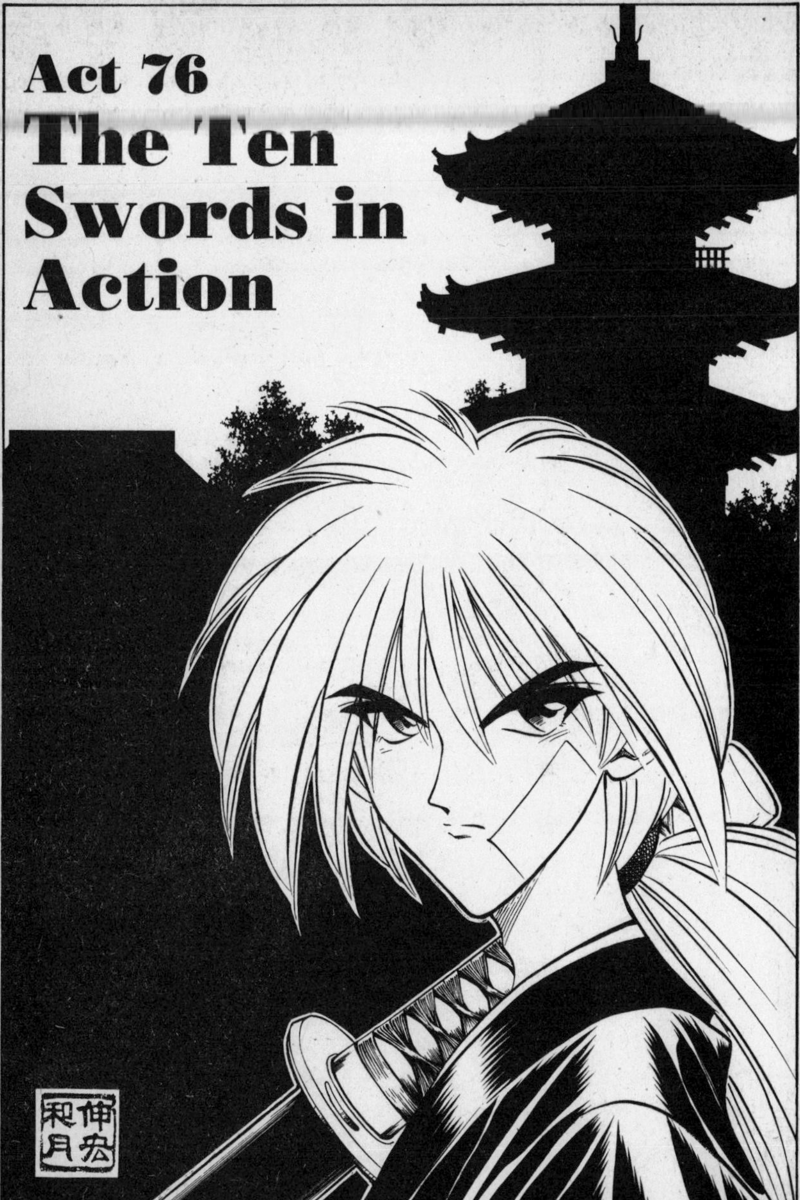
Act 76
The Ten Swords in Action

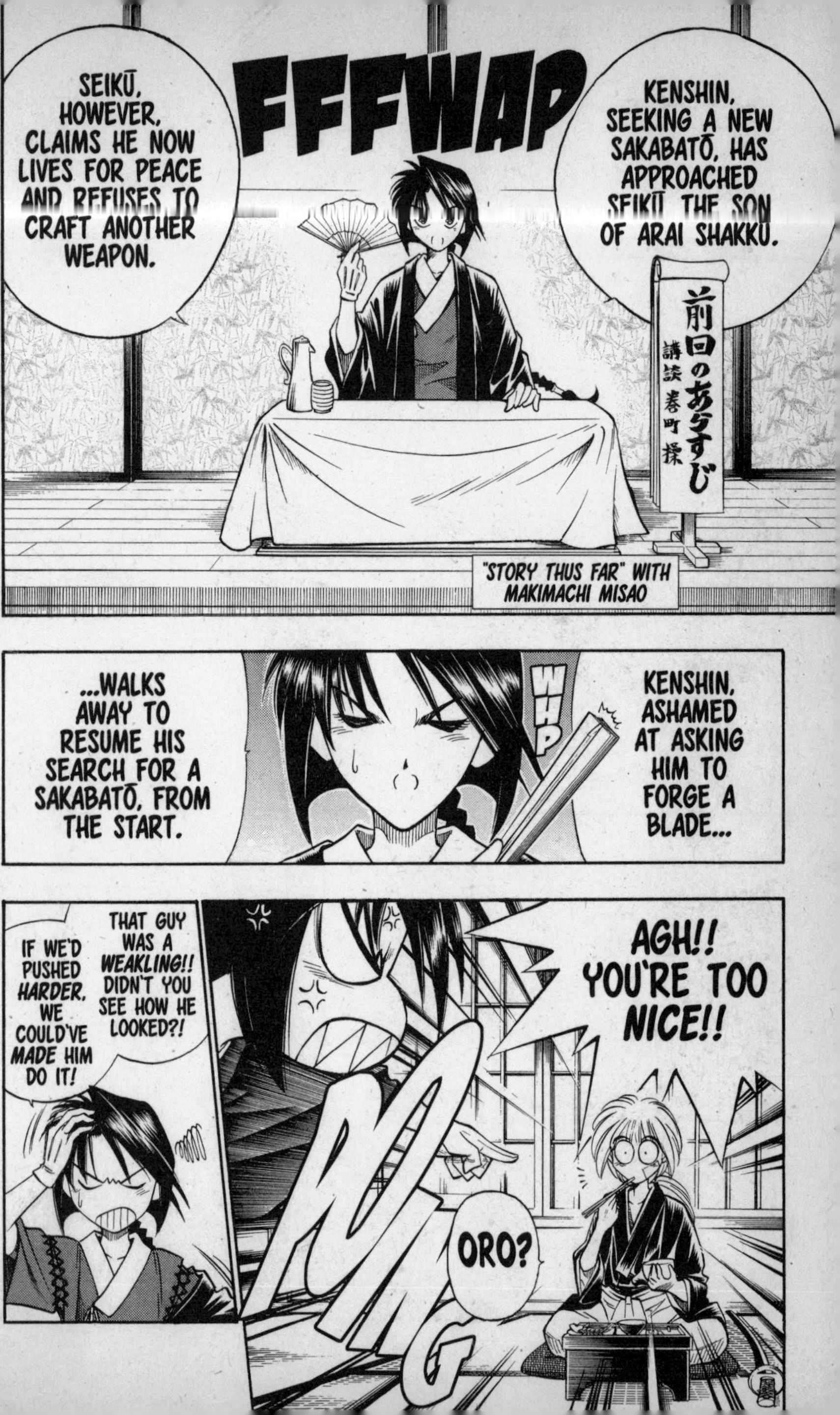
KENSHIN, SEEKING A NEW SAKABATŌ, HAS APPROACHED SEIKŪ, THE SON OF ARAI SHAKKU.
FFFWAP
SEIKŪ, HOWEVER, CLAIMS HE NOW LIVES FOR PEACE AND REFUSES TO CRAFT ANOTHER WEAPON.
前回のあらすじ
講談 巻町操
"STORY THUS FAR" WITH MAKIMACHI MISAO
KENSHIN, ASHAMED AT ASKING HIM TO FORGE A BLADE...
WHP
...WALKS AWAY TO RESUME HIS SEARCH FOR A SAKABATŌ, FROM THE START.
AGH!! YOU'RE TOO NICE!!
THAT GUY WAS A WEAKLING!! DIDN'T YOU SEE HOW HE LOOKED?!
IF WE'D PUSHED HARDER, WE COULD'VE MADE HIM DO IT!
ORO?
MG

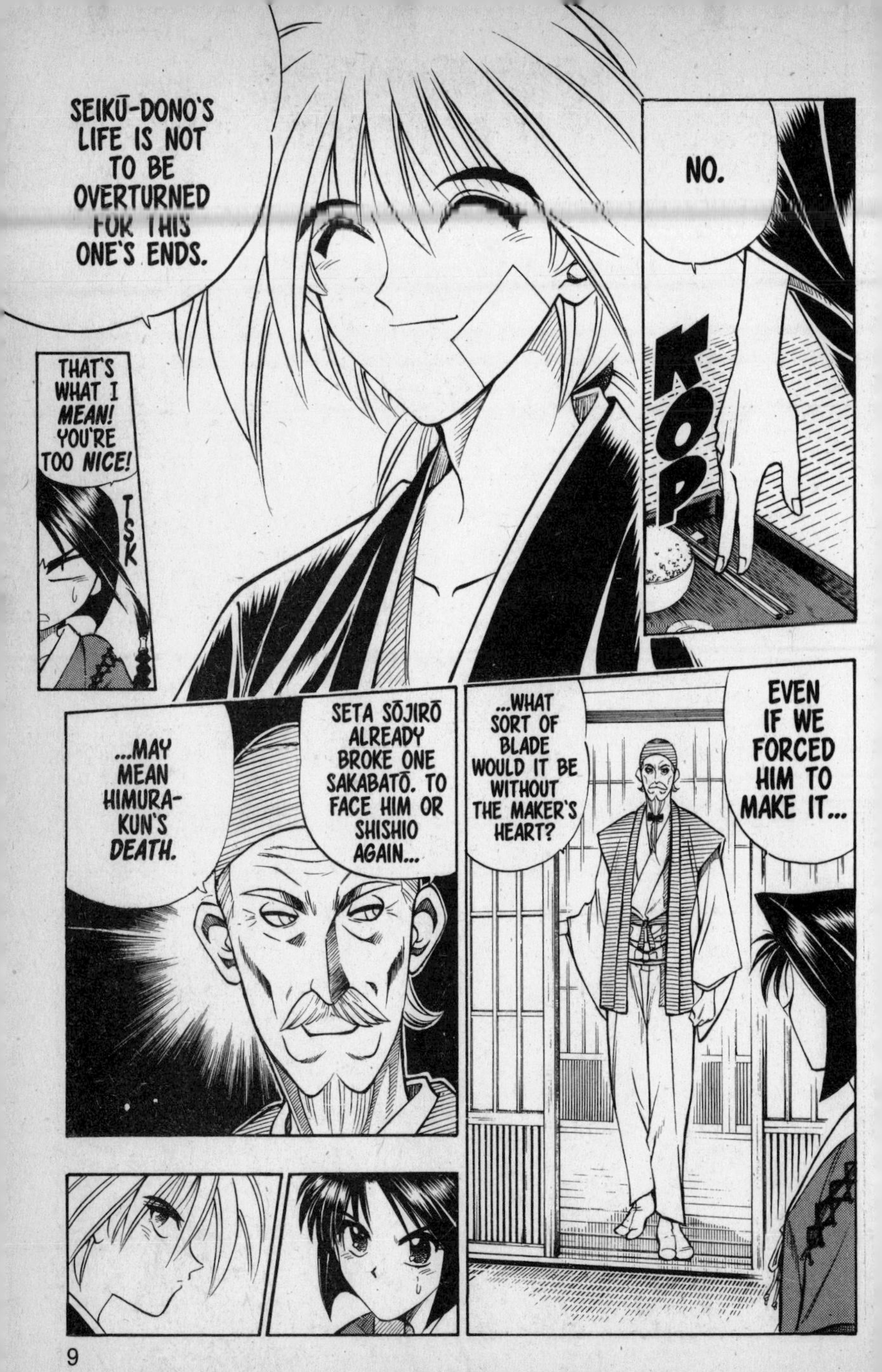
NO.
KOP
SEIKŪ-DONO'S LIFE IS NOT TO BE OVERTURNED FOR THIS ONE'S ENDS.
THAT'S WHAT I *MEAN!* YOU'RE TOO *NICE!*
TSK
EVEN IF WE FORCED HIM TO MAKE IT...
...WHAT SORT OF BLADE WOULD IT BE WITHOUT THE MAKER'S HEART?
SETA SŌJIRŌ ALREADY BROKE ONE SAKABATŌ. TO FACE HIM OR SHISHIO AGAIN...
...MAY MEAN HIMURA-KUN'S *DEATH.*

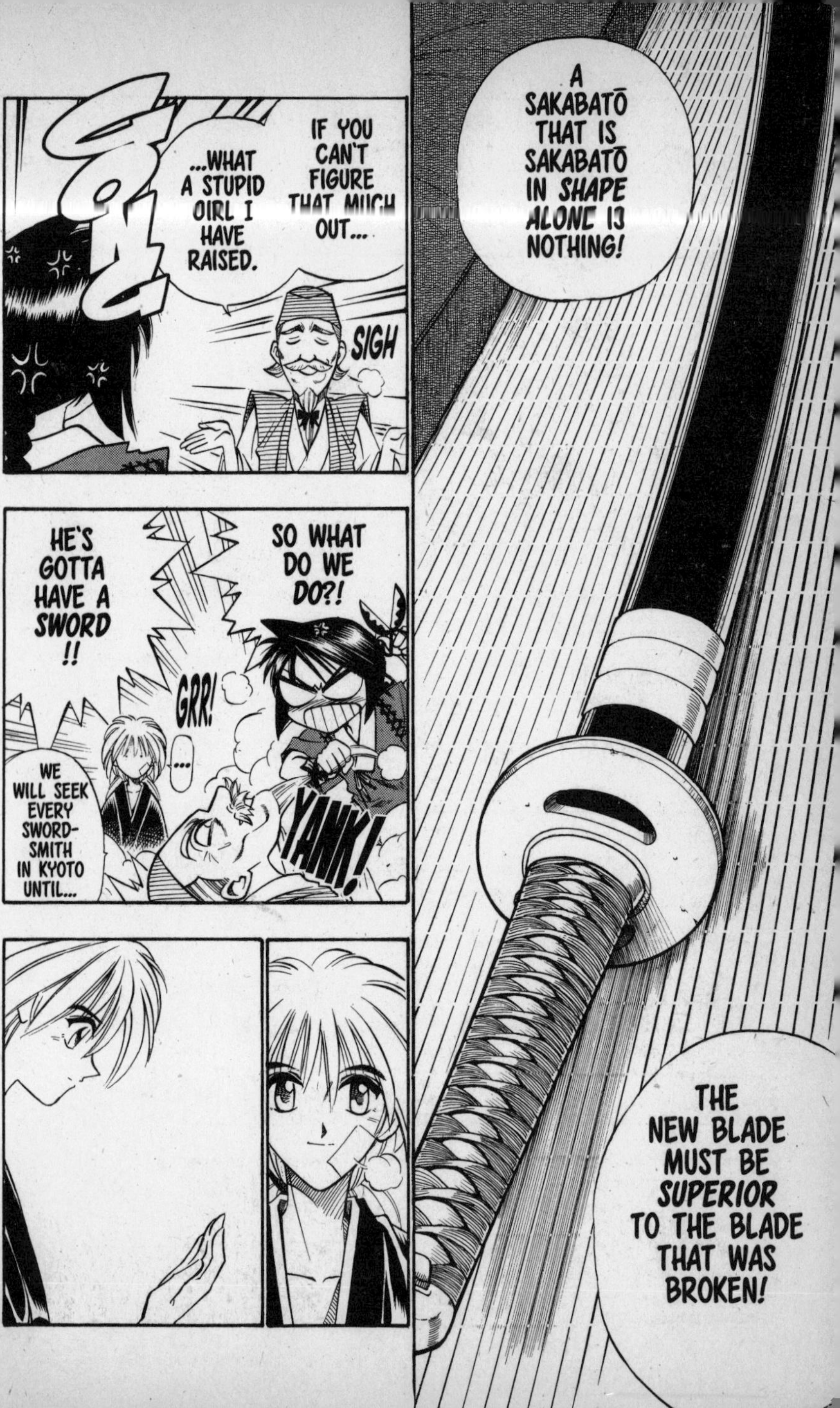
A SAKABATŌ THAT IS SAKABATŌ IN *SHAPE ALONE* IS NOTHING!
THE NEW BLADE MUST BE *SUPERIOR* TO THE BLADE THAT WAS BROKEN!
IF YOU CAN'T FIGURE THAT MUCH OUT...
...WHAT A STUPID GIRL I HAVE RAISED.
SIGH
SO WHAT DO WE *DO?!*
HE'S GOTTA HAVE A *SWORD* !!
GRR!
...
YANK!
WE WILL SEEK EVERY SWORD-SMITH IN KYOTO UNTIL...

READ THIS WAY

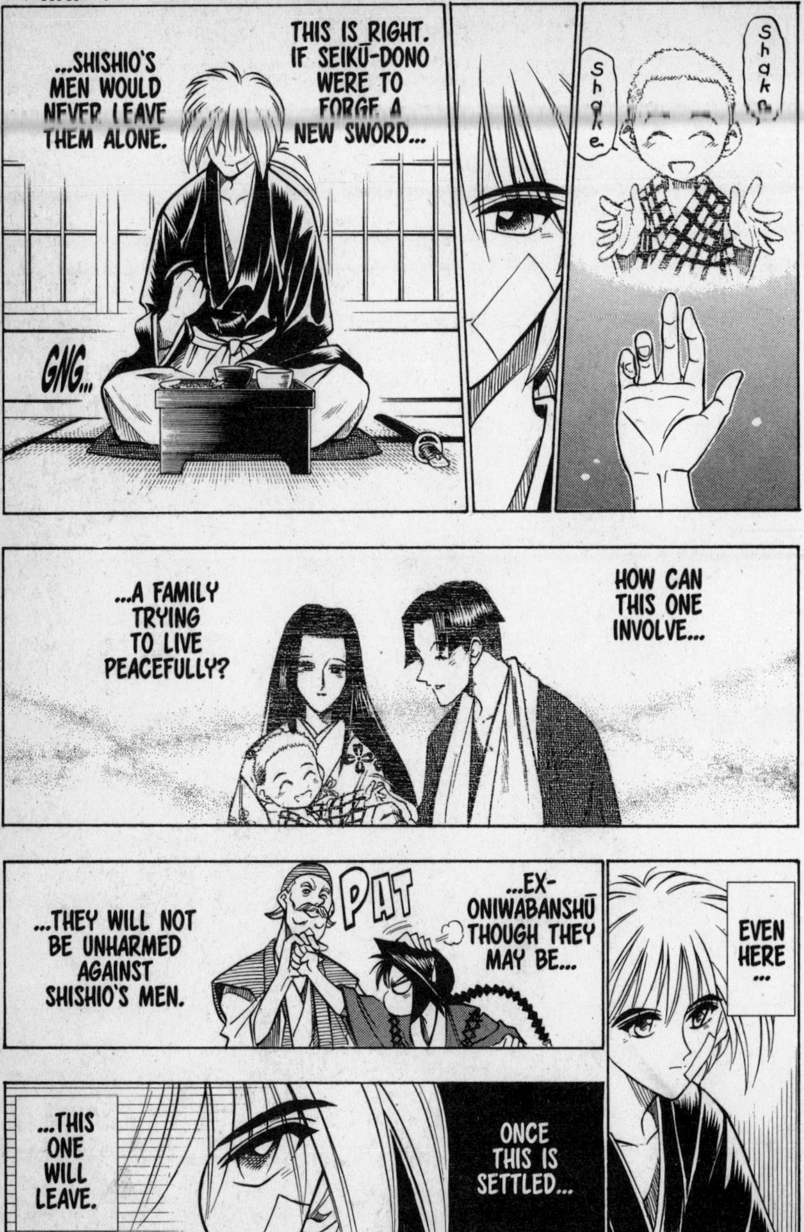

Shake
Shake
THIS IS RIGHT. IF SEIKŪ-DONO WERE TO FORGE A NEW SWORD...
...SHISHIO'S MEN WOULD NEVER LEAVE THEM ALONE.
GNG...
HOW CAN THIS ONE INVOLVE...
...A FAMILY TRYING TO LIVE PEACEFULLY?
EVEN HERE...
...EX-ONIWABANSHŪ THOUGH THEY MAY BE...
PAT
...THEY WILL NOT BE UNHARMED AGAINST SHISHIO'S MEN.
ONCE THIS IS SETTLED...
...THIS ONE WILL LEAVE.

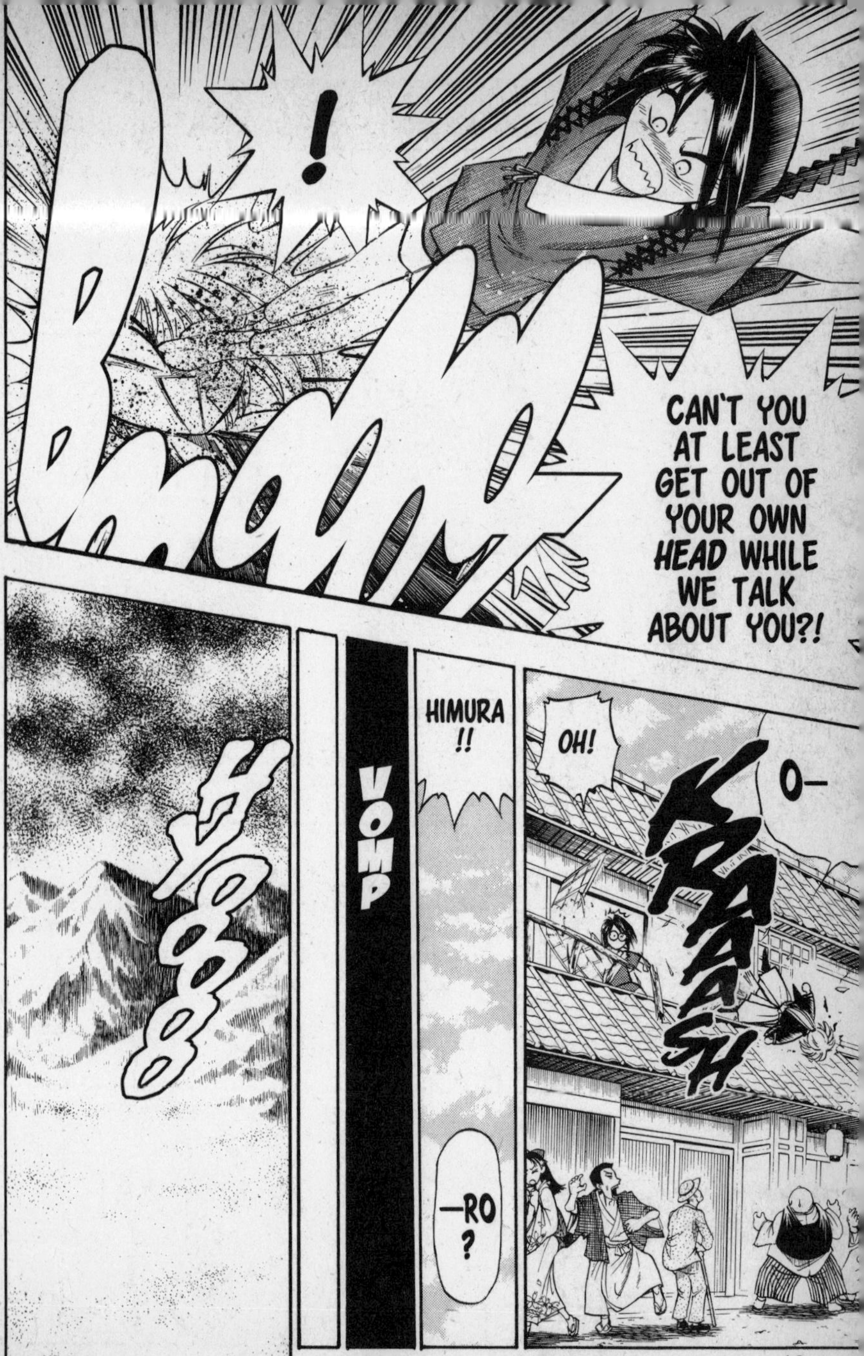
!
CAN'T YOU AT LEAST GET OUT OF YOUR OWN HEAD WHILE WE TALK ABOUT YOU?!
O—
OH!
HIMURA !!
—RO ?
VOMP

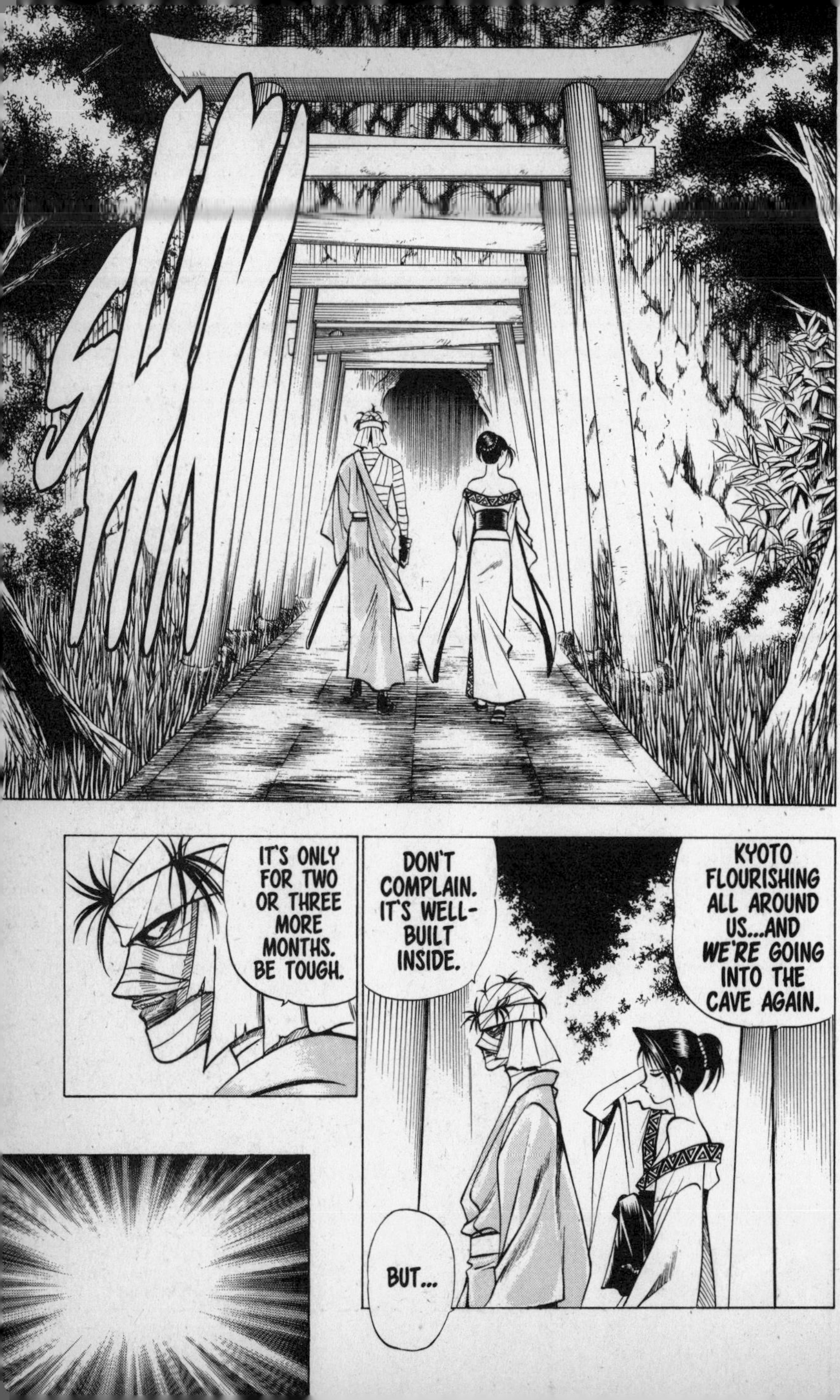
KYOTO FLOURISHING ALL AROUND US...AND WE'RE GOING INTO THE CAVE AGAIN.
DON'T COMPLAIN. IT'S WELL-BUILT INSIDE.
BUT...
IT'S ONLY FOR TWO OR THREE MORE MONTHS. BE TOUGH.

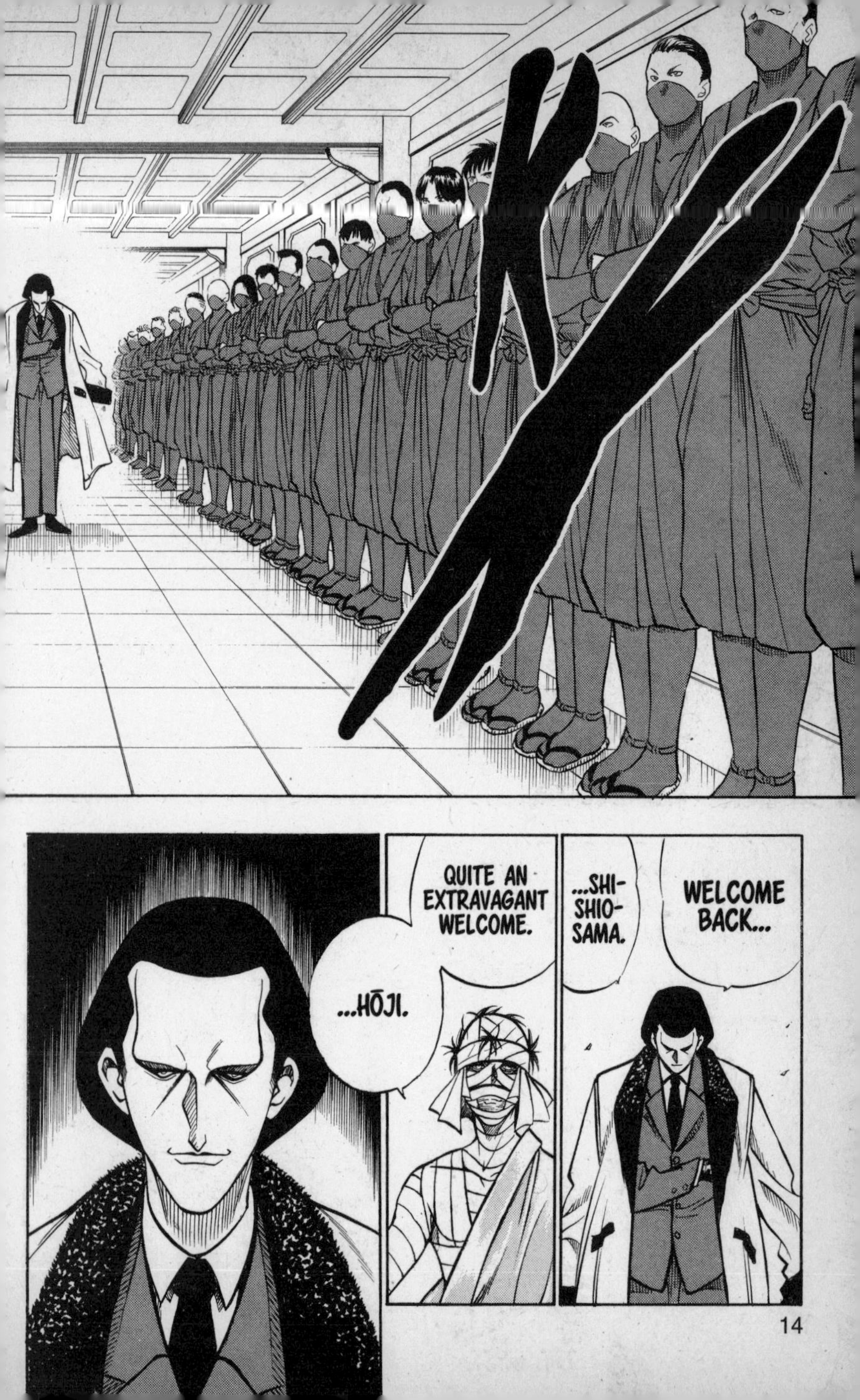
WELCOME BACK...
...SHI-SHIO-SAMA.
QUITE AN EXTRAVAGANT WELCOME.
...HŌJI.

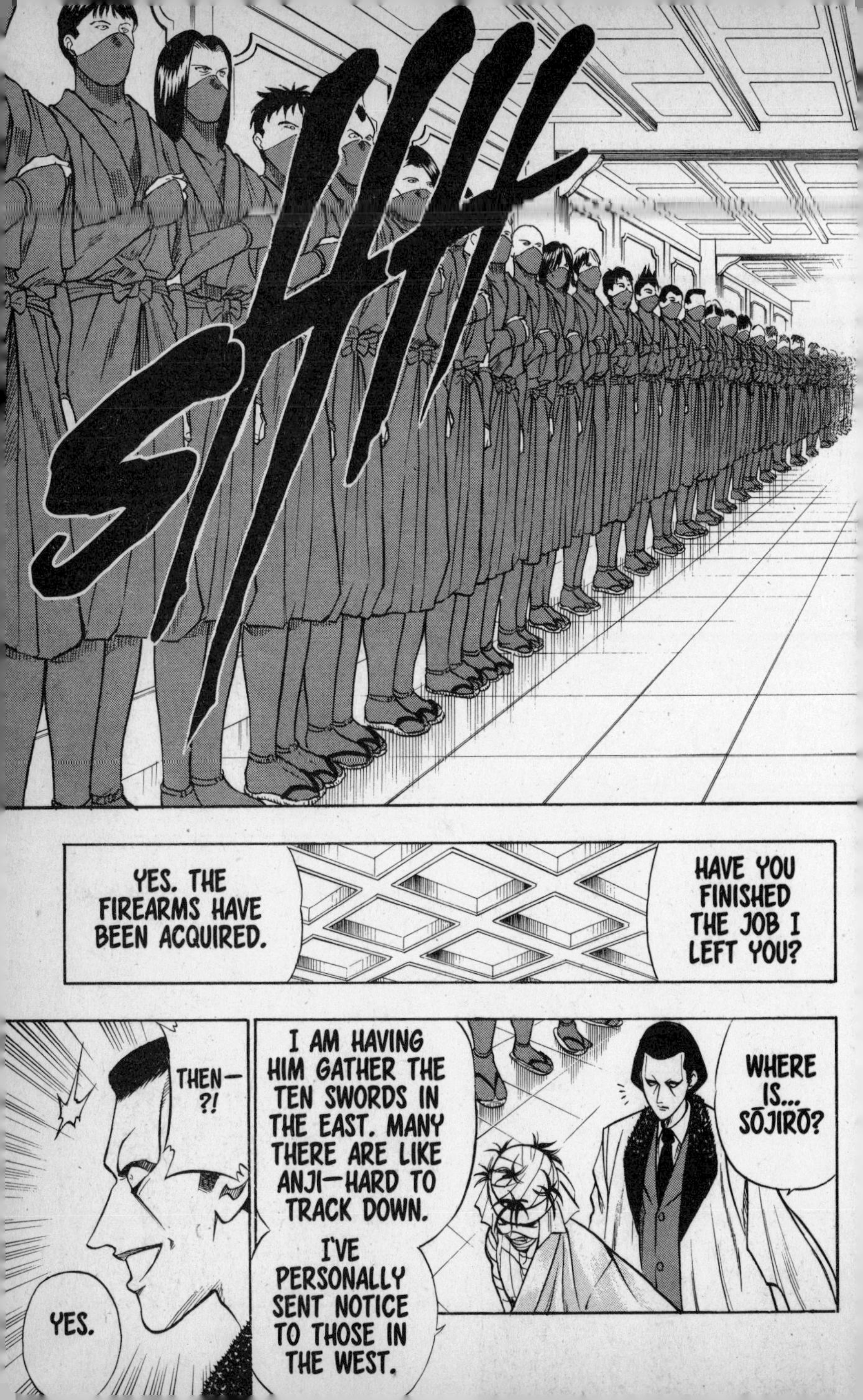
HAVE YOU FINISHED THE JOB I LEFT YOU?
YES. THE FIREARMS HAVE BEEN ACQUIRED.
WHERE IS... SŌJIRŌ?
I AM HAVING HIM GATHER THE TEN SWORDS IN THE EAST. MANY THERE ARE LIKE ANJI—HARD TO TRACK DOWN.
I'VE PERSONALLY SENT NOTICE TO THOSE IN THE WEST.
THEN—?!
YES.

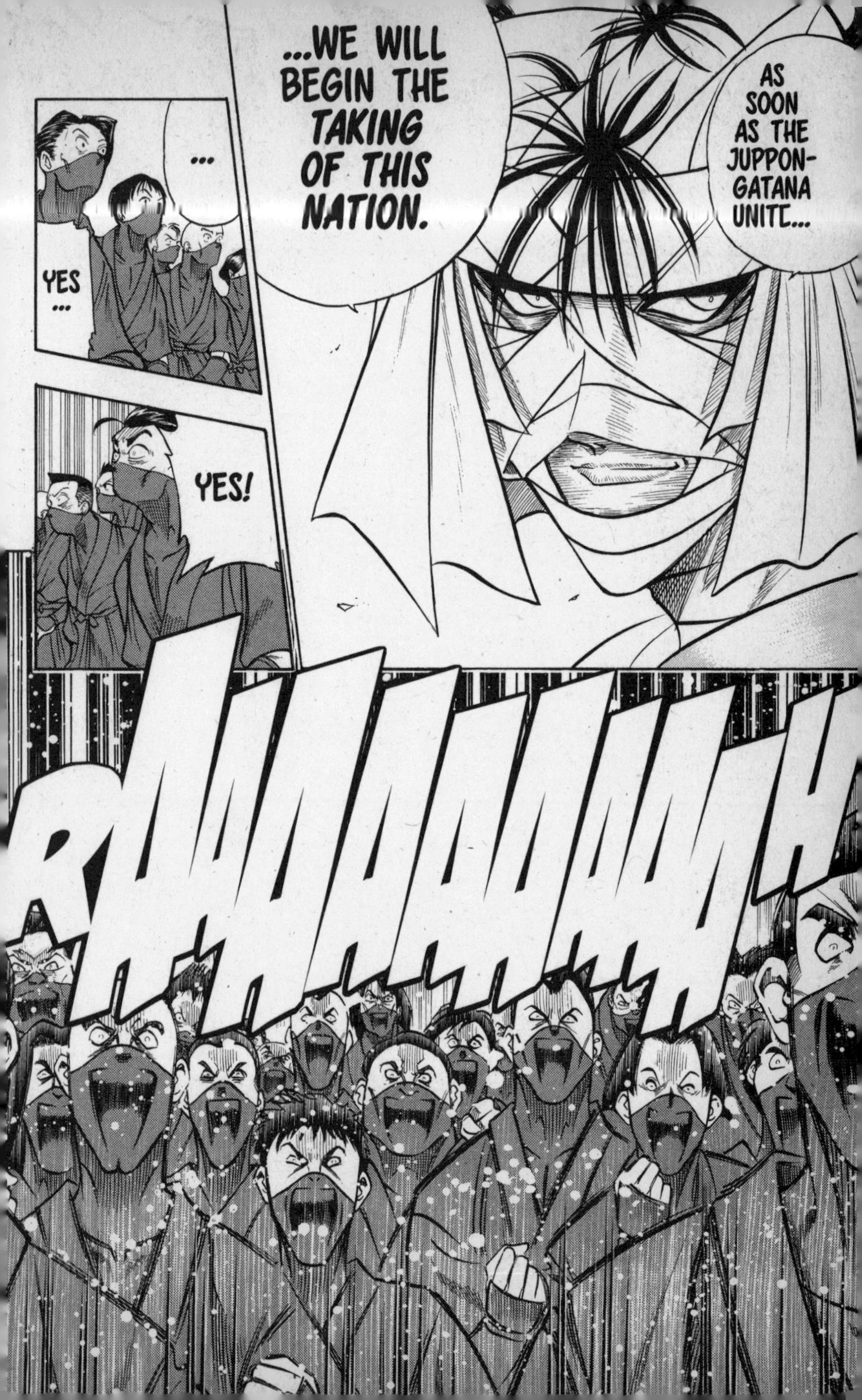
AS SOON AS THE JUPPON-GATANA UNITE...
...WE WILL BEGIN THE TAKING OF THIS NATION.
...
YES ...
YES!
RAAAAAAAH!

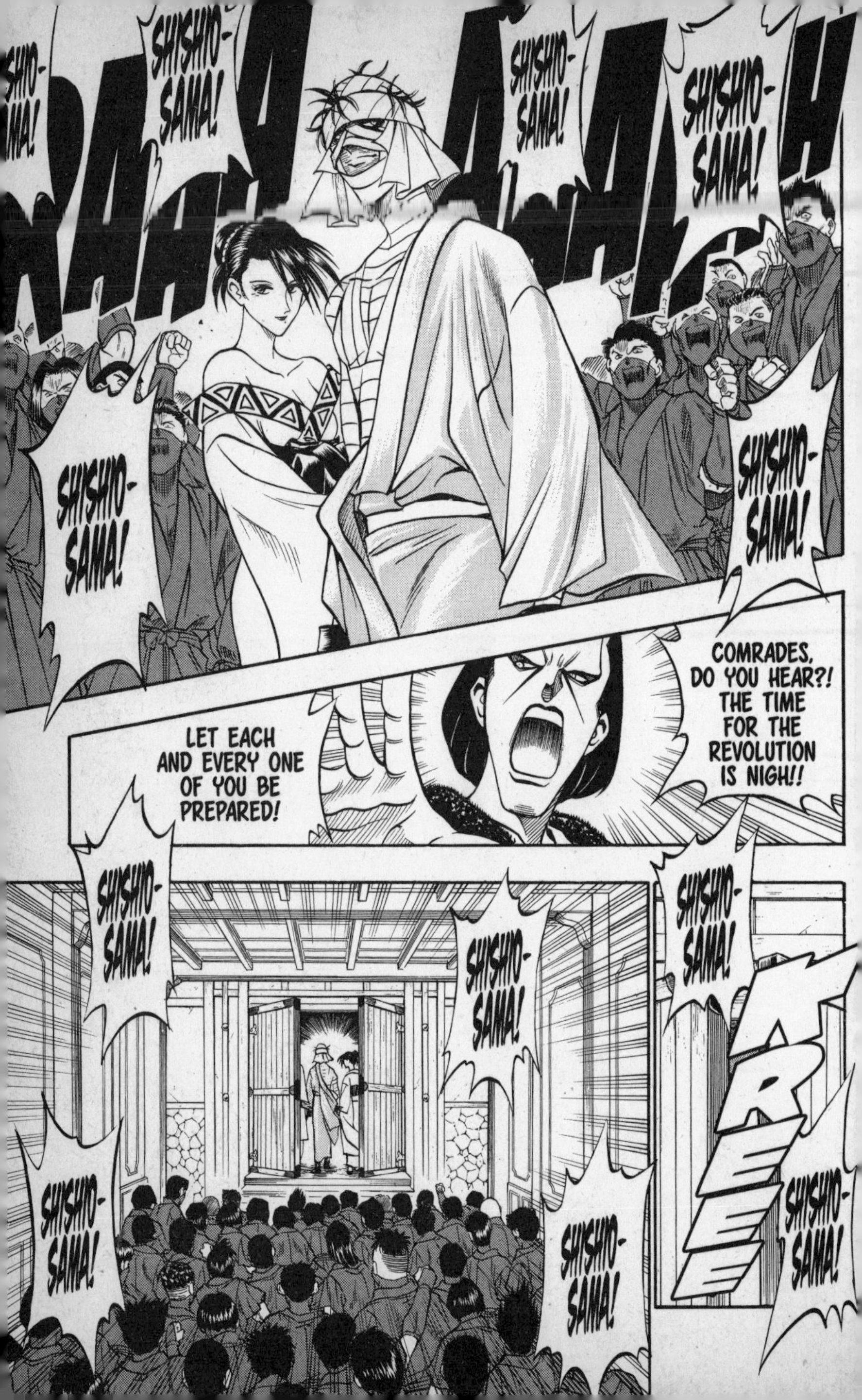
SHISHIO-SAMA!
SHISHIO-SAMA!
SHISHIO-SAMA!
SHISHIO-SAMA!
SHISHIO-SAMA!
COMRADES, DO YOU HEAR?! THE TIME FOR THE REVOLUTION IS NIGH!!
LET EACH AND EVERY ONE OF YOU BE PREPARED!
SHISHIO-SAMA!
SHISHIO-SAMA!
SHISHIO-SAMA!
SHISHIO-SAMA!
SHISHIO-SAMA!
SHISHIO-SAMA!

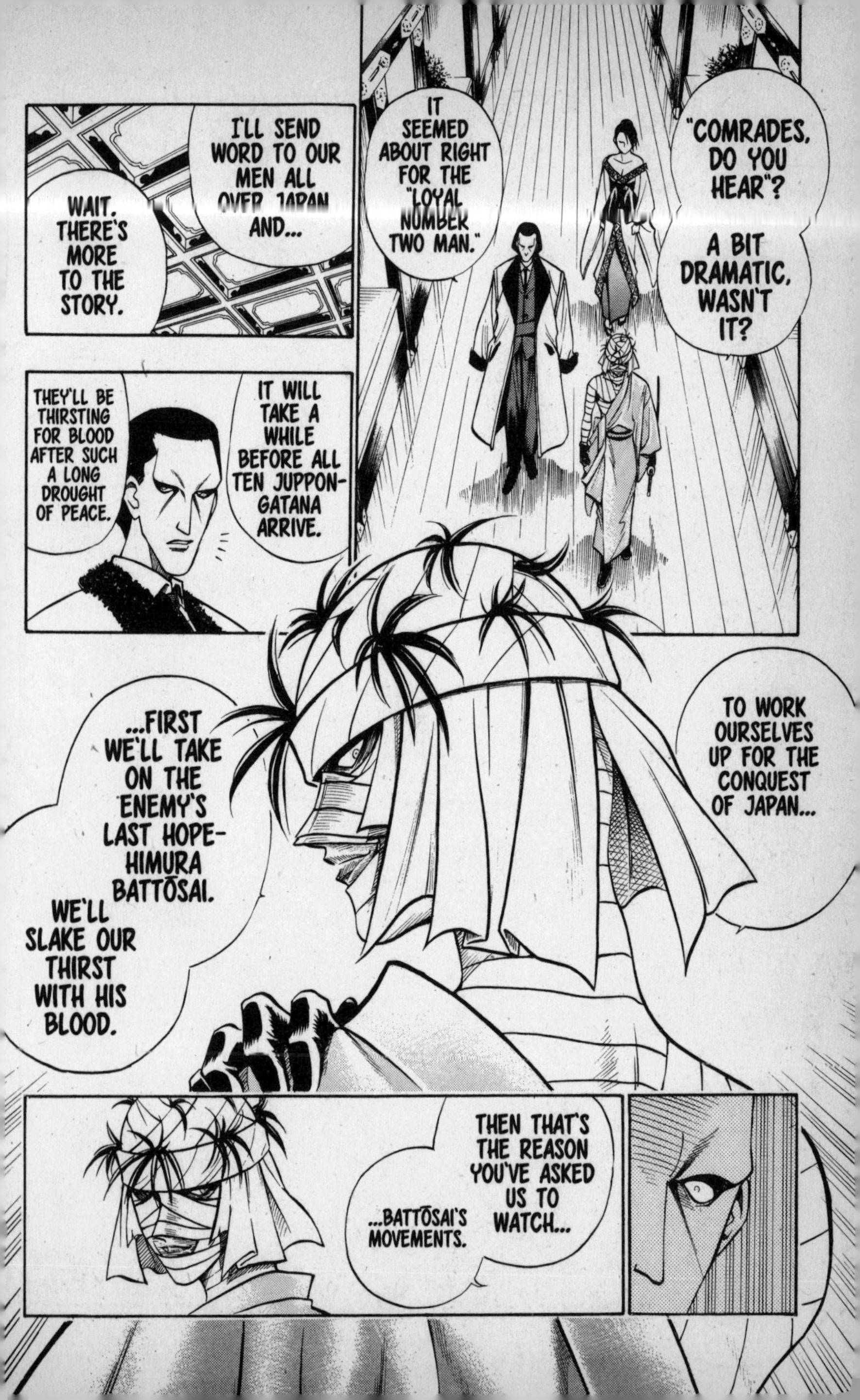
"COMRADES, DO YOU HEAR"?
A BIT DRAMATIC, WASN'T IT?
IT SEEMED ABOUT RIGHT FOR THE "LOYAL NUMBER TWO MAN."
I'LL SEND WORD TO OUR MEN ALL OVER JAPAN AND...
WAIT. THERE'S MORE TO THE STORY.
IT WILL TAKE A WHILE BEFORE ALL TEN JUPPON-GATANA ARRIVE.
THEY'LL BE THIRSTING FOR BLOOD AFTER SUCH A LONG DROUGHT OF PEACE.
TO WORK OURSELVES UP FOR THE CONQUEST OF JAPAN...
...FIRST WE'LL TAKE ON THE ENEMY'S LAST HOPE—HIMURA BATTŌSAI.
WE'LL SLAKE OUR THIRST WITH HIS BLOOD.
THEN THAT'S THE REASON YOU'VE ASKED US TO WATCH...
...BATTŌSAI'S MOVEMENTS.

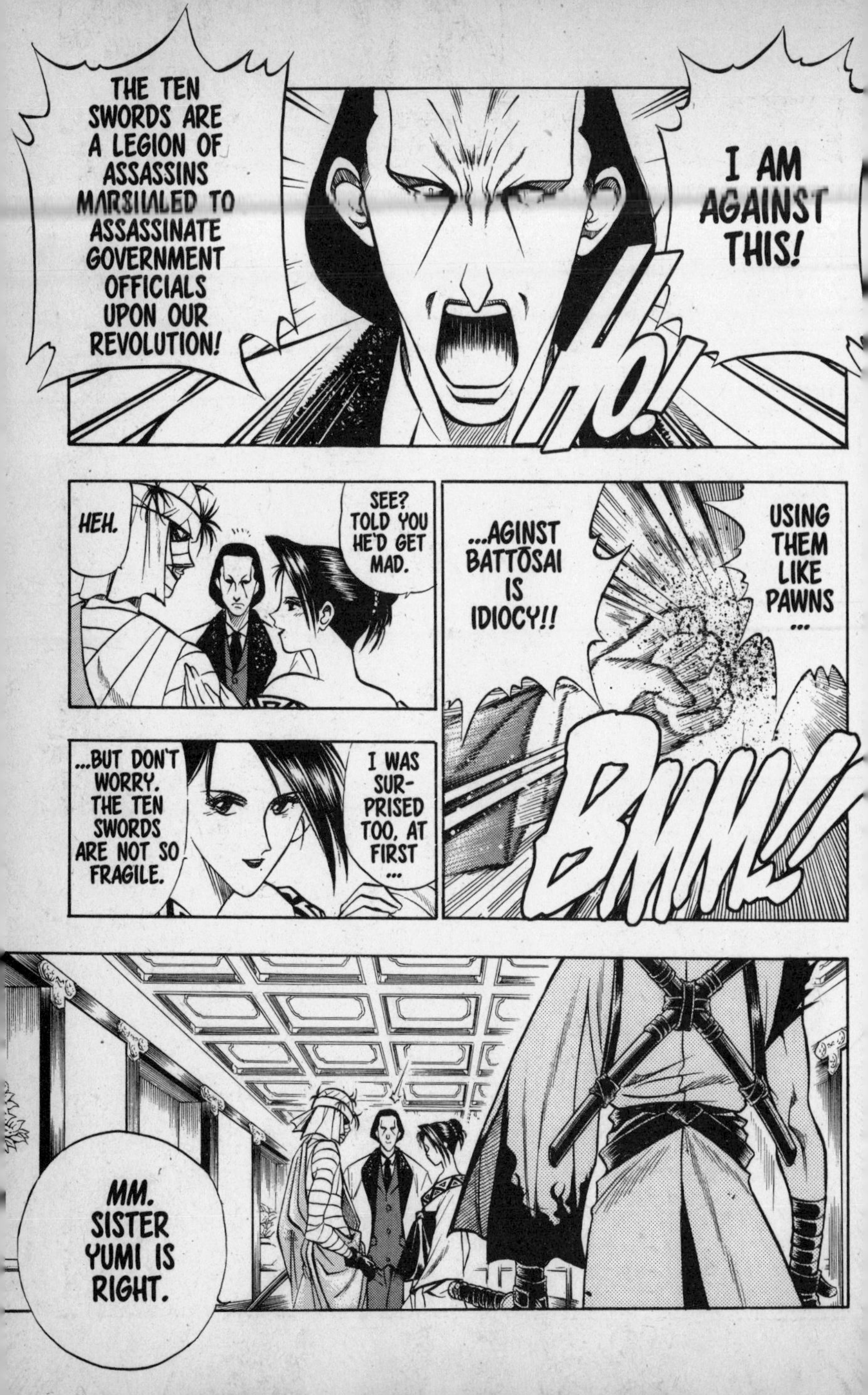
I AM AGAINST THIS!
THE TEN SWORDS ARE A LEGION OF ASSASSINS MARSHALLED TO ASSASSINATE GOVERNMENT OFFICIALS UPON OUR REVOLUTION!
HO!
USING THEM LIKE PAWNS ...
...AGINST BATTŌSAI IS IDIOCY!!
BMM!
SEE? TOLD YOU HE'D GET MAD.
HEH.
I WAS SUR-PRISED TOO, AT FIRST ...
...BUT DON'T WORRY. THE TEN SWORDS ARE NOT SO FRAGILE.
MM. SISTER YUMI IS RIGHT.

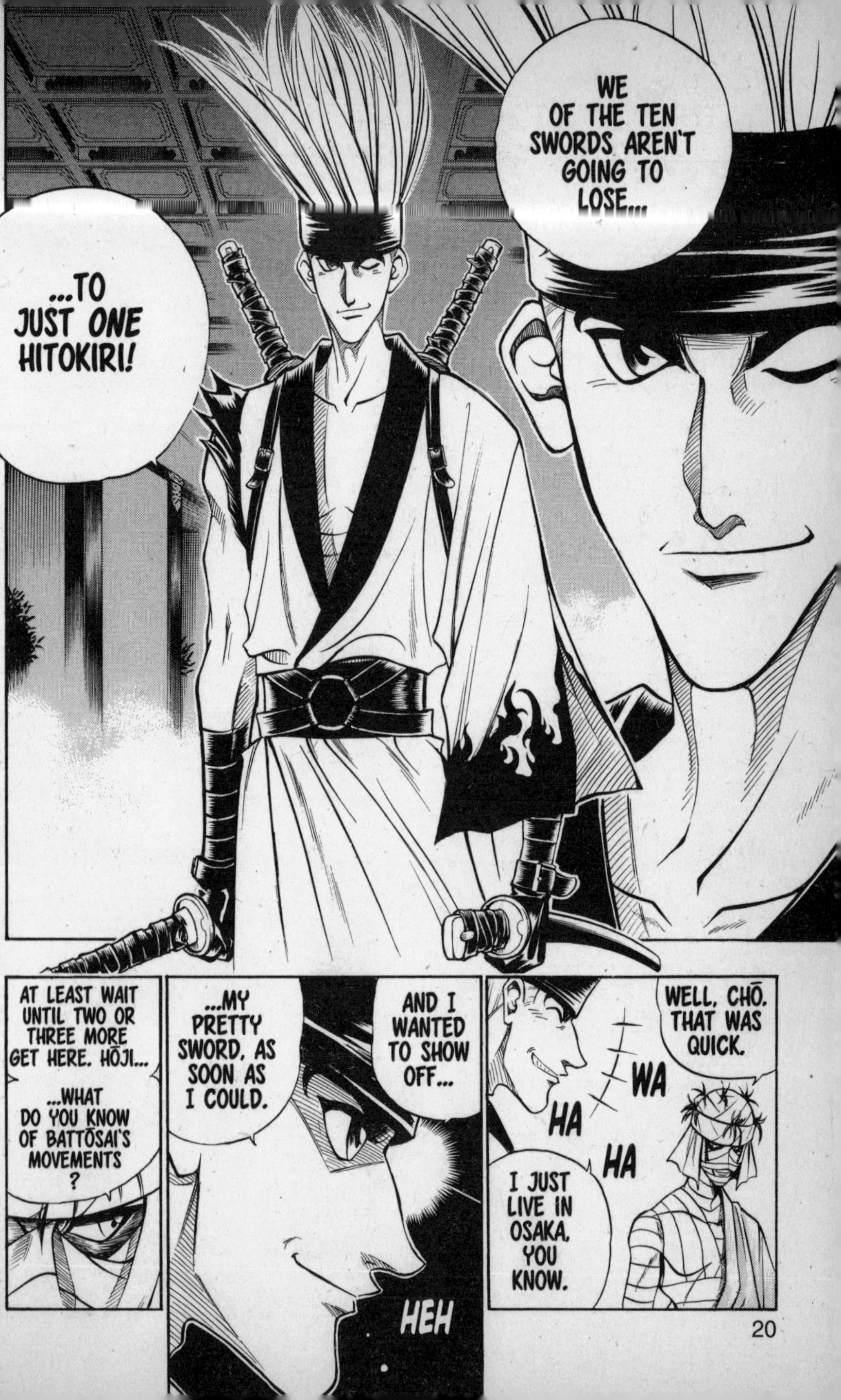
WE OF THE TEN SWORDS AREN'T GOING TO LOSE...
...TO JUST *ONE* HITOKIRI!
WELL, CHŌ. THAT WAS QUICK.
WA HA HA
I JUST LIVE IN OSAKA, YOU KNOW.
AND I WANTED TO SHOW OFF...
...MY PRETTY SWORD, AS SOON AS I COULD.
HEH
AT LEAST WAIT UNTIL TWO OR THREE MORE GET HERE. HŌJI...
...WHAT DO YOU KNOW OF BATTŌSAI'S MOVEMENTS?

READ THIS WAY

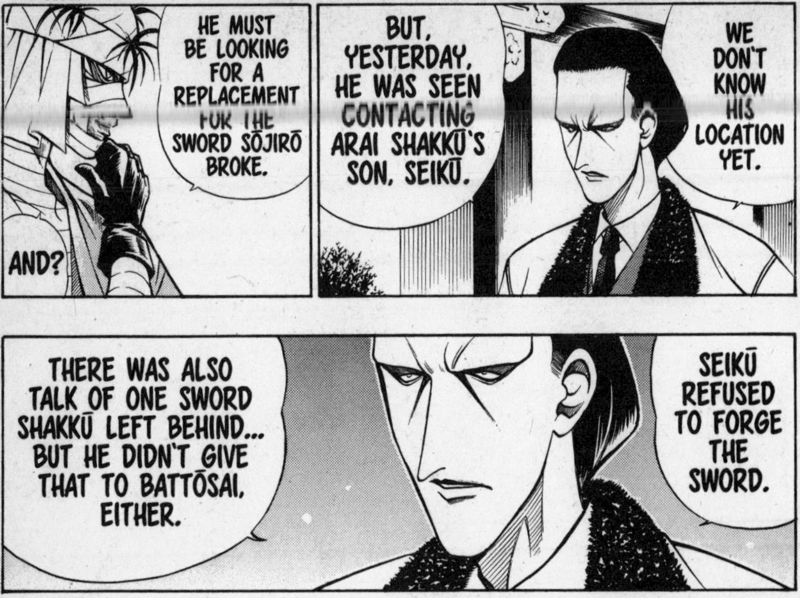
WE DON'T KNOW HIS LOCATION YET.
BUT, YESTERDAY, HE WAS SEEN CONTACTING ARAI SHAKKŪ'S SON, SEIKŪ.
HE MUST BE LOOKING FOR A REPLACEMENT FOR THE SWORD SŌJIRŌ BROKE.
AND?
SEIKŪ REFUSED TO FORGE THE SWORD.
THERE WAS ALSO TALK OF ONE SWORD SHAKKŪ LEFT BEHIND... BUT HE DIDN'T GIVE THAT TO BATTŌSAI, EITHER.

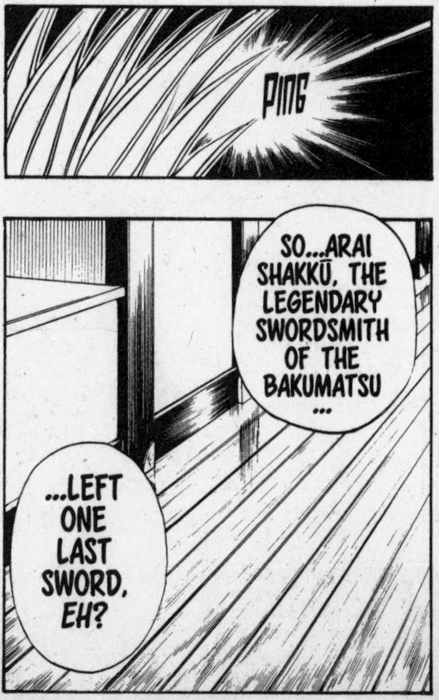
PING
SO...ARAI SHAKKŪ, THE LEGENDARY SWORDSMITH OF THE BAKUMATSU ...
...LEFT ONE LAST SWORD, EH?

Long time no see. Watsuki here. It's been three months already since the TV anime started. What are your thoughts about it? To my eyes, it turned out better than imagined, so I'm relieved. I'm a tough critic where art's concerned, but I can see it was done with the pride and soul of professionals, so I'm happy. Otherwise, I have issues with some of the timing problems, with the condensing of the script (I can't see Jin-e's story being only two episodes), and with those off-the-wall, embarrassing subtitles. But I've talked to the director, and I think it'll be improving gradually from here on in. Stay tuned!

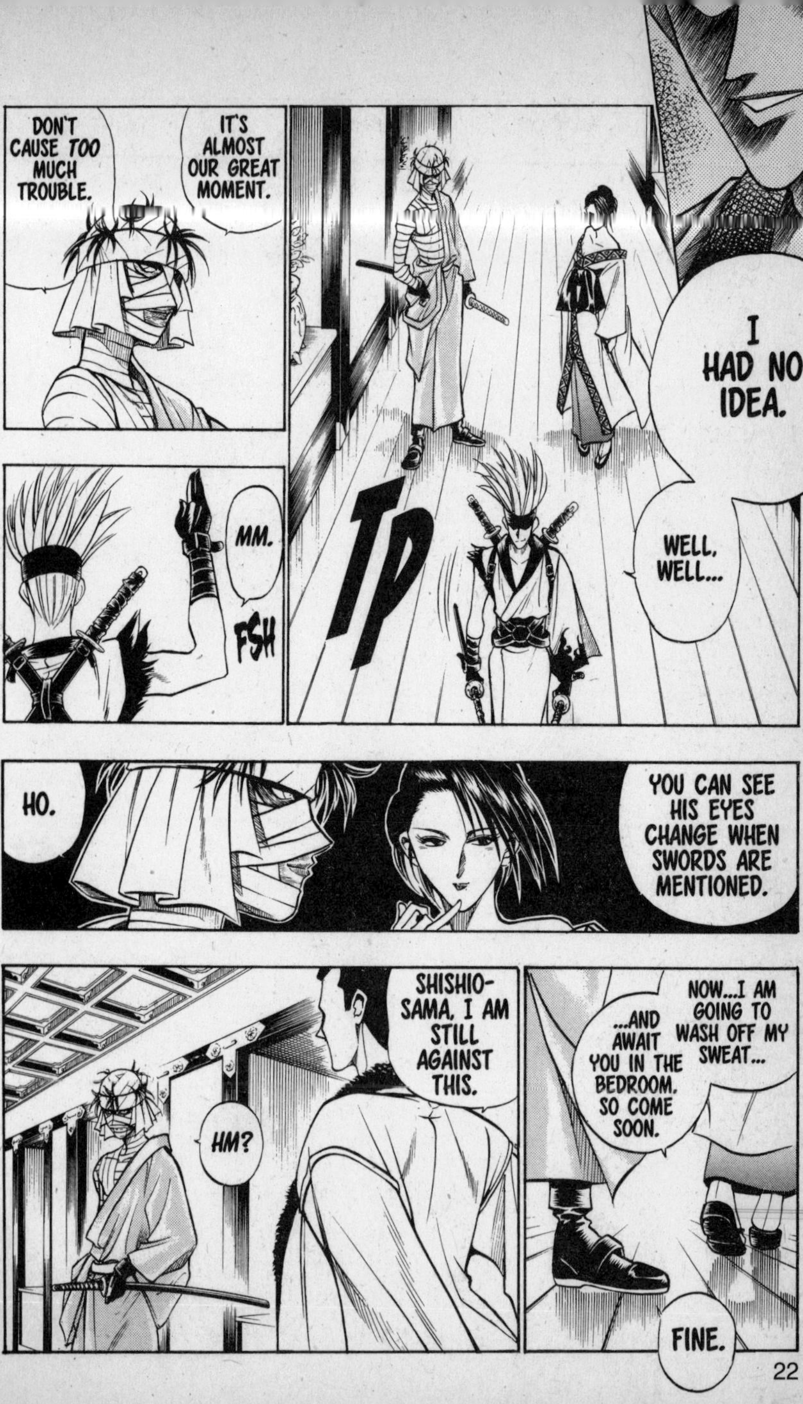
I HAD NO IDEA.
WELL, WELL...
TP
IT'S ALMOST OUR GREAT MOMENT.
DON'T CAUSE *TOO* MUCH TROUBLE.
MM.
FSH
YOU CAN SEE HIS EYES CHANGE WHEN SWORDS ARE MENTIONED.
HO.
NOW...I AM GOING TO WASH OFF MY SWEAT...
...AND AWAIT YOU IN THE BEDROOM. SO COME SOON.
FINE.
SHISHIO-SAMA, I AM STILL AGAINST THIS.
HM?

READ THIS WAY

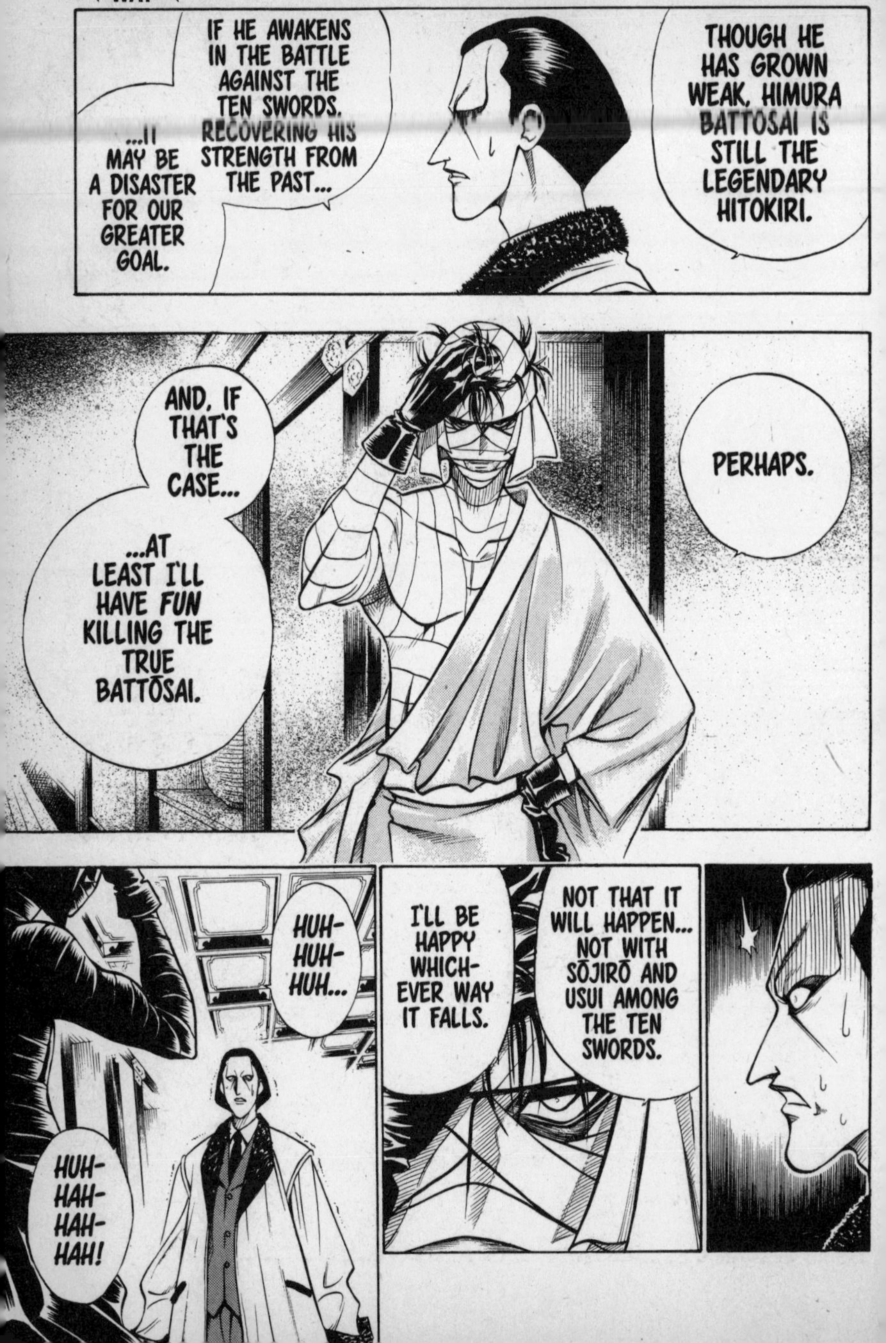
THOUGH HE HAS GROWN WEAK, HIMURA BATTOSAI IS STILL THE LEGENDARY HITOKIRI.
IF HE AWAKENS IN THE BATTLE AGAINST THE TEN SWORDS, RECOVERING HIS STRENGTH FROM THE PAST...
...IT MAY BE A DISASTER FOR OUR GREATER GOAL.
PERHAPS.
AND, IF THAT'S THE CASE...
...AT LEAST I'LL HAVE *FUN* KILLING THE TRUE BATTŌSAI.
NOT THAT IT WILL HAPPEN... NOT WITH SŌJIRŌ AND USUI AMONG THE TEN SWORDS.
I'LL BE HAPPY WHICHEVER WAY IT FALLS.
HUH-HUH-HUH...
HUH-HAH-HAH-HAH!

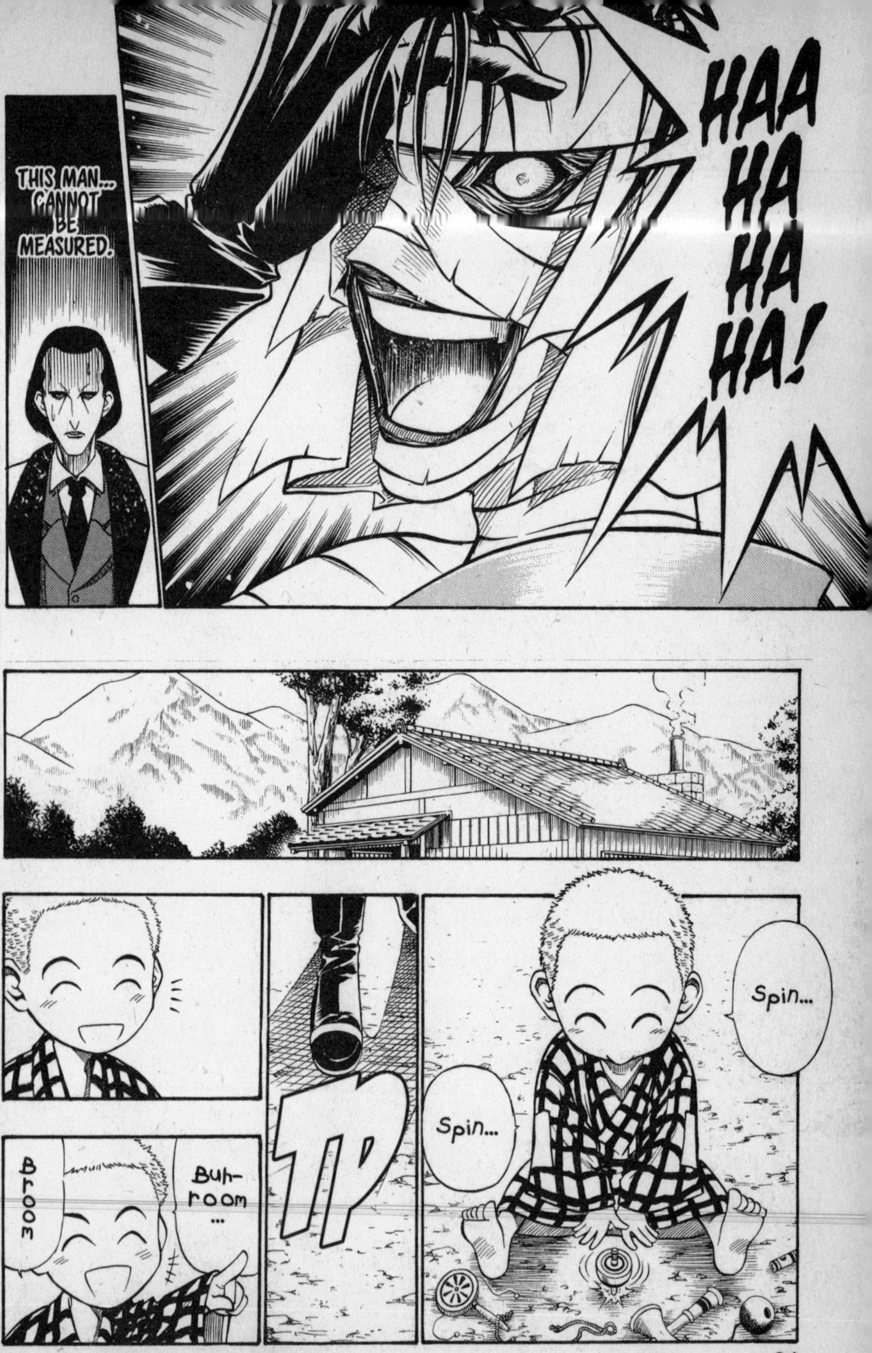
HAA HA HA HA HA!
THIS MAN... CANNOT BE MEASURED.
Spin...
Spin...
TP
Buh-room...
Broom

READ THIS WAY

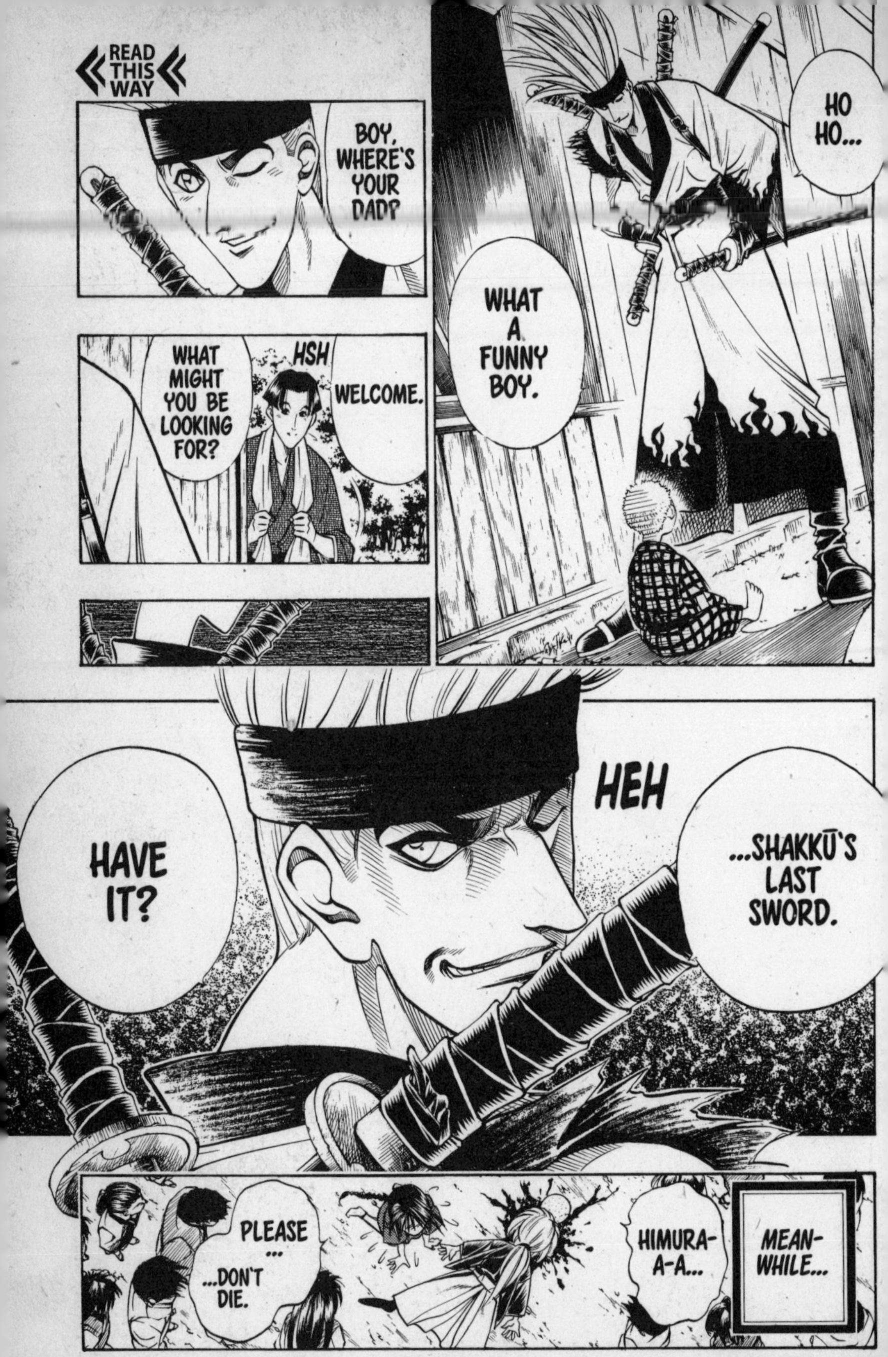
HO HO...
WHAT A FUNNY BOY.
BOY, WHERE'S YOUR DAD?
WELCOME.
HSH
WHAT MIGHT YOU BE LOOKING FOR?
...SHAKKŪ'S LAST SWORD.
HEH
HAVE IT?
MEAN-WHILE...
HIMURA-A-A...
PLEASE... ...DON'T DIE.

Rurouni Kenshin

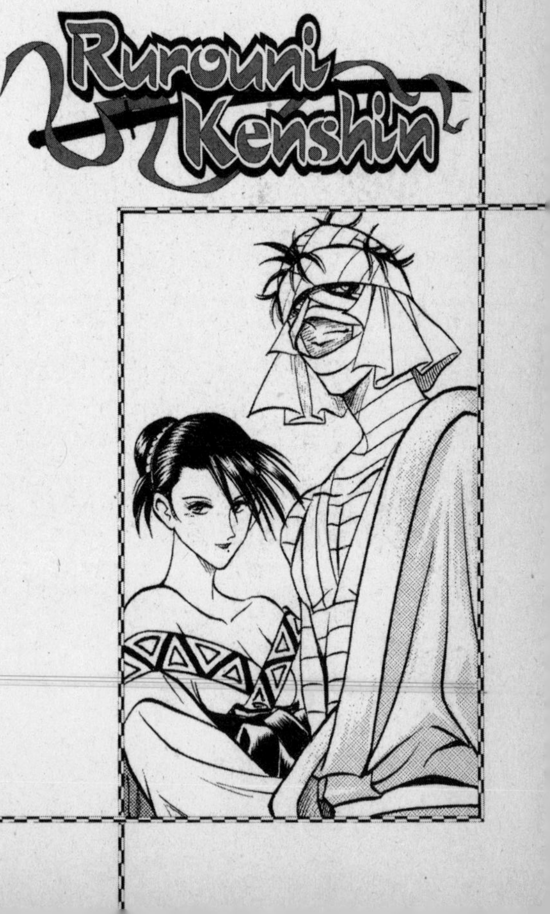

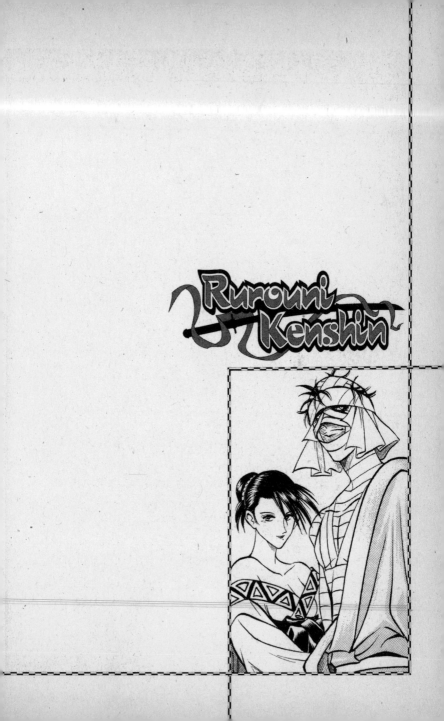

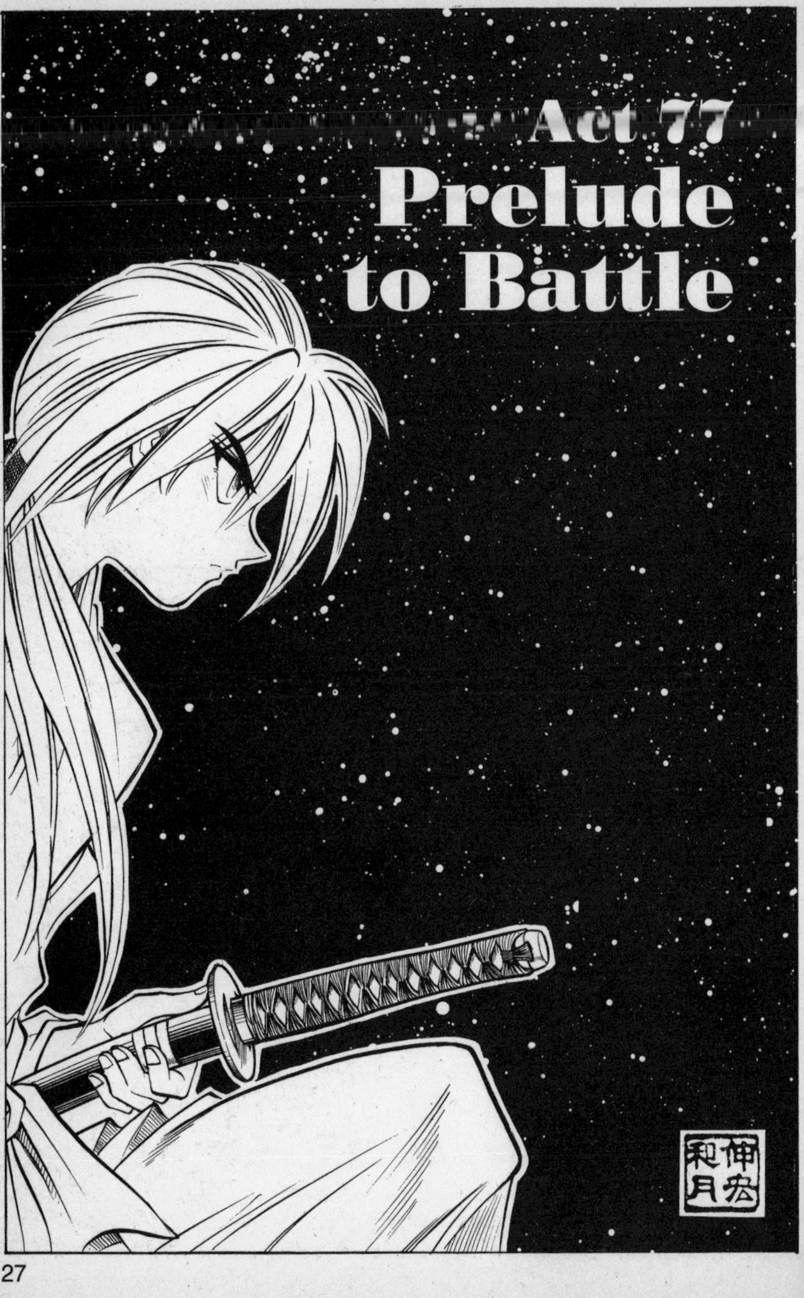
Act 77
Prelude to Battle

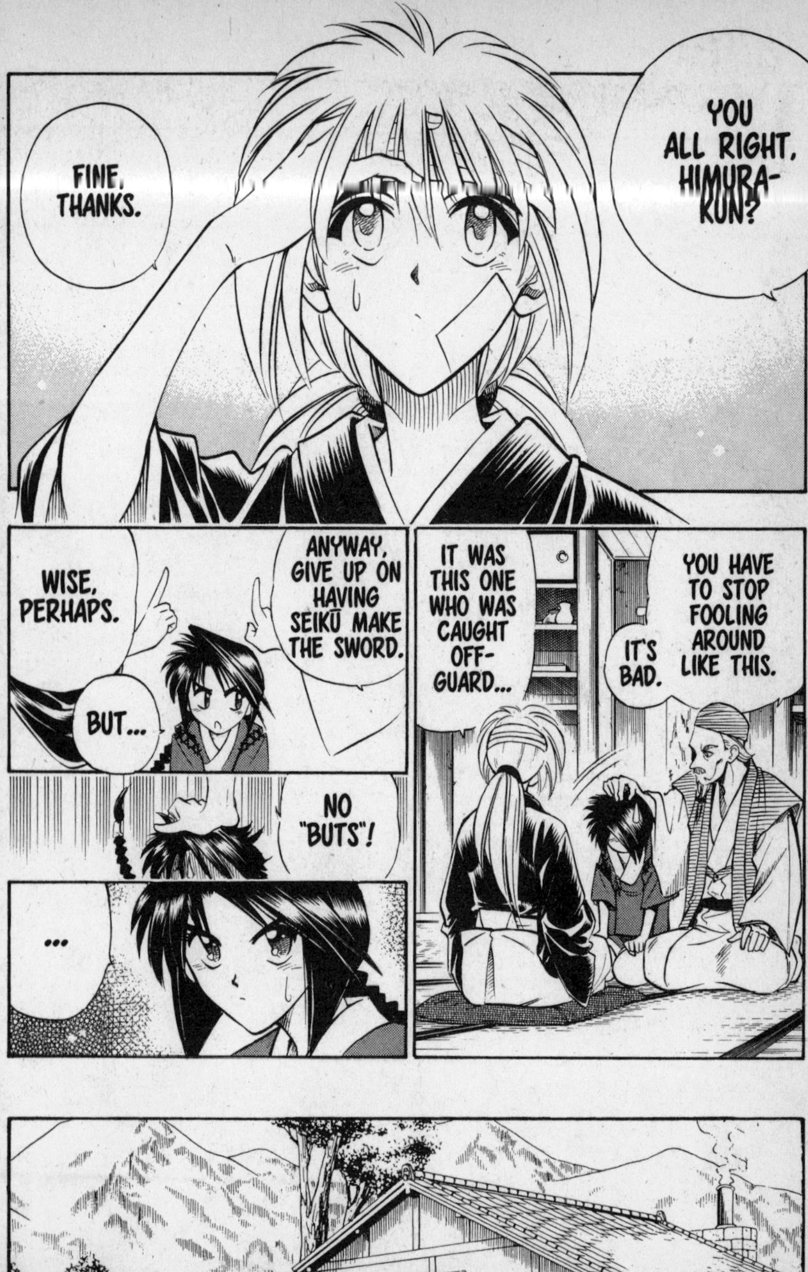
YOU ALL RIGHT, HIMURA-KUN?
FINE, THANKS.
YOU HAVE TO STOP FOOLING AROUND LIKE THIS.
IT'S BAD.
IT WAS THIS ONE WHO WAS CAUGHT OFF-GUARD...
ANYWAY, GIVE UP ON HAVING SEIKŪ MAKE THE SWORD.
WISE, PERHAPS.
BUT...
NO "BUTS"!
...

READ THIS WAY

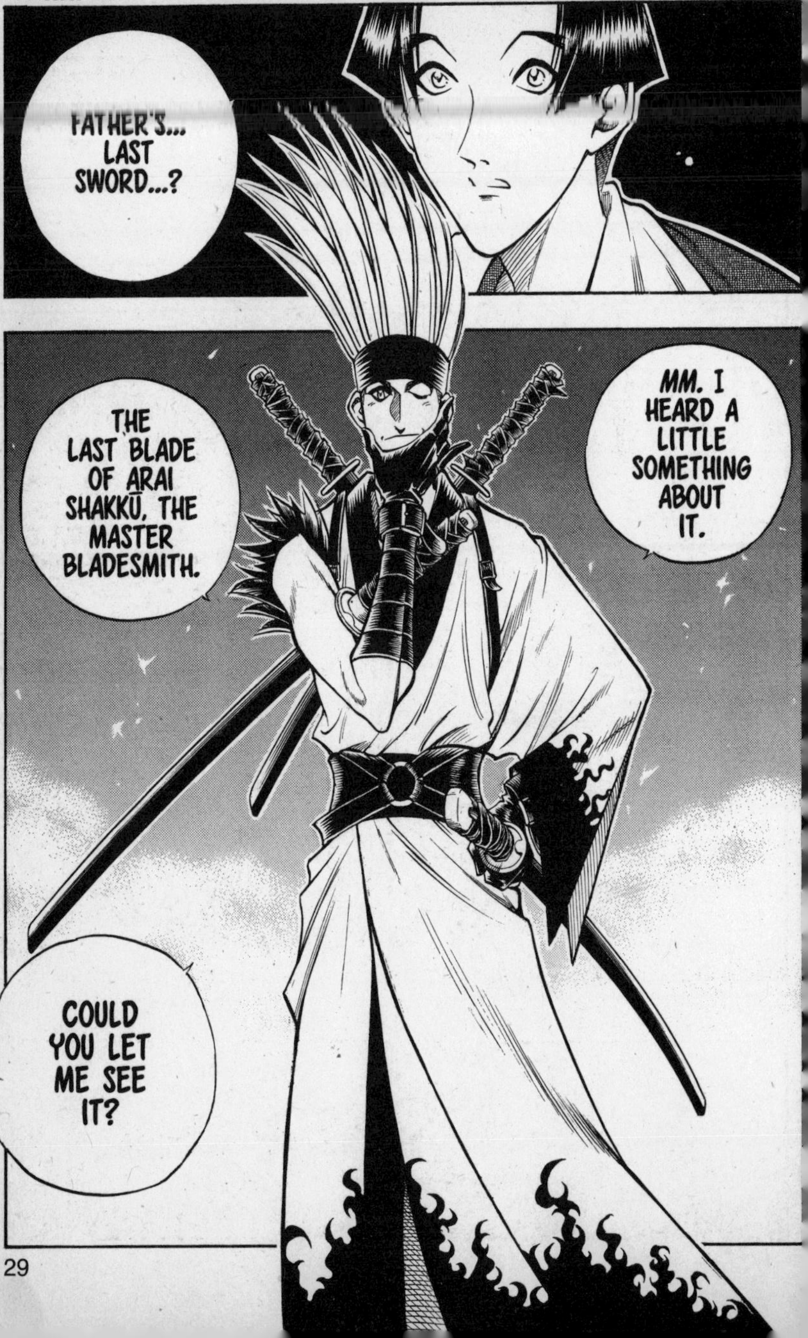

FATHER'S... LAST SWORD...?
MM. I HEARD A LITTLE SOMETHING ABOUT IT.
THE LAST BLADE OF ARAI SHAKKŪ, THE MASTER BLADESMITH.
COULD YOU LET ME SEE IT?

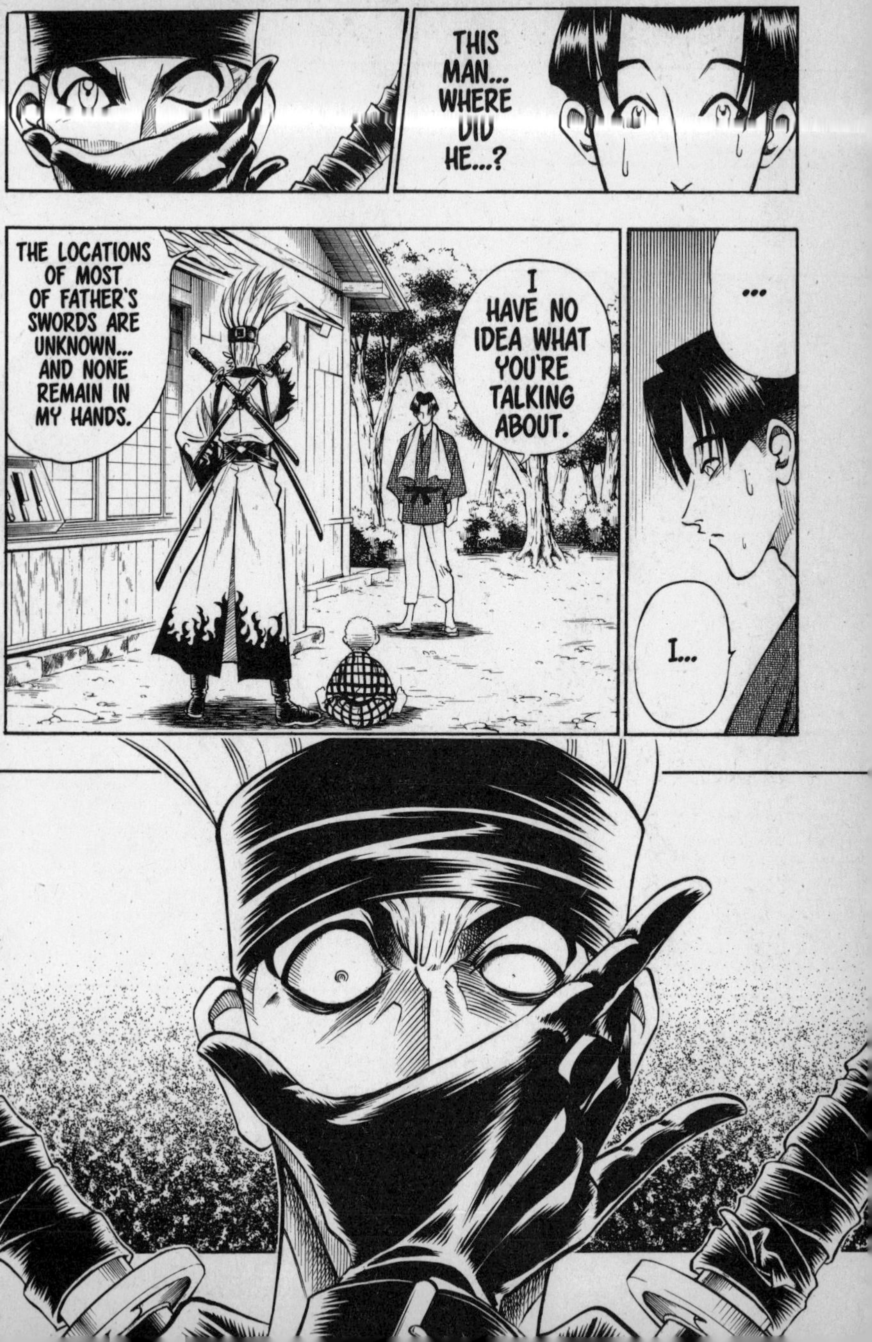
THIS MAN... WHERE DID HE...?
...
I...
I HAVE NO IDEA WHAT YOU'RE TALKING ABOUT.
THE LOCATIONS OF MOST OF FATHER'S SWORDS ARE UNKNOWN... AND NONE REMAIN IN MY HANDS.

READ THIS WAY

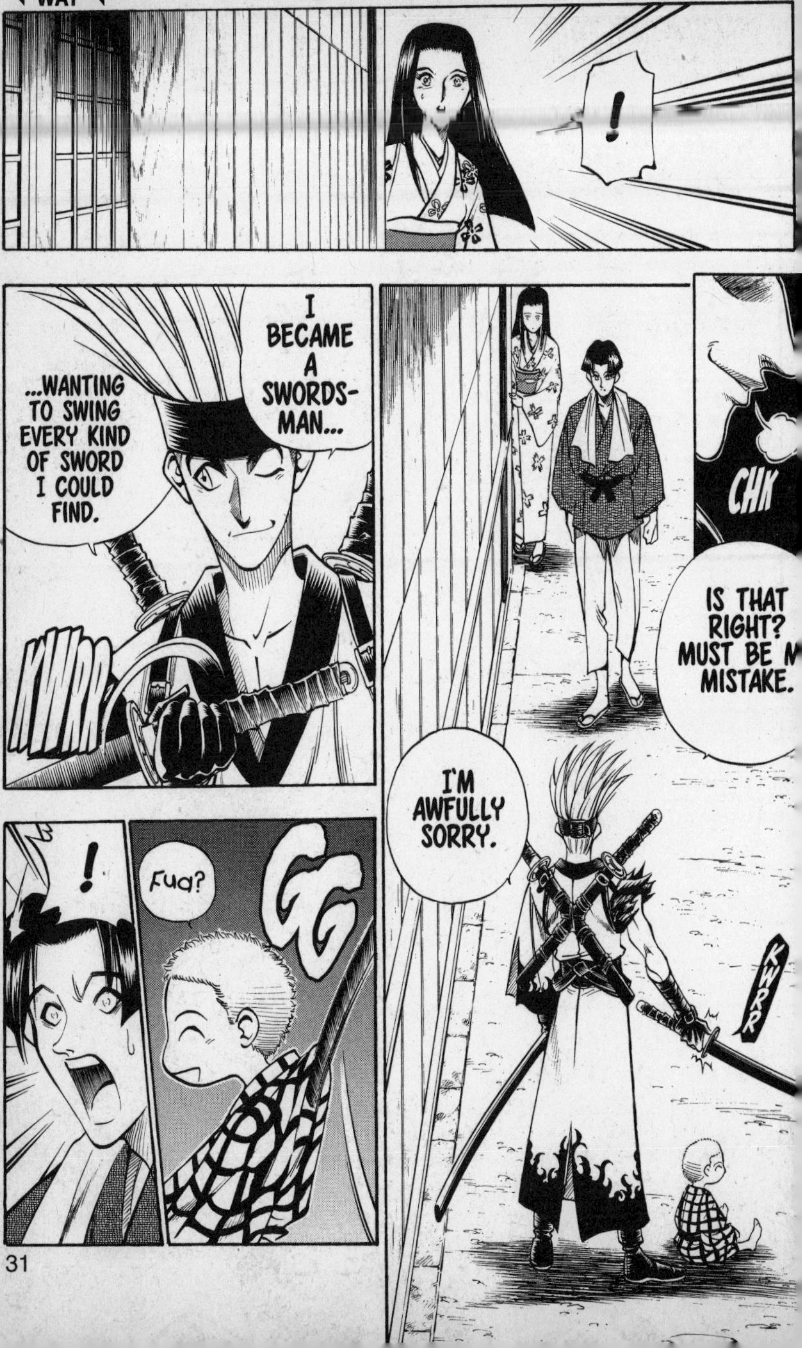
!
CHK
IS THAT RIGHT? MUST BE M
MISTAKE.
I'M AWFULLY SORRY.
KWRR
I BECAME A SWORDS-MAN...
...WANTING TO SWING EVERY KIND OF SWORD I COULD FIND.
KWRR
GG
Fua?
!

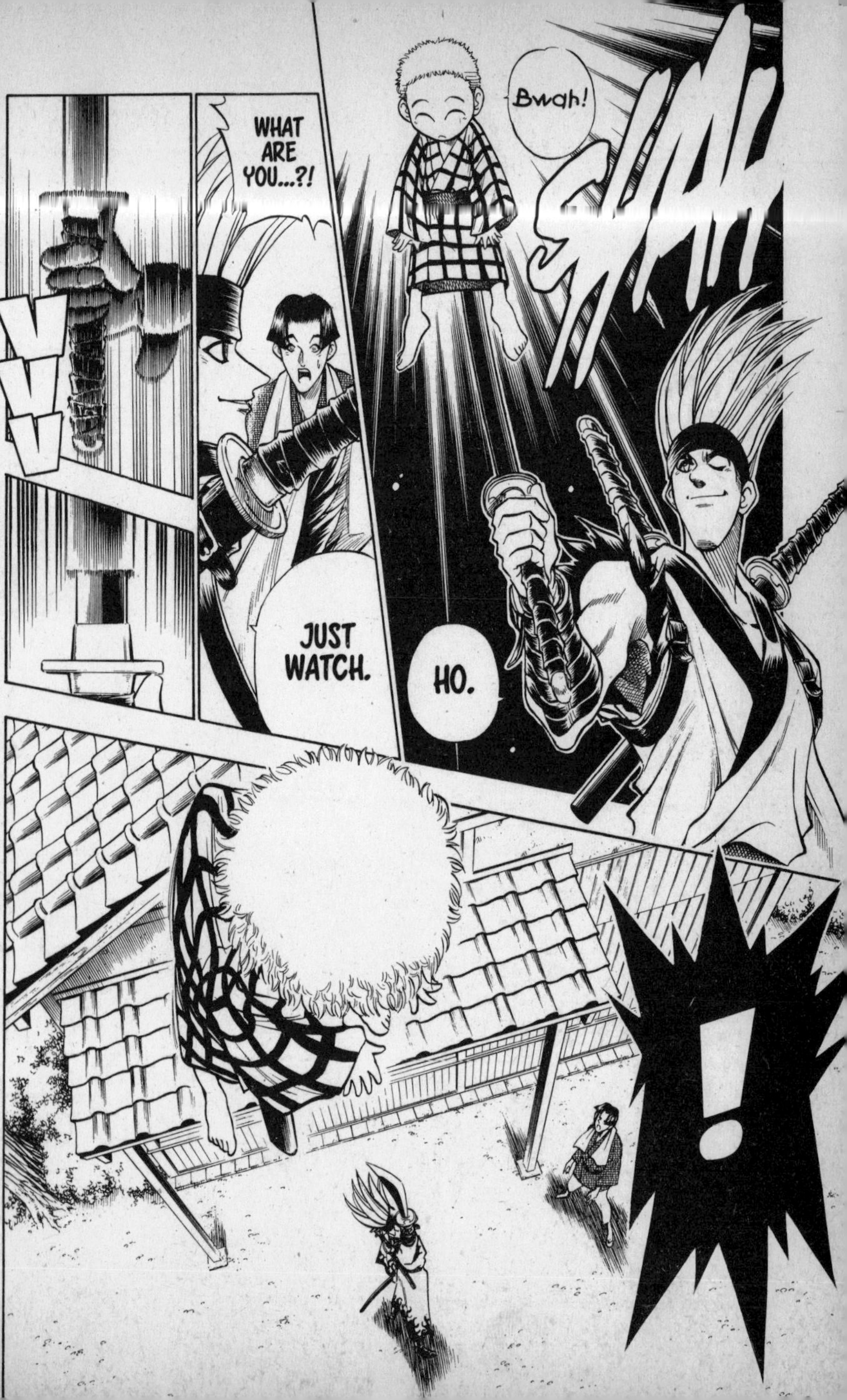
Bwah!
HO.
WHAT ARE YOU...?!
JUST WATCH.
VVV
!

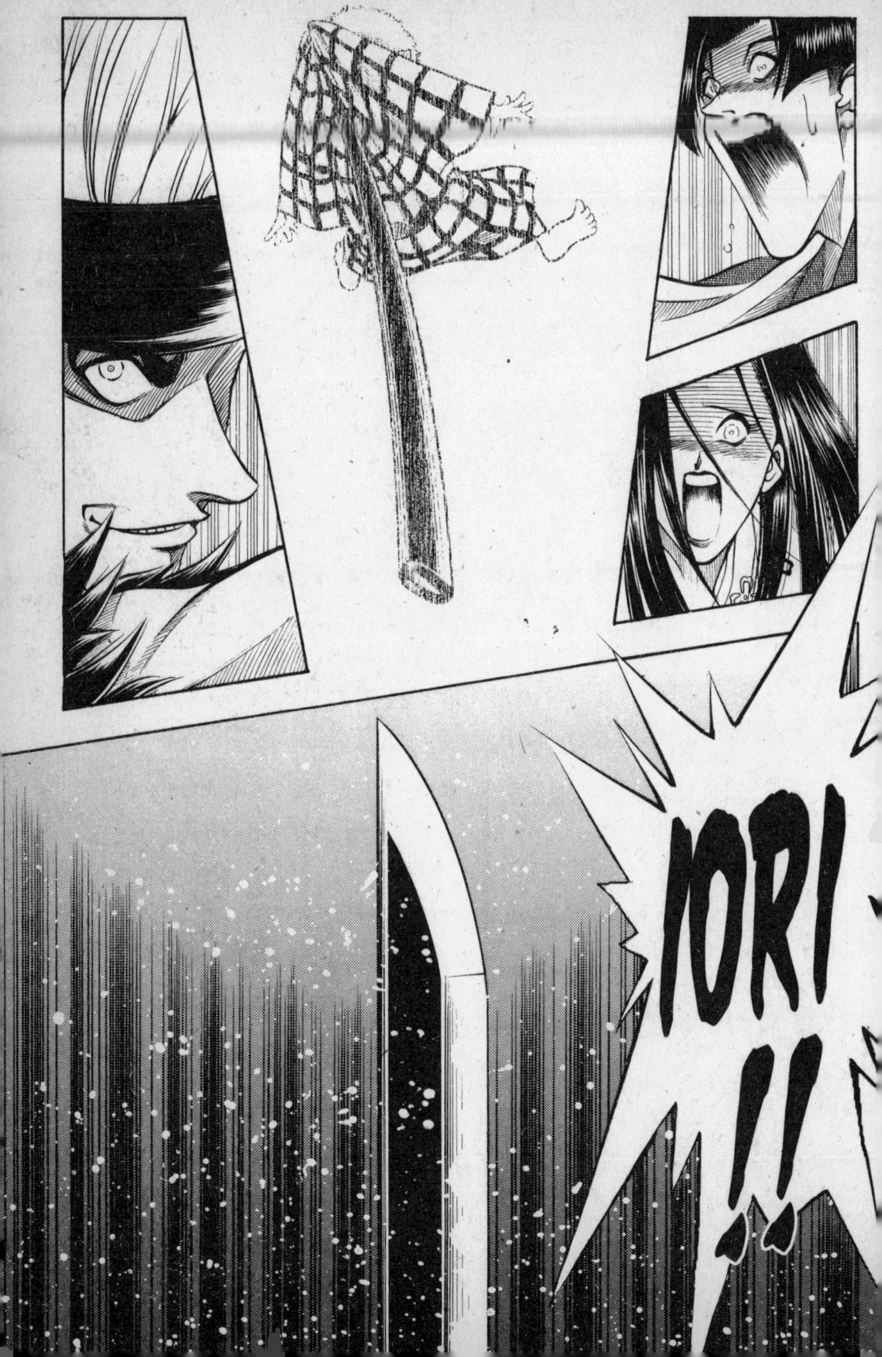
IORI!!

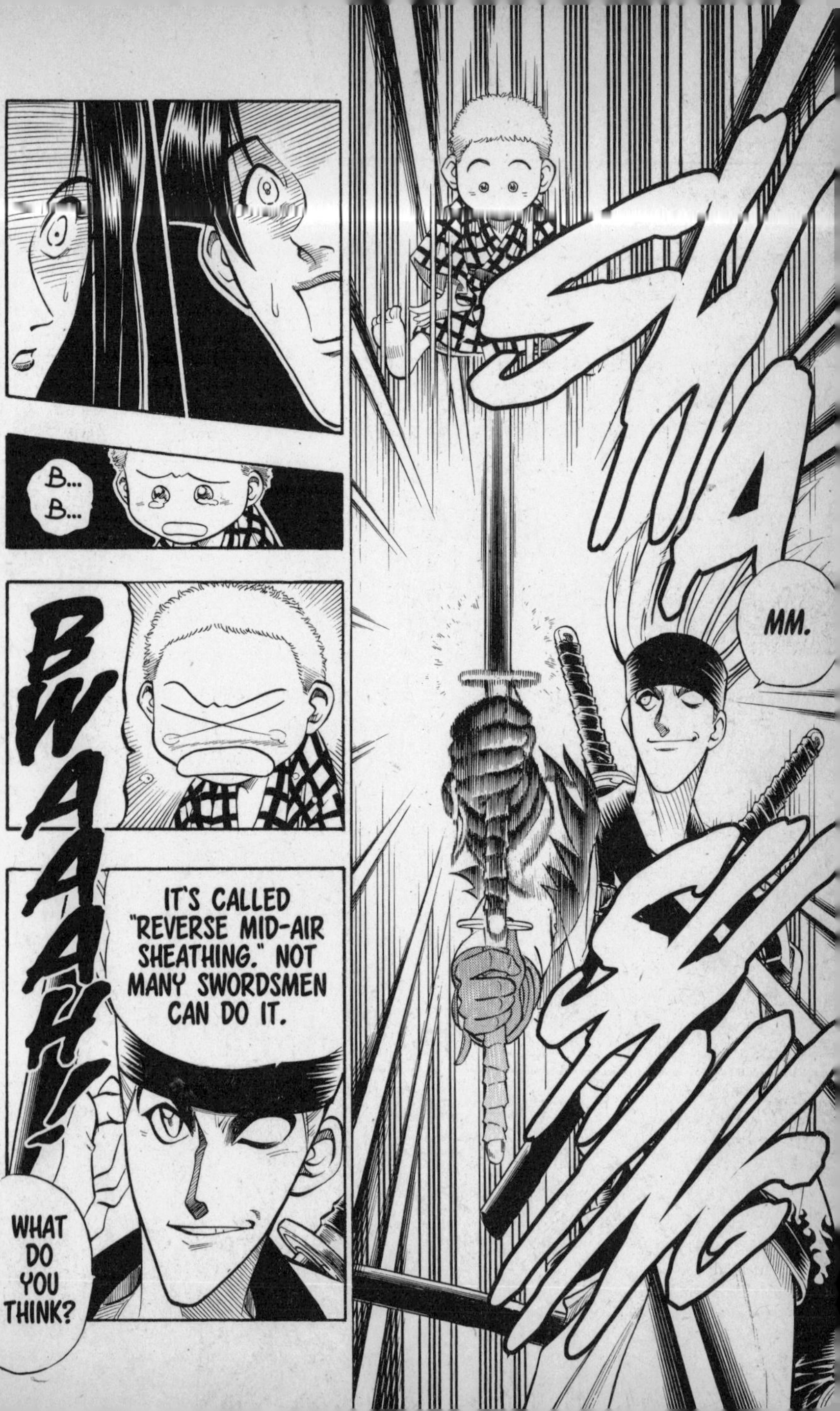
MM.
B... B...
BWAAAH!
IT'S CALLED "REVERSE MID-AIR SHEATHING." NOT MANY SWORDSMEN CAN DO IT.
WHAT DO YOU THINK?

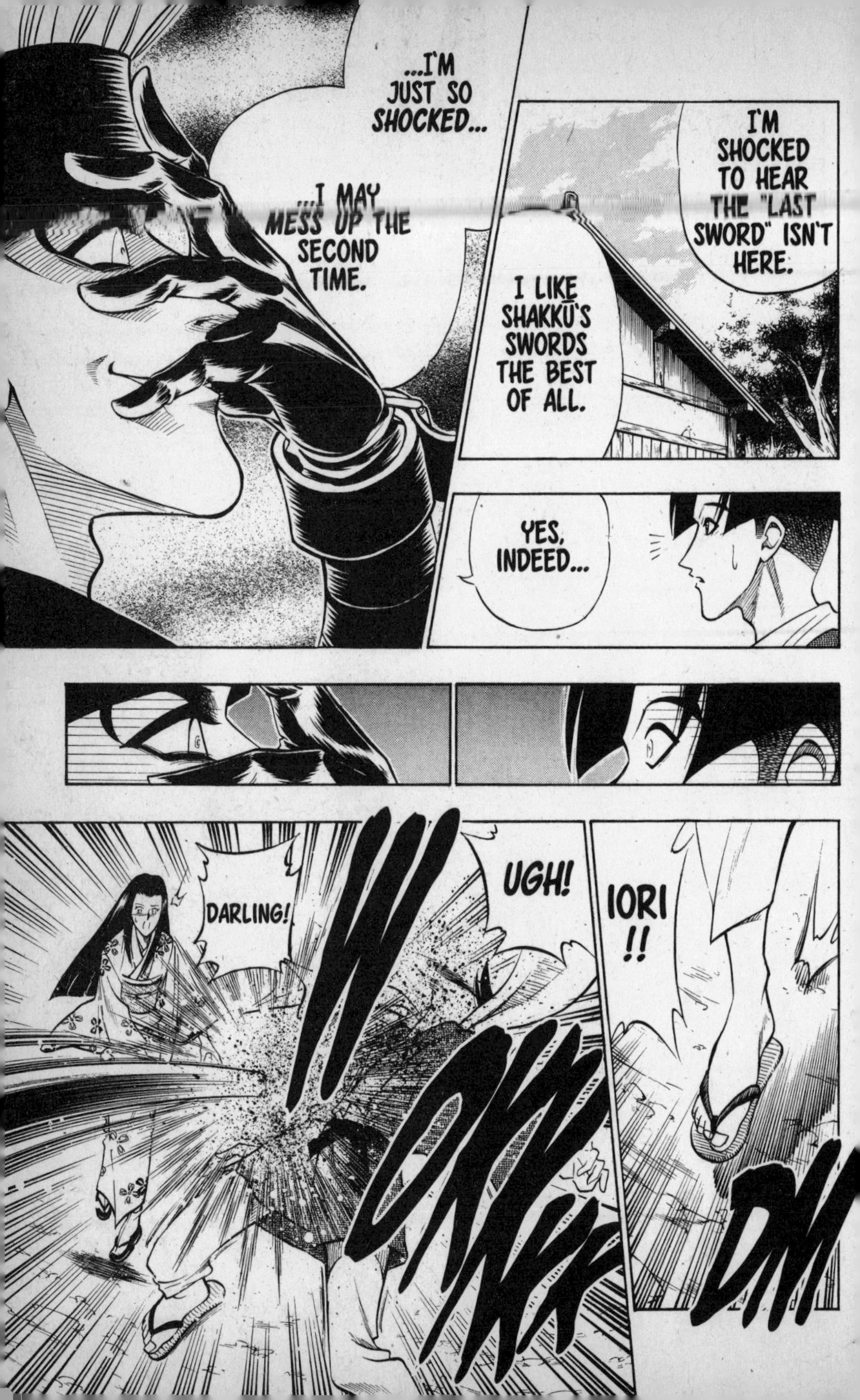
I'M SHOCKED TO HEAR THE "LAST SWORD" ISN'T HERE.
I LIKE SHAKKŪ'S SWORDS THE BEST OF ALL.
YES, INDEED...
...I'M JUST SO SHOCKED...
...I MAY MESS UP THE SECOND TIME.
IORI !!
UGH!
DARLING!

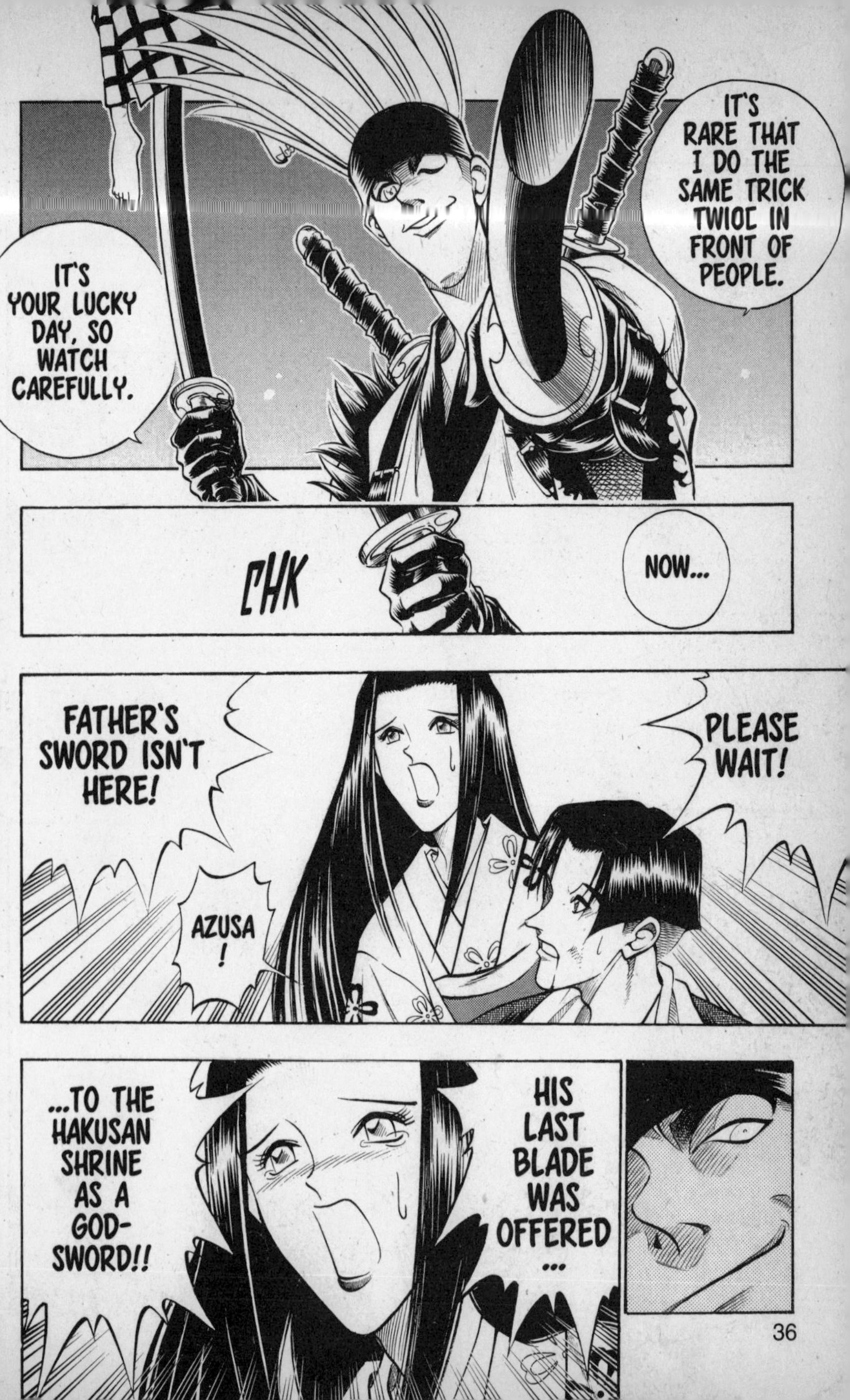
IT'S RARE THAT I DO THE SAME TRICK TWICE IN FRONT OF PEOPLE.
IT'S YOUR LUCKY DAY, SO WATCH CAREFULLY.
NOW...
CHK
PLEASE WAIT!
FATHER'S SWORD ISN'T HERE!
AZUSA!
HIS LAST BLADE WAS OFFERED...
...TO THE HAKUSAN SHRINE AS A GOD-SWORD!!

READ THIS WAY

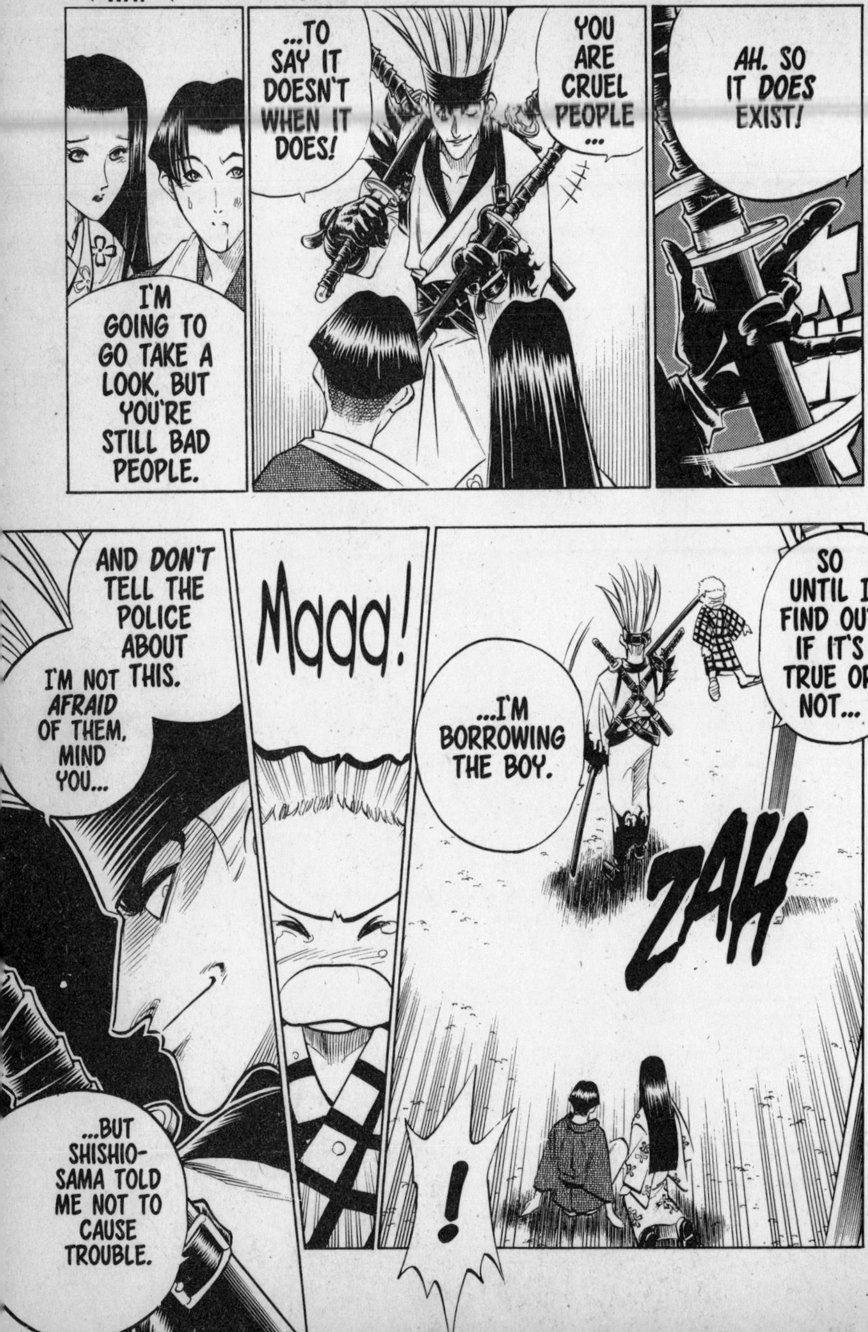
AH. SO IT DOES EXIST!
YOU ARE CRUEL PEOPLE...
...TO SAY IT DOESN'T WHEN IT DOES!
I'M GOING TO GO TAKE A LOOK, BUT YOU'RE STILL BAD PEOPLE.
SO UNTIL I FIND OUT IF IT'S TRUE OR NOT...
...I'M BORROWING THE BOY.
ZAH
!
Maaa!
AND DON'T TELL THE POLICE ABOUT THIS.
I'M NOT AFRAID OF THEM, MIND YOU...
...BUT SHISHIO-SAMA TOLD ME NOT TO CAUSE TROUBLE.

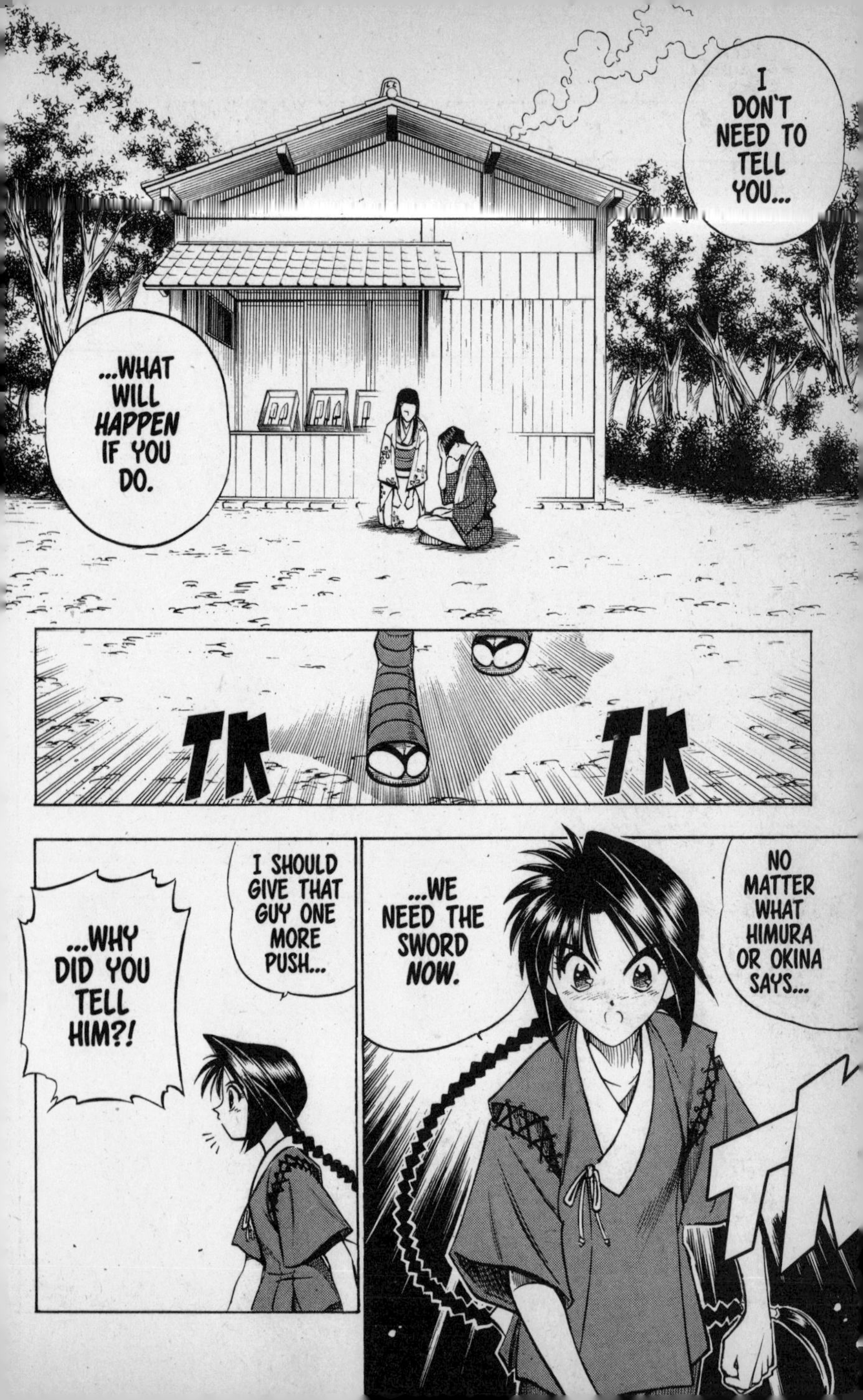
I DON'T NEED TO TELL YOU...
...WHAT WILL HAPPEN IF YOU DO.
TK
TK
NO MATTER WHAT HIMURA OR OKINA SAYS...
...WE NEED THE SWORD NOW.
I SHOULD GIVE THAT GUY ONE MORE PUSH...
...WHY DID YOU TELL HIM?!

READ THIS WAY

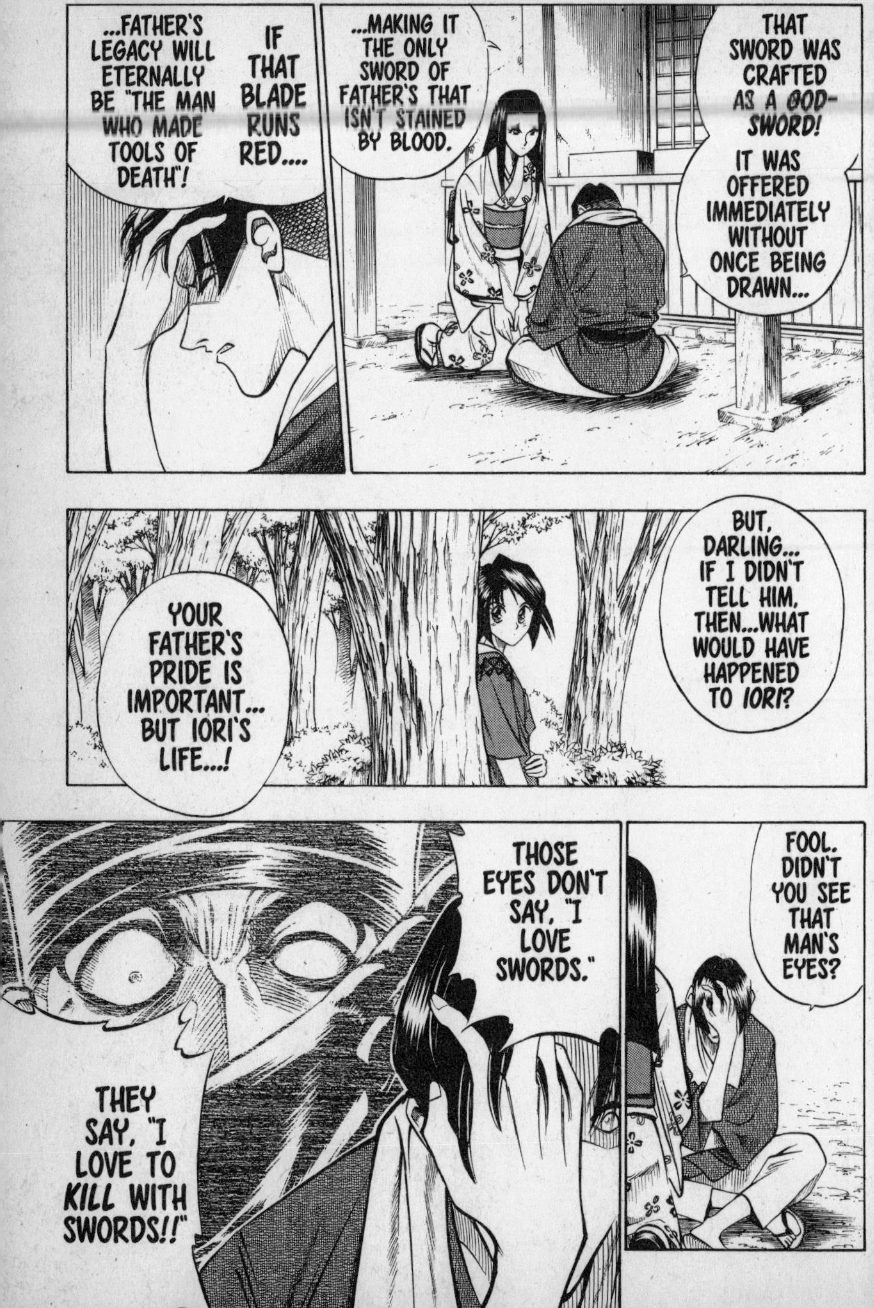
THAT SWORD WAS CRAFTED AS A GOD-SWORD!
IT WAS OFFERED IMMEDIATELY WITHOUT ONCE BEING DRAWN...
...MAKING IT THE ONLY SWORD OF FATHER'S THAT ISN'T STAINED BY BLOOD.
IF THAT BLADE RUNS RED....
...FATHER'S LEGACY WILL ETERNALLY BE "THE MAN WHO MADE TOOLS OF DEATH"!
BUT, DARLING... IF I DIDN'T TELL HIM, THEN...WHAT WOULD HAVE HAPPENED TO IORI?
YOUR FATHER'S PRIDE IS IMPORTANT... BUT IORI'S LIFE...!
FOOL. DIDN'T YOU SEE THAT MAN'S EYES?
THOSE EYES DON'T SAY, "I LOVE SWORDS."
THEY SAY, "I LOVE TO KILL WITH SWORDS!!"

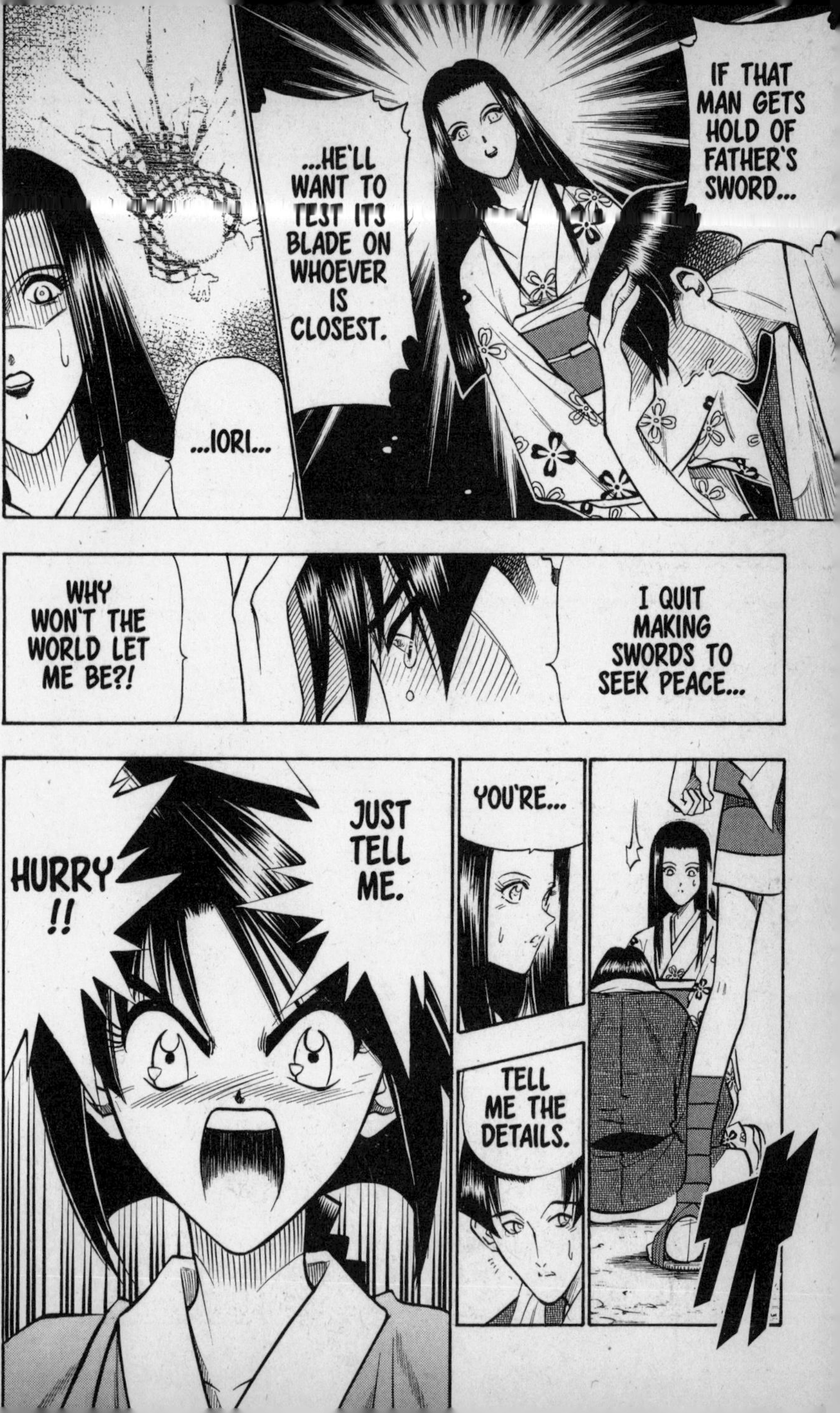
IF THAT MAN GETS HOLD OF FATHER'S SWORD...
...HE'LL WANT TO TEST ITS BLADE ON WHOEVER IS CLOSEST.
...IORI...
I QUIT MAKING SWORDS TO SEEK PEACE...
WHY WON'T THE WORLD LET ME BE?!
YOU'RE...
TELL ME THE DETAILS.
JUST TELL ME.
HURRY!!

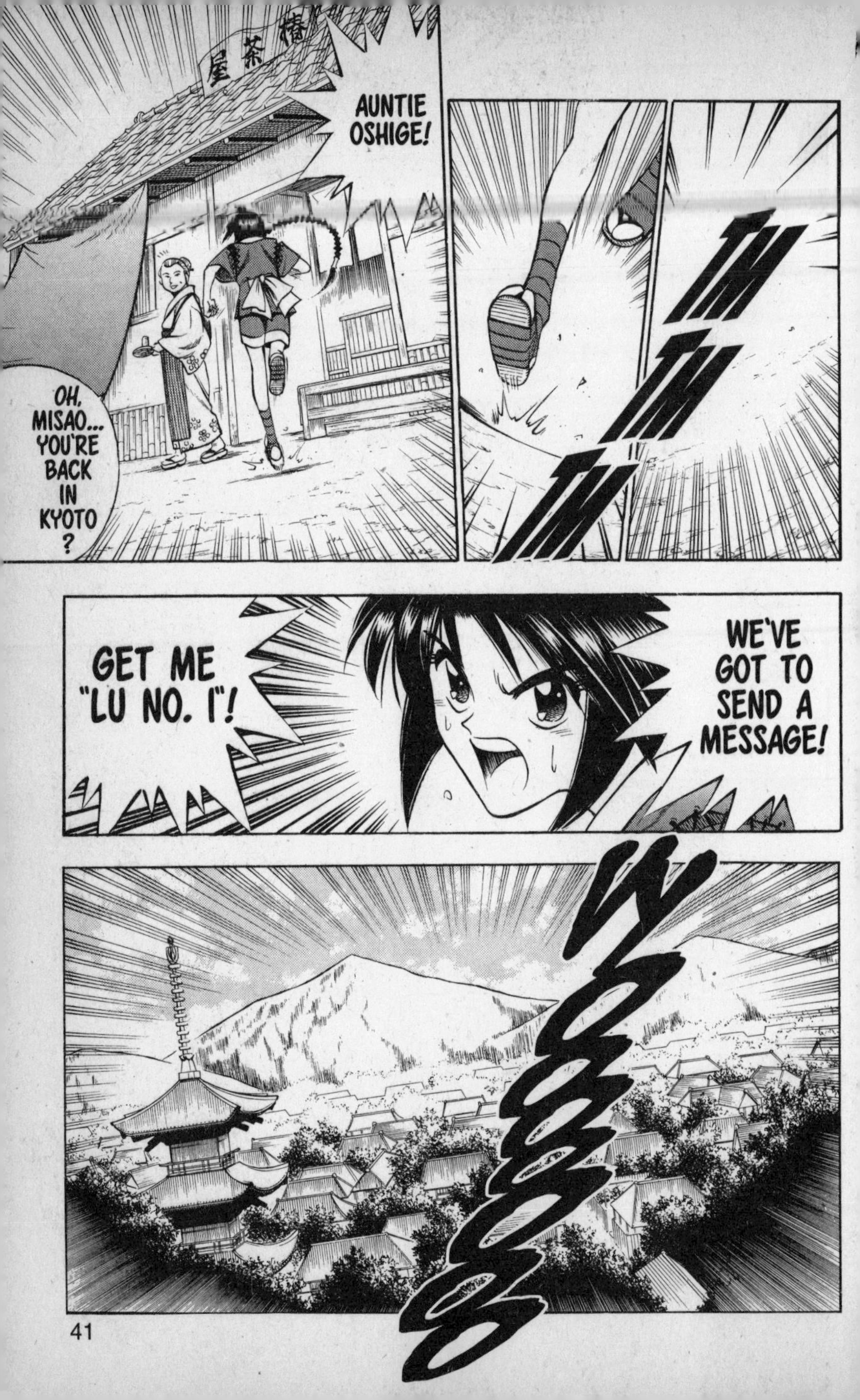
AUNTIE OSHIGE!
OH, MISAO... YOU'RE BACK IN KYOTO?
WE'VE GOT TO SEND A MESSAGE!
GET ME "LU NO. 1"!

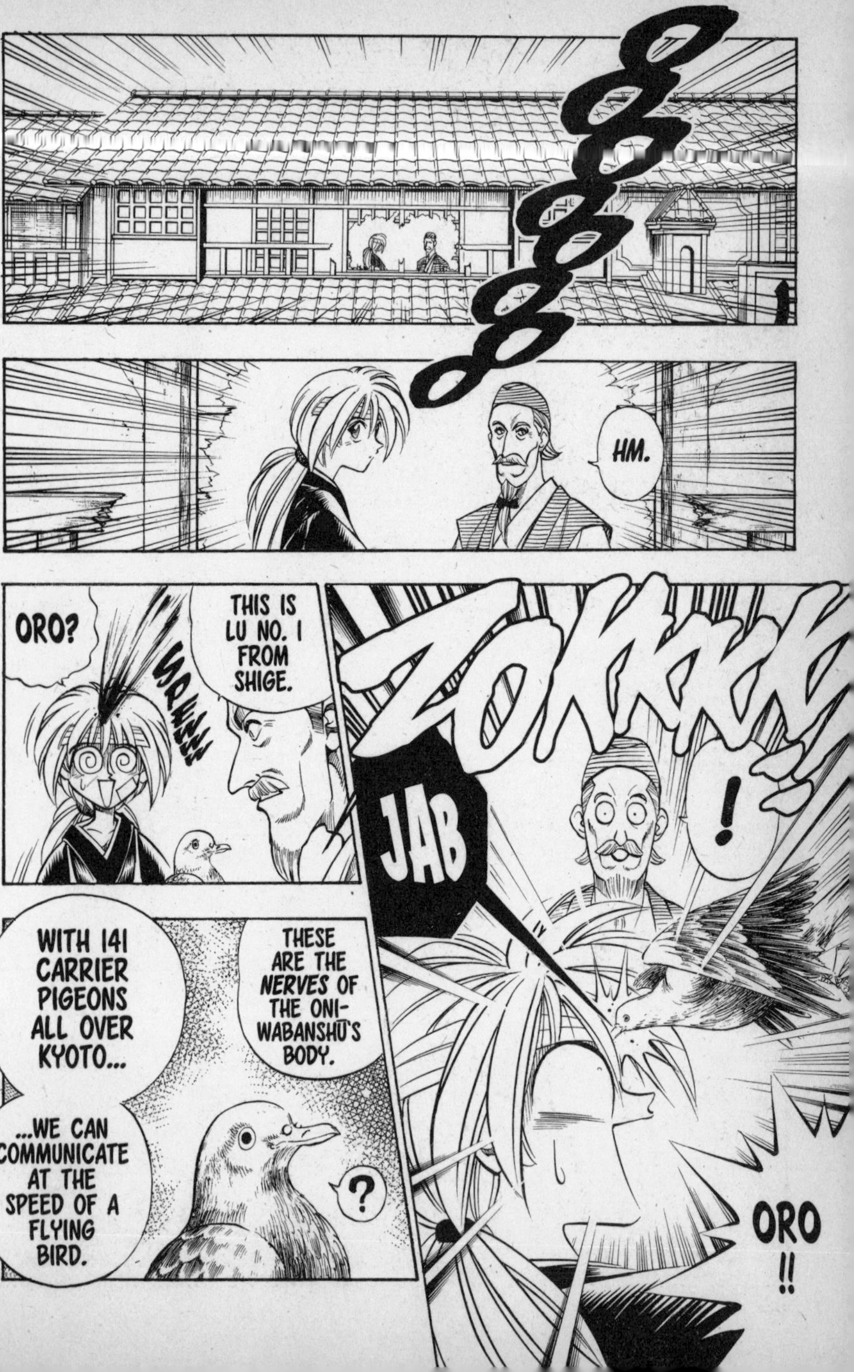
HM.
JAB
!
ORO!!
THIS IS LU NO. 1 FROM SHIGE.
ORO?
THESE ARE THE NERVES OF THE ONI-WABANSHŪ'S BODY.
WITH 141 CARRIER PIGEONS ALL OVER KYOTO...
...WE CAN COMMUNICATE AT THE SPEED OF A FLYING BIRD.
?

READ THIS WAY

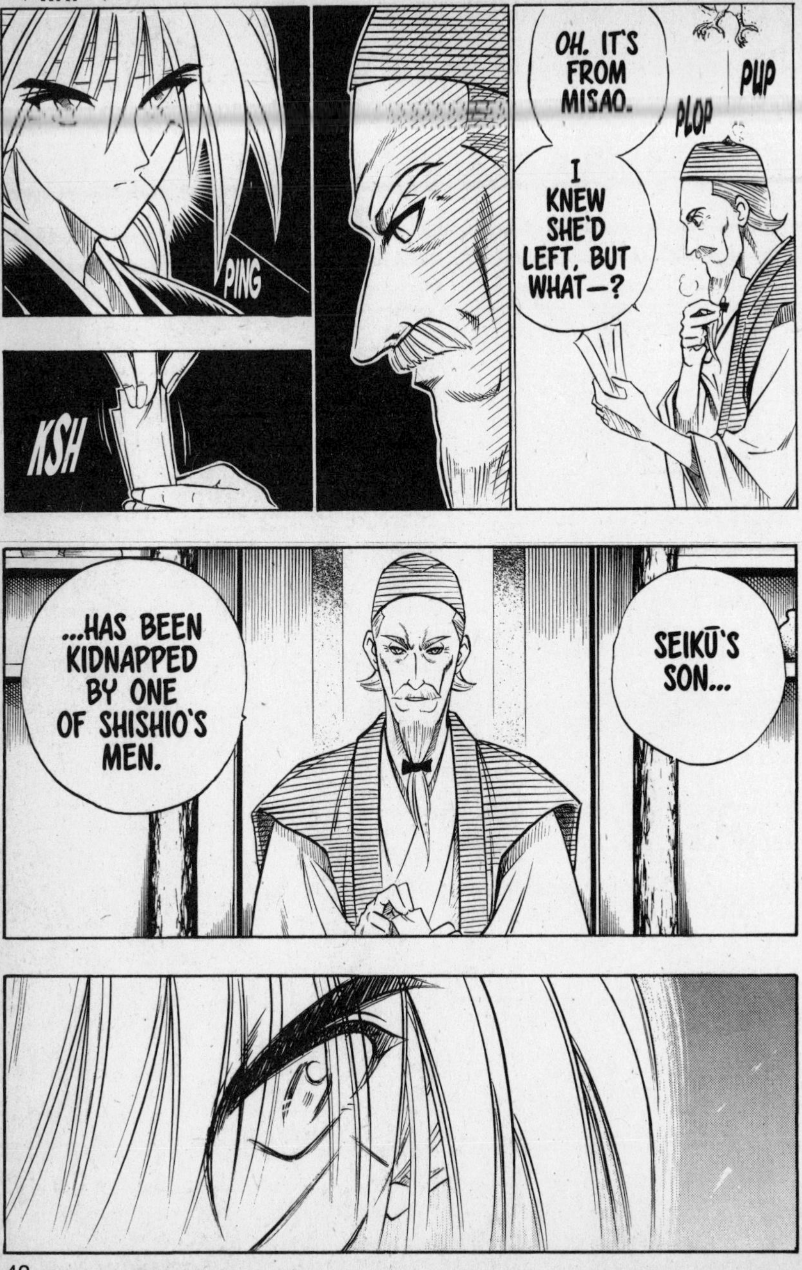

OH. IT'S FROM MISAO.
I KNEW SHE'D LEFT, BUT WHAT—?
PUP
PLOP
PING
KSH
SEIKŪ'S SON...
...HAS BEEN KIDNAPPED BY ONE OF SHISHIO'S MEN.

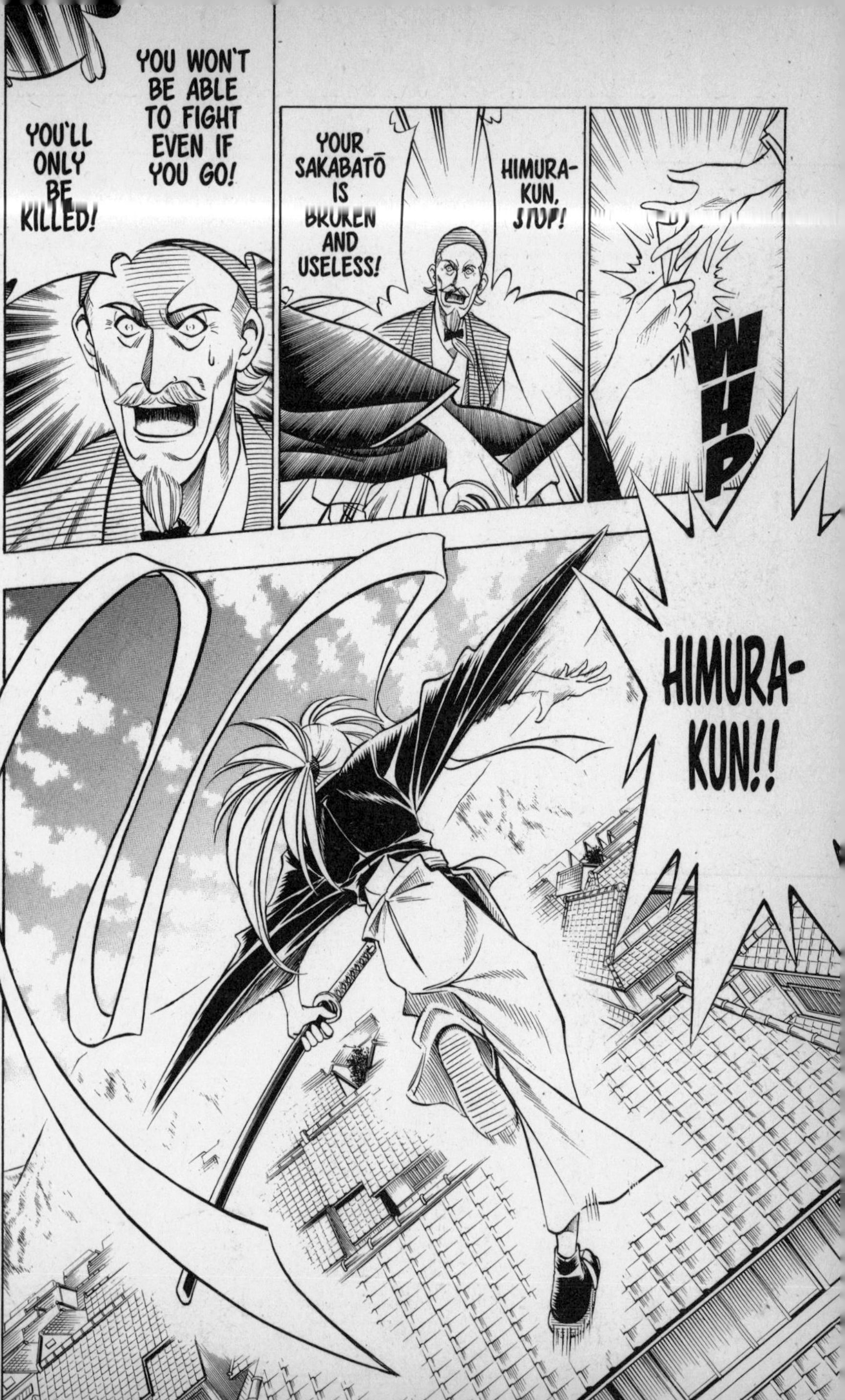
WHP
HIMURA-KUN, STOP!
YOUR SAKABATŌ IS BROKEN AND USELESS!
YOU WON'T BE ABLE TO FIGHT EVEN IF YOU GO!
YOU'LL ONLY BE KILLED!
HIMURA-KUN!!

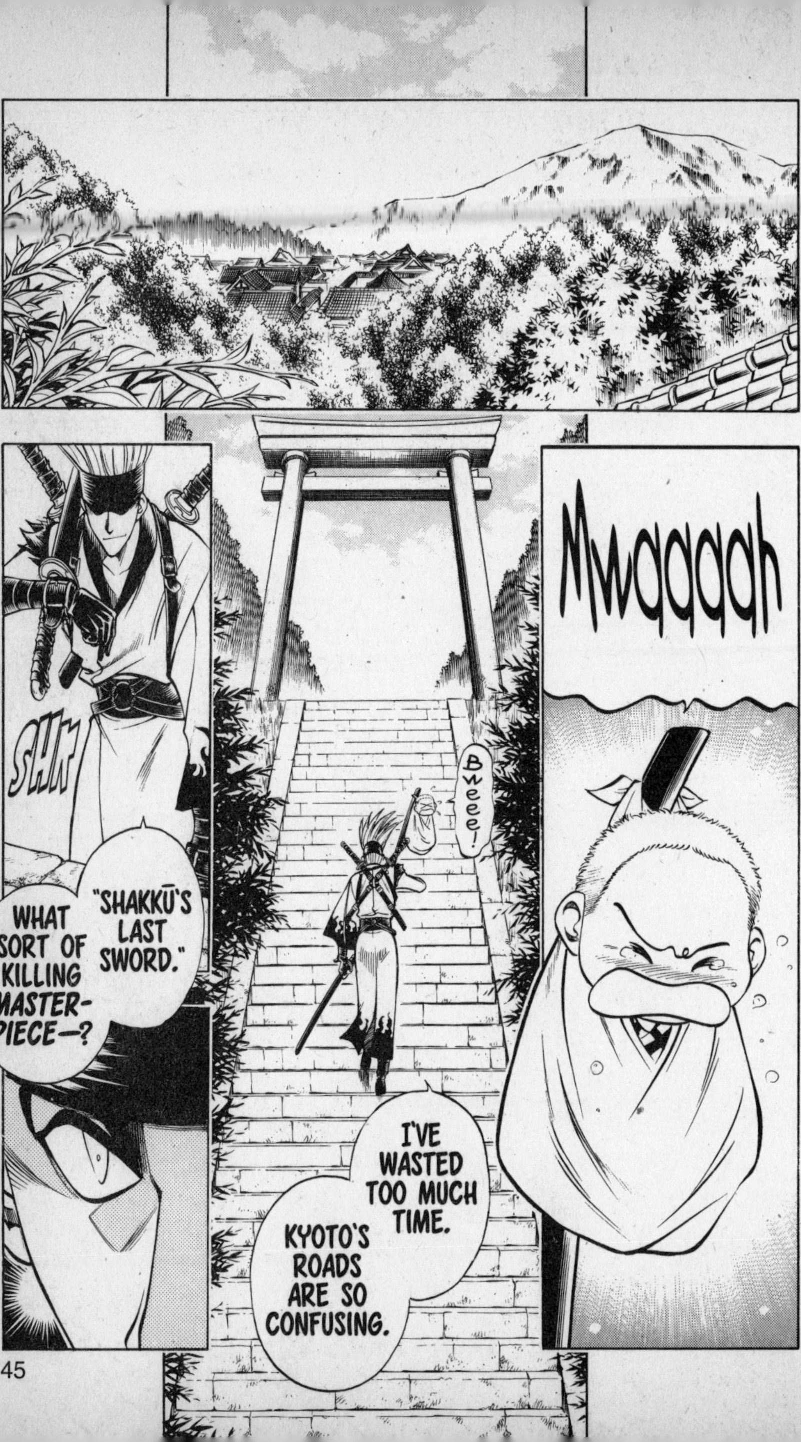
Mwaaah
Bweee!
I'VE WASTED TOO MUCH TIME.
KYOTO'S ROADS ARE SO CONFUSING.
SHK
"SHAKKŪ'S LAST SWORD."
WHAT SORT OF KILLING MASTER-PIECE—?

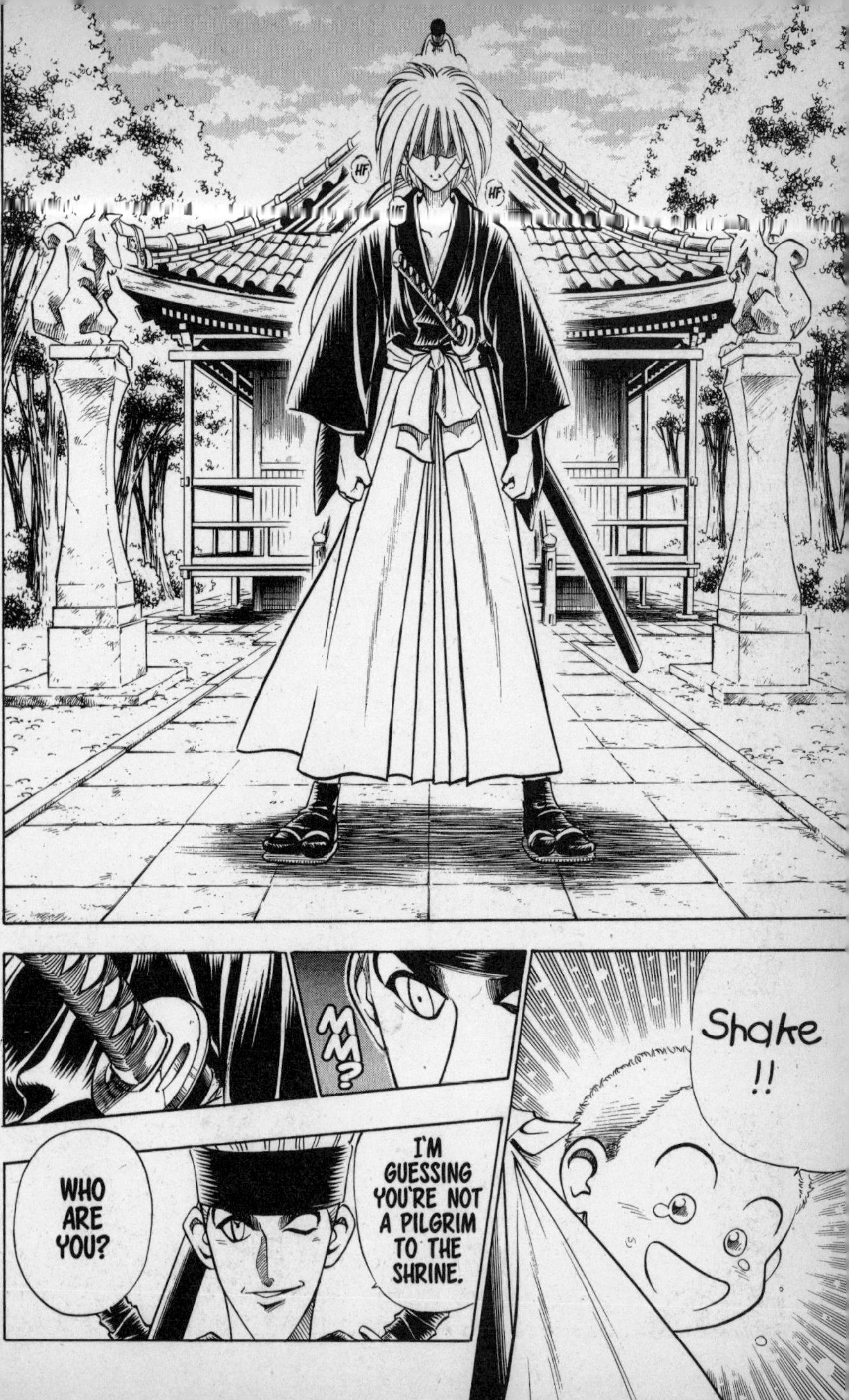
HF
HF
HF
Shake !!
MM?
I'M GUESSING YOU'RE NOT A PILGRIM TO THE SHRINE.
WHO ARE YOU?

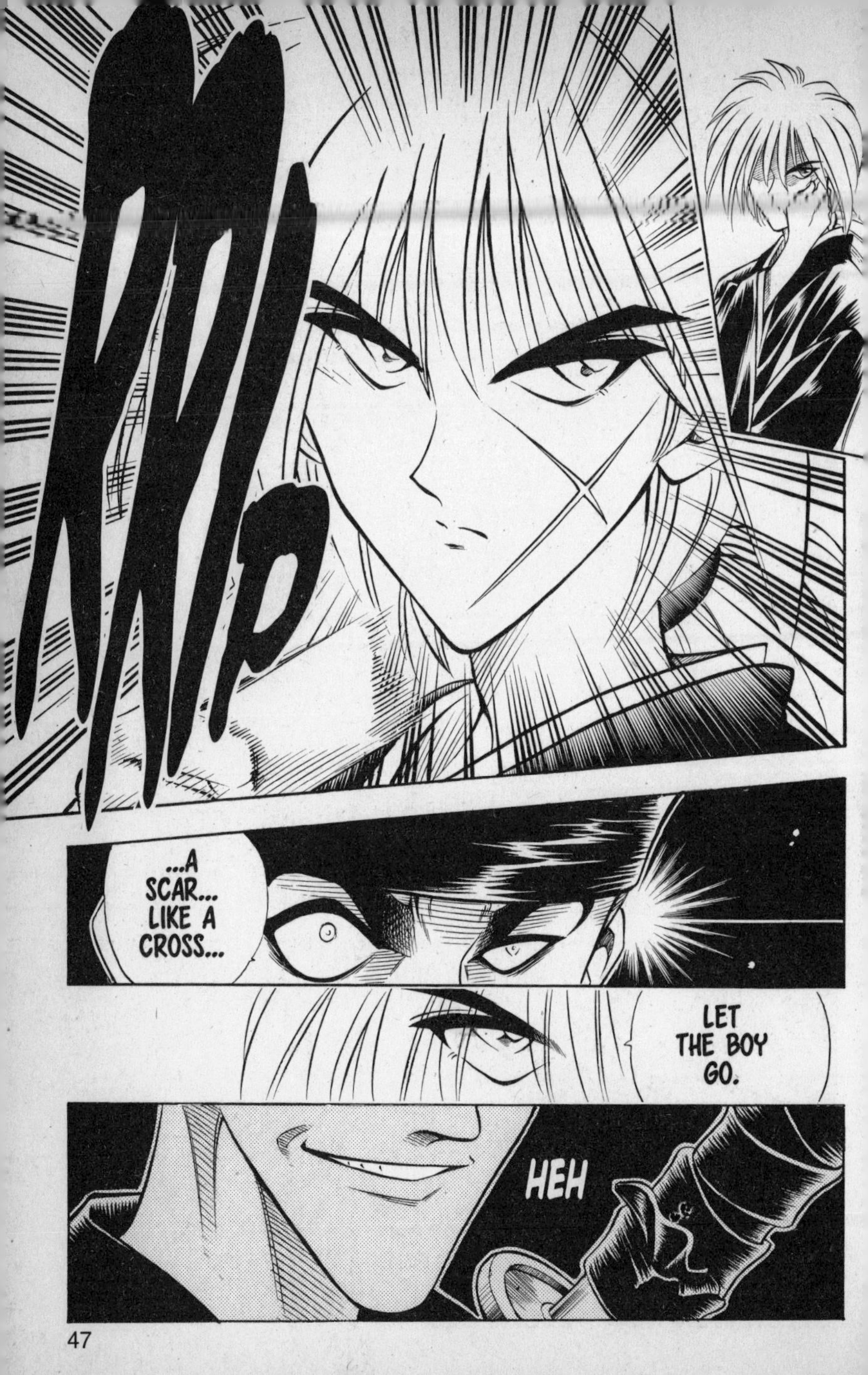
KRIP
...A SCAR... LIKE A CROSS...
LET THE BOY GO.
HEH

Rurouni Kenshin

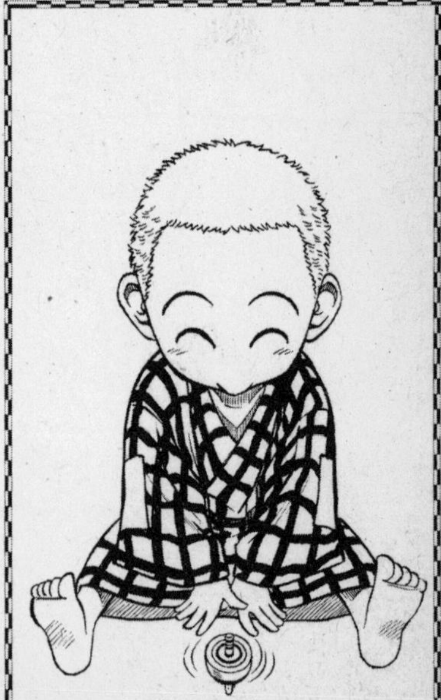

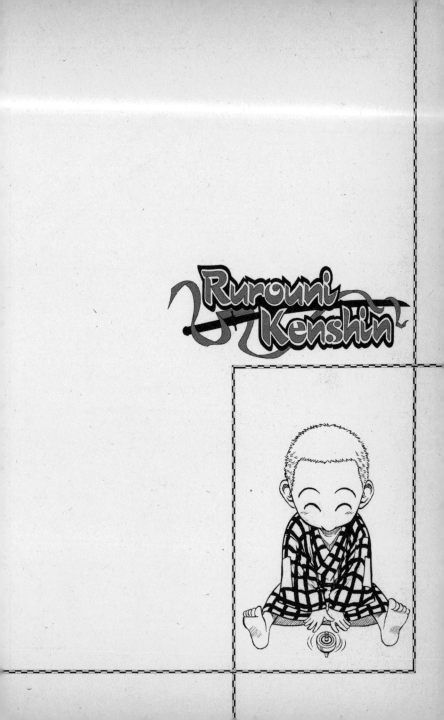

Act 78
Chō of the Ten Swords

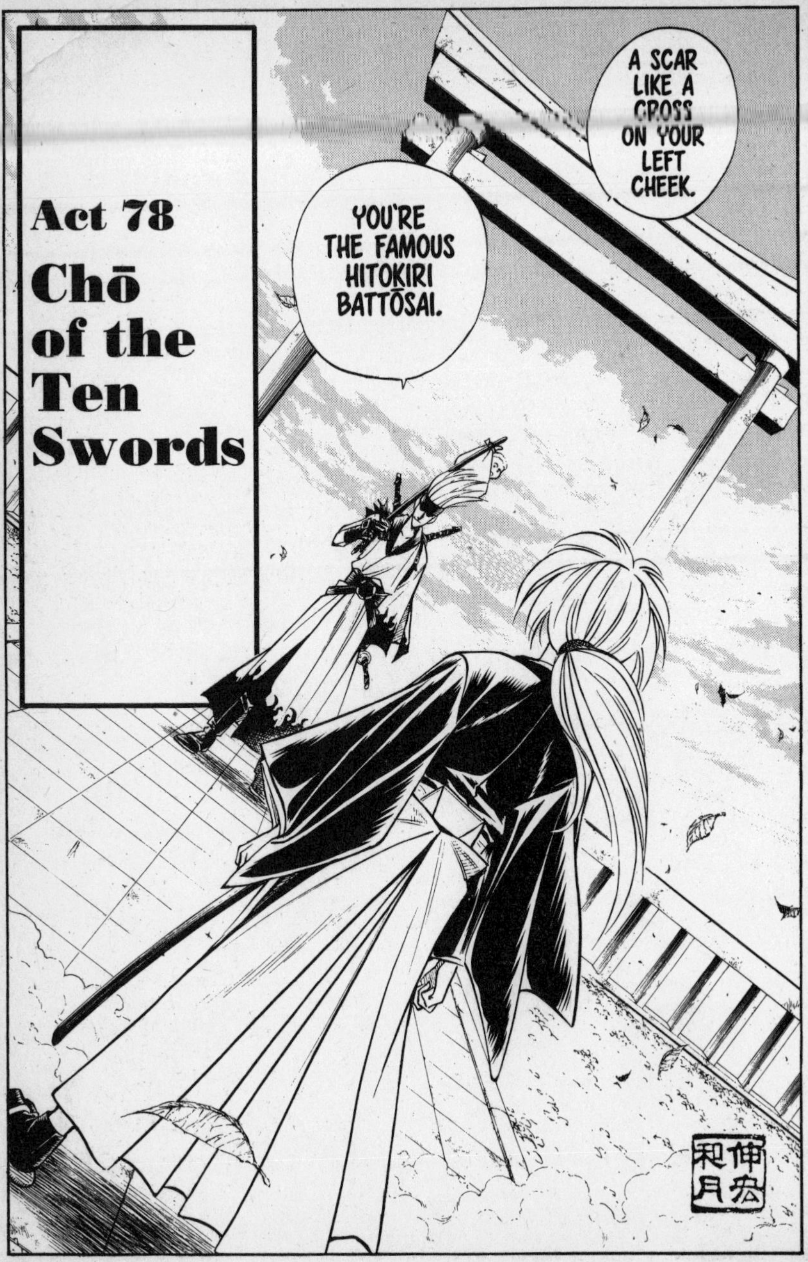
A SCAR LIKE A CROSS ON YOUR LEFT CHEEK.
YOU'RE THE FAMOUS HITOKIRI BATTŌSAI.
伸宏和月

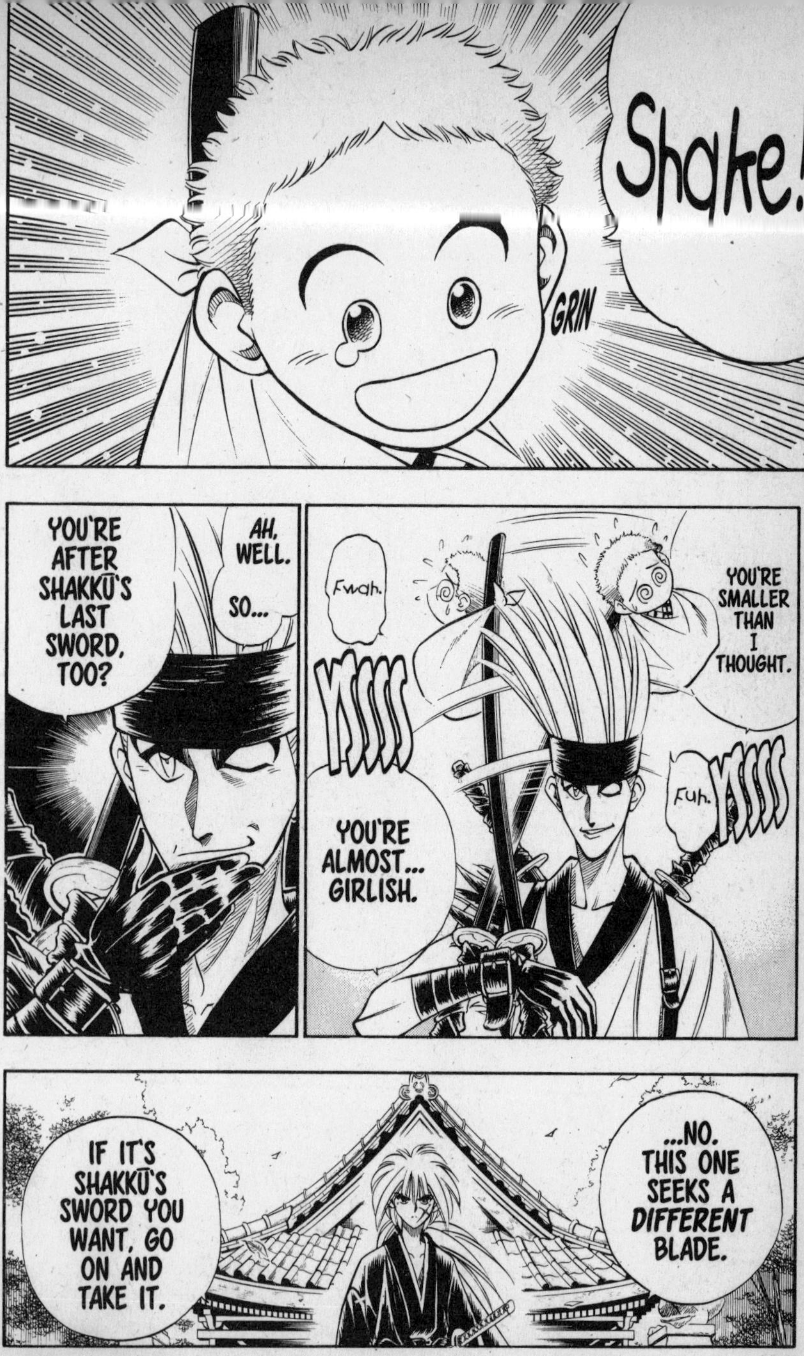
Shake!
GRIN
YOU'RE SMALLER THAN I THOUGHT.
Fwah.
YSSSS
Fuh.
YSSSS
YOU'RE ALMOST... GIRLISH.
AH, WELL.
SO...
YOU'RE AFTER SHAKKŪ'S LAST SWORD, TOO?
...NO. THIS ONE SEEKS A DIFFERENT BLADE.
IF IT'S SHAKKŪ'S SWORD YOU WANT, GO ON AND TAKE IT.

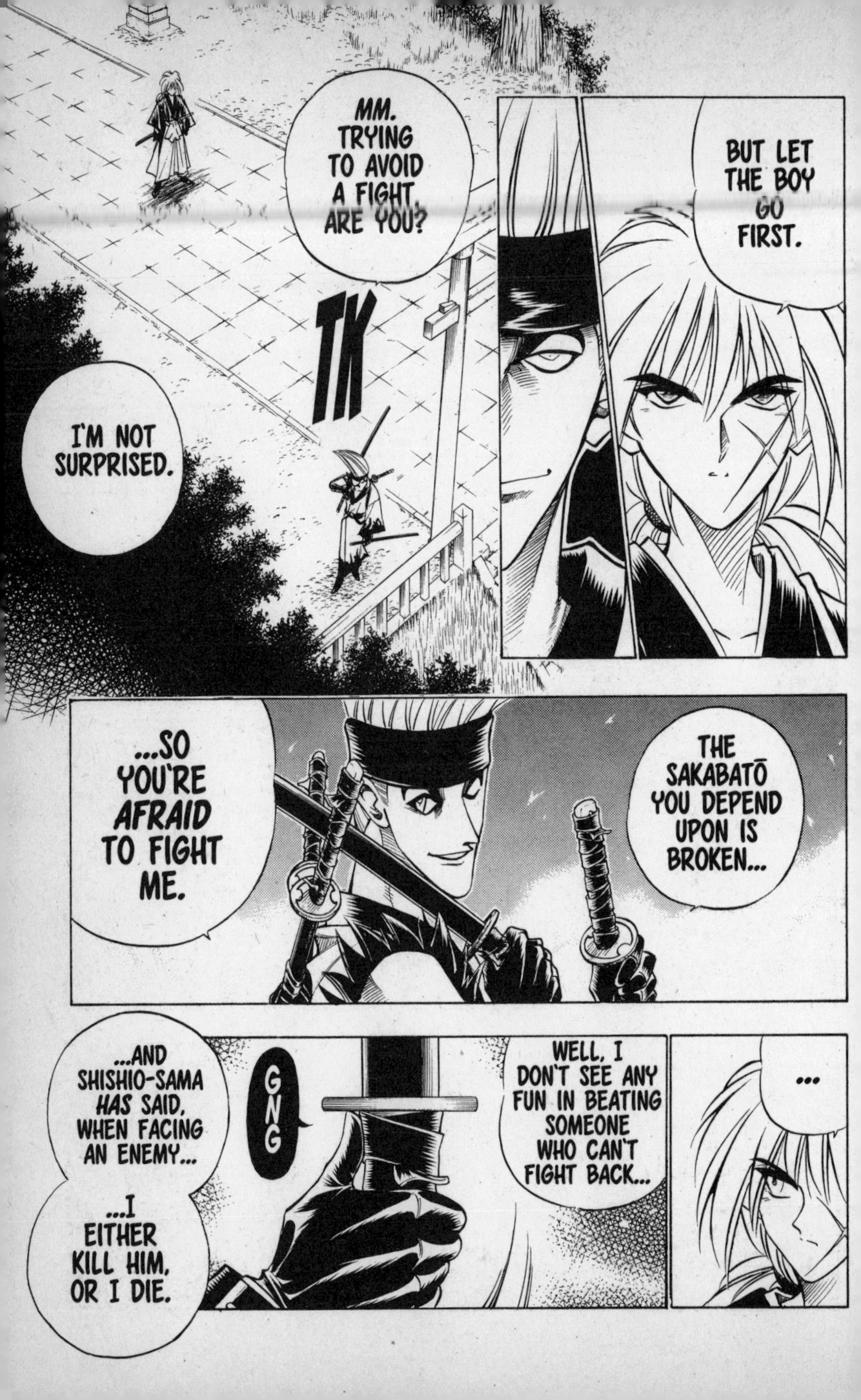
BUT LET THE BOY GO FIRST.
MM. TRYING TO AVOID A FIGHT, ARE YOU?
TK
I'M NOT SURPRISED.
THE SAKABATŌ YOU DEPEND UPON IS BROKEN...
...SO YOU'RE *AFRAID* TO FIGHT ME.
...
WELL, I DON'T SEE ANY FUN IN BEATING SOMEONE WHO CAN'T FIGHT BACK...
GNG
...AND SHISHIO-SAMA *HAS* SAID, WHEN FACING AN ENEMY...
...I EITHER KILL HIM, OR I DIE.

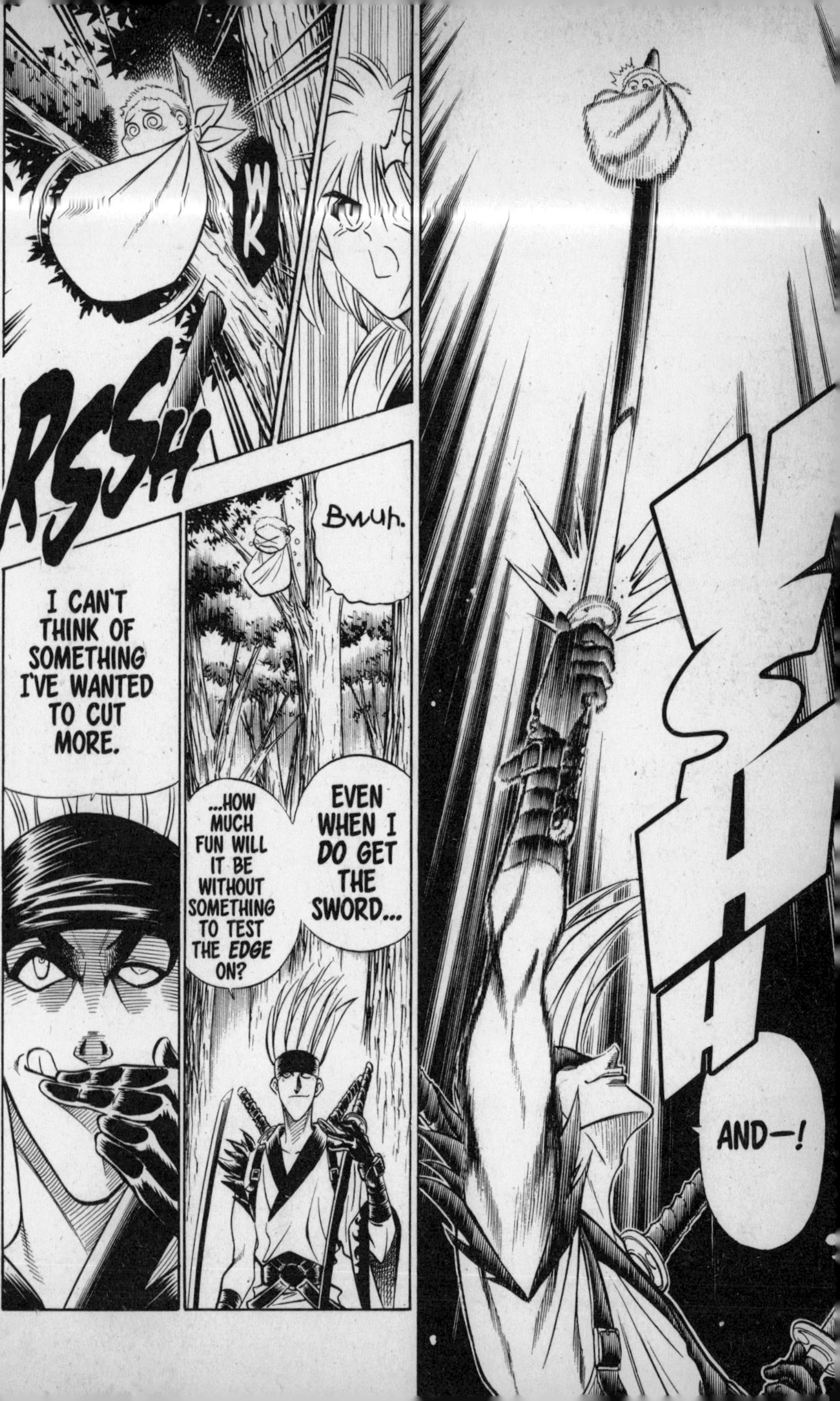
AND—!
WK
RSSH
Bwuh.
EVEN WHEN I DO GET THE SWORD...
...HOW MUCH FUN WILL IT BE WITHOUT SOMETHING TO TEST THE EDGE ON?
I CAN'T THINK OF SOMETHING I'VE WANTED TO CUT MORE.

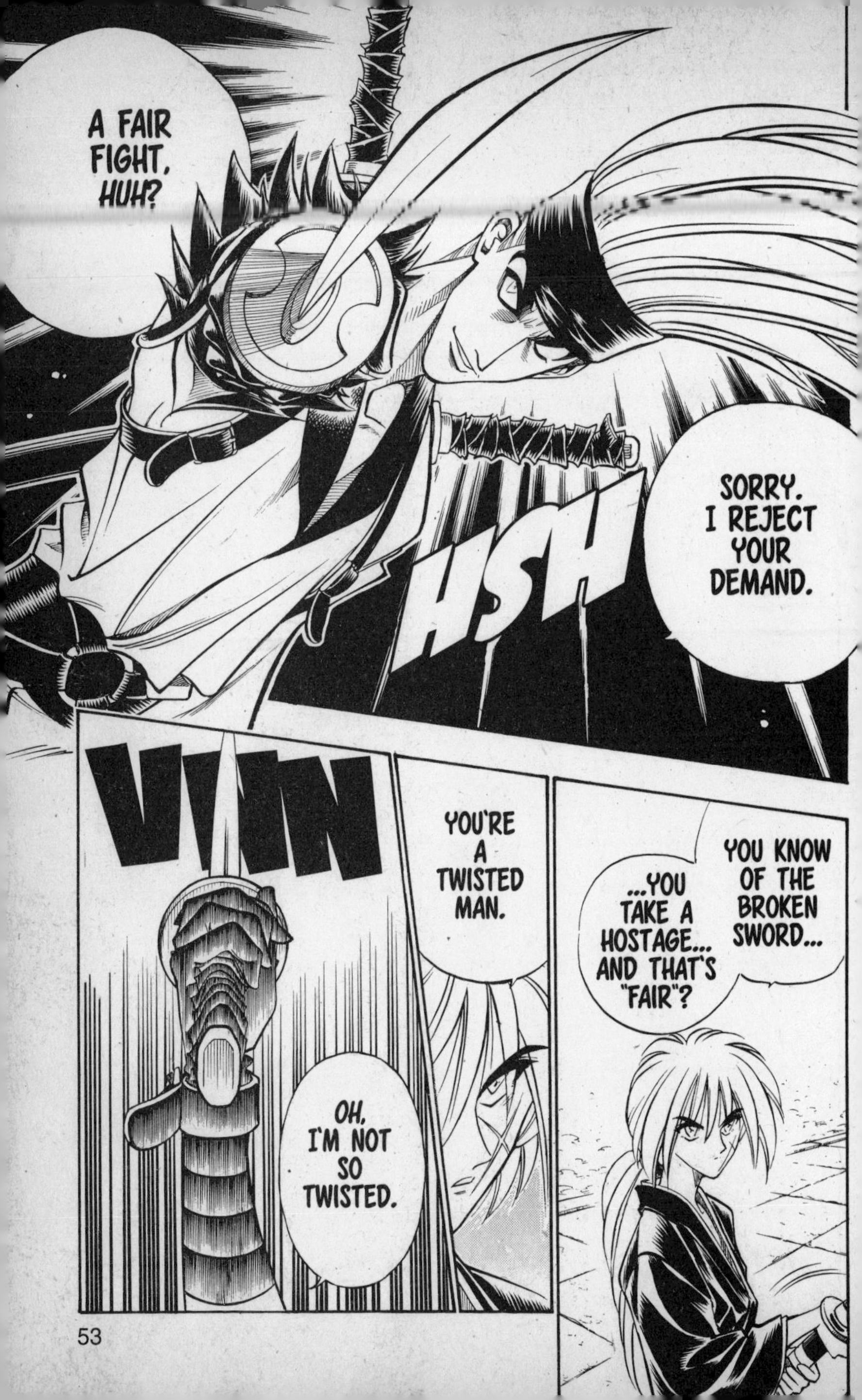
A FAIR FIGHT, HUH?
HSH
SORRY. I REJECT YOUR DEMAND.
YOU KNOW OF THE BROKEN SWORD...
...YOU TAKE A HOSTAGE... AND THAT'S "FAIR"?
YOU'RE A TWISTED MAN.
VIIN
OH, I'M NOT SO TWISTED.

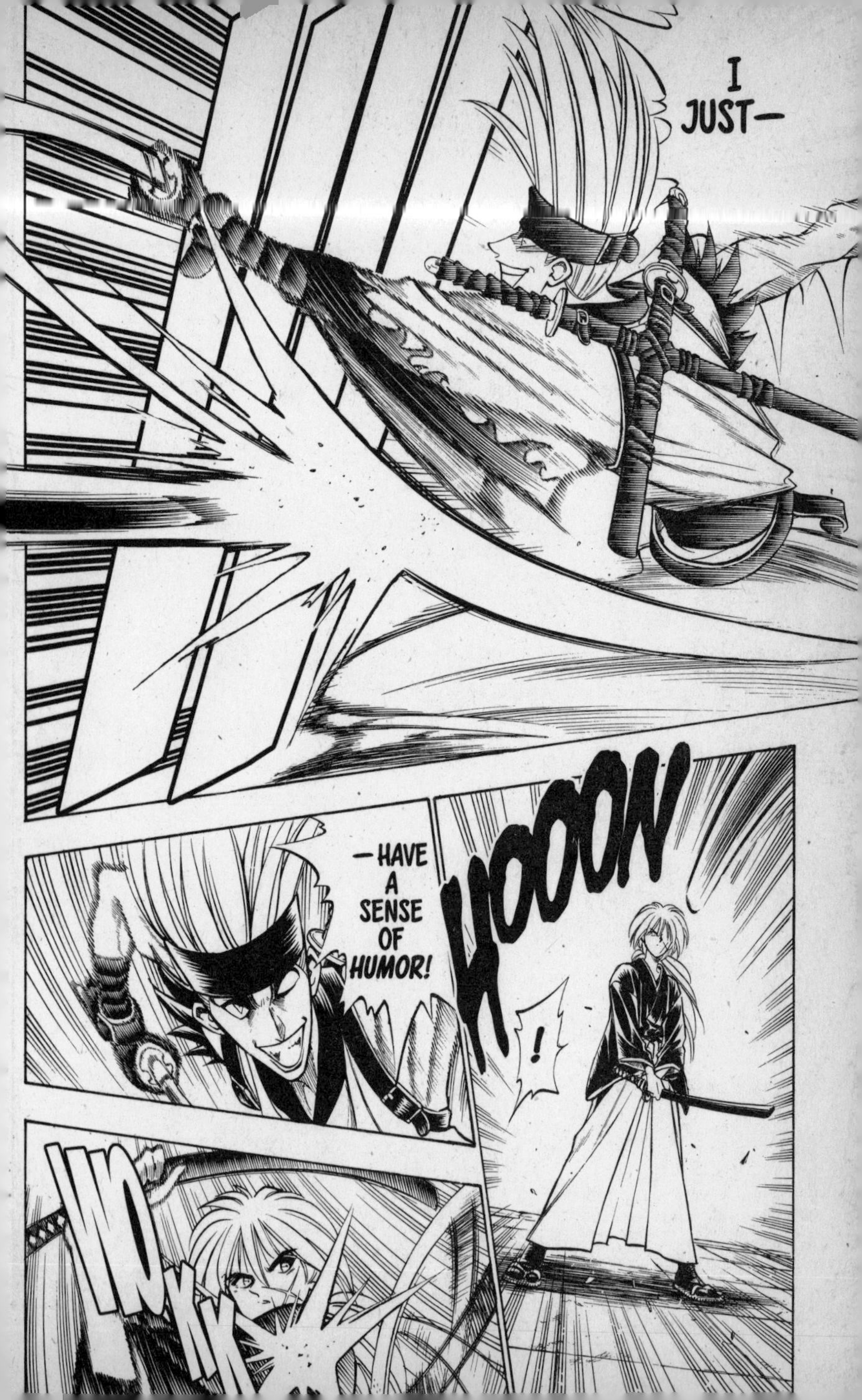
I JUST—
HOOON
!
—HAVE A SENSE OF HUMOR!

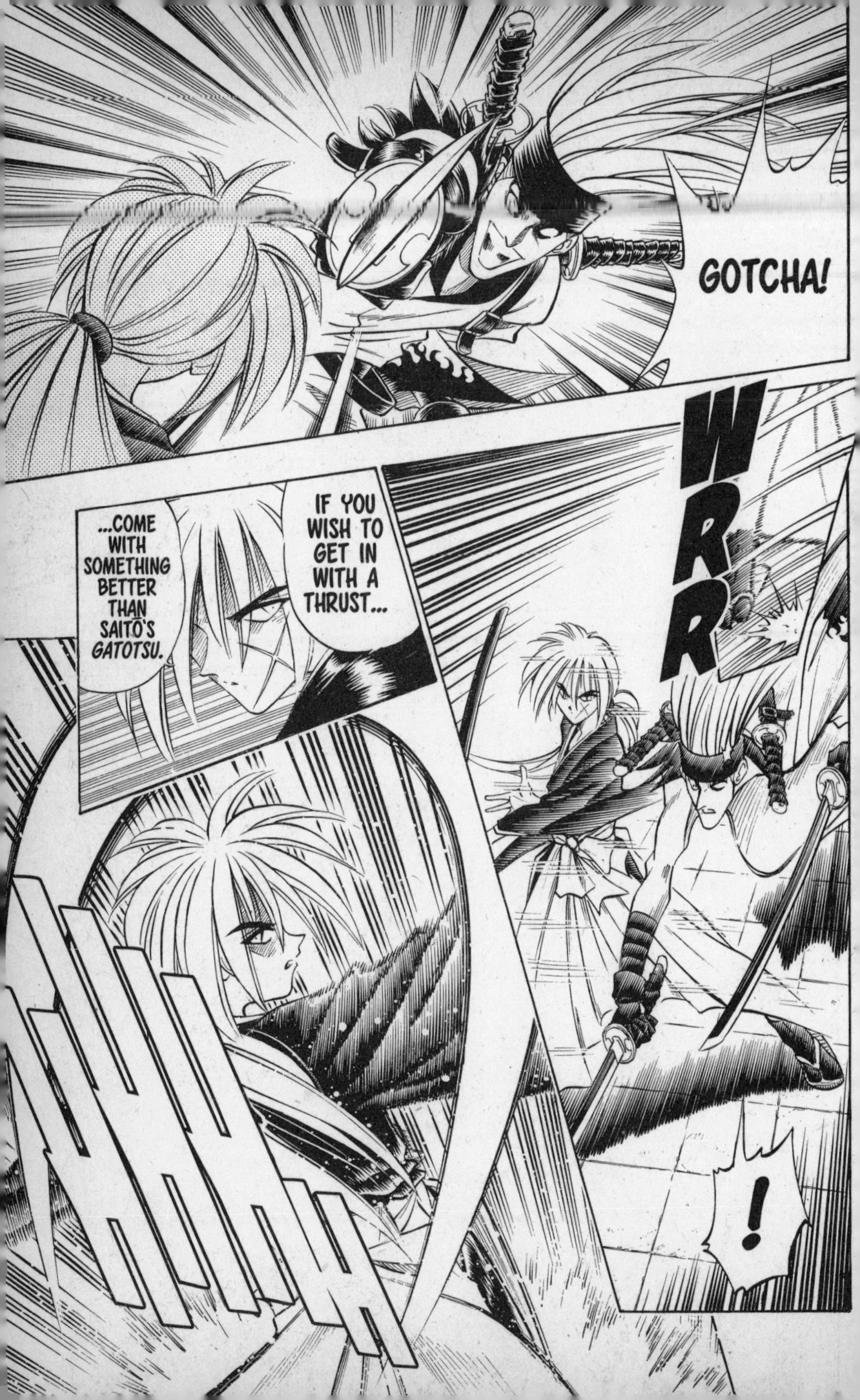
GOTCHA!
WRR
IF YOU WISH TO GET IN WITH A THRUST...
...COME WITH SOMETHING BETTER THAN SAITŌ'S GATOTSU.
!

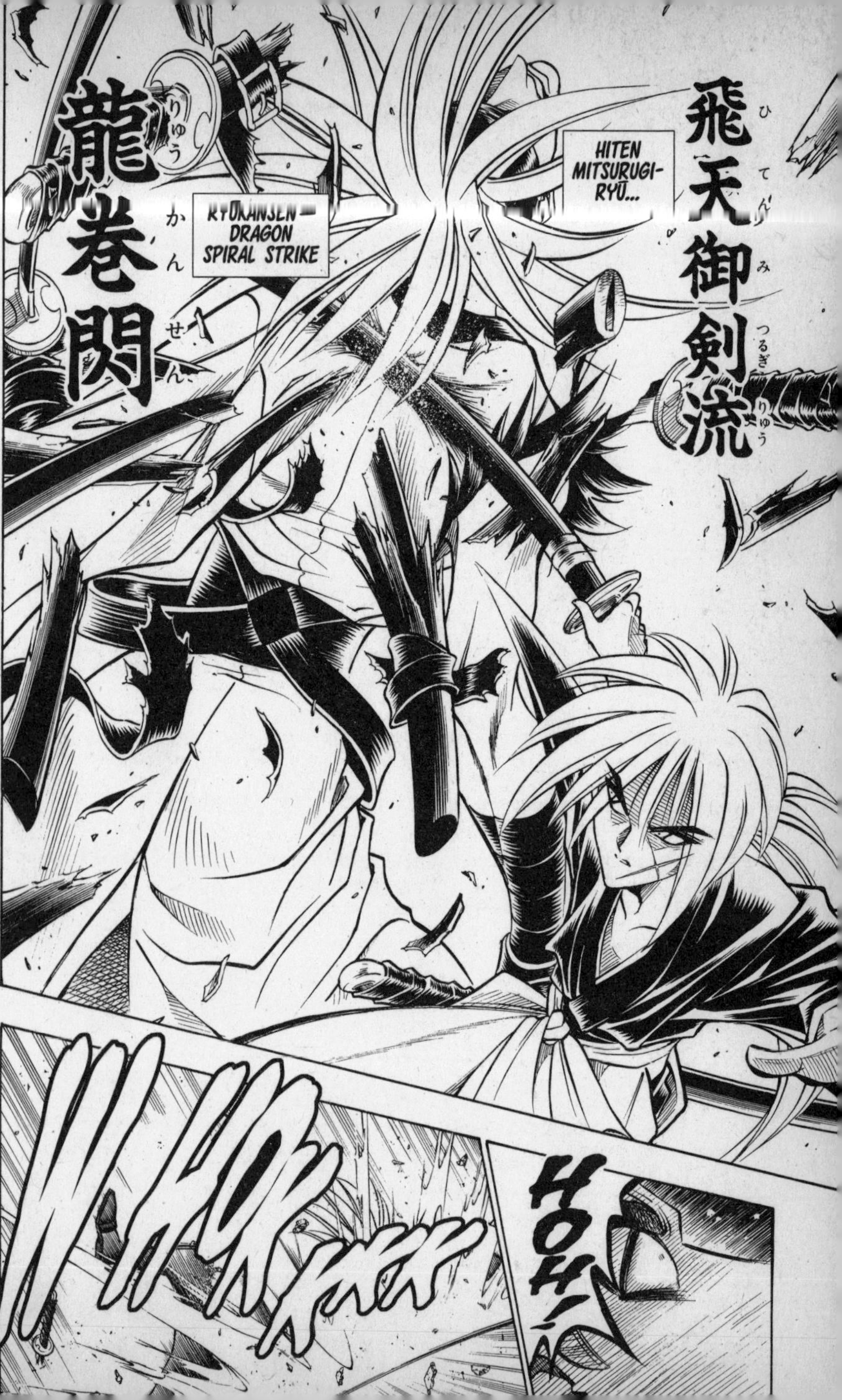
飛天御剣流
HITEN MITSURUGI-RYŪ...
龍巻閃
RYŪKANSEN — DRAGON SPIRAL STRIKE
HOH!!

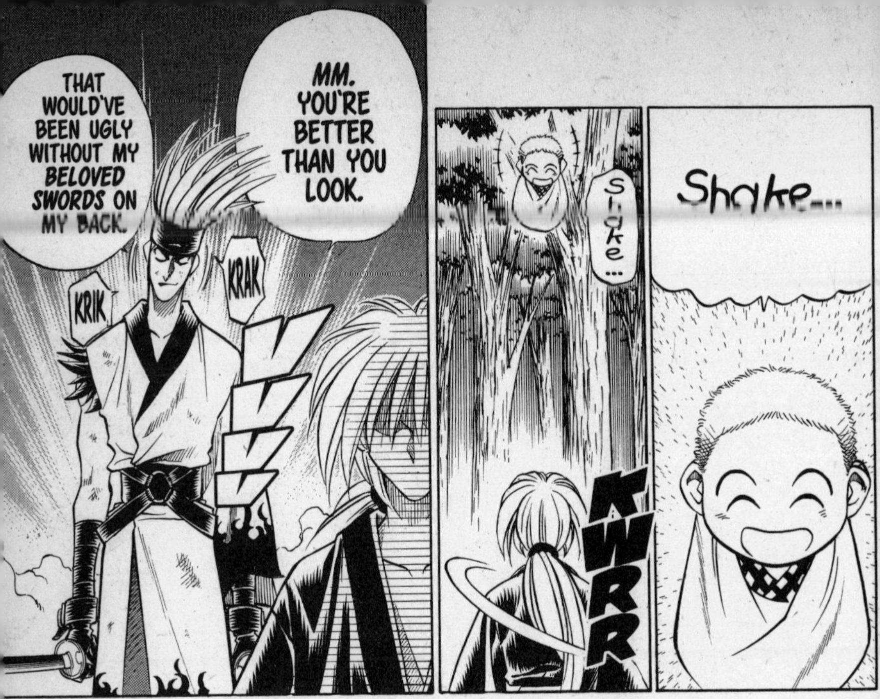
Shake...
Shake...
KWRR
MM. YOU'RE BETTER THAN YOU LOOK.
KRAK
KRIK
THAT WOULD'VE BEEN UGLY WITHOUT MY BELOVED SWORDS ON MY BACK.

_More on the anime. The first series is almost over, and the second will have original storylines (nothing you've seen in the manga). A lot of people dislike "TV originals," but for Watsuki, it's exciting. What will happen when someone *else* does "RuroKen"? Since the first half of the original storyline was jammed into the first series (I know the producers didn't mean for it to feel that way, but to me that's how it felt—sorry!), I'm looking forward to a way more entertaining second series. That the anime staff put their hearts and souls into the first series was obvious, but the second series will be a much better stage for their talents. I hope they keep giving it their all!

This is sort of off-topic, but I'd like to say something about the difference in voice-actors between the CD books and the anime. As I wrote in Volume 9, I basically had nothing to do with the production of the anime—my schedule and their schedule just conflict too much. The only thing I can really do is give my opinion on decisions already made...and that's how it was with the hiring of the voice-actors. Compared to the CD, the TV production has far more companies involved in it, so an industry power-structure comes into play, and that ultimately resulted in different voice-actors than those used for the CD books.

Personally? I feel sorry for the voice-actors in the CD books. (To be continued.)

和月伸宏

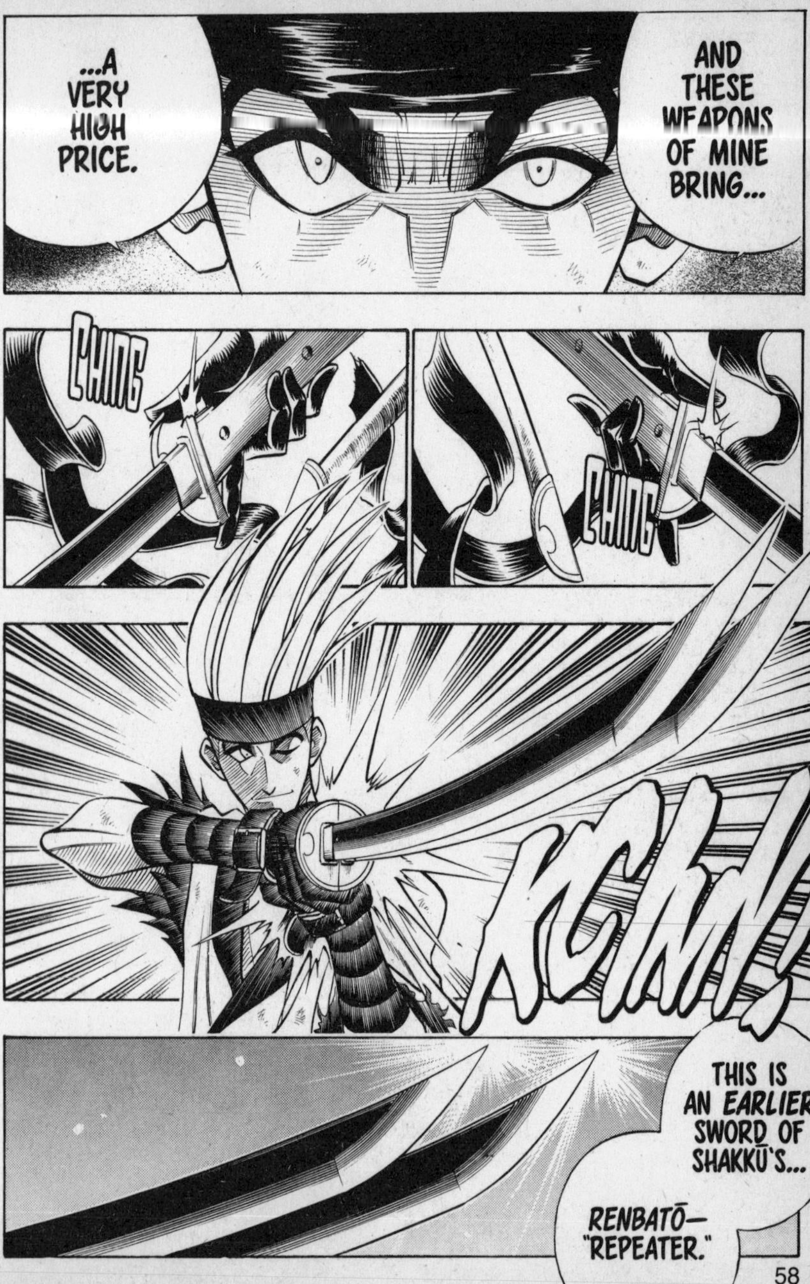
AND THESE WEAPONS OF MINE BRING...
...A VERY HIGH PRICE.
CHING
CHING
KCHN!!
THIS IS AN EARLIER SWORD OF SHAKKŪ'S...
RENBATŌ—"REPEATER."

READ THIS WAY

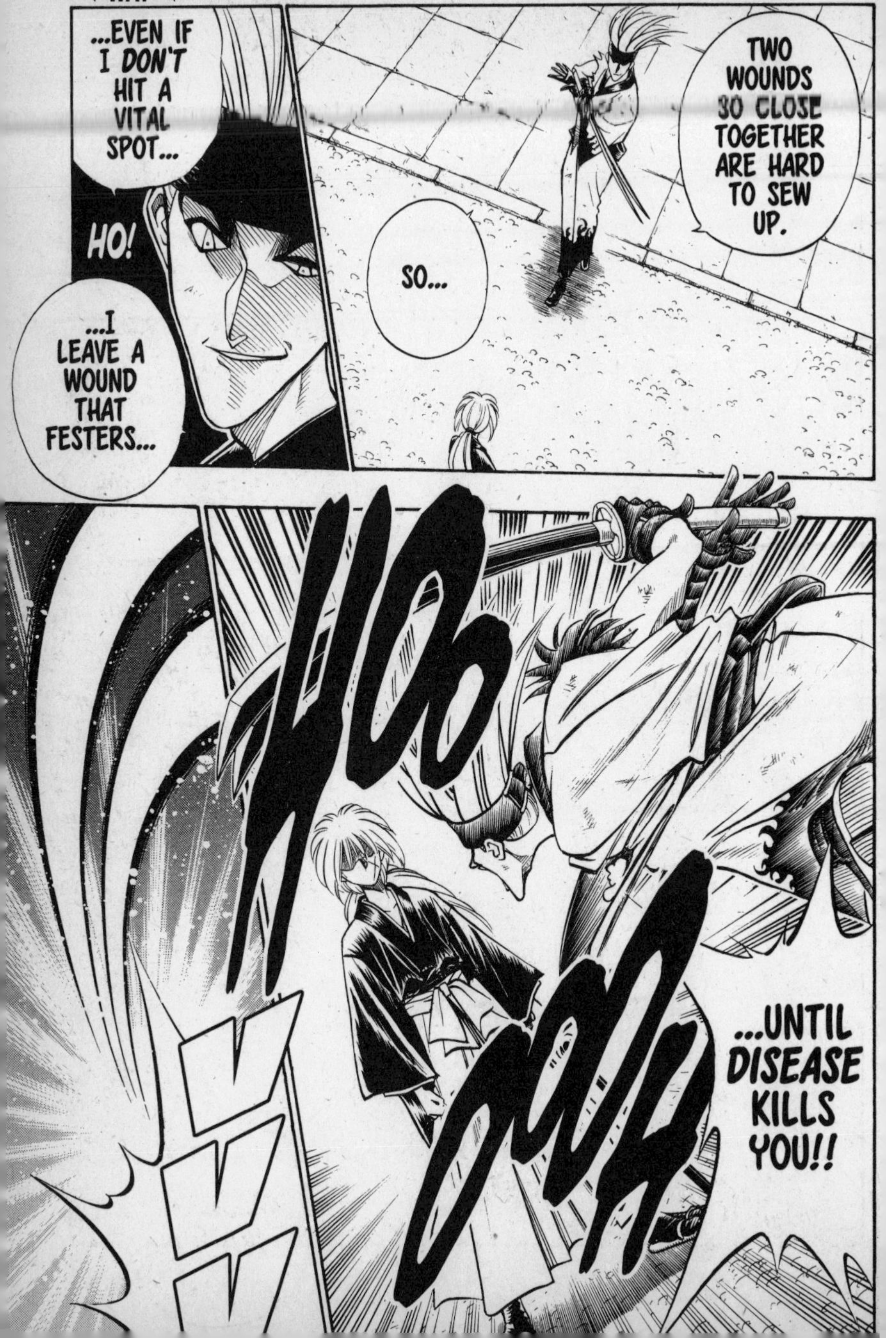
TWO WOUNDS SO CLOSE TOGETHER ARE HARD TO SEW UP.
SO...
...EVEN IF I DON'T HIT A VITAL SPOT...
HO!
...I LEAVE A WOUND THAT FESTERS...
...UNTIL DISEASE KILLS YOU!!

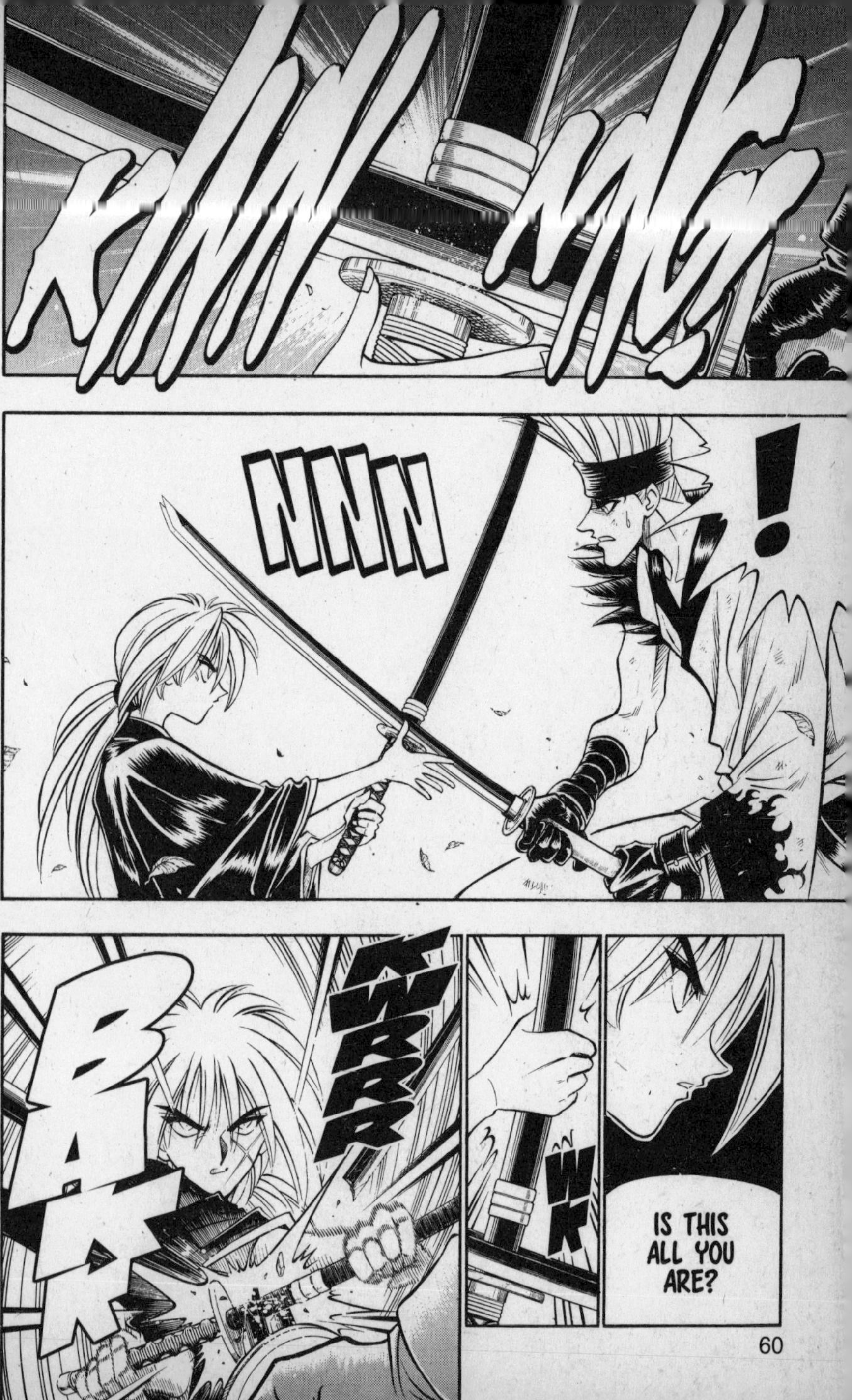
NNNN
!
IS THIS ALL YOU ARE?

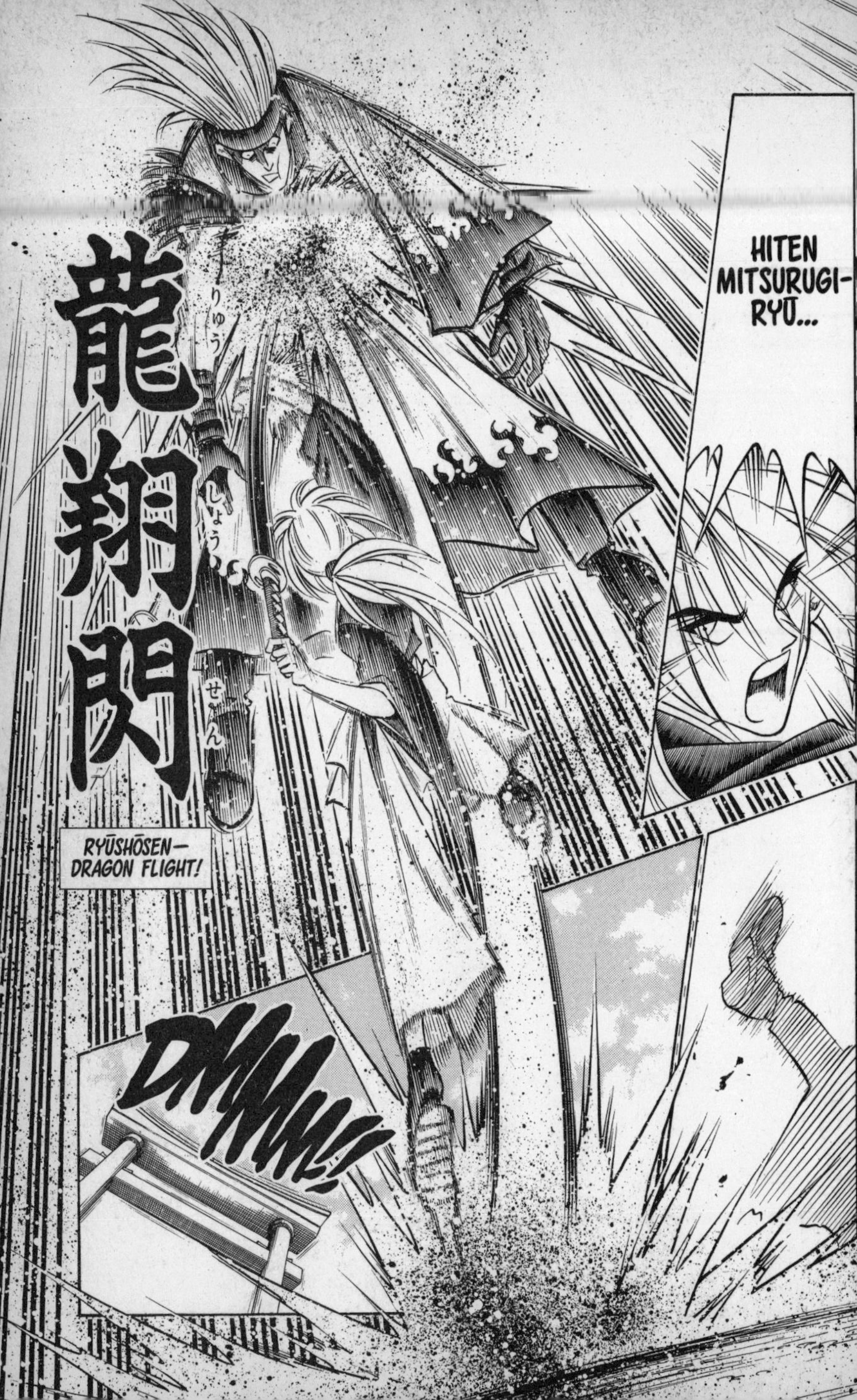
HITEN MITSURUGI-RYŪ...
龍翔閃
りゅうしょうせん
RYŪSHŌSEN—DRAGON FLIGHT!

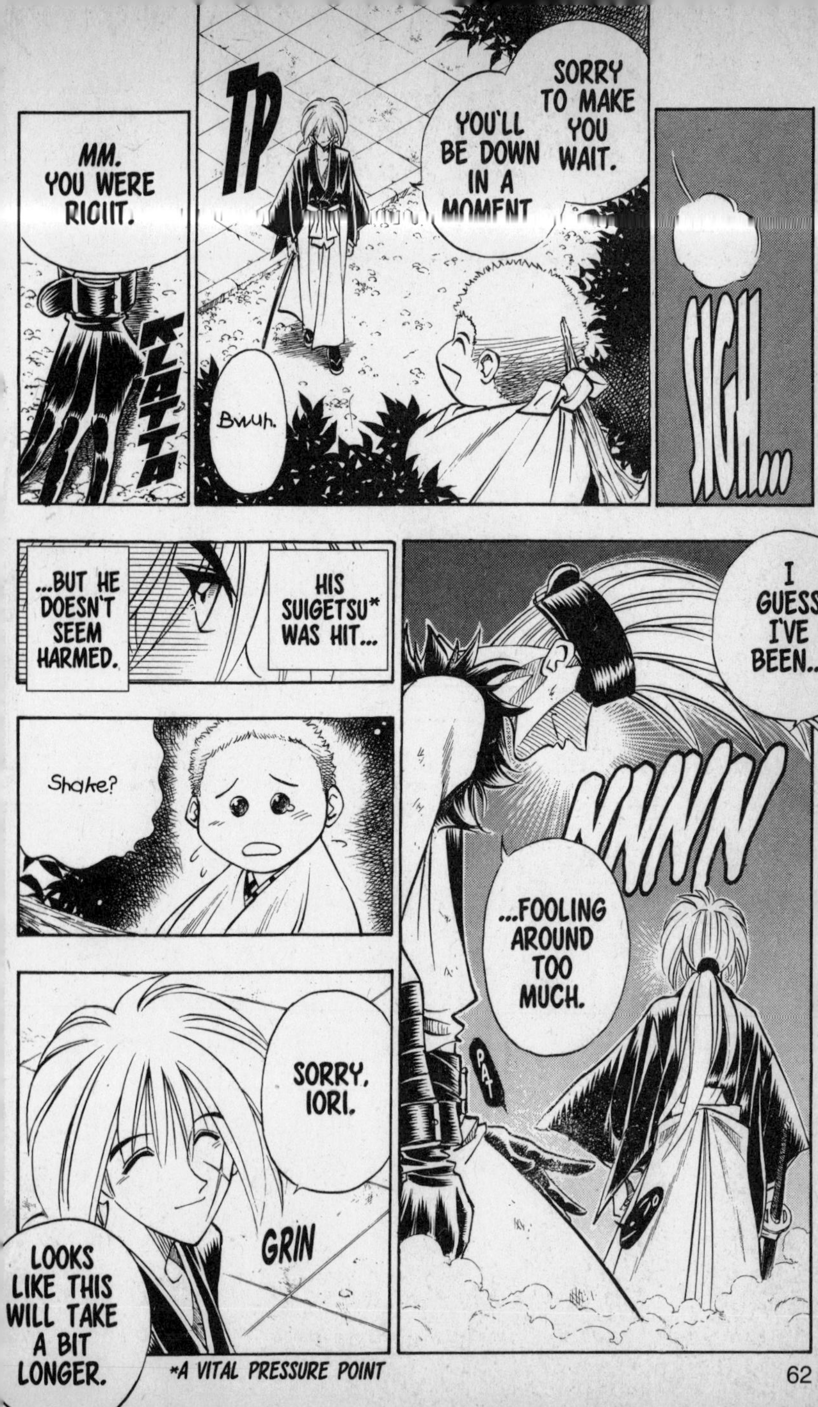
SIGH...
SORRY TO MAKE YOU WAIT.
YOU'LL BE DOWN IN A MOMENT.
TP
Bwuh.
MM. YOU WERE RIGHT.
KLATTA
I GUESS I'VE BEEN...
NNNN
...FOOLING AROUND TOO MUCH.
PAT
HIS SUIGETSU* WAS HIT...
...BUT HE DOESN'T SEEM HARMED.
Shake?
SORRY, IORI.
GRIN
LOOKS LIKE THIS WILL TAKE A BIT LONGER.

*A VITAL PRESSURE POINT

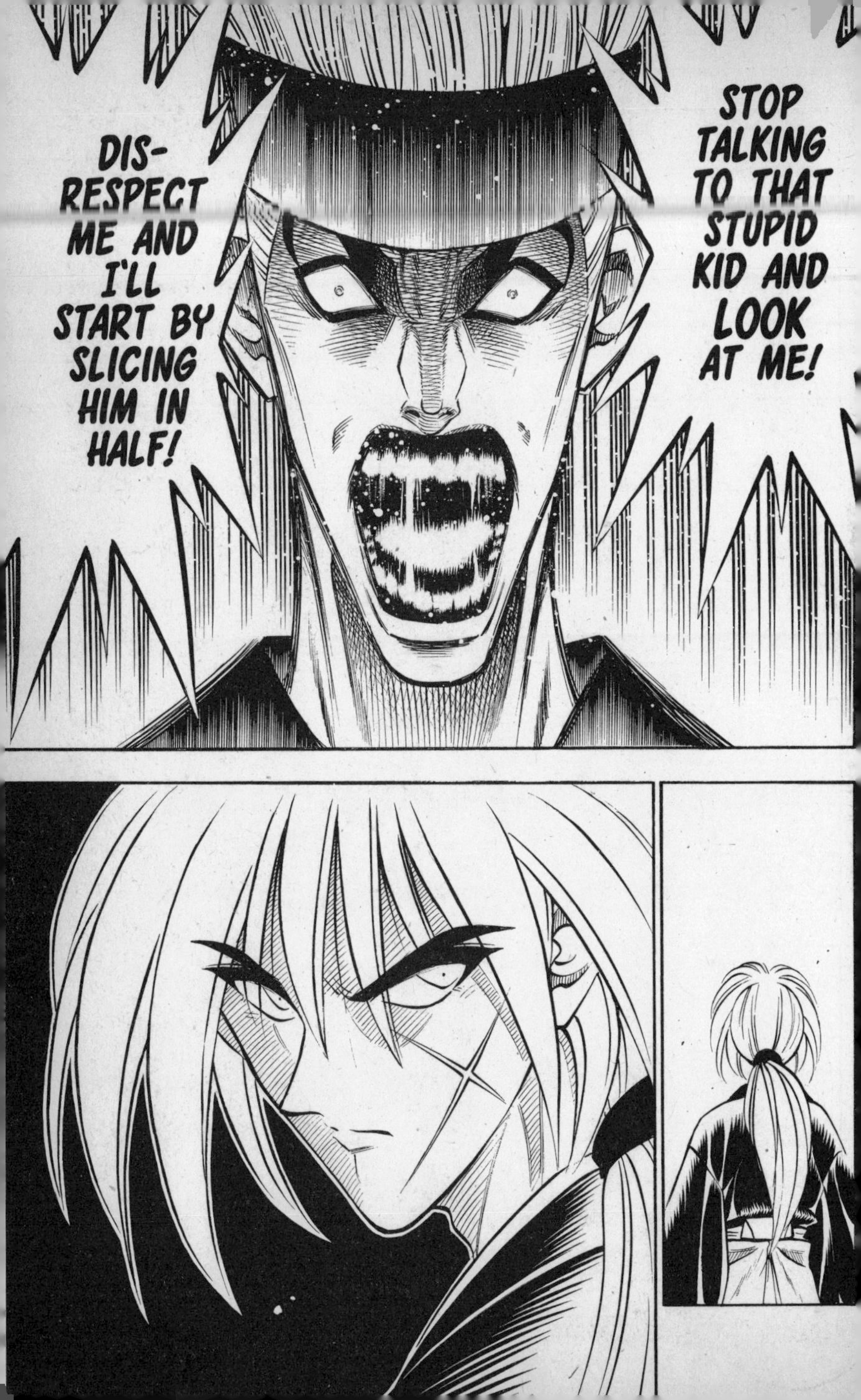
STOP TALKING TO THAT STUPID KID AND LOOK AT ME!
DIS-RESPECT ME AND I'LL START BY SLICING HIM IN HALF!

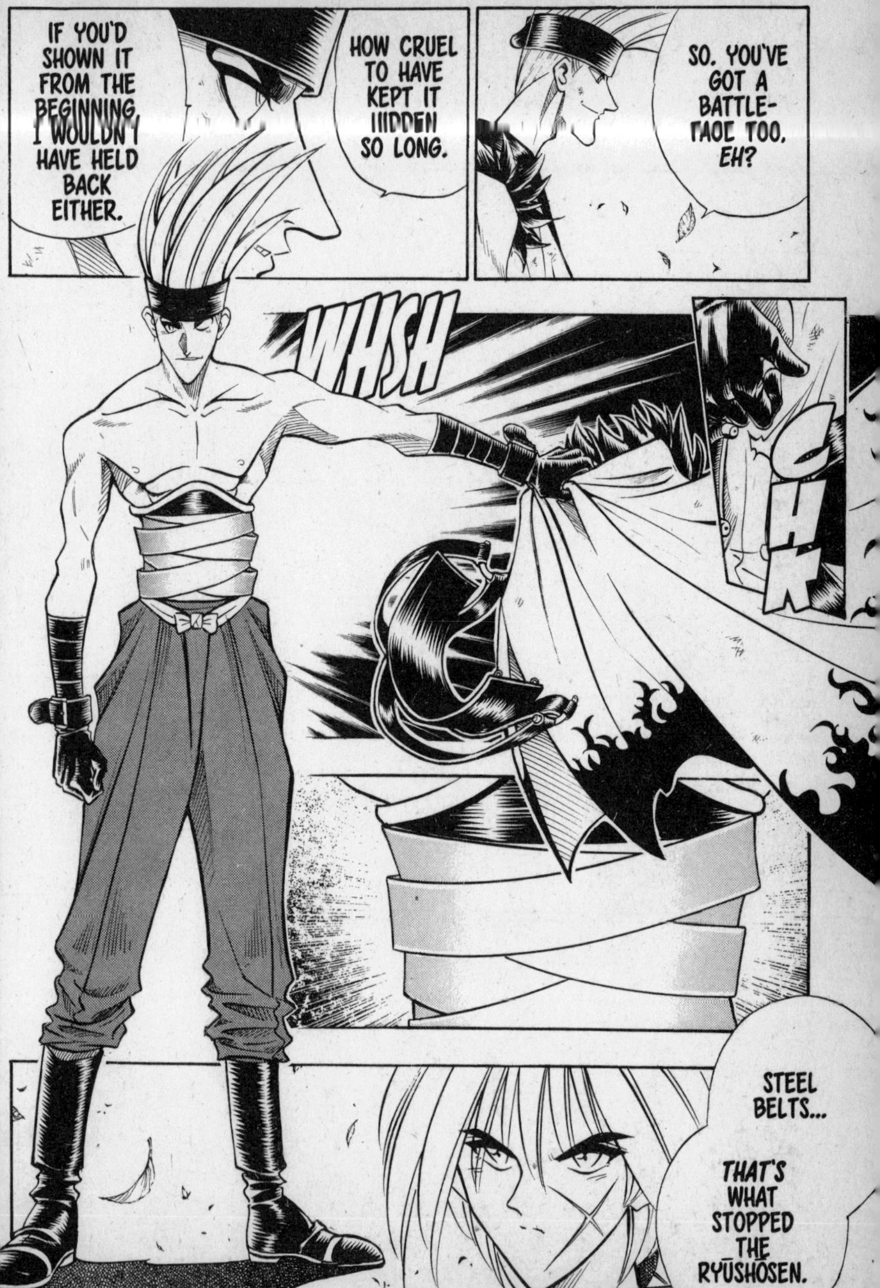
SO. YOU'VE GOT A BATTLE-FACE TOO, EH?
HOW CRUEL TO HAVE KEPT IT HIDDEN SO LONG.
IF YOU'D SHOWN IT FROM THE BEGINNING, I WOULDN'T HAVE HELD BACK EITHER.
CHK
WHSH
STEEL BELTS...
THAT'S WHAT STOPPED THE RYŪSHOSEN.

READ THIS WAY

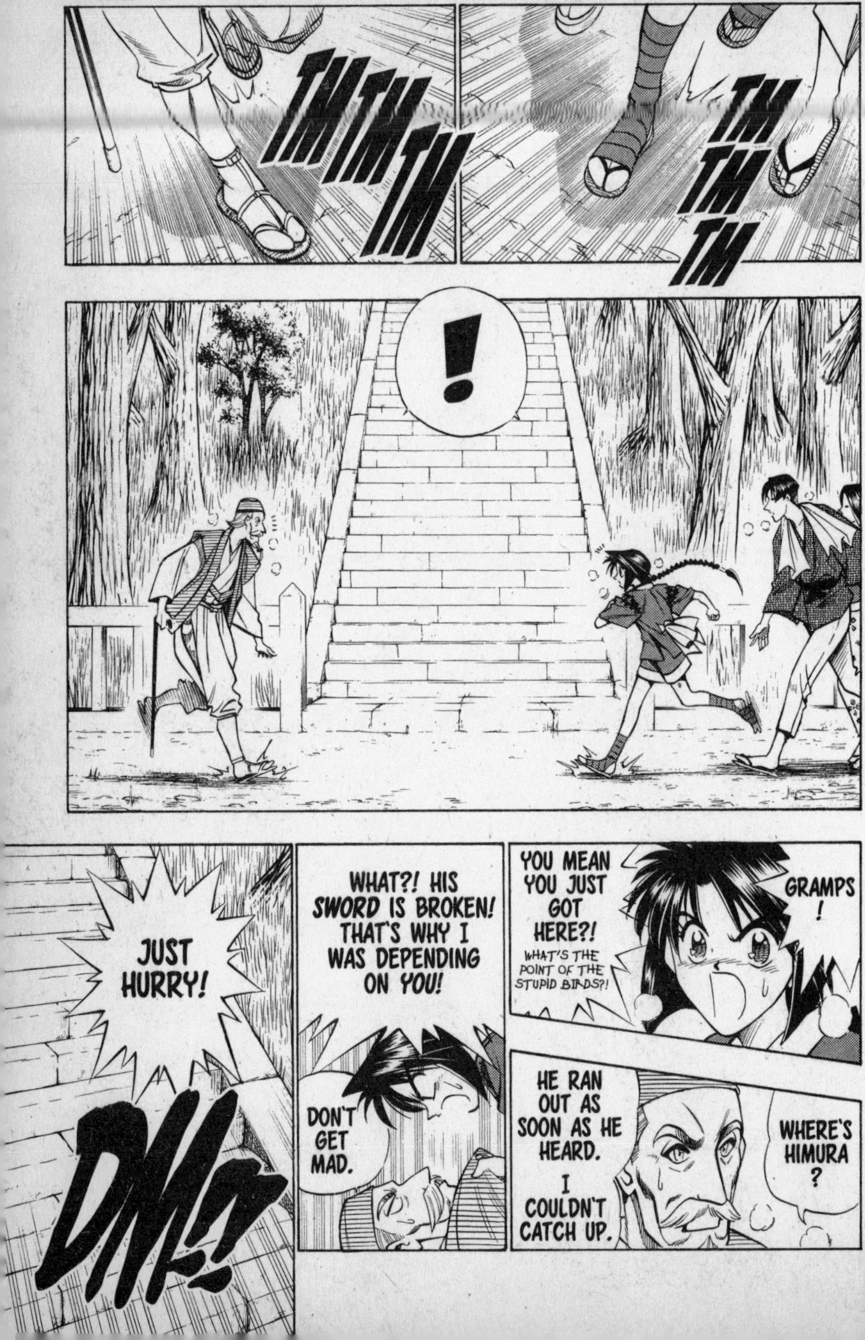
TM TM TM TM
TM TM TM TM
!
GRAMPS!
YOU MEAN YOU JUST GOT HERE?!
WHAT'S THE POINT OF THE STUPID BIRDS?!
WHERE'S HIMURA?
HE RAN OUT AS SOON AS HE HEARD.
I COULDN'T CATCH UP.
WHAT?! HIS SWORD IS BROKEN! THAT'S WHY I WAS DEPENDING ON YOU!
DON'T GET MAD.
JUST HURRY!

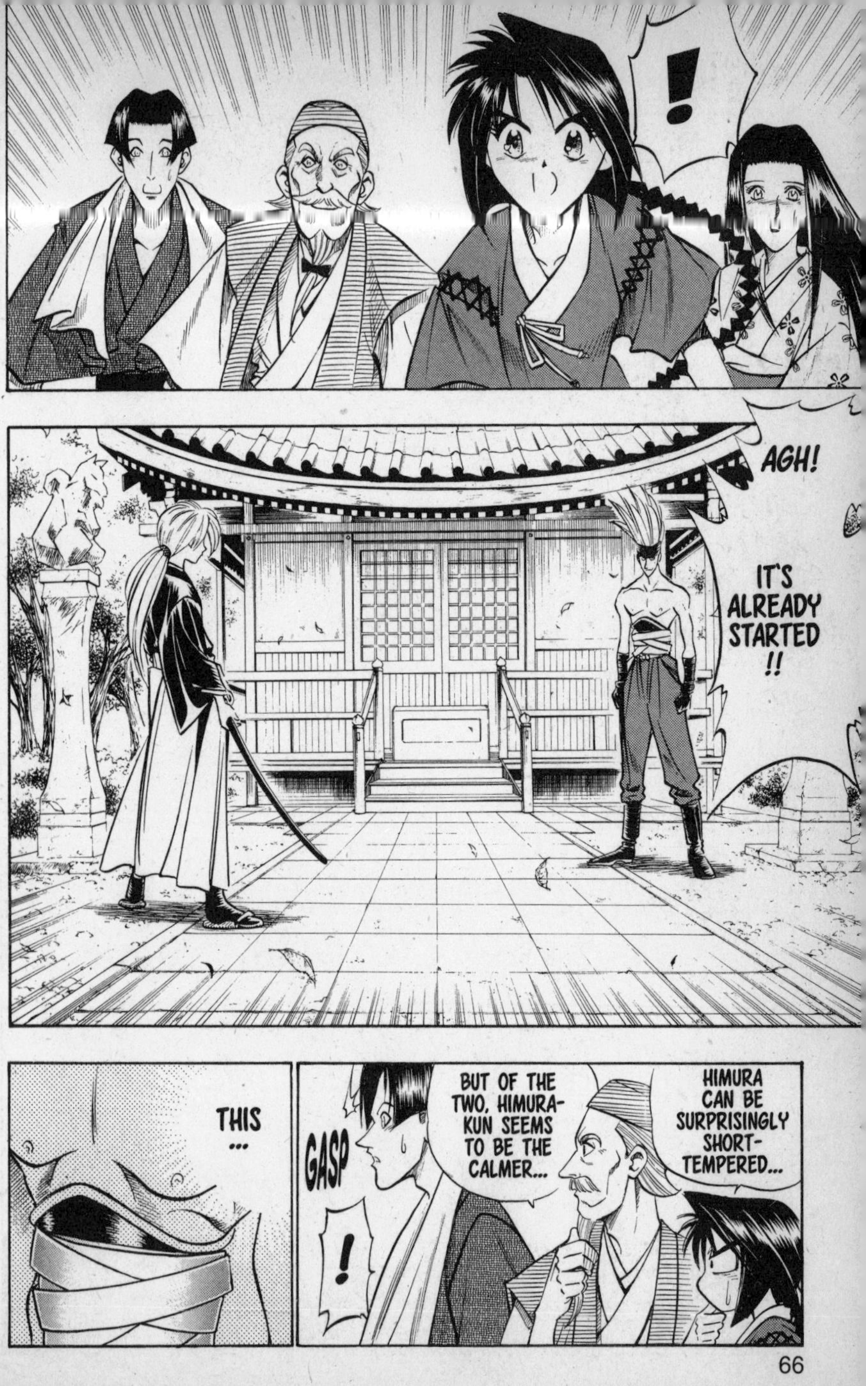
!
AGH!
IT'S ALREADY STARTED !!
HIMURA CAN BE SURPRISINGLY SHORT-TEMPERED...
BUT OF THE TWO, HIMURA-KUN SEEMS TO BE THE CALMER...
GASP
!
THIS ...

READ THIS WAY

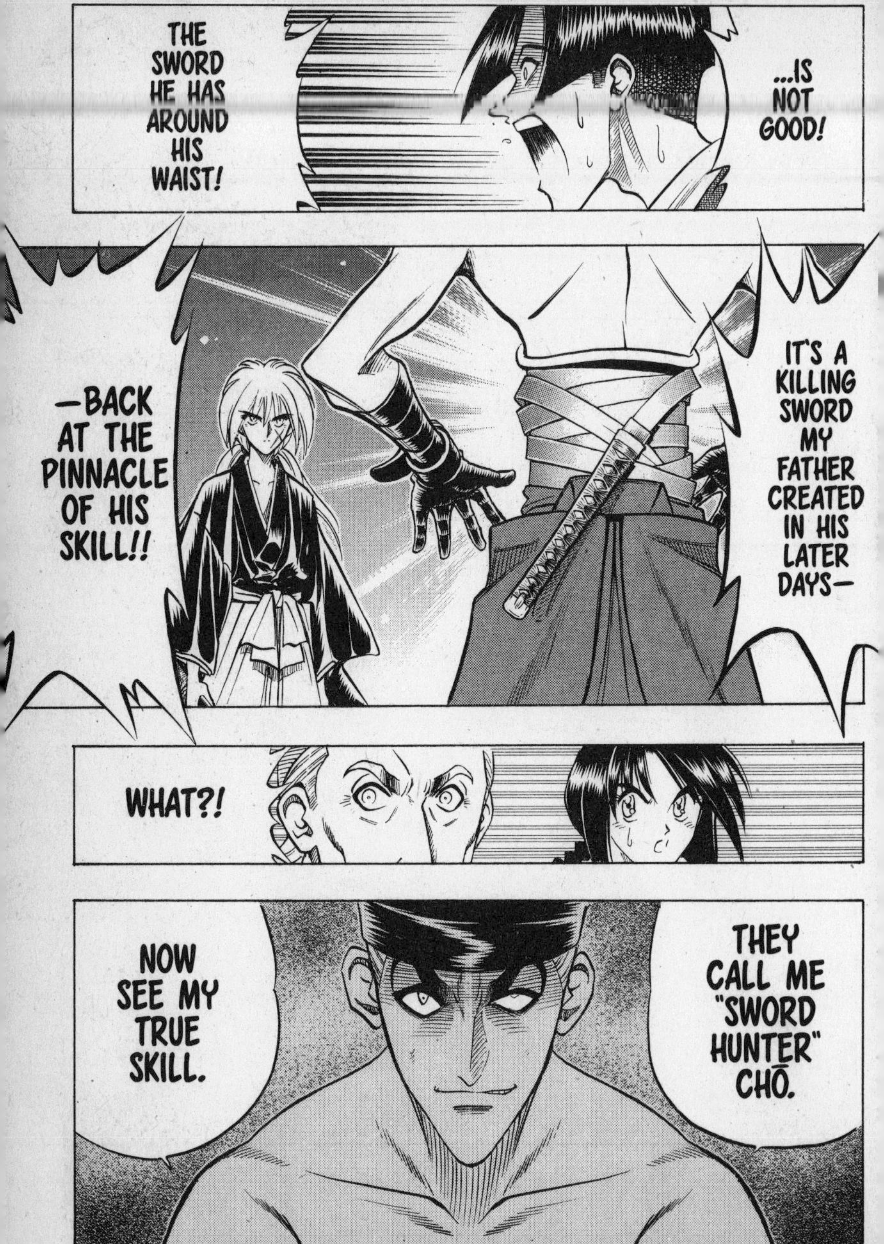
...IS NOT GOOD!
THE SWORD HE HAS AROUND HIS WAIST!
IT'S A KILLING SWORD MY FATHER CREATED IN HIS LATER DAYS—
—BACK AT THE PINNACLE OF HIS SKILL!!
WHAT?!
THEY CALL ME "SWORD HUNTER" CHŌ.
NOW SEE MY TRUE SKILL.

Rurouni Kenshin

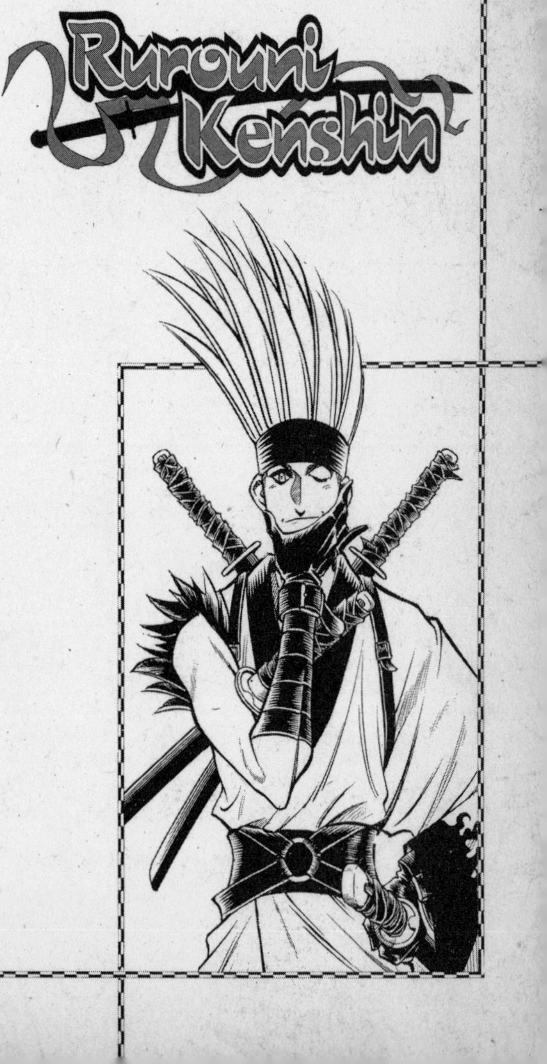

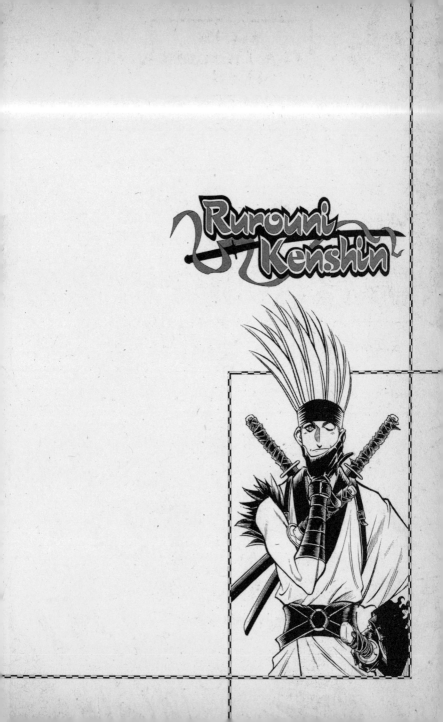

Act 79
The Thinnest Blade

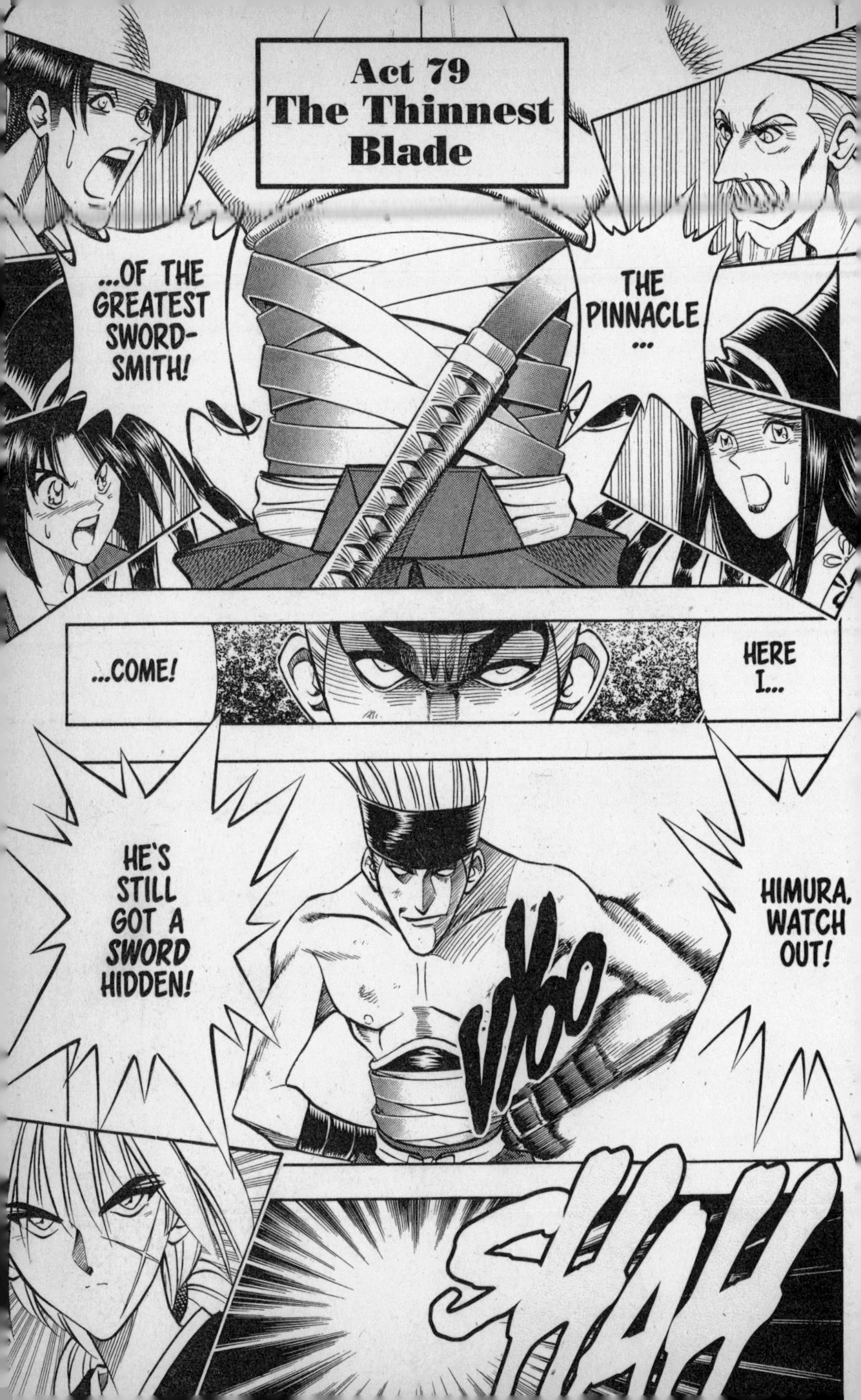
THE PINNACLE ...
...OF THE GREATEST SWORD-SMITH!
HERE I...
...COME!
HIMURA, WATCH OUT!
HE'S STILL GOT A SWORD HIDDEN!
VHOO
SHAH

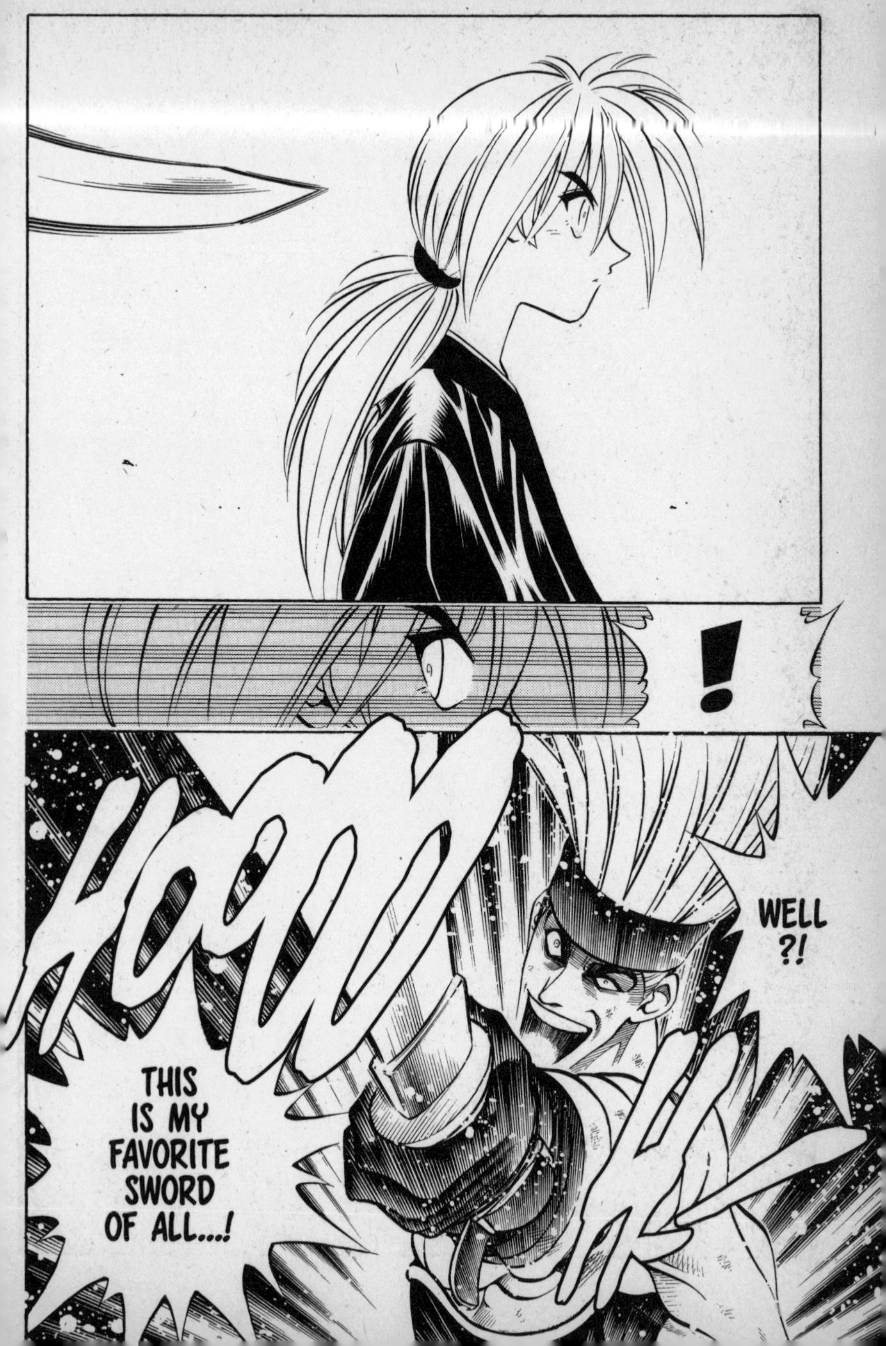
!
WELL ?!
THIS IS MY FAVORITE SWORD OF ALL...!

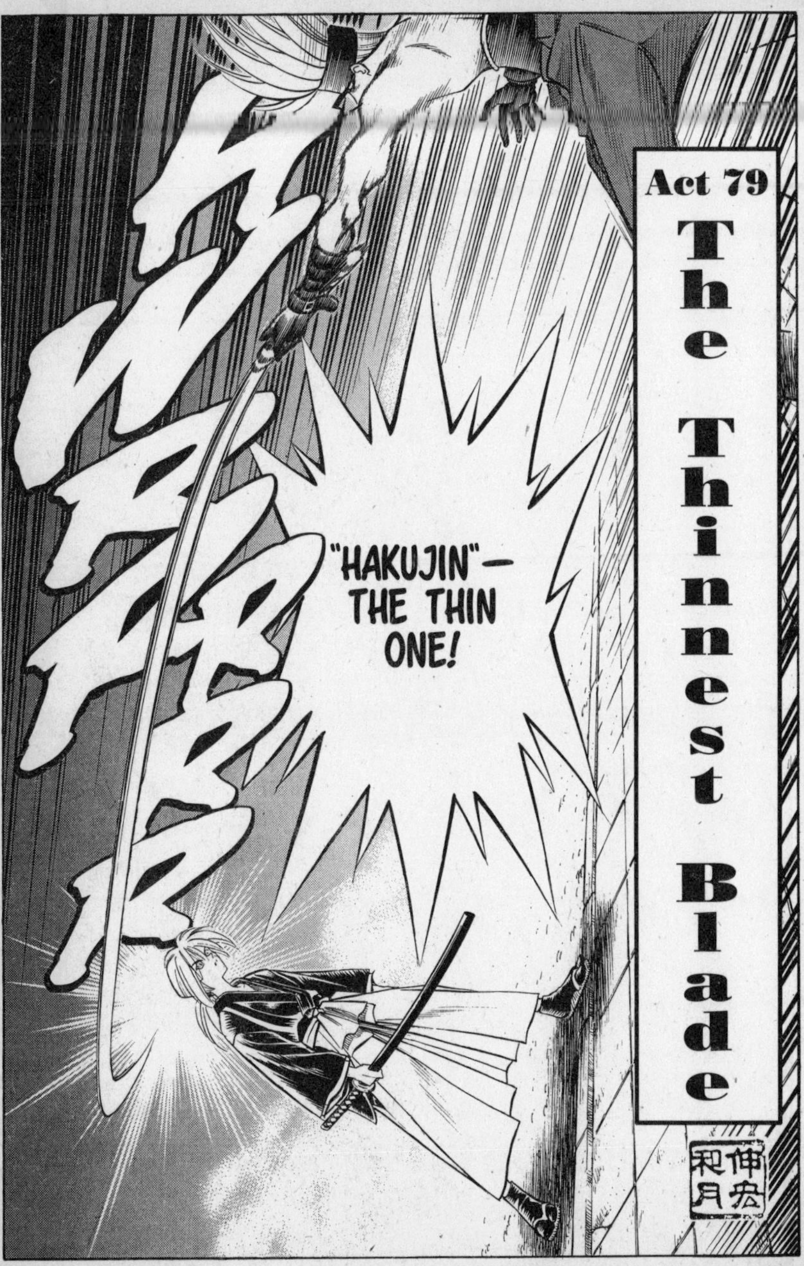
Act 79
The Thinnest Blade
"HAKUJIN"—
THE THIN ONE!

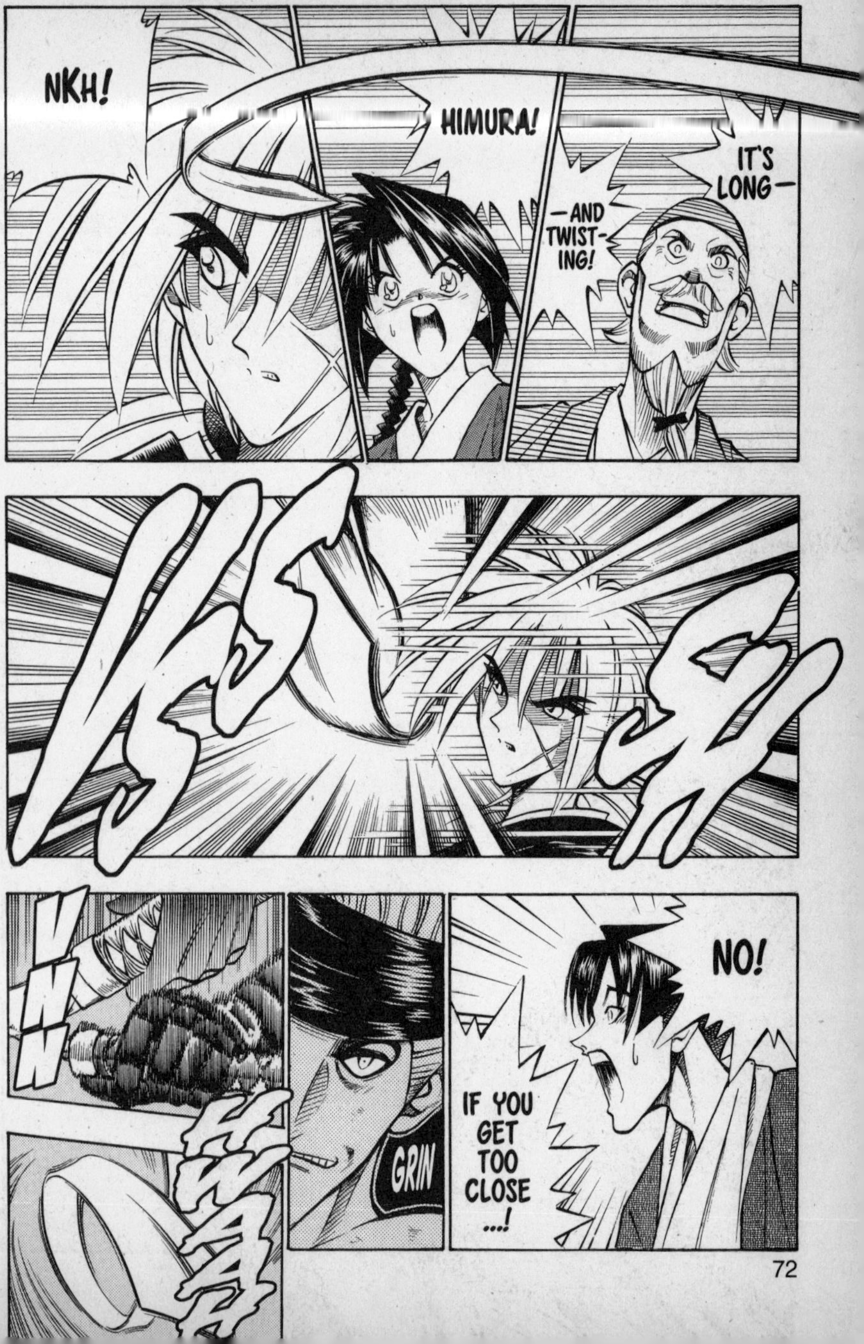
IT'S LONG—
—AND TWISTING!
HIMURA!
NKH!
NO!
IF YOU GET TOO CLOSE ...!
GRIN
VNNN

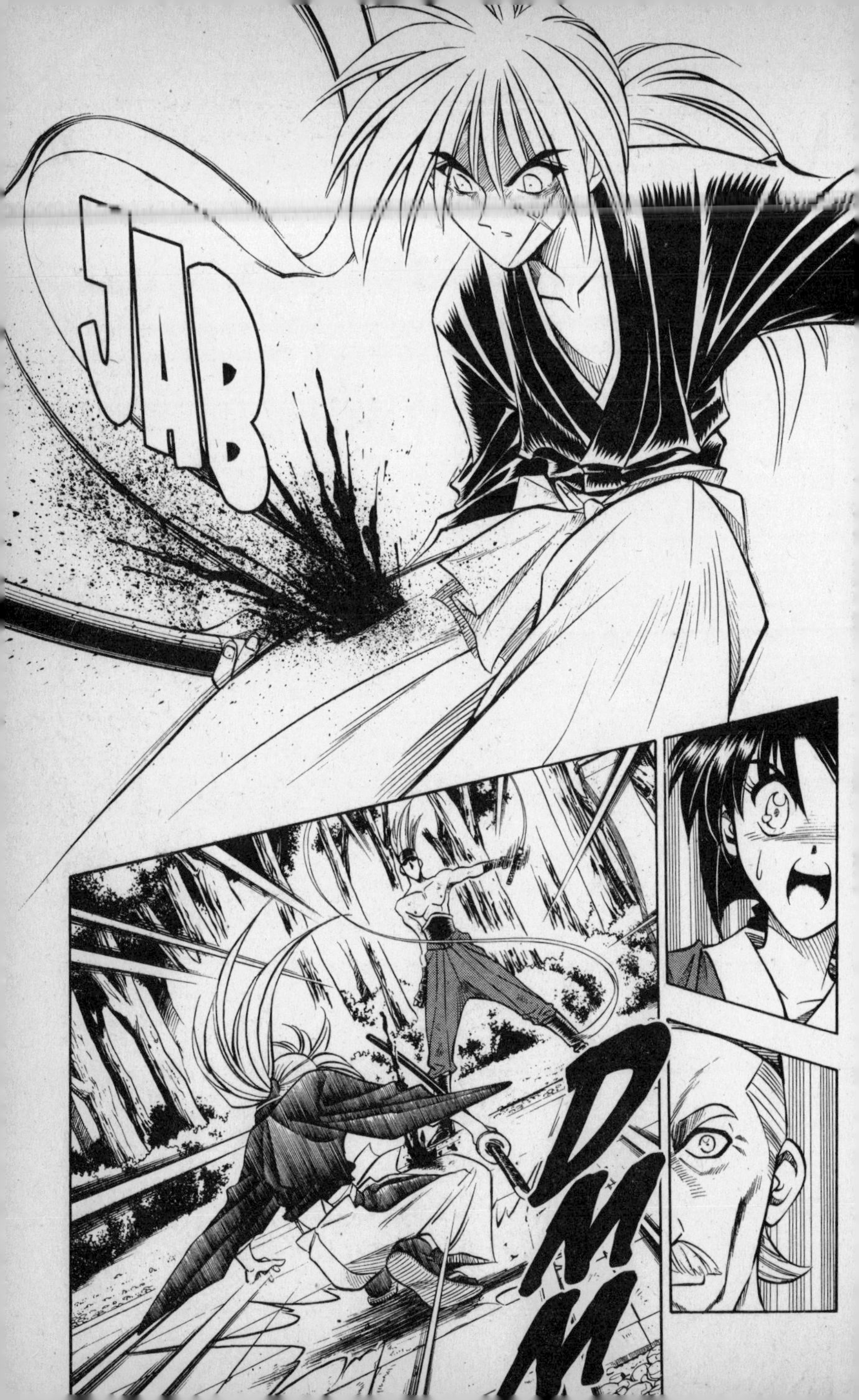
JAB
DMM

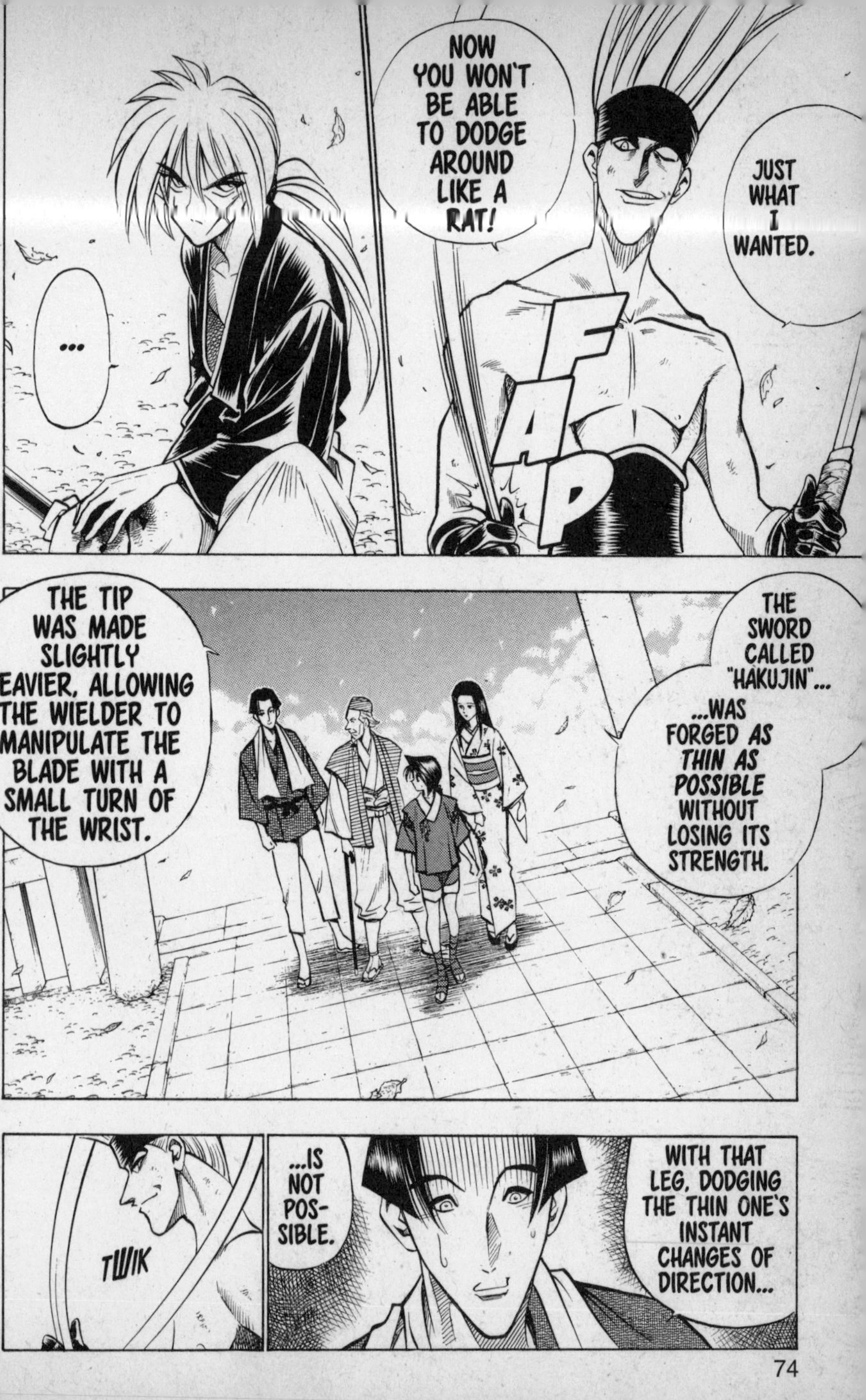
JUST WHAT I WANTED.
NOW YOU WON'T BE ABLE TO DODGE AROUND LIKE A RAT!
FAP
...
THE SWORD CALLED "HAKUJIN"...
...WAS FORGED AS THIN AS POSSIBLE WITHOUT LOSING ITS STRENGTH.
THE TIP WAS MADE SLIGHTLY HEAVIER, ALLOWING THE WIELDER TO MANIPULATE THE BLADE WITH A SMALL TURN OF THE WRIST.
WITH THAT LEG, DODGING THE THIN ONE'S INSTANT CHANGES OF DIRECTION...
...IS NOT POSSIBLE.
TWIK

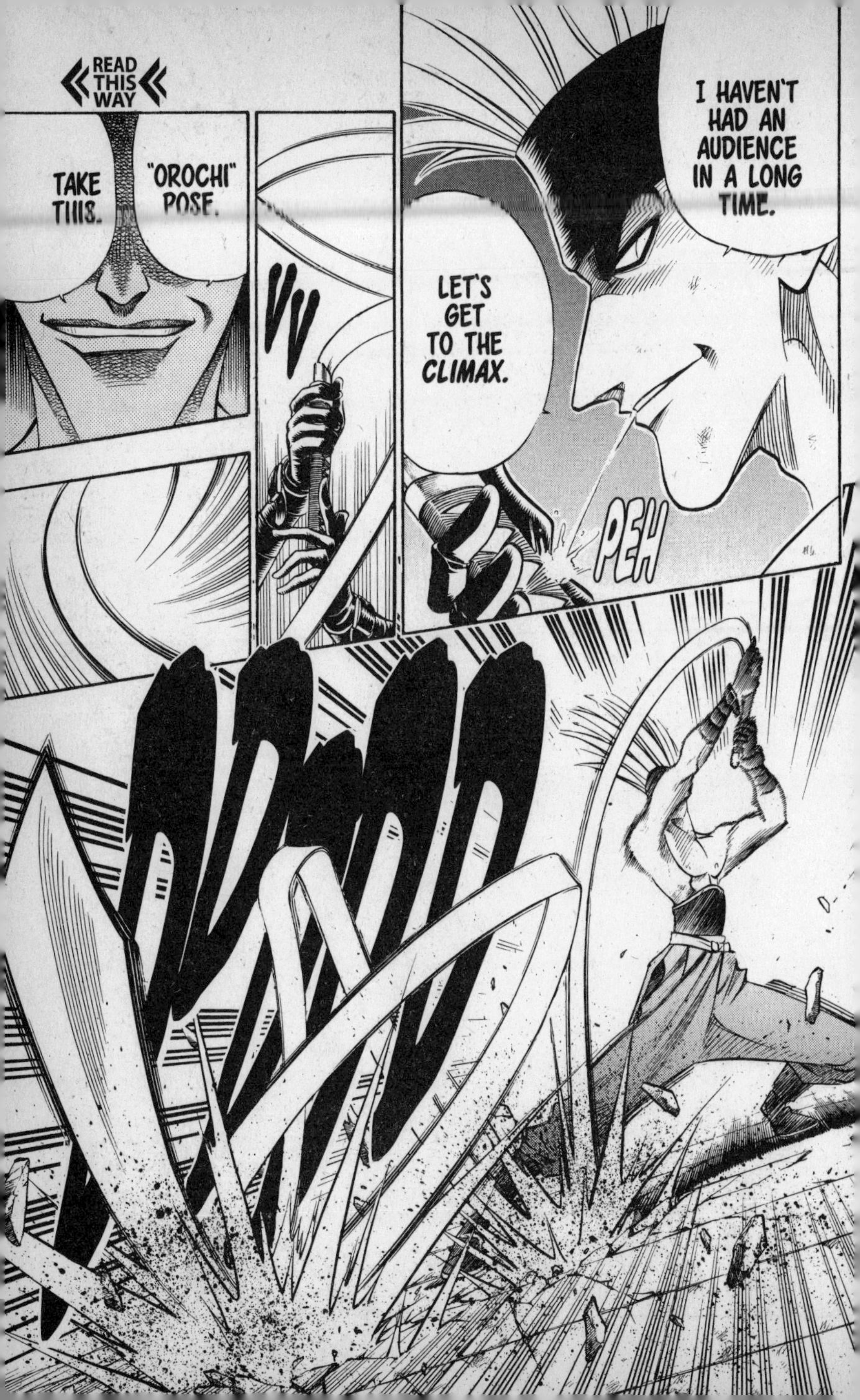
READ THIS WAY
I HAVEN'T HAD AN AUDIENCE IN A LONG TIME.
LET'S GET TO THE CLIMAX.
PEH
VV
"OROCHI" POSE.
TAKE THIS.

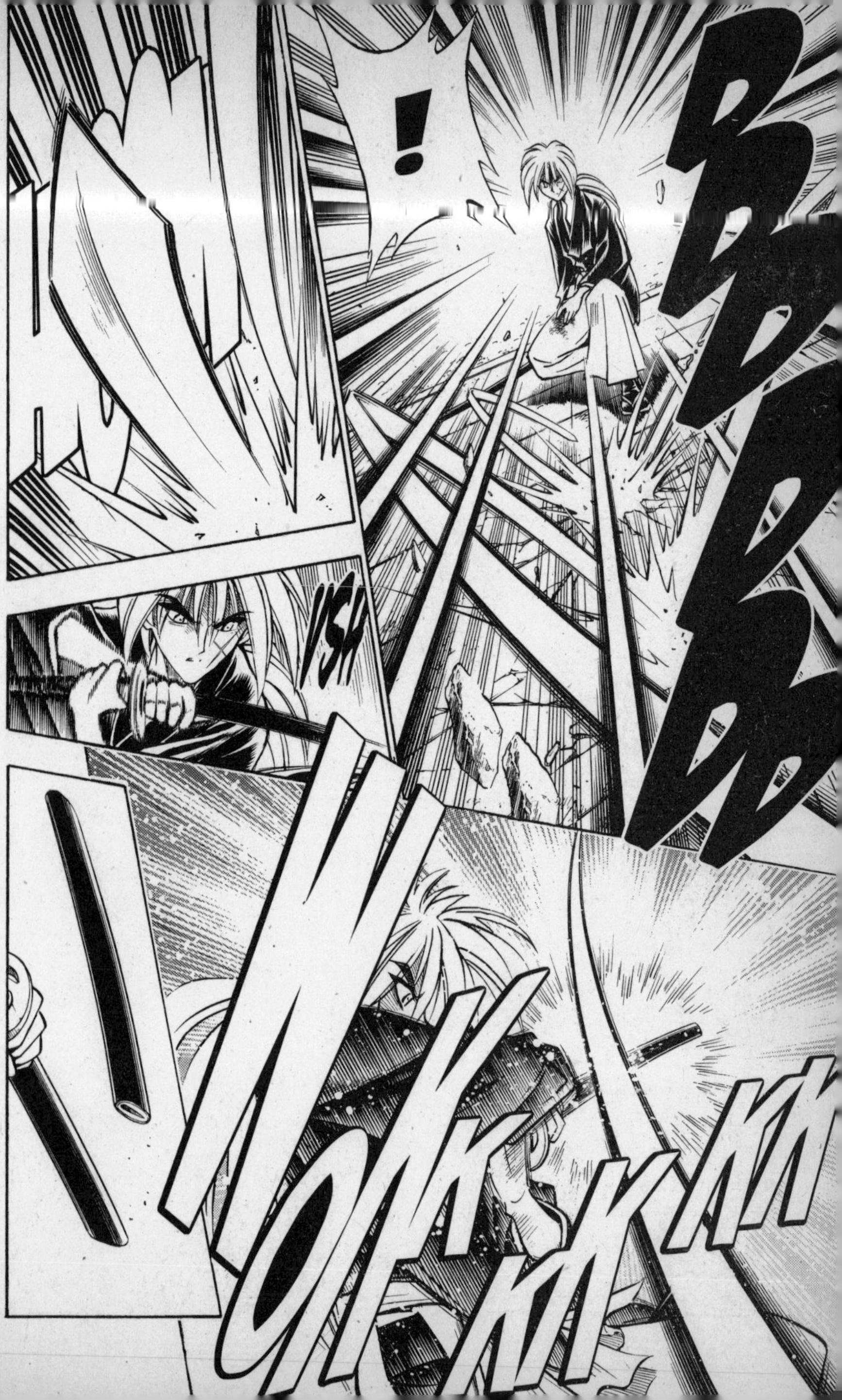

!
VSH

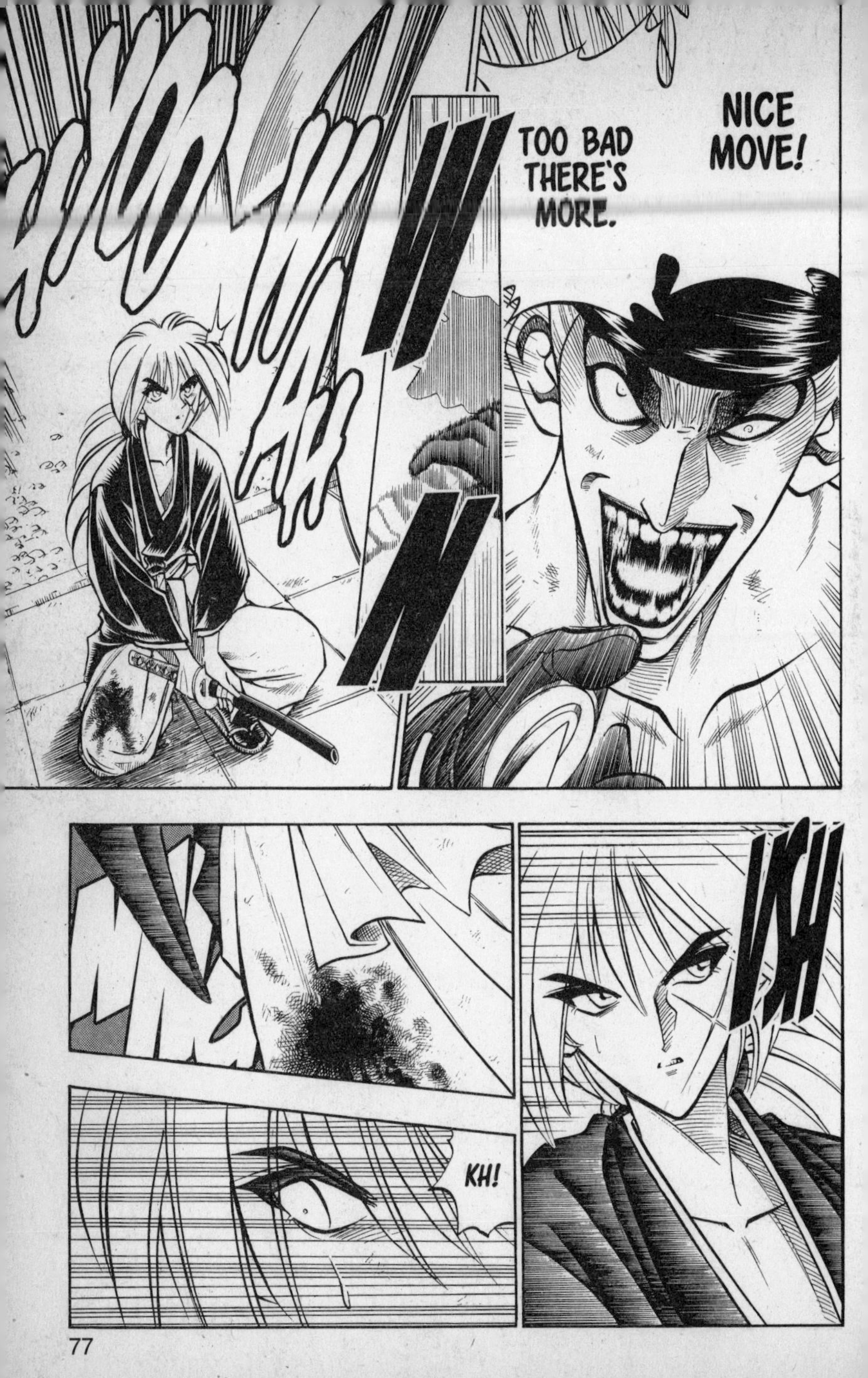
NICE MOVE!
TOO BAD THERE'S MORE.
KH!

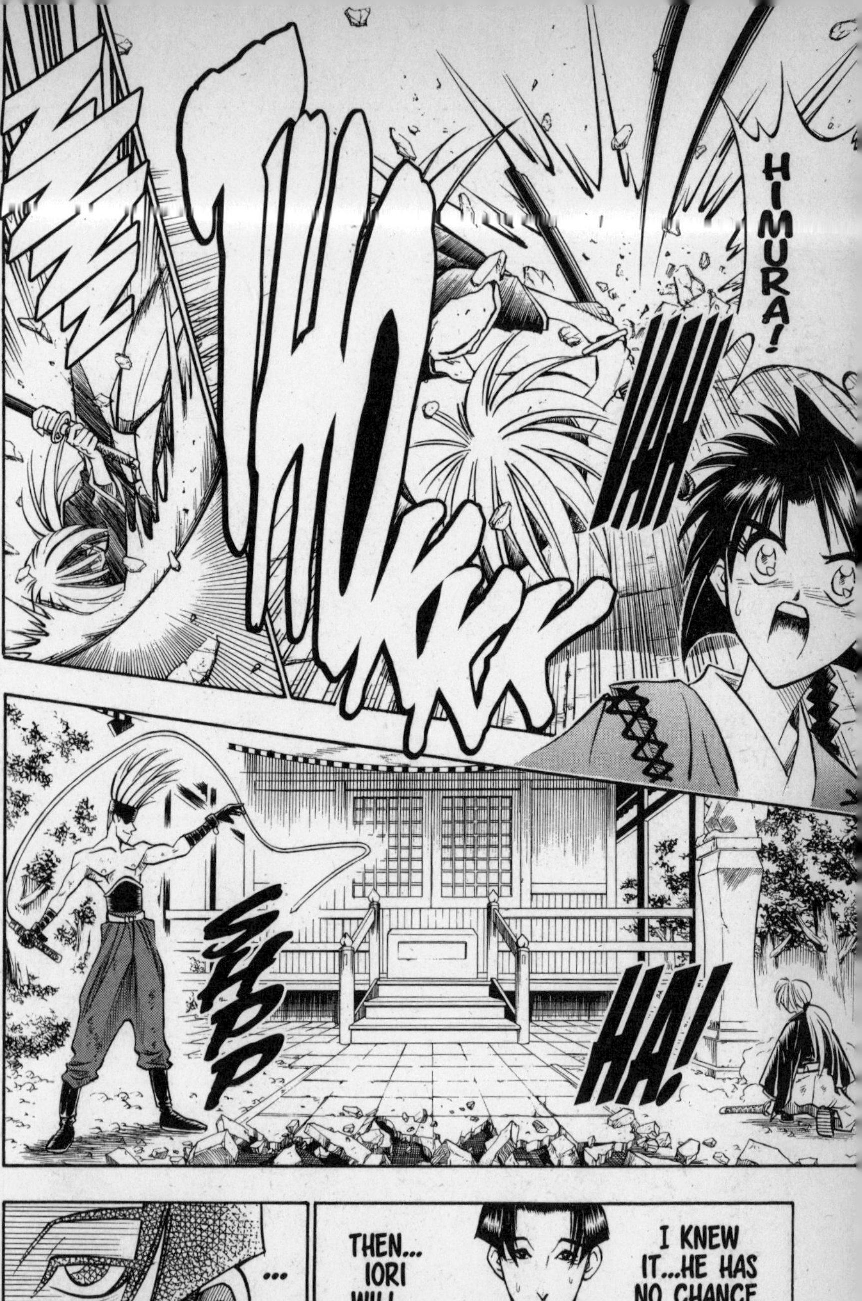
HIMURA!
THWACK
HAH
HA!
I KNEW IT...HE HAS NO CHANCE.
THEN... IORI WILL...
...

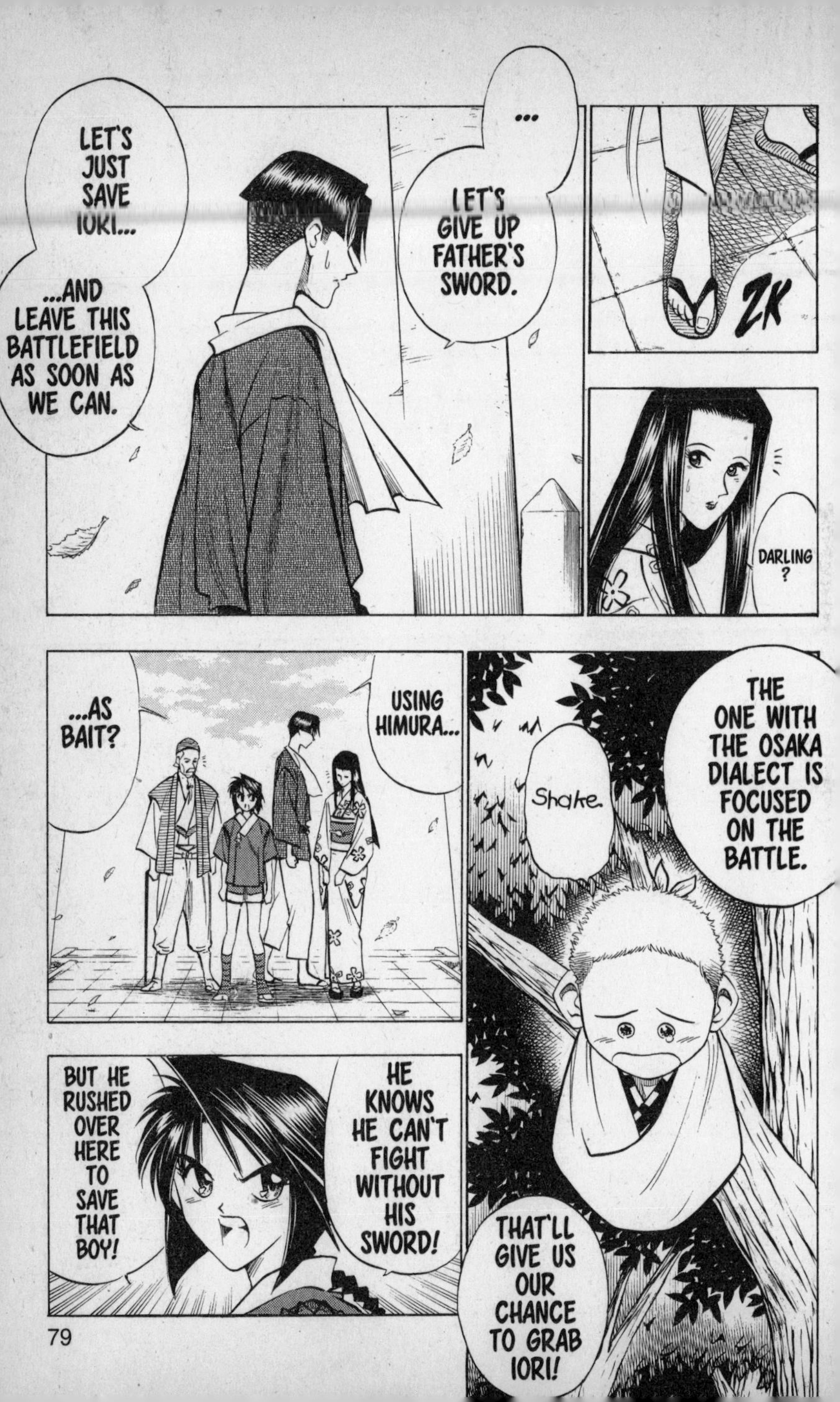
ZK
DARLING ?
...
LET'S GIVE UP FATHER'S SWORD.
LET'S JUST SAVE IORI...
...AND LEAVE THIS BATTLEFIELD AS SOON AS WE CAN.
THE ONE WITH THE OSAKA DIALECT IS FOCUSED ON THE BATTLE.
Shake.
THAT'LL GIVE US OUR CHANCE TO GRAB IORI!
USING HIMURA...
...AS BAIT?
HE KNOWS HE CAN'T FIGHT WITHOUT HIS SWORD!
BUT HE RUSHED OVER HERE TO SAVE THAT BOY!

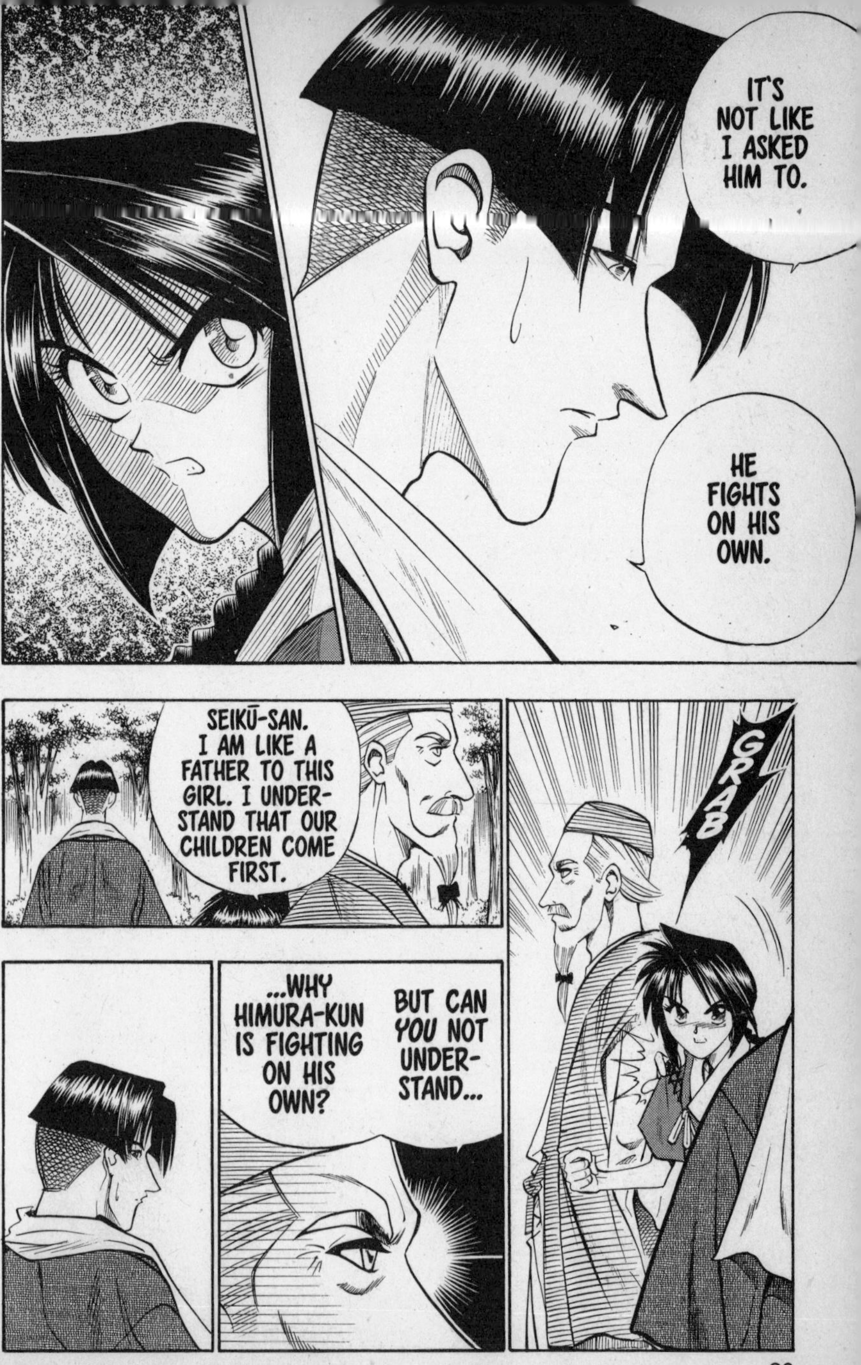
IT'S NOT LIKE I ASKED HIM TO.
HE FIGHTS ON HIS OWN.
GRAB
SEIKŪ-SAN. I AM LIKE A FATHER TO THIS GIRL. I UNDER-STAND THAT OUR CHILDREN COME FIRST.
BUT CAN *YOU* NOT UNDER-STAND...
...WHY HIMURA-KUN IS FIGHTING ON HIS OWN?

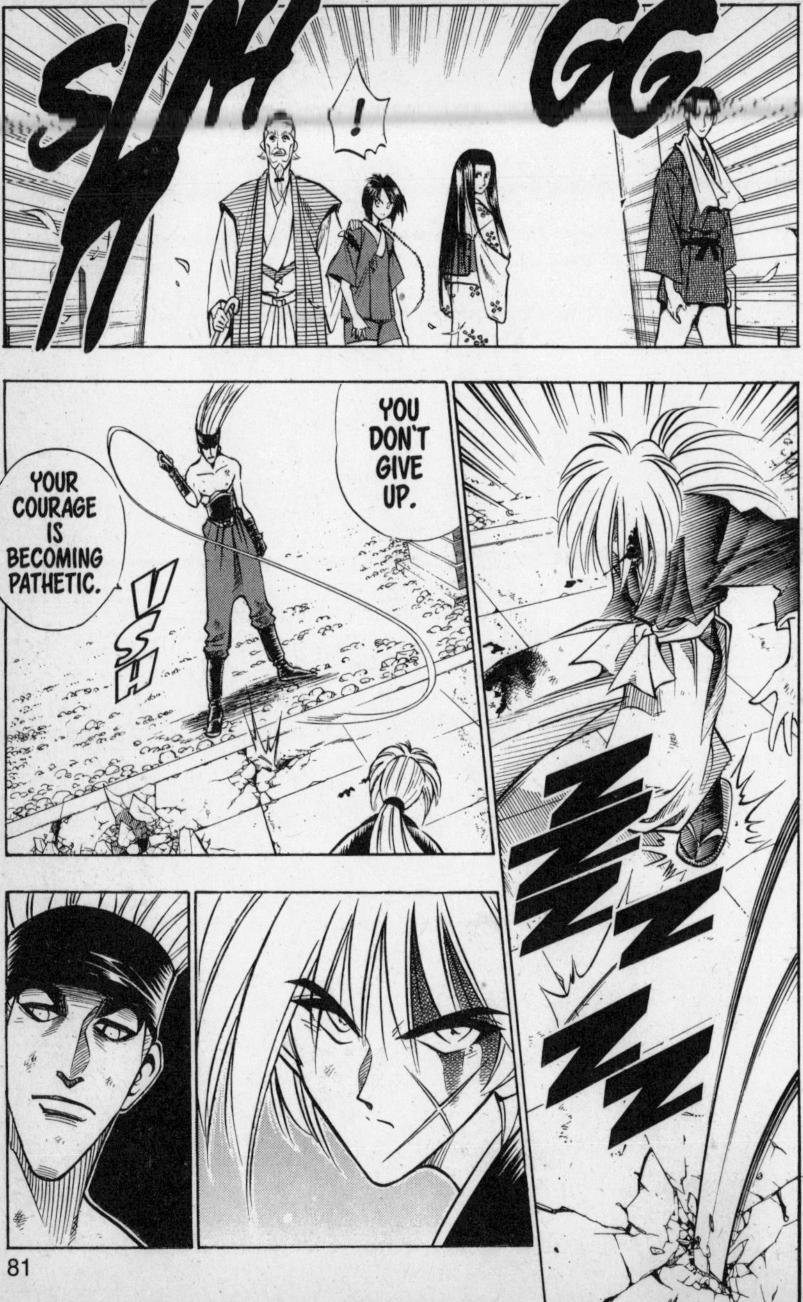
!
SHH GG
ZZZZZZ
YOU DON'T GIVE UP.
YOUR COURAGE IS BECOMING PATHETIC.
VISH

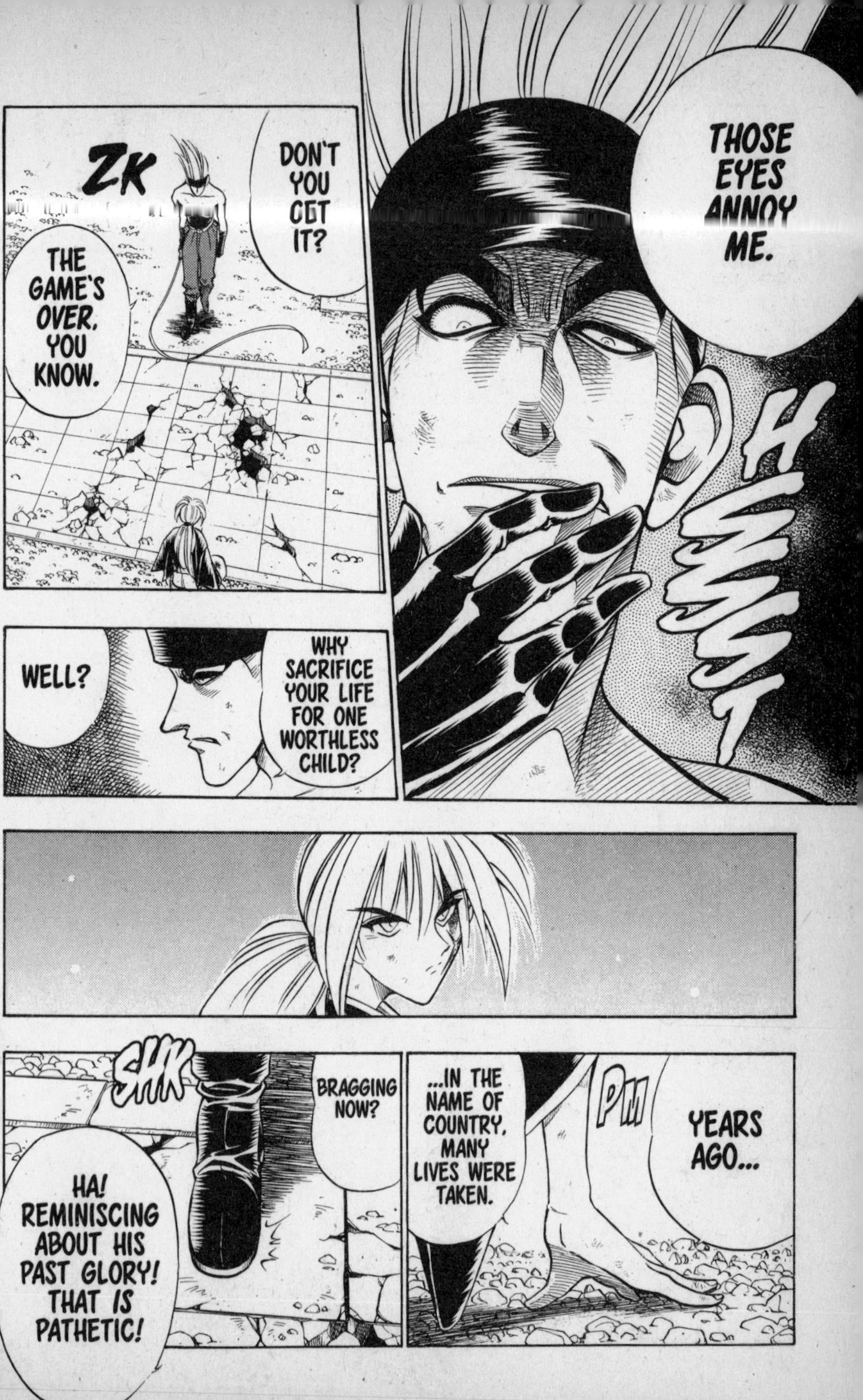
THOSE EYES ANNOY ME.
HWSST
DON'T YOU GET IT?
ZK
THE GAME'S OVER, YOU KNOW.
WHY SACRIFICE YOUR LIFE FOR ONE WORTHLESS CHILD?
WELL?
YEARS AGO...
PM
...IN THE NAME OF COUNTRY, MANY LIVES WERE TAKEN.
BRAGGING NOW?
SHK
HA! REMINISCING ABOUT HIS PAST GLORY! THAT IS PATHETIC!

« READ THIS WAY «

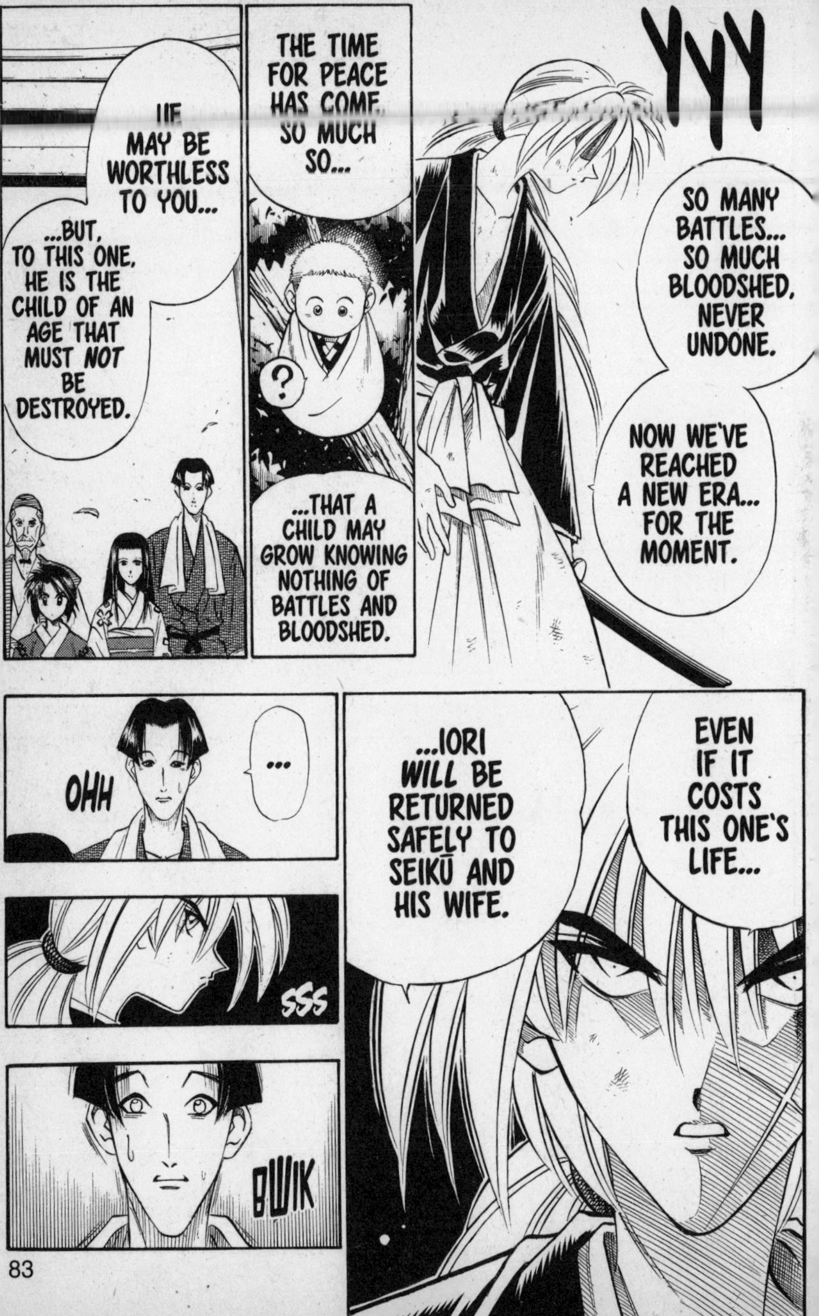
YYY
SO MANY BATTLES... SO MUCH BLOODSHED, NEVER UNDONE.
NOW WE'VE REACHED A NEW ERA... FOR THE MOMENT.
THE TIME FOR PEACE HAS COME, SO MUCH SO...
?
...THAT A CHILD MAY GROW KNOWING NOTHING OF BATTLES AND BLOODSHED.
LIFE MAY BE WORTHLESS TO YOU...
...BUT, TO THIS ONE, HE IS THE CHILD OF AN AGE THAT MUST *NOT* BE DESTROYED.
EVEN IF IT COSTS THIS ONE'S LIFE...
...IORI *WILL* BE RETURNED SAFELY TO SEIKŪ AND HIS WIFE.
...
OHH
SSS
BWIK

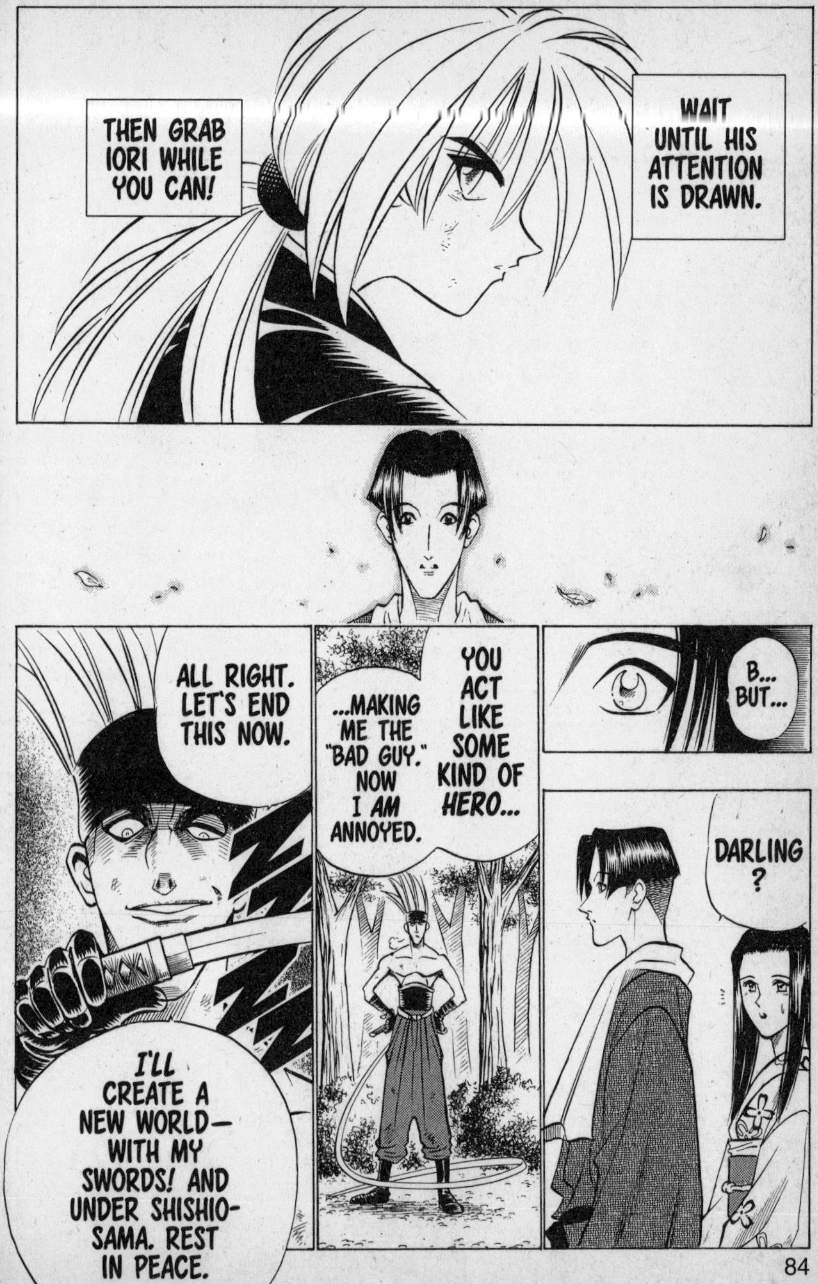
WAIT UNTIL HIS ATTENTION IS DRAWN.
THEN GRAB IORI WHILE YOU CAN!
B... BUT...
DARLING?
YOU ACT LIKE SOME KIND OF HERO...
...MAKING ME THE "BAD GUY." NOW I *AM* ANNOYED.
ALL RIGHT. LET'S END THIS NOW.
I'LL CREATE A NEW WORLD—WITH MY SWORDS! AND UNDER SHISHIO-SAMA. REST IN PEACE.

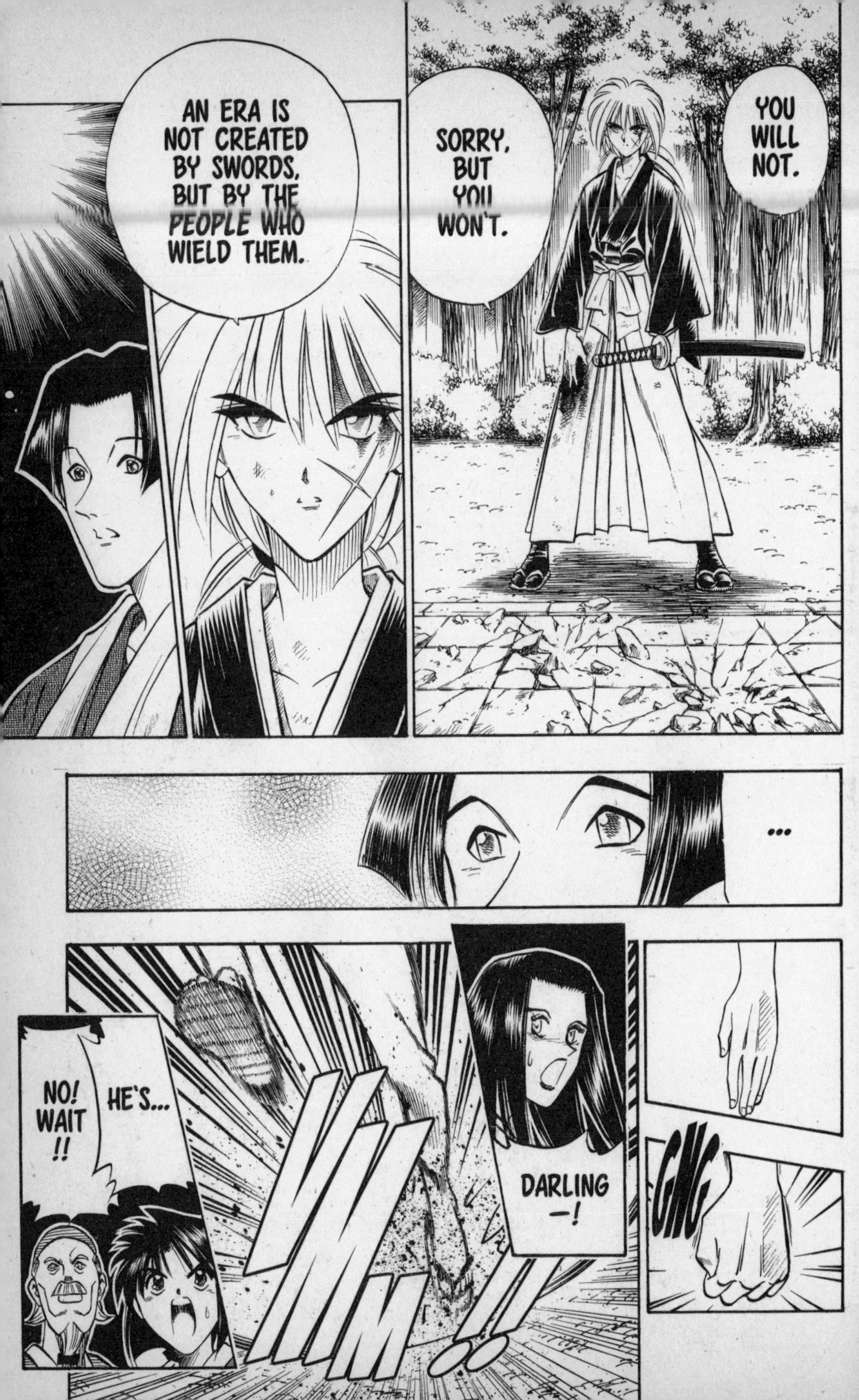
YOU WILL NOT.
SORRY, BUT YOU WON'T.
AN ERA IS NOT CREATED BY SWORDS, BUT BY THE *PEOPLE* WHO WIELD THEM.
...
GNG
DARLING —!
VWM!!
HE'S...
NO! WAIT !!

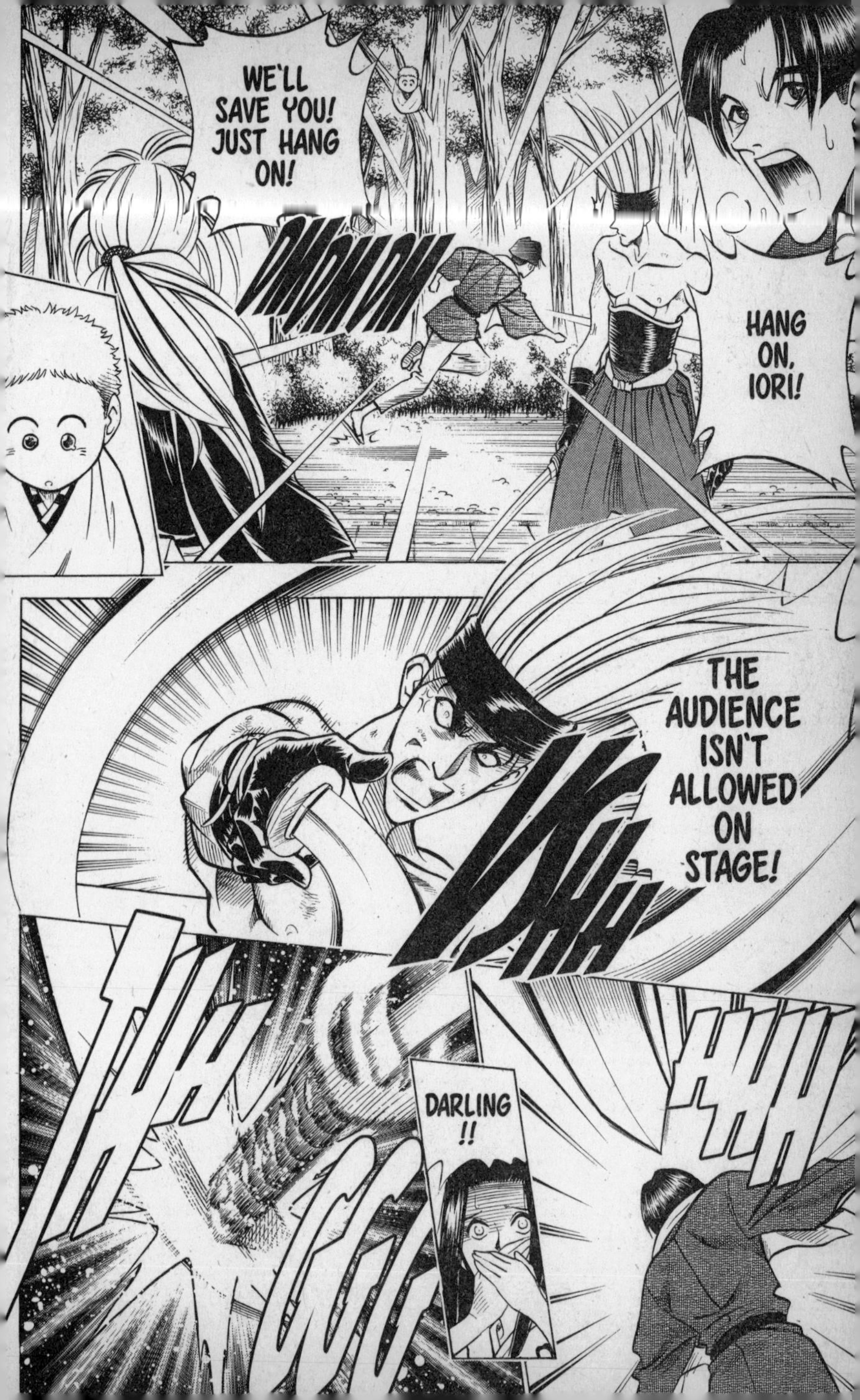
HANG ON, IORI!
WE'LL SAVE YOU! JUST HANG ON!
THE AUDIENCE ISN'T ALLOWED ON STAGE!
DARLING !!

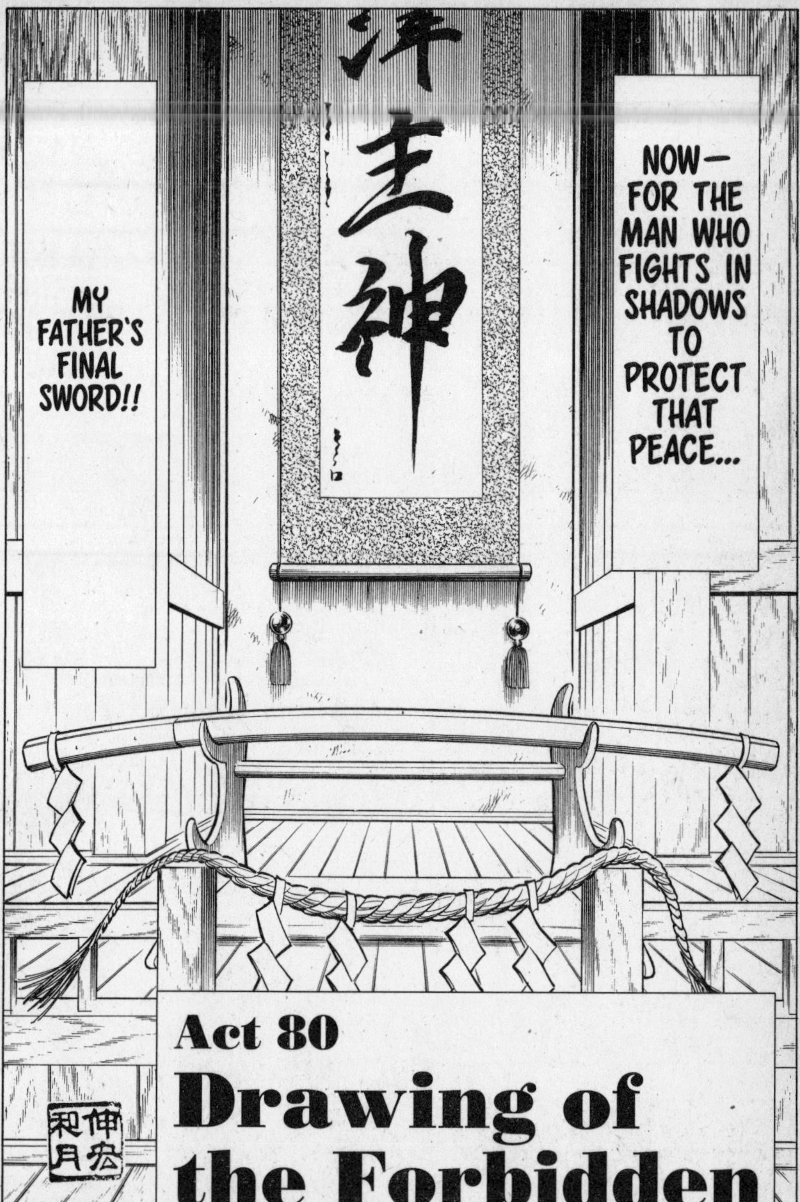
NOW— FOR THE MAN WHO FIGHTS IN SHADOWS TO PROTECT THAT PEACE...
MY FATHER'S FINAL SWORD!!

Act 80
Drawing of the Forbidden

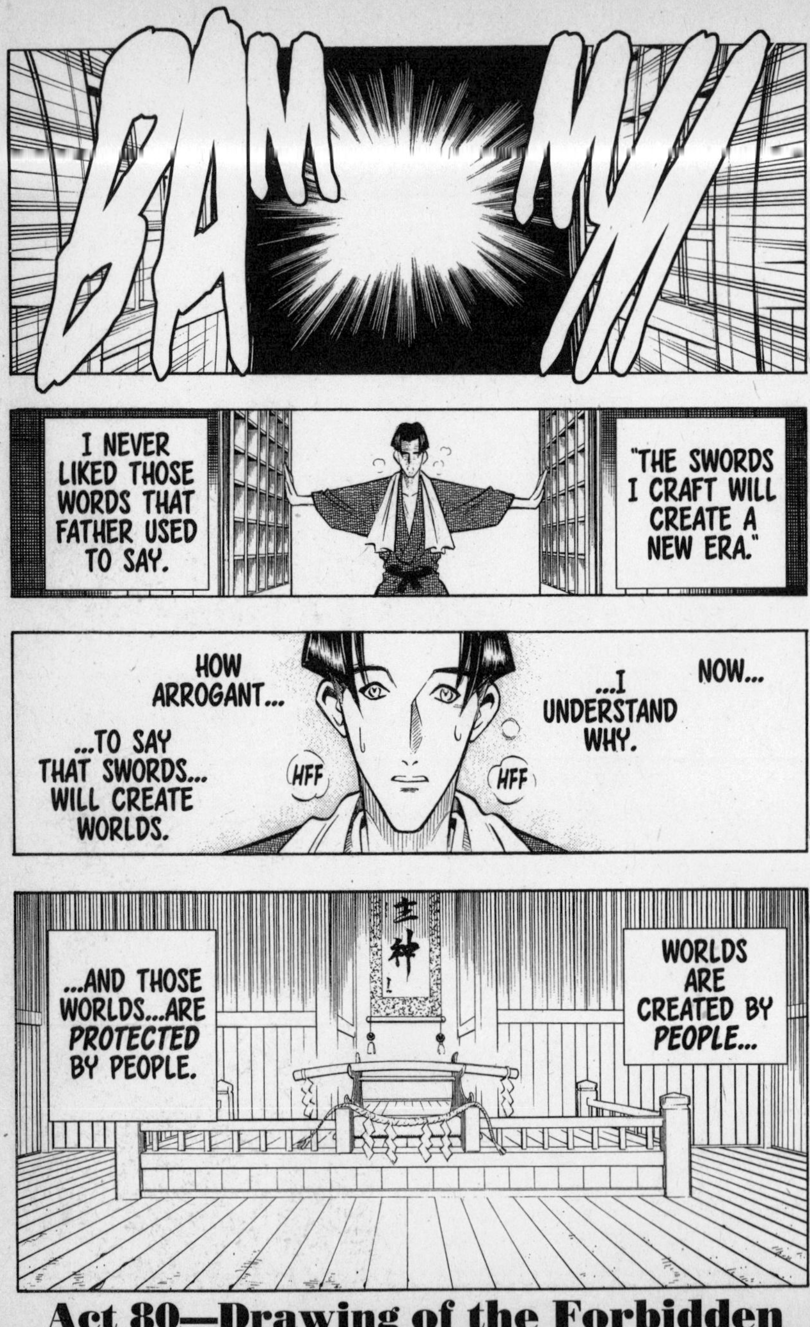
BAM
"THE SWORDS I CRAFT WILL CREATE A NEW ERA."
I NEVER LIKED THOSE WORDS THAT FATHER USED TO SAY.
NOW...
...I UNDERSTAND WHY.
HFF
HOW ARROGANT...
...TO SAY THAT SWORDS... WILL CREATE WORLDS.
HFF
WORLDS ARE CREATED BY PEOPLE...
...AND THOSE WORLDS...ARE PROTECTED BY PEOPLE.

Act 80—Drawing of the Forbidden

Rurouni Kenshin

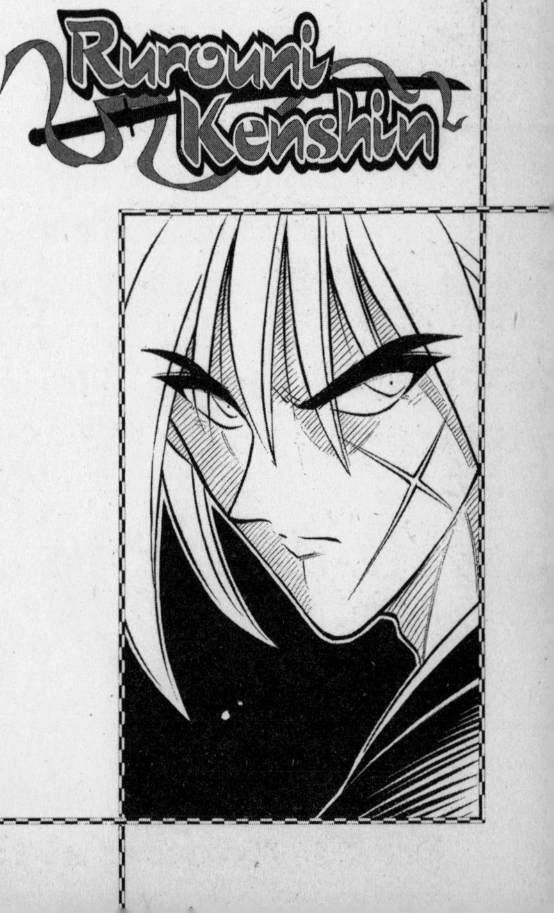

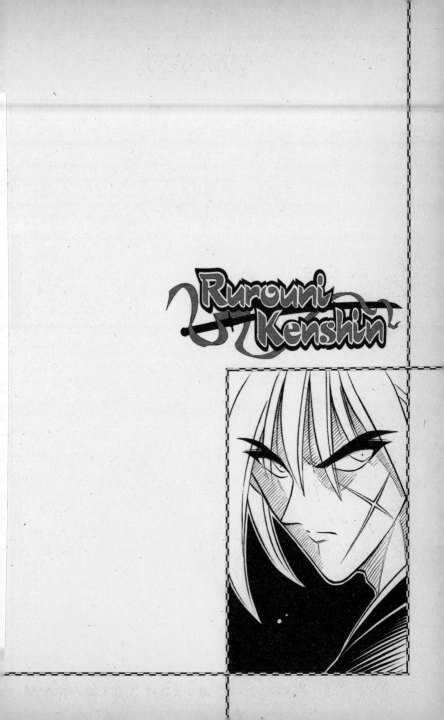

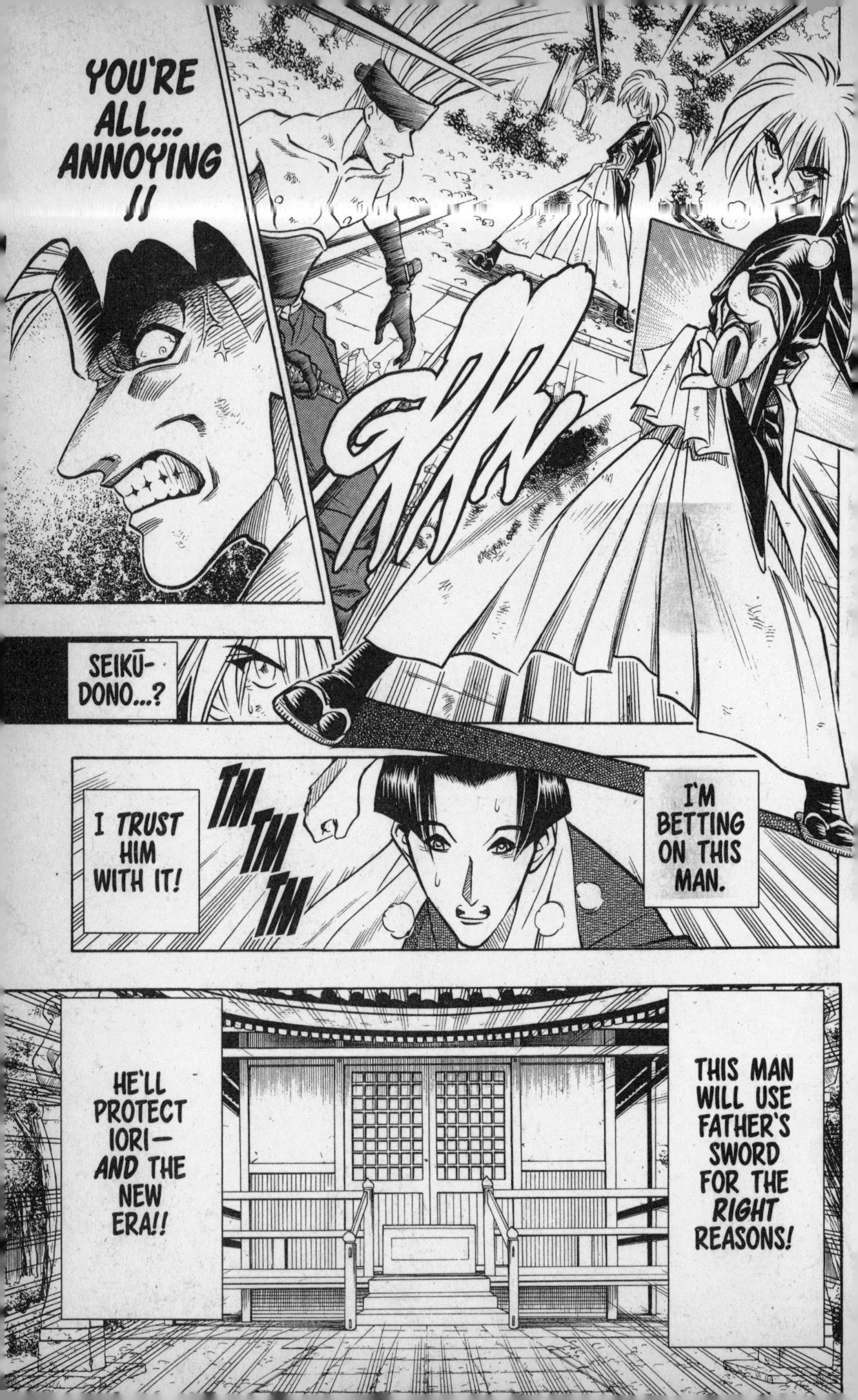
GYAN
YOU'RE ALL... ANNOYING!!
SEIKŪ-DONO...?
I'M BETTING ON THIS MAN.
TM TM TM
I TRUST HIM WITH IT!
THIS MAN WILL USE FATHER'S SWORD FOR THE RIGHT REASONS!
HE'LL PROTECT IORI— AND THE NEW ERA!!

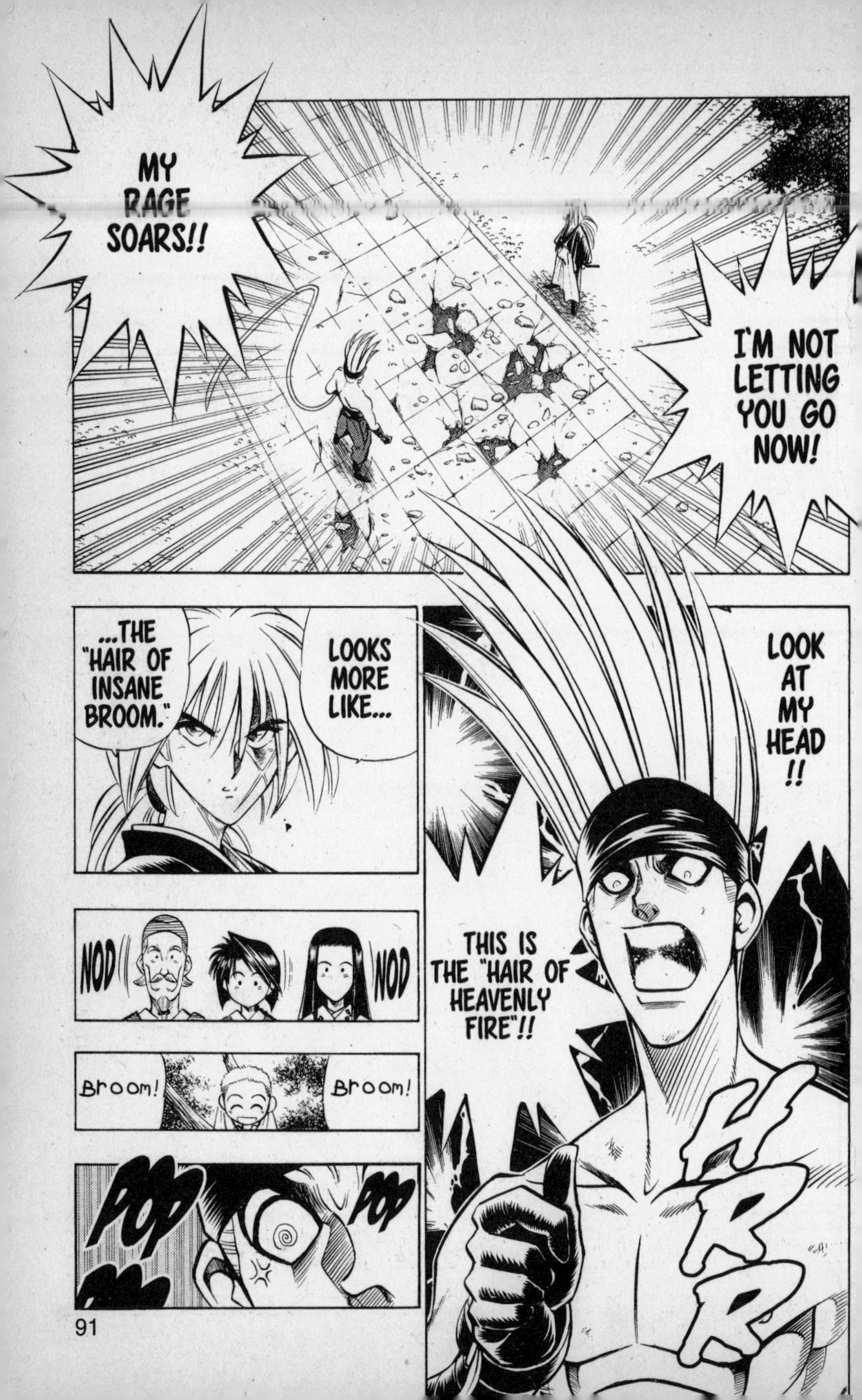
I'M NOT LETTING YOU GO NOW!
MY RAGE SOARS!!
LOOK AT MY HEAD!!
THIS IS THE "HAIR OF HEAVENLY FIRE"!!
LOOKS MORE LIKE...
...THE "HAIR OF INSANE BROOM."
NOD
NOD
Broom!
Broom!
POP
POP

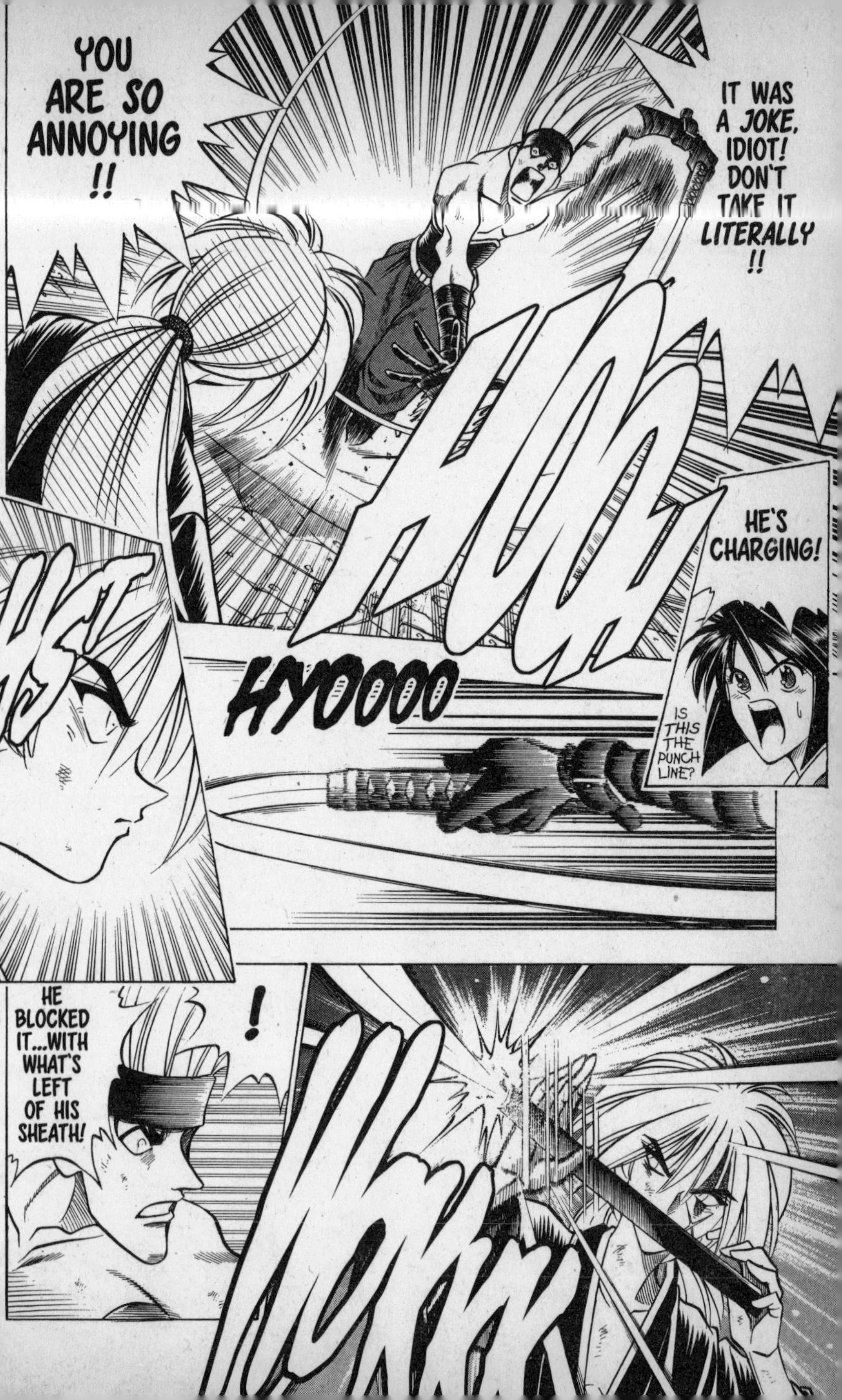
IT WAS A JOKE, IDIOT! DON'T TAKE IT LITERALLY !!
YOU ARE SO ANNOYING !!
HE'S CHARGING!
IS THIS THE PUNCH LINE?
HYOOOO
!
HE BLOCKED IT...WITH WHAT'S LEFT OF HIS SHEATH!

« READ THIS WAY «

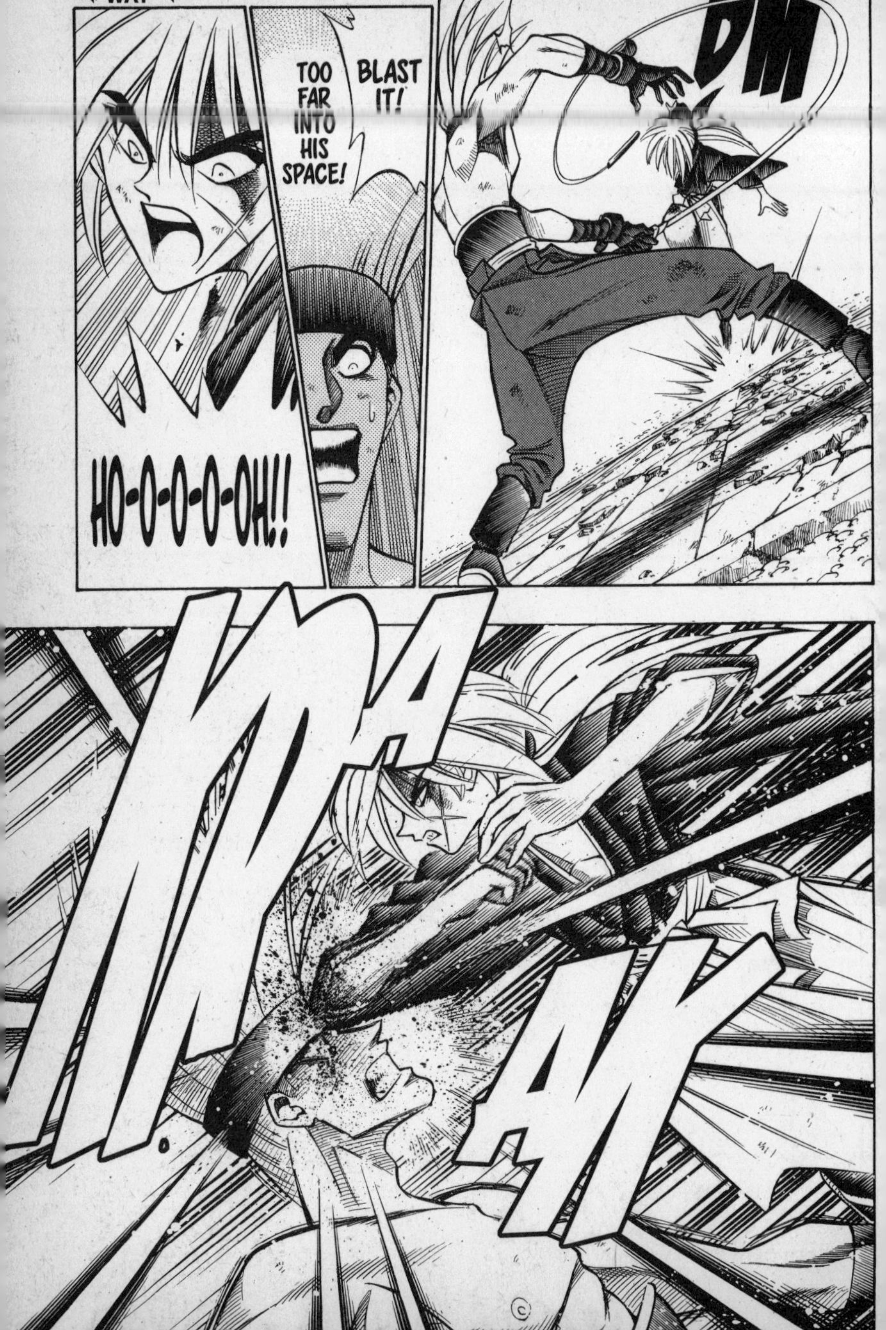
DM
BLAST IT!
TOO FAR INTO HIS SPACE!
HO-O-O-O-OH!!
WHAAK

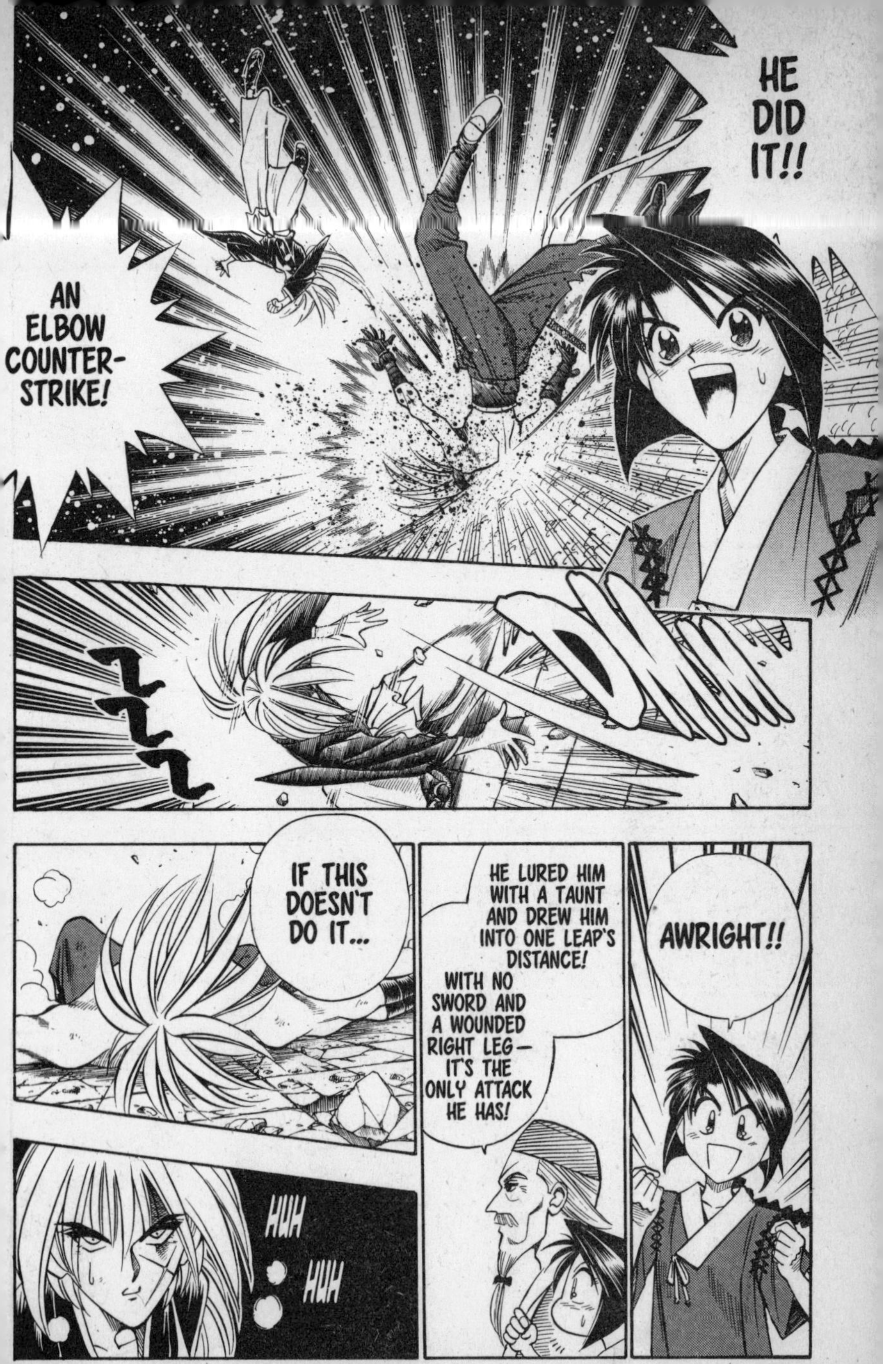
HE DID IT!!
AN ELBOW COUNTER-STRIKE!
AWRIGHT!!
HE LURED HIM WITH A TAUNT AND DREW HIM INTO ONE LEAP'S DISTANCE!
WITH NO SWORD AND A WOUNDED RIGHT LEG— IT'S THE ONLY ATTACK HE HAS!
IF THIS DOESN'T DO IT...
HUH
HUH

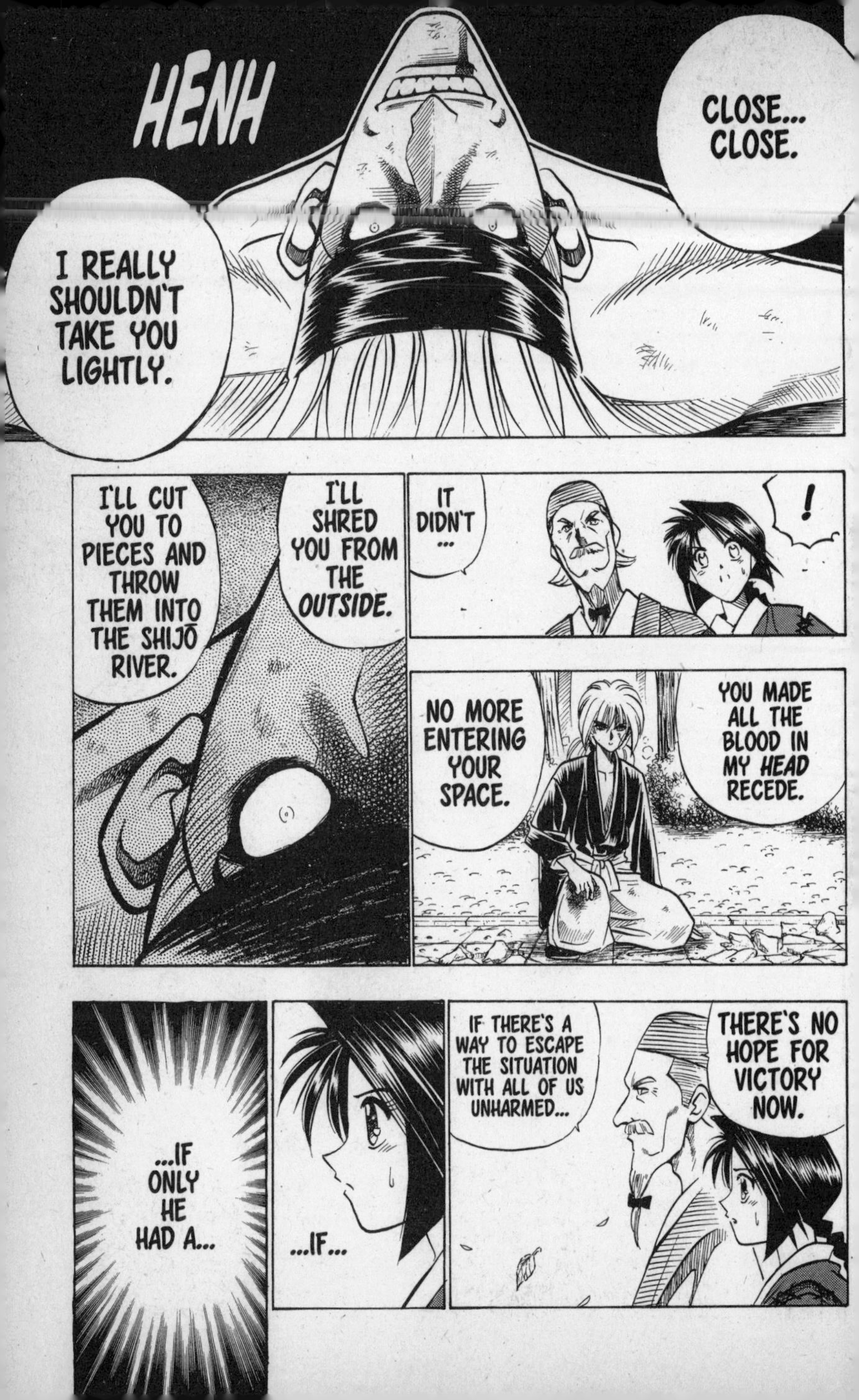

CLOSE... CLOSE.
HENH
I REALLY SHOULDN'T TAKE YOU LIGHTLY.
!
IT DIDN'T ...
YOU MADE ALL THE BLOOD IN MY *HEAD* RECEDE.
NO MORE ENTERING YOUR SPACE.
I'LL SHRED YOU FROM THE *OUTSIDE.*
I'LL CUT YOU TO PIECES AND THROW THEM INTO THE SHIJŌ RIVER.
THERE'S NO HOPE FOR VICTORY NOW.
IF THERE'S A WAY TO ESCAPE THE SITUATION WITH ALL OF US UNHARMED...
...IF...
...IF ONLY HE HAD A...

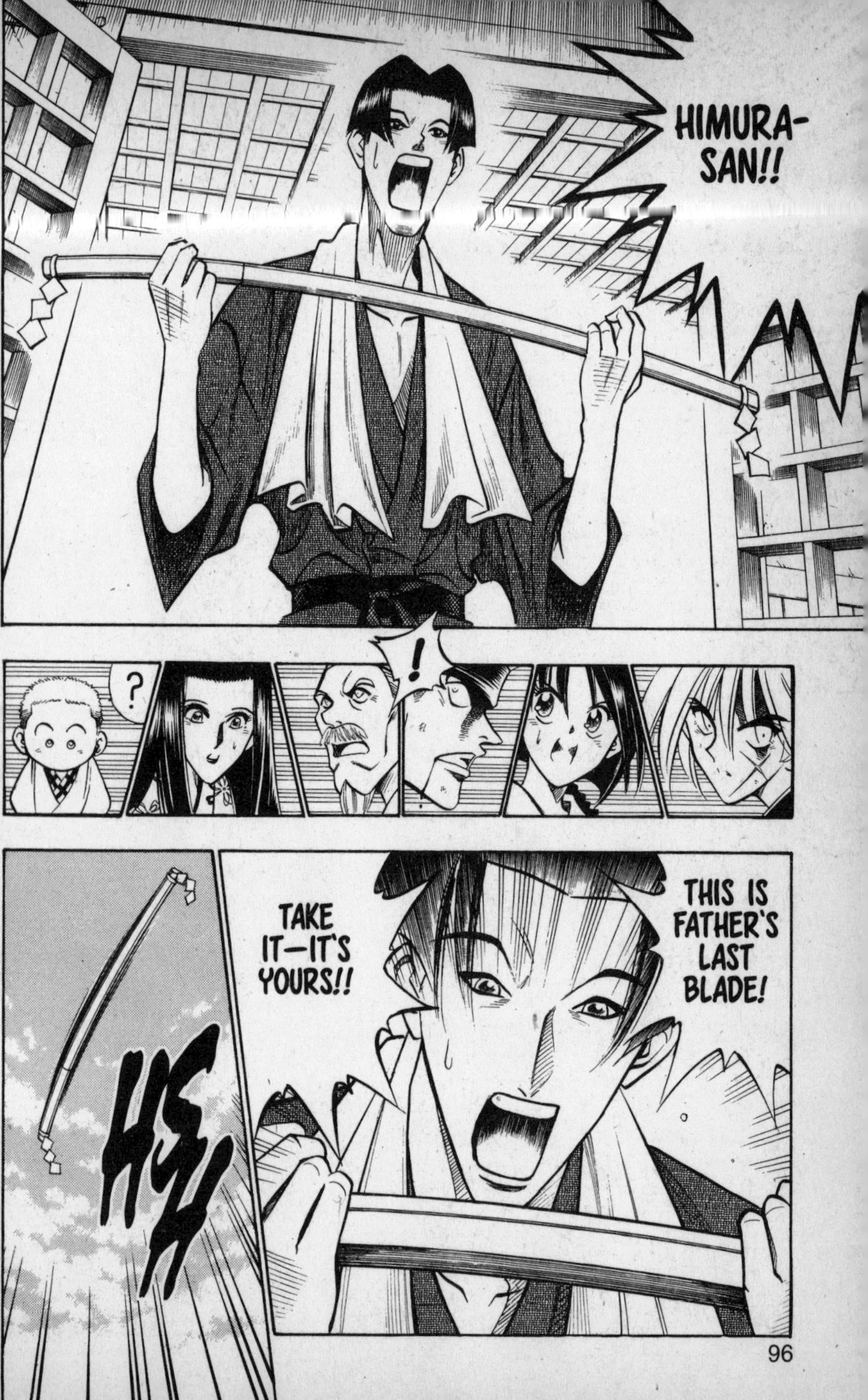
HIMURA-SAN!!
!
?
THIS IS FATHER'S LAST BLADE!
TAKE IT—IT'S YOURS!!

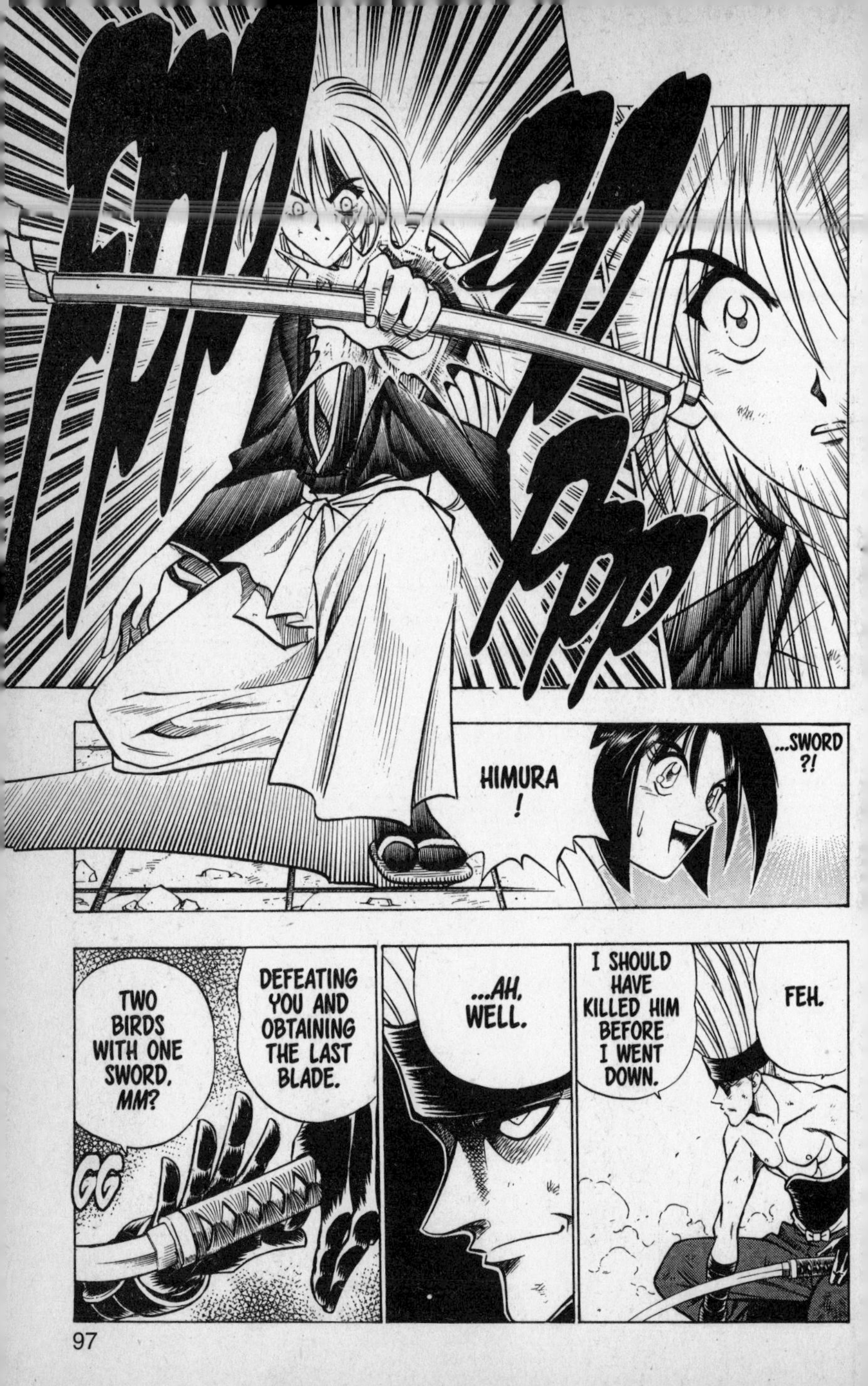
...SWORD ?!
HIMURA !
FEH.
I SHOULD HAVE KILLED HIM BEFORE I WENT DOWN.
...AH, WELL.
DEFEATING YOU AND OBTAINING THE LAST BLADE.
TWO BIRDS WITH ONE SWORD. MM?
GG

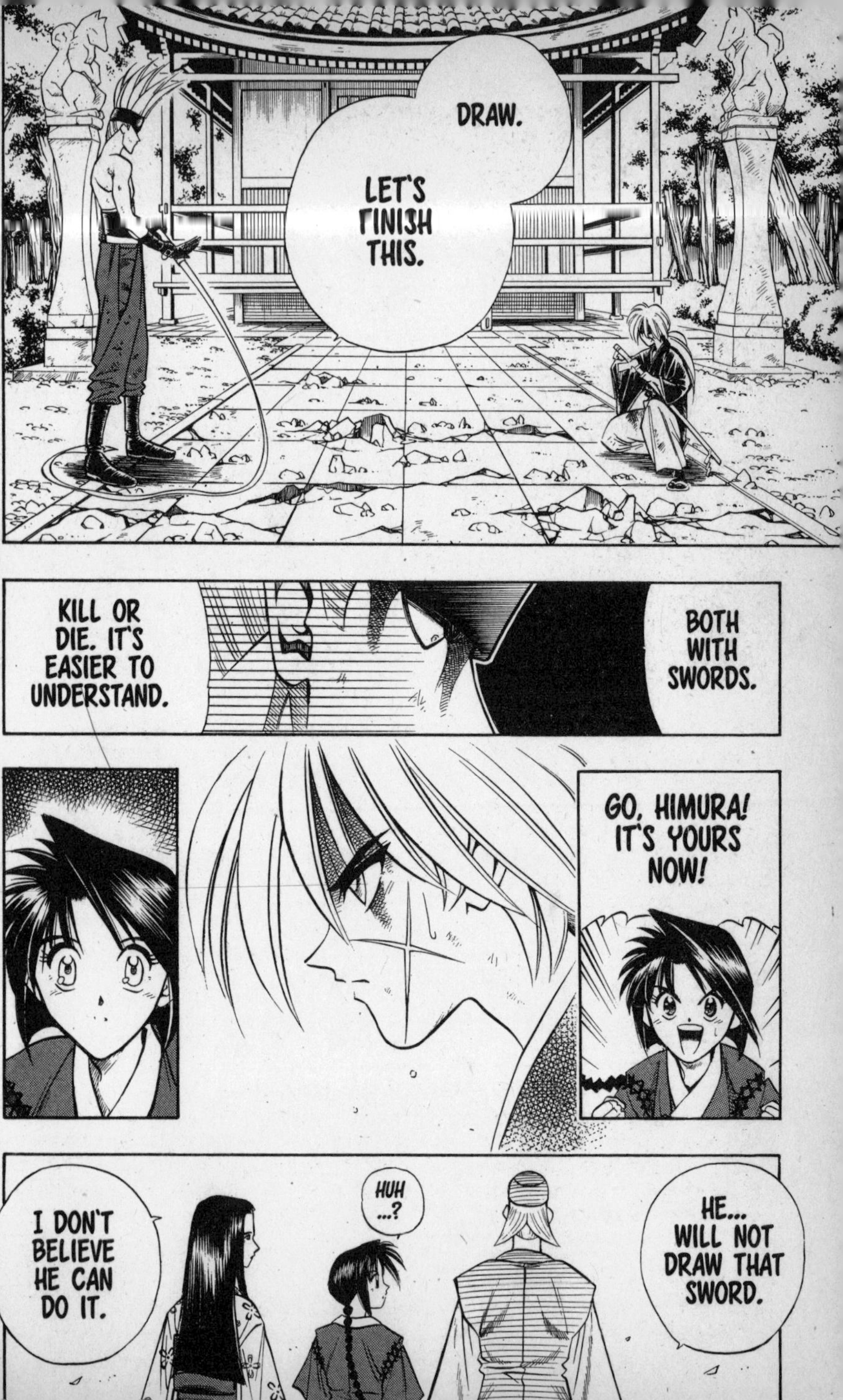
DRAW.
LET'S FINISH THIS.
BOTH WITH SWORDS.
KILL OR DIE. IT'S EASIER TO UNDERSTAND.
GO, HIMURA! IT'S YOURS NOW!
HE... WILL NOT DRAW THAT SWORD.
HUH ...?
I DON'T BELIEVE HE CAN DO IT.

READ THIS WAY

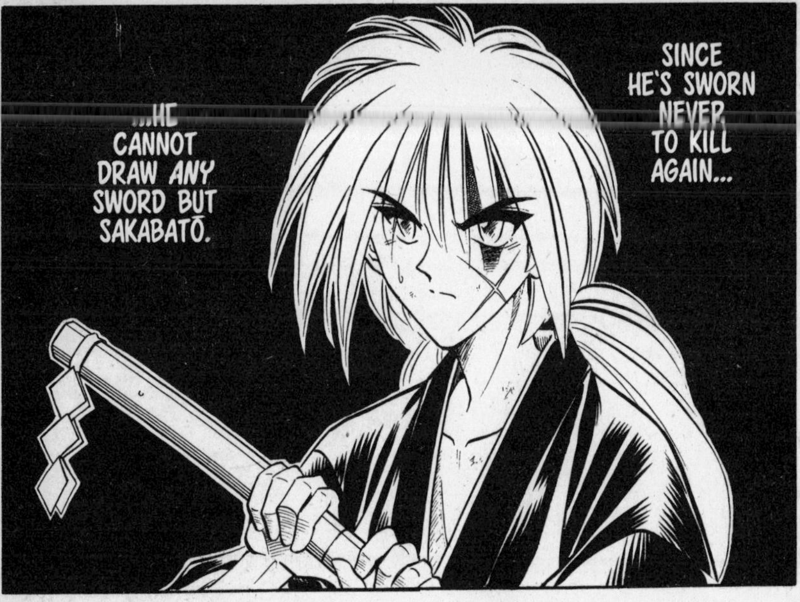
SINCE HE'S SWORN NEVER TO KILL AGAIN...
...HE CANNOT DRAW ANY SWORD BUT SAKABATŌ.

The voice-actors for the CD book were pros, in both name and skill...almost too good for the likes of Watsuki. I was completely ignorant about voice-actors until then, but they showed me so much pride and dedication that I immediately began to respect their craft—and that's what made it disappointing to have had the voice-actors change, especially **Ogata Megumi** as "Kenshin," and **Seki Tomokazu** as "Sanosuke." I thought both were equally well suited to their parts. I had a chance to apologize to Seki-san when we met once during a dinner arranged by a friend of mine. (I'm sorry I wasn't able to make the premiere of "Gekidan Hero, Hero Q." I'll go the next chance I get.) I still haven't had a chance to talk to Ogata-san (please don't bother pointing out that that's to be expected). So, even if it is indirectly, I'll take this opportunity to say it: Ogata-san, I'm very sorry.

Recently I've received quite a few letters of protest, and also letters to the effect, "If (Ogata-san) can't do 'Kenshin,' at least have her do 'Sōjirō.'" As far as I'm concerned, though, I'd like her for "Misao." (I thought she'd find a "stubborn girl" more challenging than the "pretty boy" parts she usually gets—though I'm sure she'll have no problem pulling it off.) However it works out, I'd like to see Ogata-san and the rest of the CD book cast get parts in the anime. And, as part of my apology, I'd like them to get parts that are worth playing. Of course, this is merely Watsuki's own, very selfish opinion...

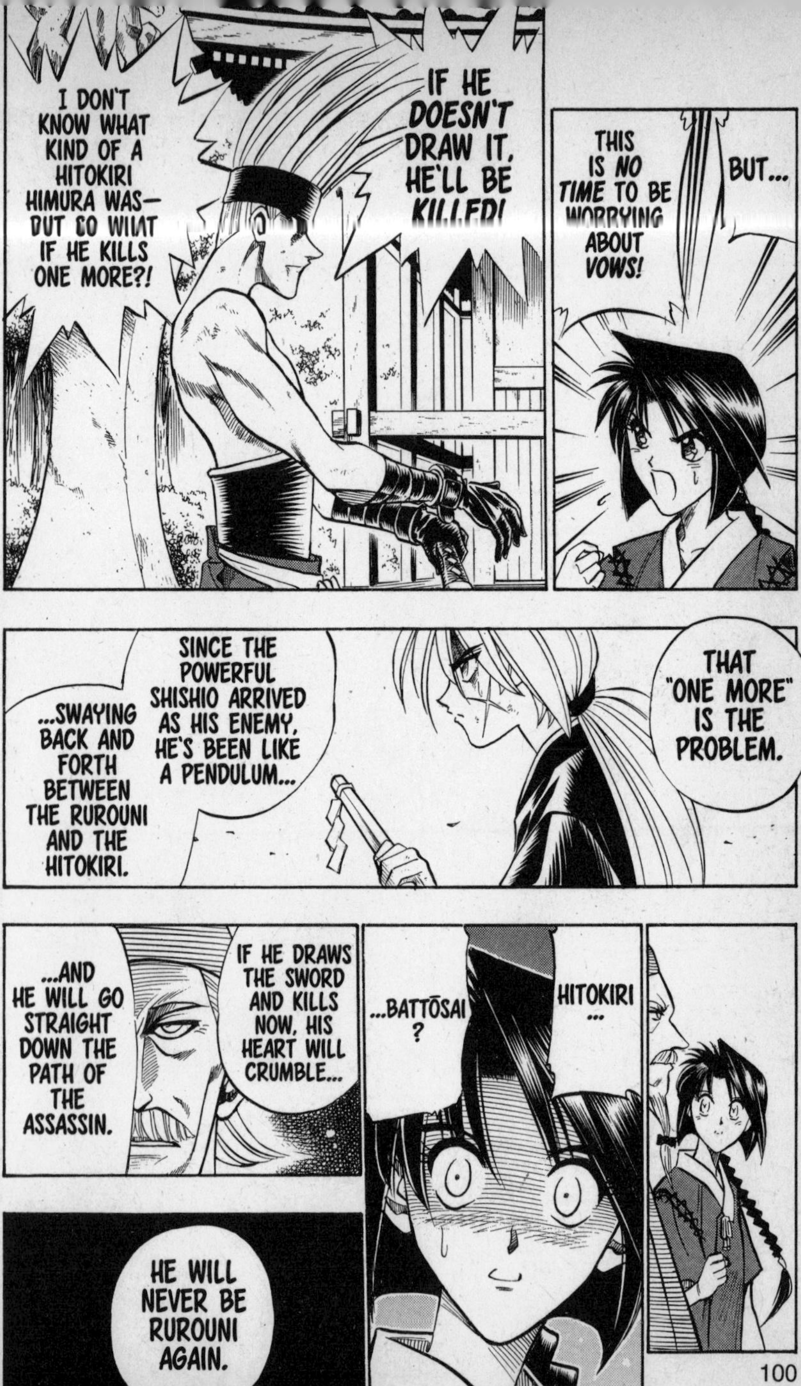
BUT...
THIS IS NO TIME TO BE WORRYING ABOUT VOWS!
IF HE DOESN'T DRAW IT, HE'LL BE KILLED!
I DON'T KNOW WHAT KIND OF A HITOKIRI HIMURA WAS—BUT SO WHAT IF HE KILLS ONE MORE?!
THAT "ONE MORE" IS THE PROBLEM.
SINCE THE POWERFUL SHISHIO ARRIVED AS HIS ENEMY, HE'S BEEN LIKE A PENDULUM...
...SWAYING BACK AND FORTH BETWEEN THE RUROUNI AND THE HITOKIRI.
HITOKIRI ...
...BATTŌSAI ?
IF HE DRAWS THE SWORD AND KILLS NOW, HIS HEART WILL CRUMBLE...
...AND HE WILL GO STRAIGHT DOWN THE PATH OF THE ASSASSIN.
HE WILL NEVER BE RUROUNI AGAIN.

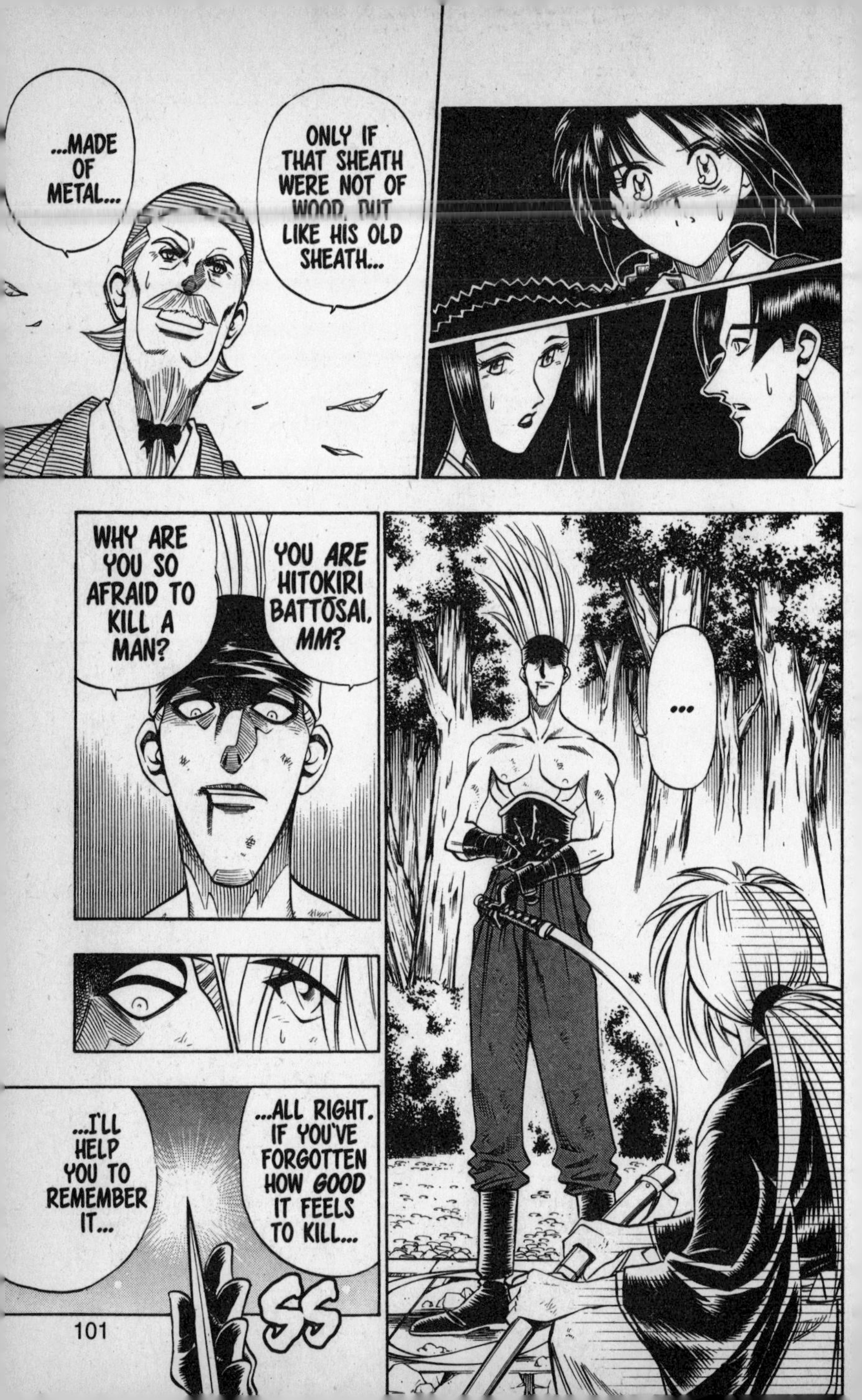
ONLY IF THAT SHEATH WERE NOT OF WOOD, BUT LIKE HIS OLD SHEATH...
...MADE OF METAL...
...
YOU ARE HITOKIRI BATTŌSAI, MM?
WHY ARE YOU SO AFRAID TO KILL A MAN?
...ALL RIGHT. IF YOU'VE FORGOTTEN HOW GOOD IT FEELS TO KILL...
...I'LL HELP YOU TO REMEMBER IT...
SS

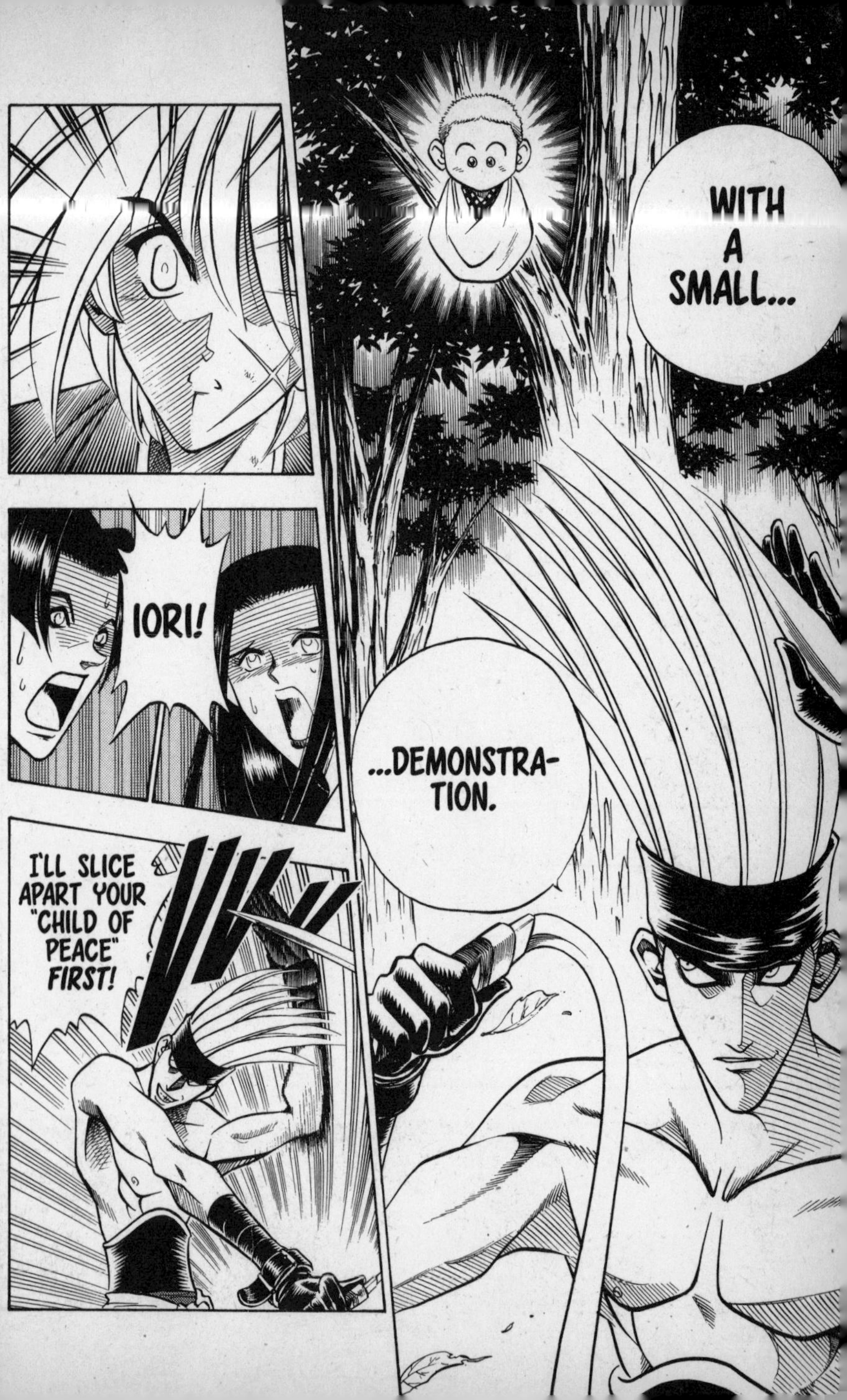
WITH A SMALL...
...DEMONSTRATION.
IORI!
I'LL SLICE APART YOUR "CHILD OF PEACE" FIRST!

READ THIS WAY

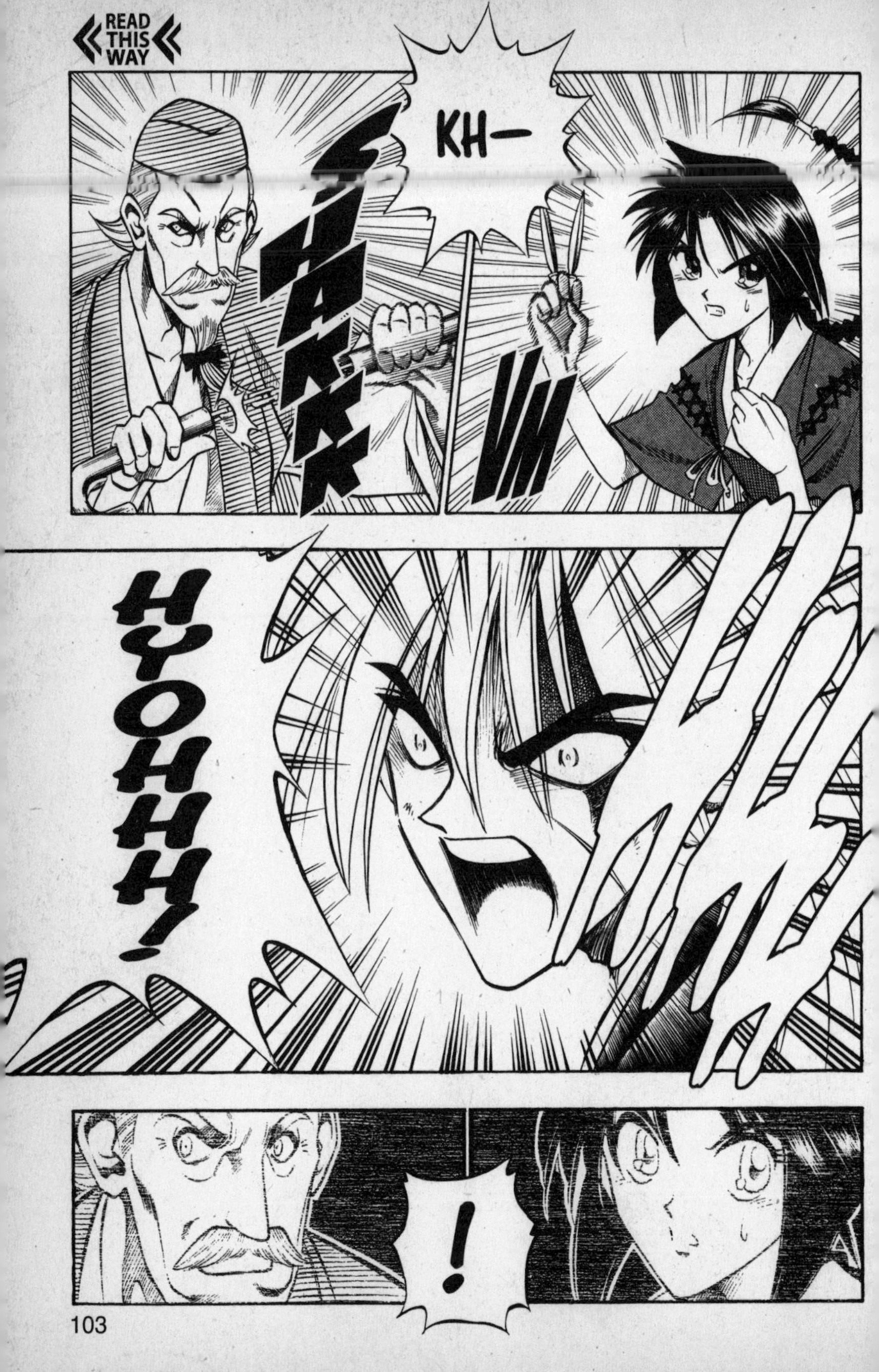
KH—
SHAKK
HYOHHH!
!

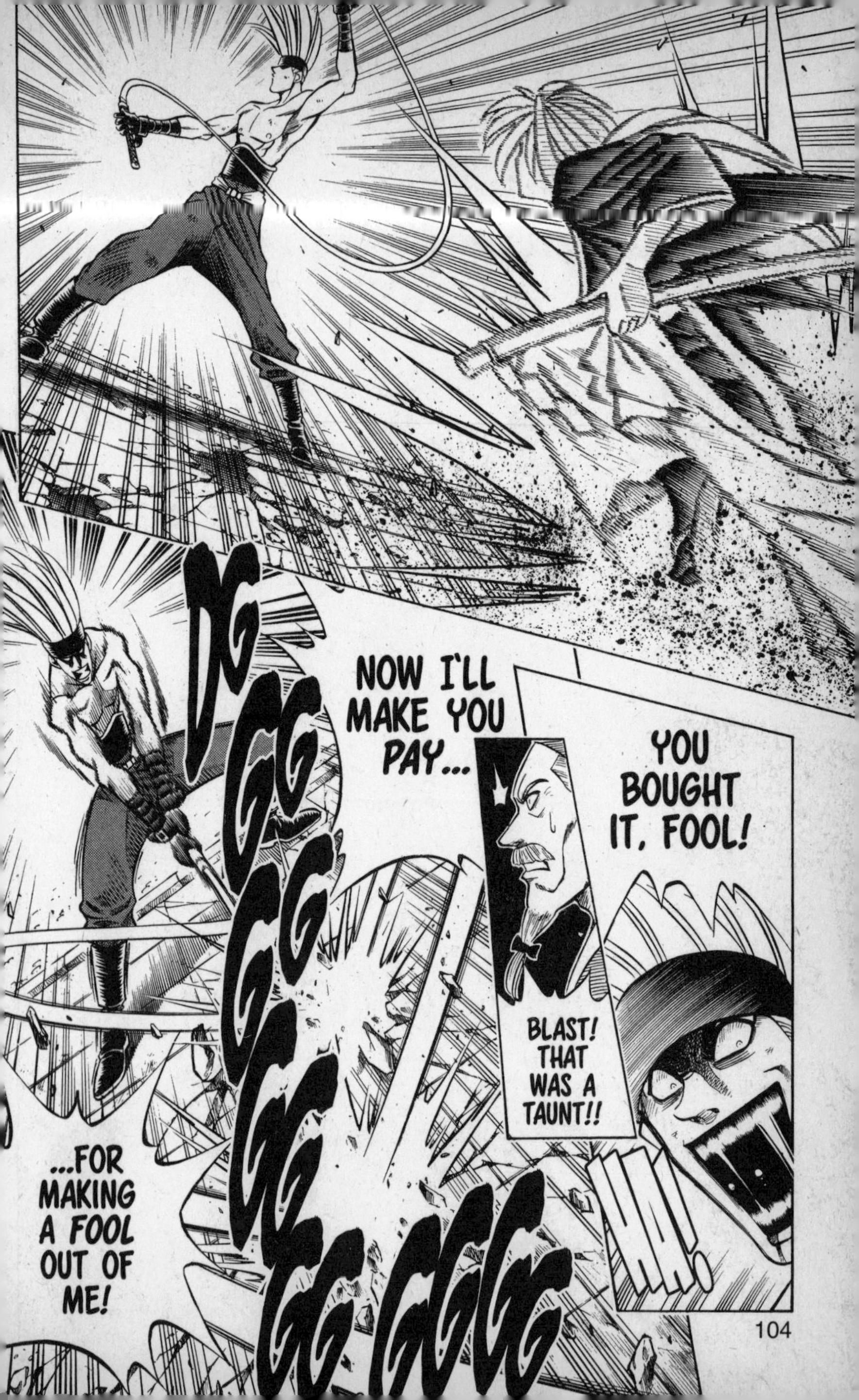
YOU BOUGHT IT, FOOL!
BLAST! THAT WAS A TAUNT!!
NOW I'LL MAKE YOU PAY...
...FOR MAKING A FOOL OUT OF ME!

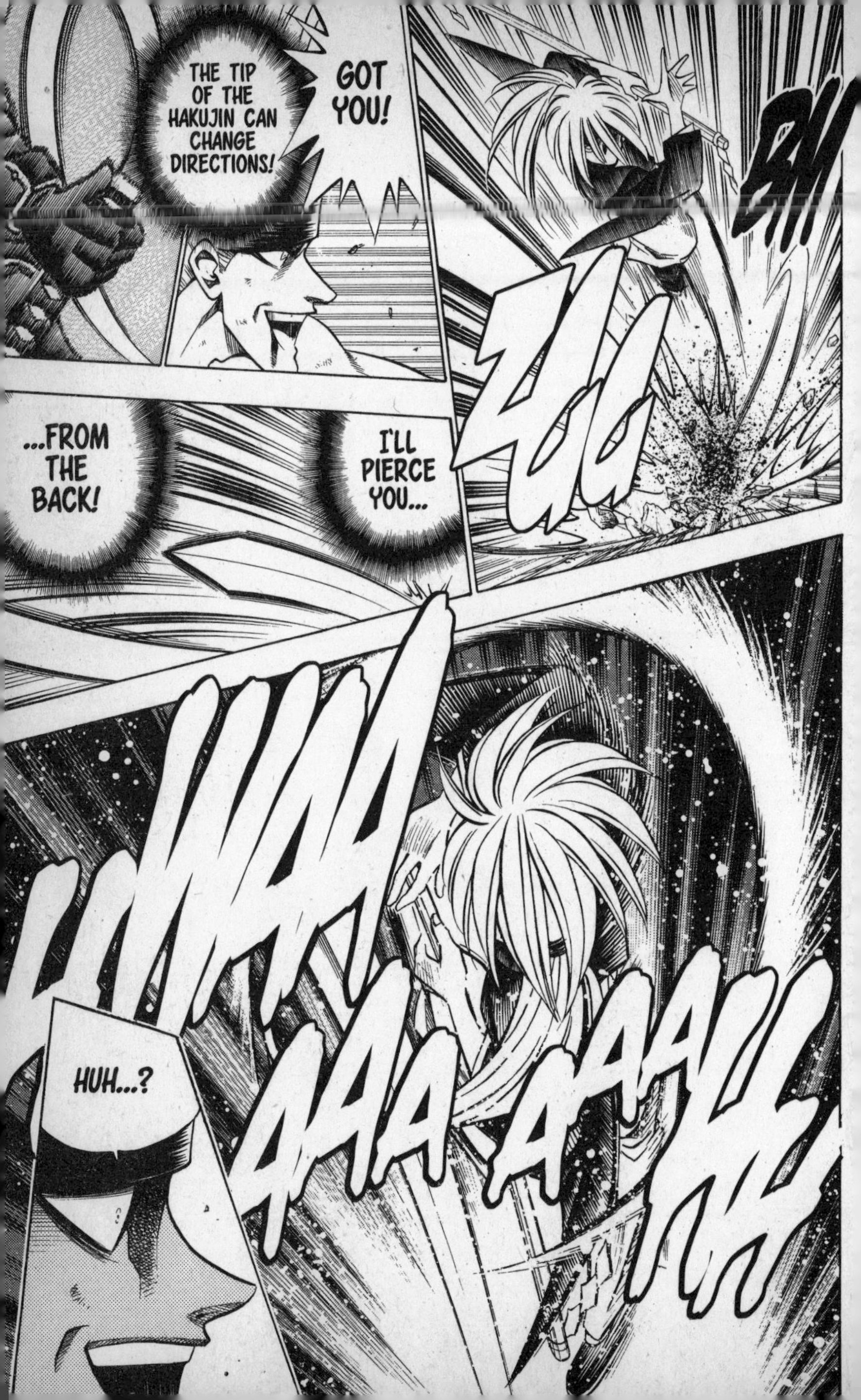
GOT YOU!
THE TIP OF THE HAKUJIN CAN CHANGE DIRECTIONS!
I'LL PIERCE YOU...
...FROM THE BACK!
HUH...?

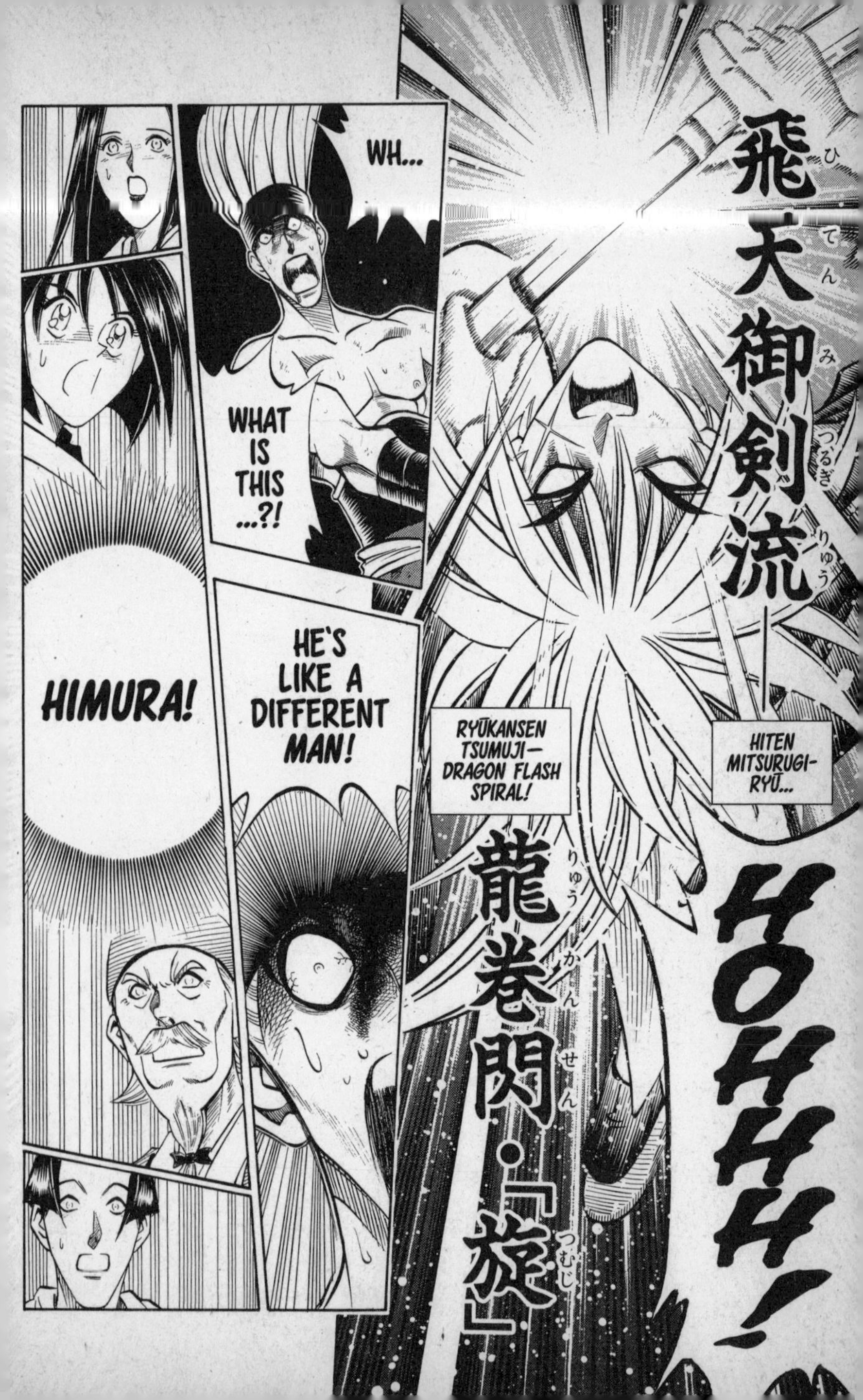
飛天御剣流
HITEN MITSURUGI-RYŪ...
龍巻閃・「旋」
RYŪKANSEN TSUMUJI—DRAGON FLASH SPIRAL!
GOHHH!
WH...
WHAT IS THIS ...?!
HE'S LIKE A DIFFERENT MAN!
HIMURA!

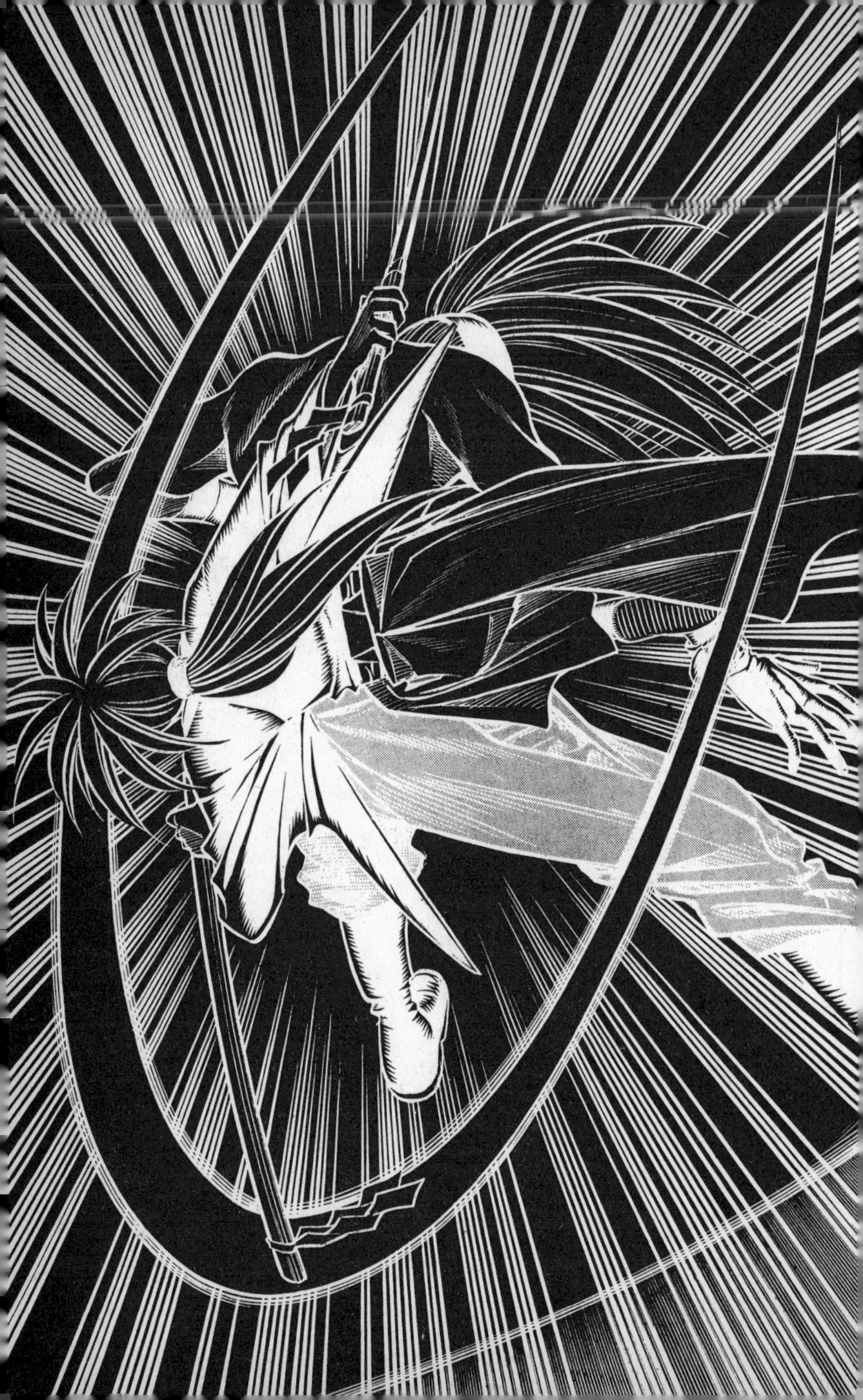

The Secret Life of Characters (29)
—Sawagejō Chō—

I've no real model for his personality, but if I had to pick one, it would be the public's stereotyped image of people from Kansai. Some of my assistants and mentors are "*Kansaijin*," and they're all fun and good people. Watsuki thinks that, in his next life, he'd like to be reincarnated as one of them. Chō isn't meant to represent Kansai people in reality, so please don't take him as such....

Despite being a villain, he was still very popular (though characters with Osaka dialects are *always* pretty popular). He was fun for me to draw, too, so I thought it was a waste to finish him off here and made him reappear later in the story. (It would be weird for him to become friendly with Kenshin and the others, though, so I've given him a bit more of a neutral position.)

As an aside, sketches of Chō sent in by fans usually have Iori in them, too, which gives me quite a laugh.

As for models in terms of design, the assistants say [*Samurai Shodown's*] "Galford" and readers say *King of Fighters*' "Benimaru," but frankly, they're both wrong. Chō's basic design was created when Watsuki was 20 years old... and was designed to be an alien (really!). That was ultimately rejected, but that horse-headed monkey-face was hard to throw out completely, so I used it this time around. The original design had given him black, messy hair, all swept back—different from the Chō of today—but to give him more impact as the first of the *Juppongatana* assassins, I incorporated a "punk rock" quality, making him what he is. I guess I can understand why people think "Benimaru"....

Incidentally, the Kansai dialect used by Chō was checked over by an assistant from Kansai, but was then broken down to make it easier for everyone all over Japan to understand... meaning, it's different from actual Kansai dialect. Some of my Kansai readers may not approve, but "*RuroKen*" is manga aimed at everyone, so cut me some slack, huh?

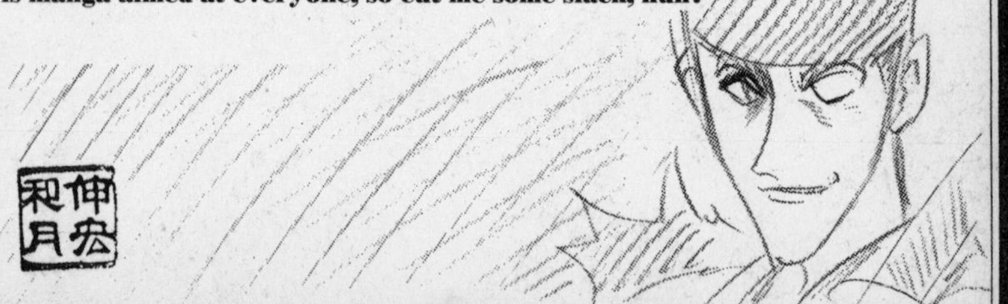
伸宏
和月

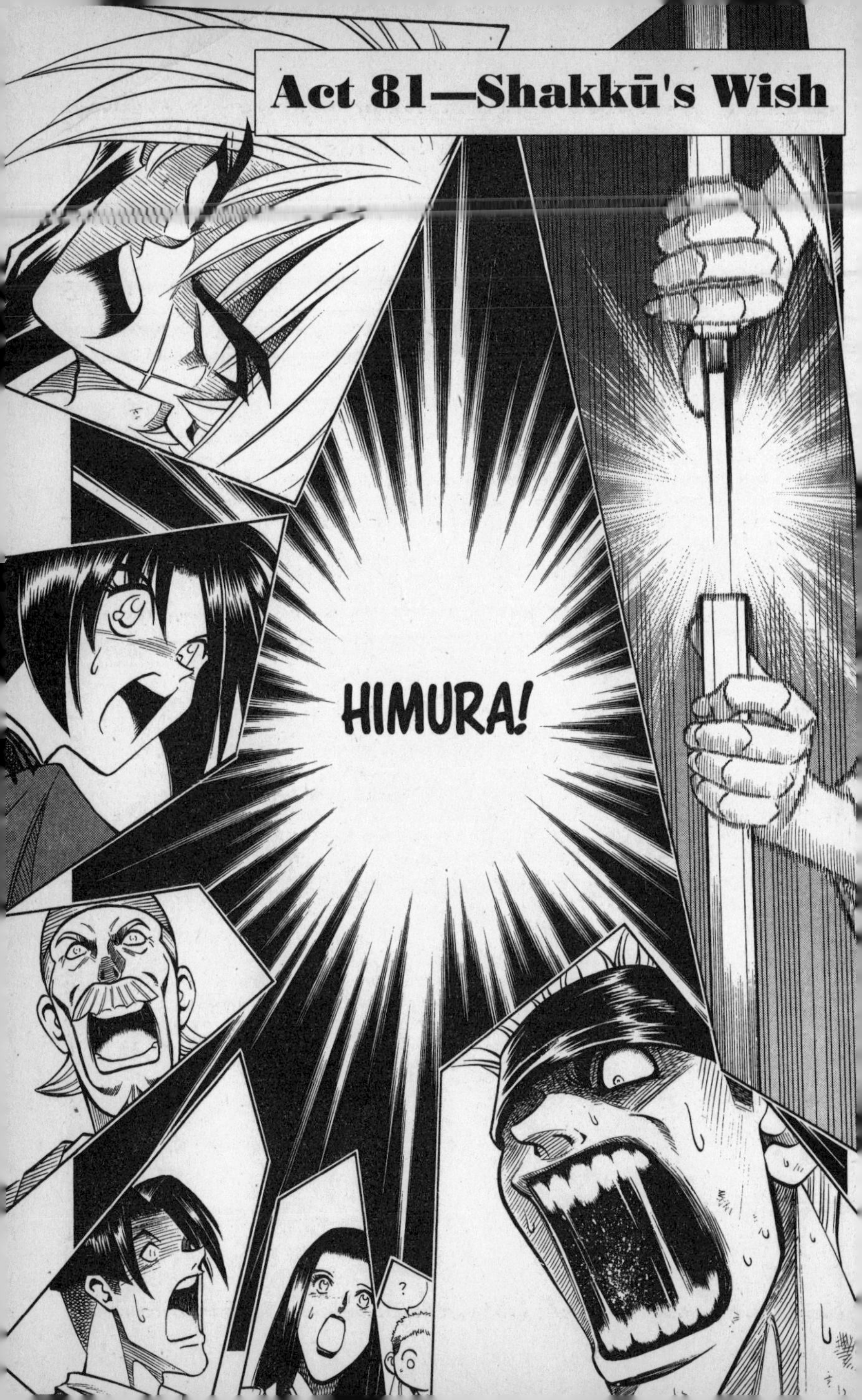
Act 81—Shakkū's Wish
HIMURA!
?

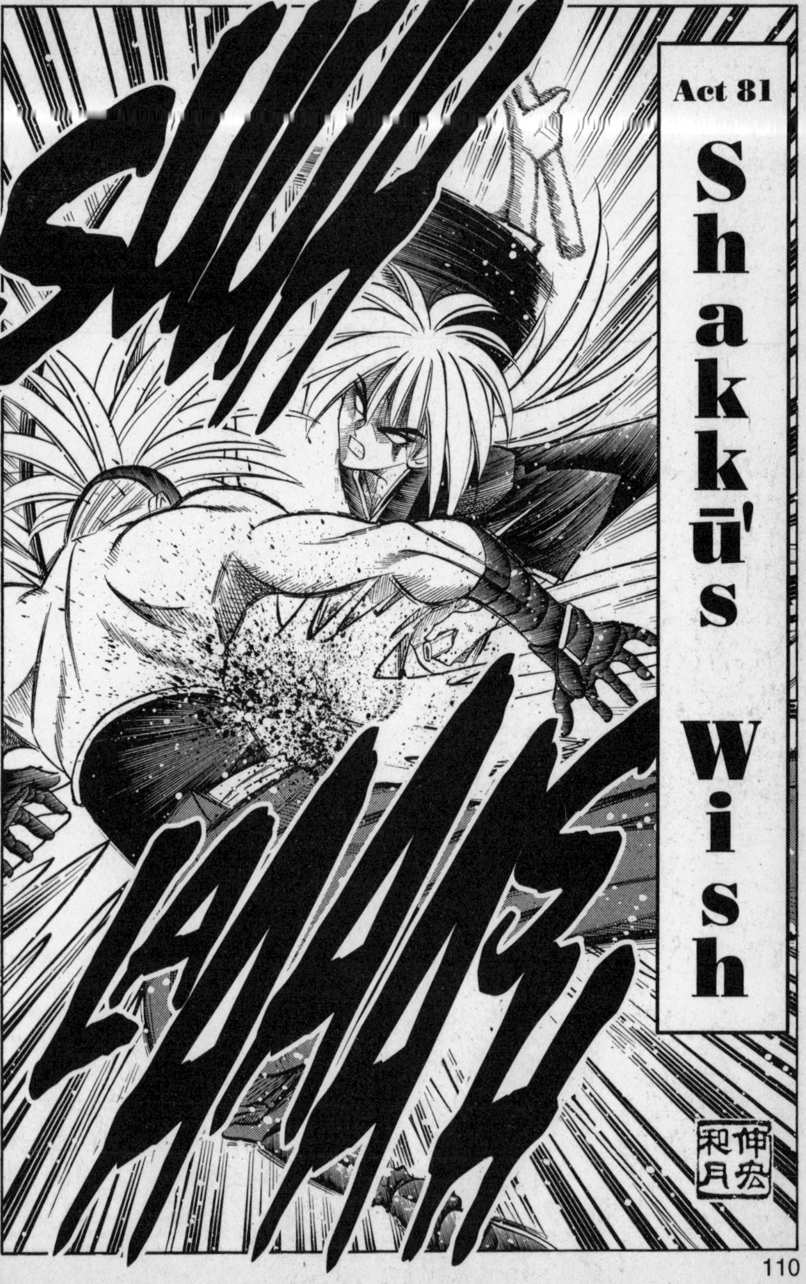
Act 81
Shakkū's Wish
伸宏
和月

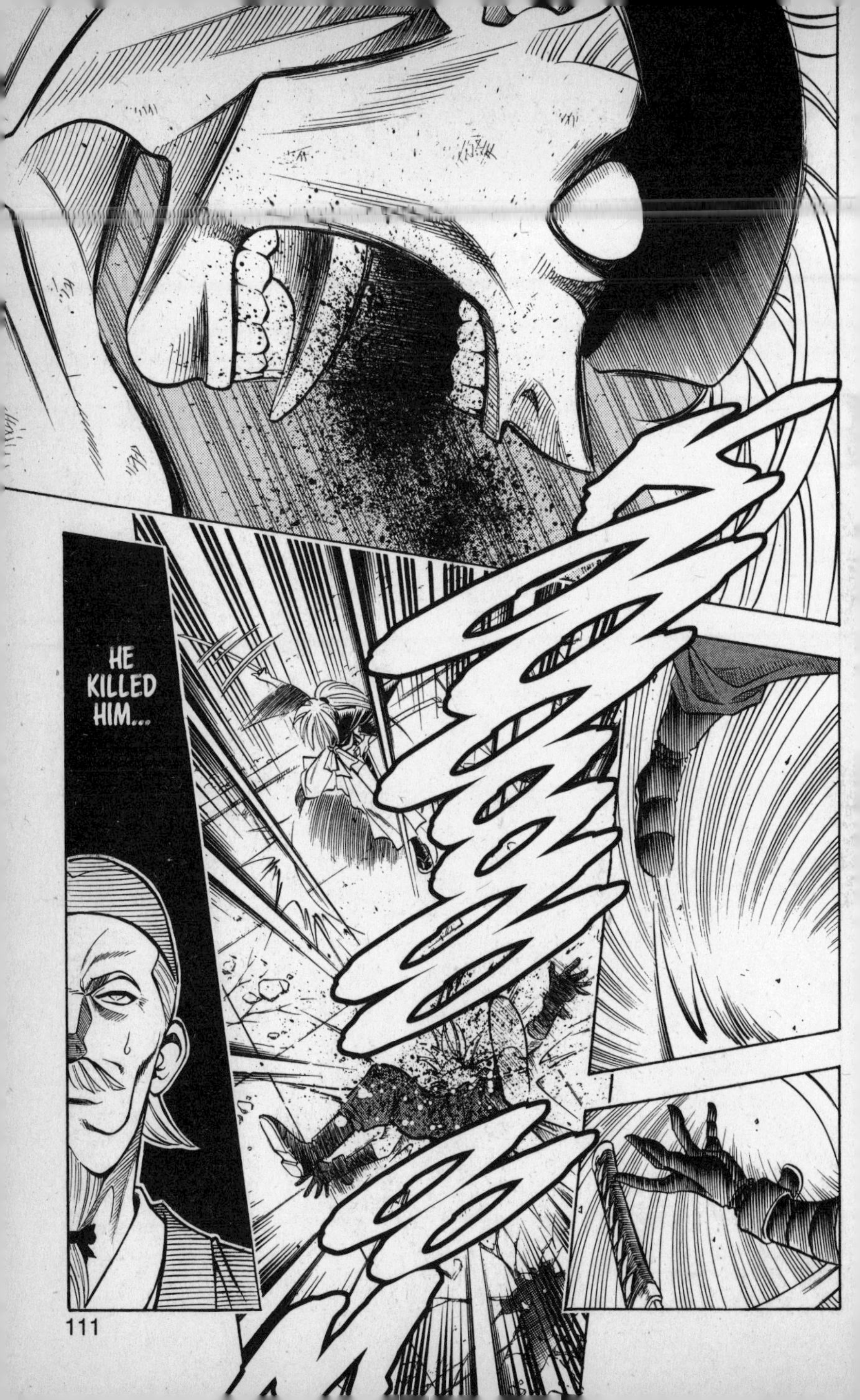
HE KILLED HIM...

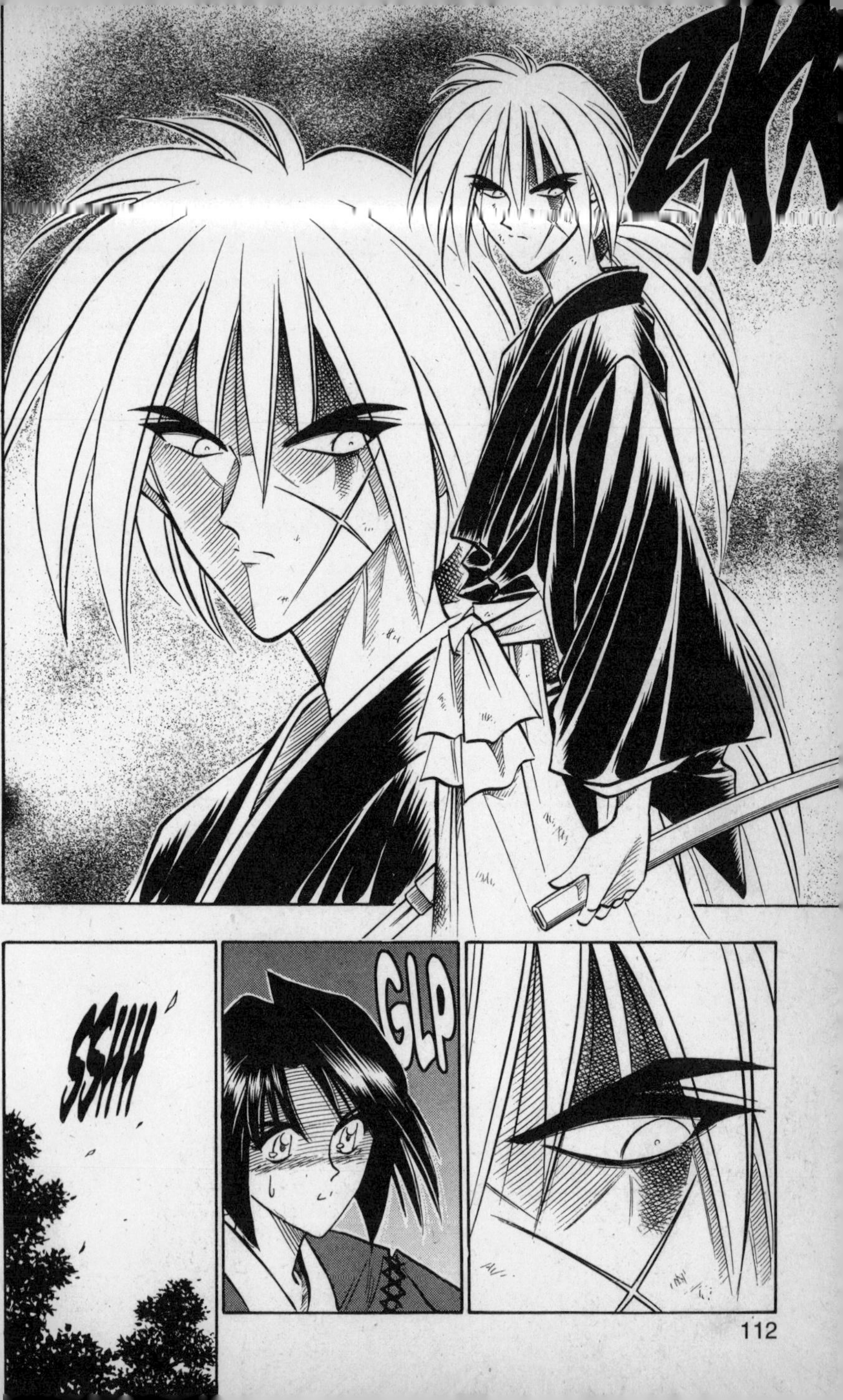
GLP
SSHH

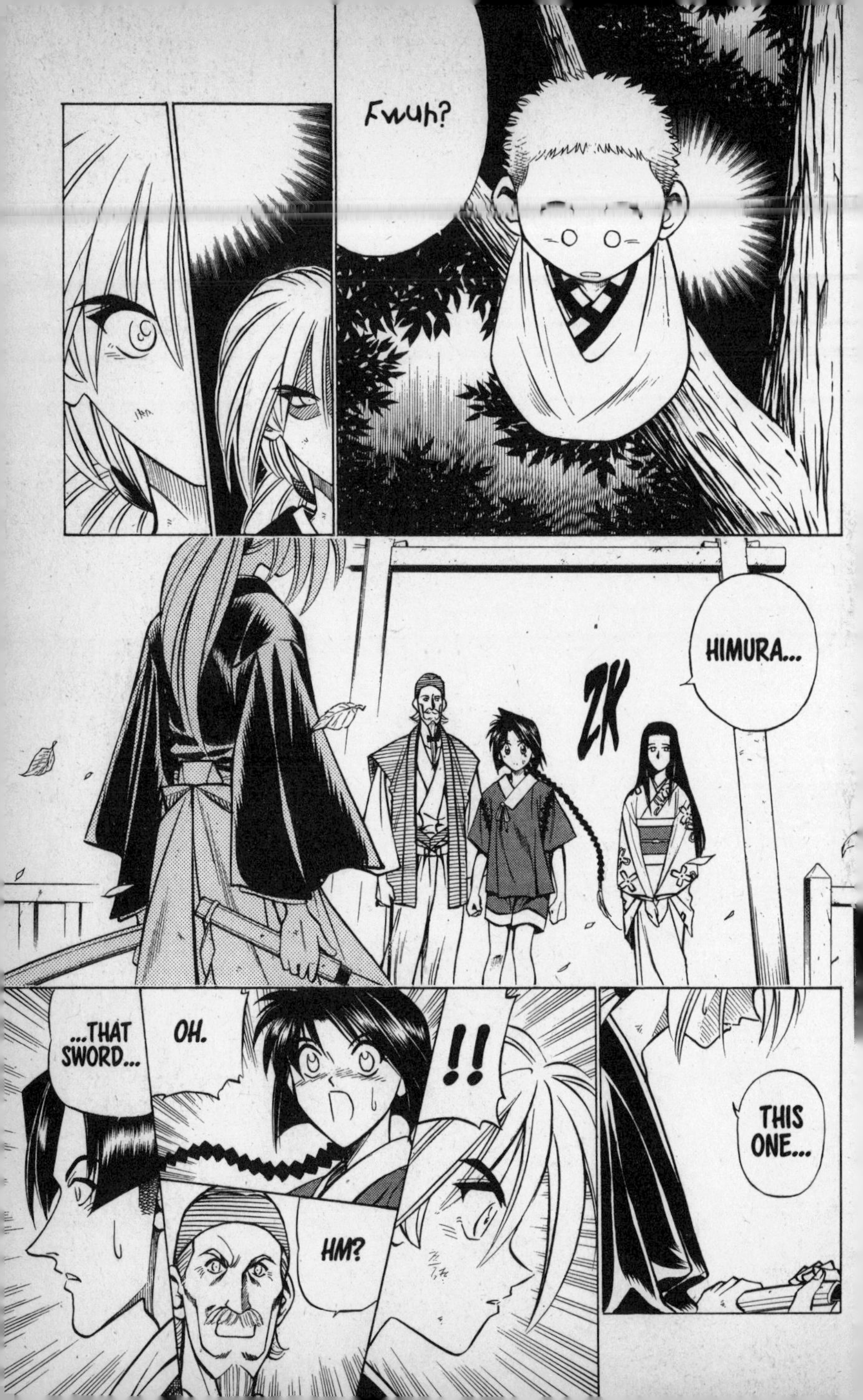
Fwuh?
HIMURA...
ZK
THIS ONE...
!!
OH.
...THAT SWORD...
HM?

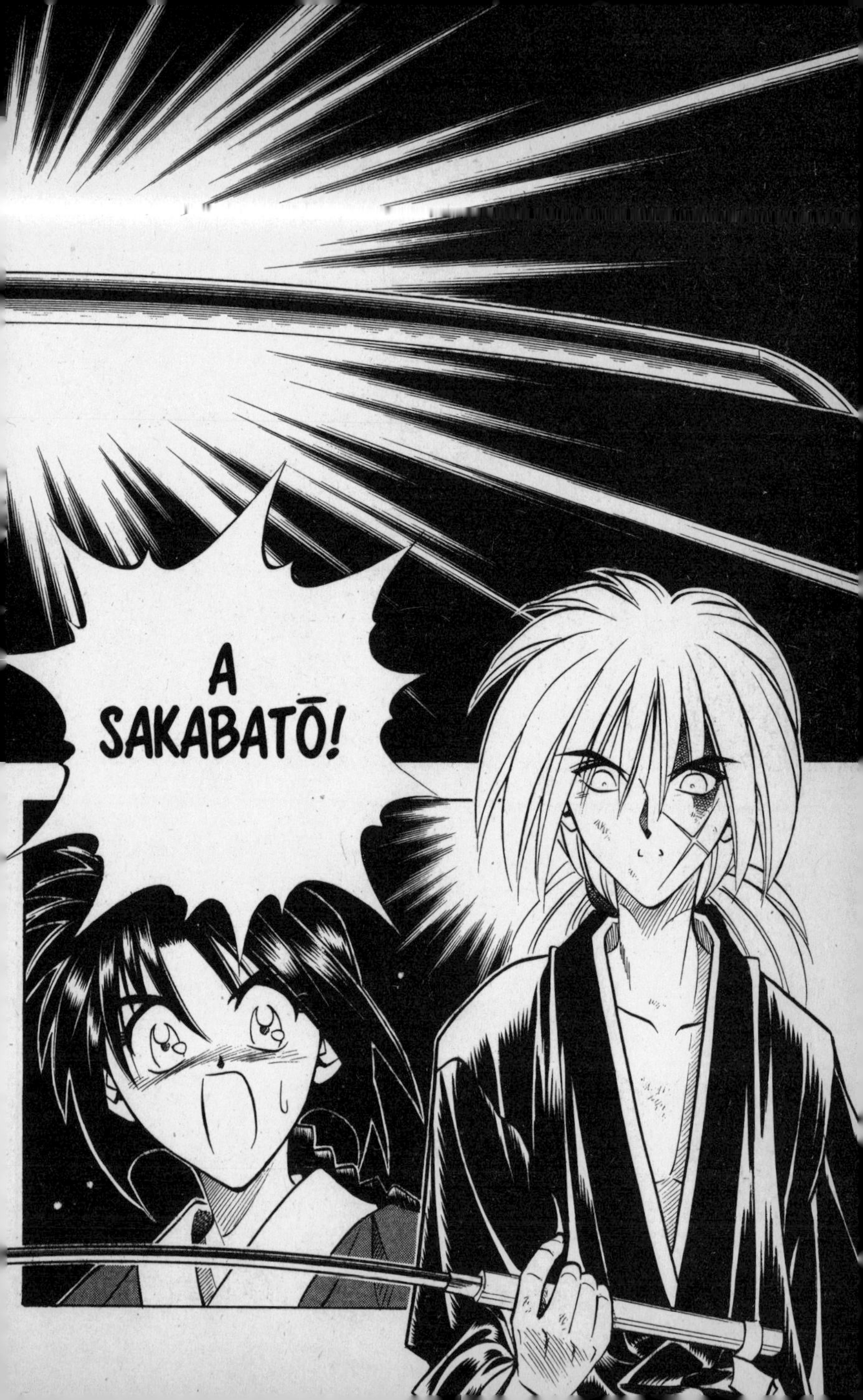
A SAKABATŌ!

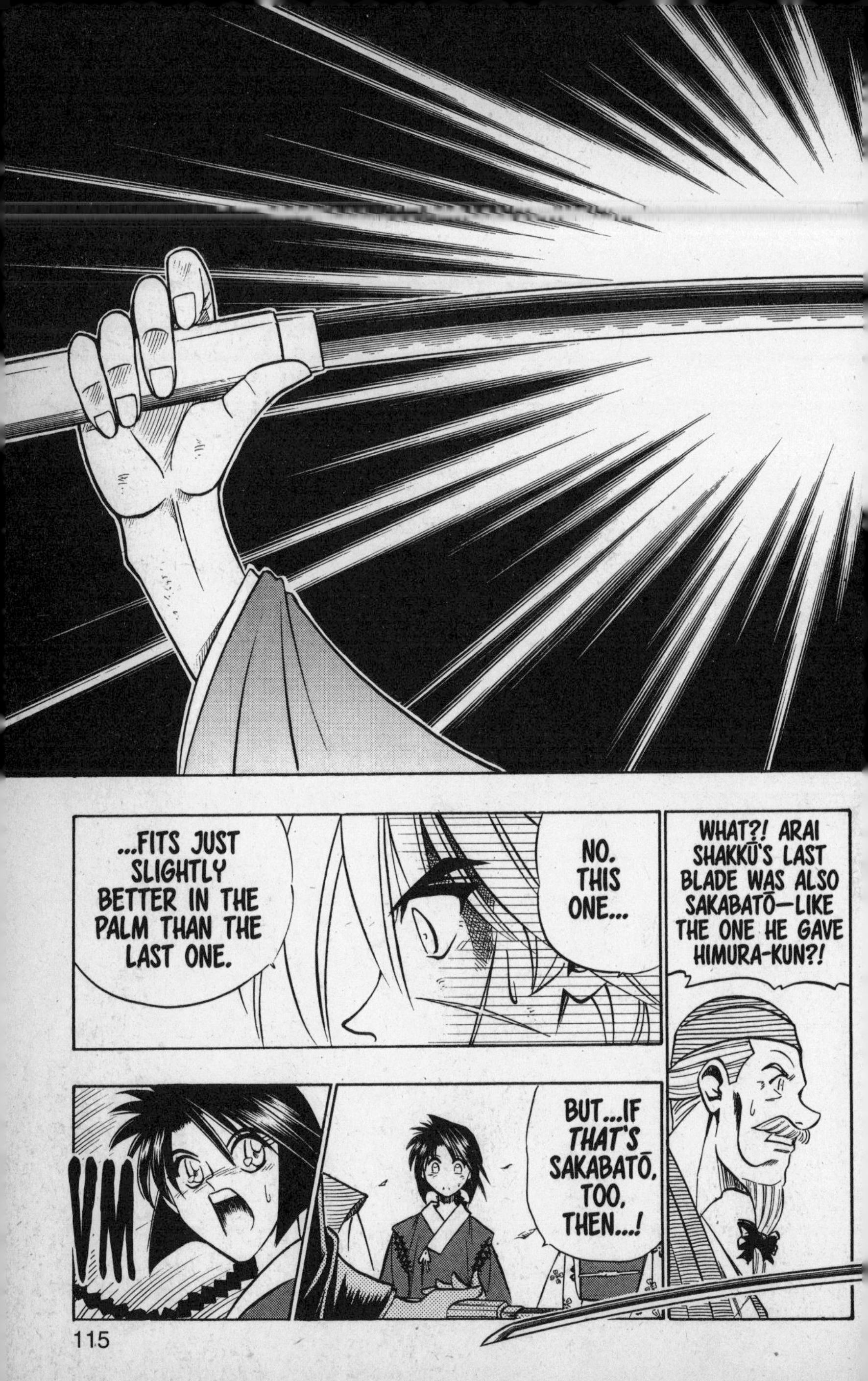
WHAT?! ARAI SHAKKŪ'S LAST BLADE WAS ALSO SAKABATŌ—LIKE THE ONE HE GAVE HIMURA-KUN?!
NO. THIS ONE...
...FITS JUST SLIGHTLY BETTER IN THE PALM THAN THE LAST ONE.
BUT...IF THAT'S SAKABATŌ, TOO, THEN...!
VM

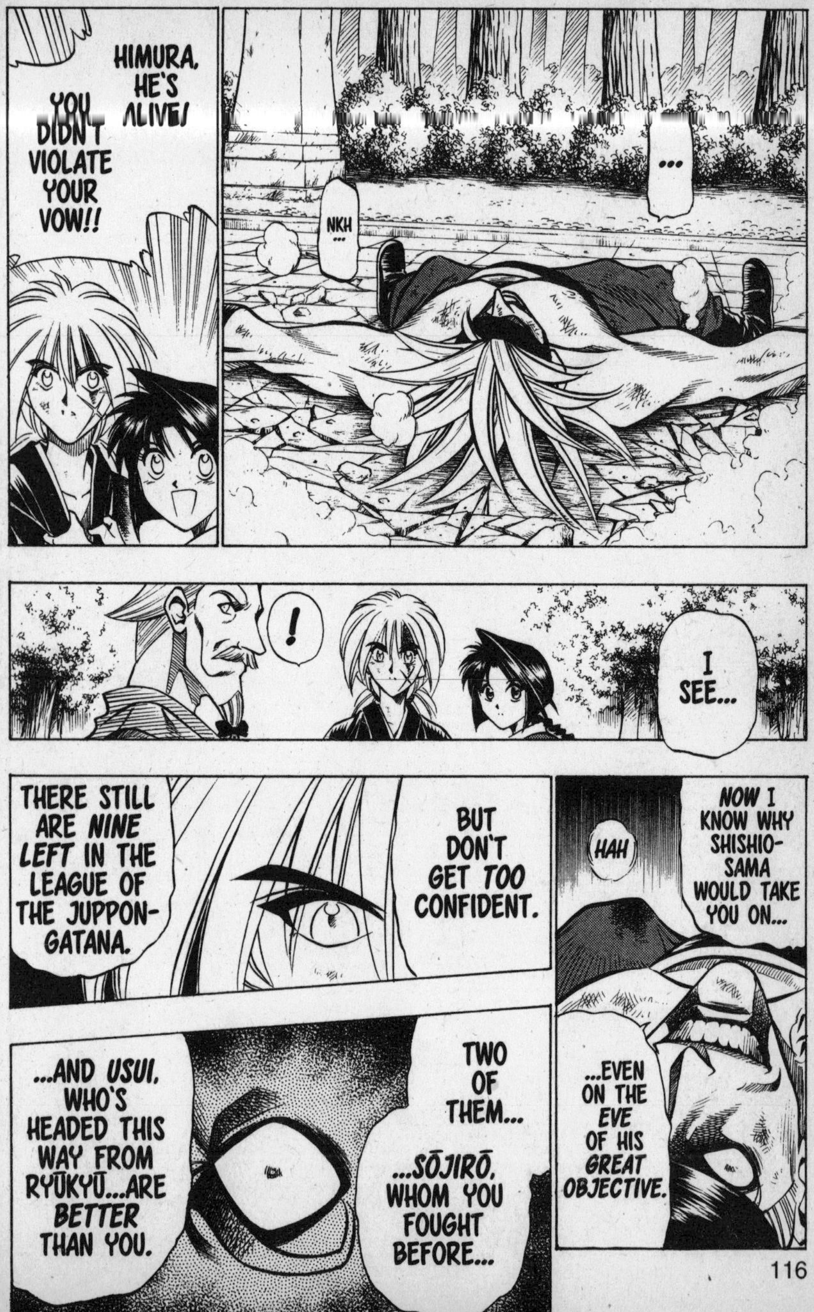
...
NKH ...
HIMURA, HE'S ALIVE!
YOU DIDN'T VIOLATE YOUR VOW!!
I SEE...
!
NOW I KNOW WHY SHISHIO-SAMA WOULD TAKE YOU ON...
HAH
...EVEN ON THE EVE OF HIS GREAT OBJECTIVE.
BUT DON'T GET TOO CONFIDENT.
THERE STILL ARE NINE LEFT IN THE LEAGUE OF THE JUPPON-GATANA.
TWO OF THEM...
...SŌJIRŌ, WHOM YOU FOUGHT BEFORE...
...AND USUI, WHO'S HEADED THIS WAY FROM RYŪKYŪ...ARE BETTER THAN YOU.

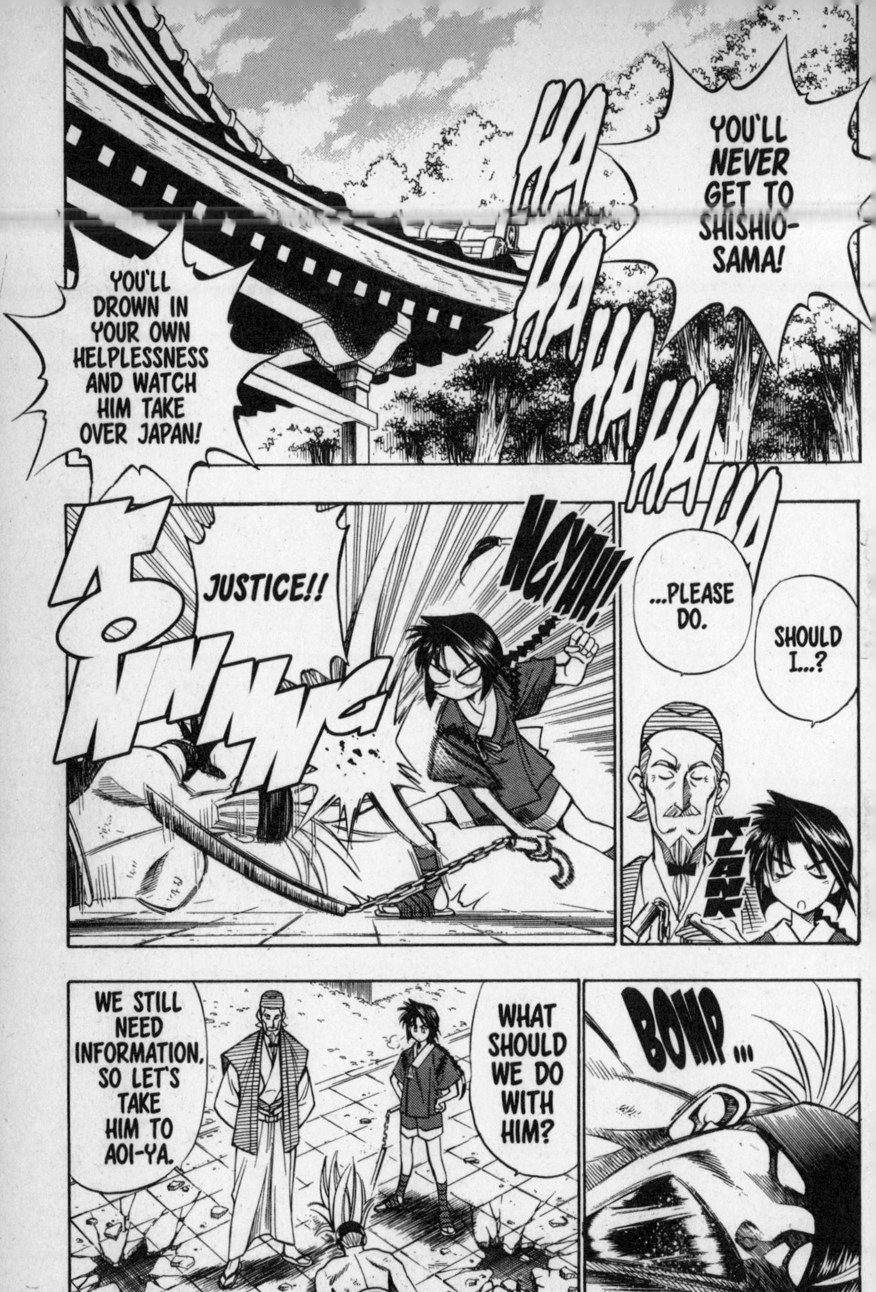
YOU'LL NEVER GET TO SHISHIO-SAMA!
HA HA HA HA HA HA
YOU'LL DROWN IN YOUR OWN HELPLESSNESS AND WATCH HIM TAKE OVER JAPAN!
SHOULD I...?
...PLEASE DO.
KLANK
HEYAH!!
JUSTICE!!
BOMP...
WHAT SHOULD WE DO WITH HIM?
WE STILL NEED INFORMATION, SO LET'S TAKE HIM TO AOI-YA.

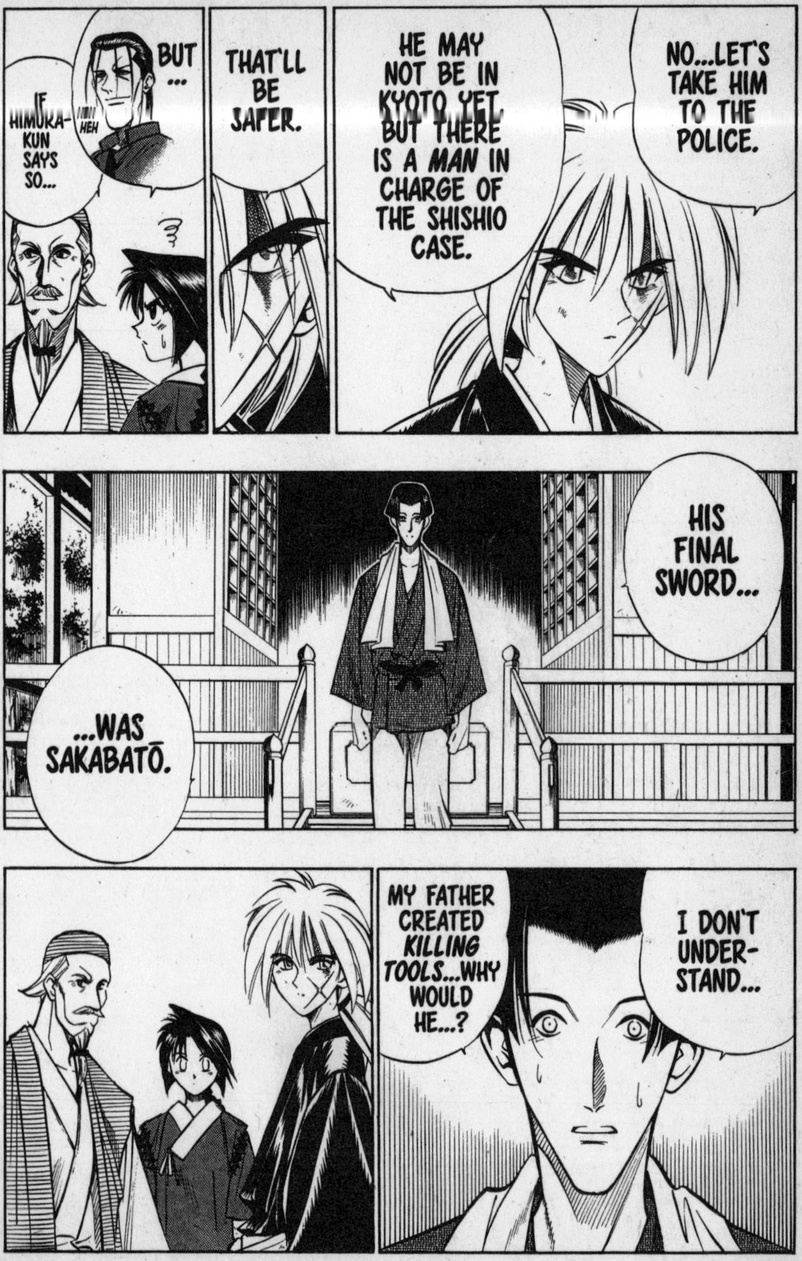
NO...LET'S TAKE HIM TO THE POLICE.
HE MAY NOT BE IN KYOTO YET, BUT THERE IS A *MAN* IN CHARGE OF THE SHISHIO CASE.
THAT'LL BE SAFER.
BUT ...
HEH
IF HIMURA-KUN SAYS SO...
HIS FINAL SWORD...
...WAS SAKABATŌ.
I DON'T UNDER-STAND...
MY FATHER CREATED *KILLING TOOLS*...WHY WOULD HE...?

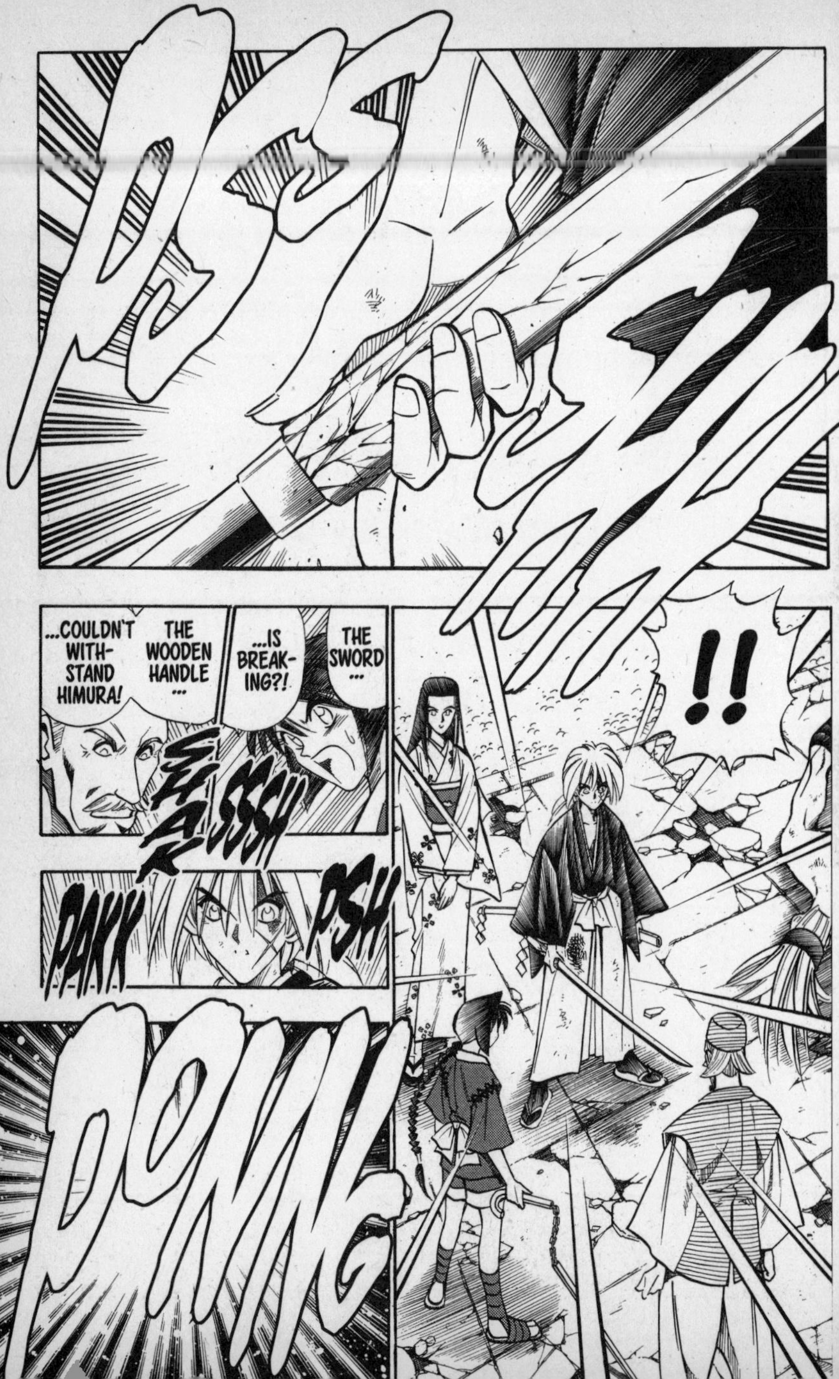

!!
THE SWORD ...
...IS BREAK-ING?!
THE WOODEN HANDLE ...
...COULDN'T WITH-STAND HIMURA!
PSH
DOING

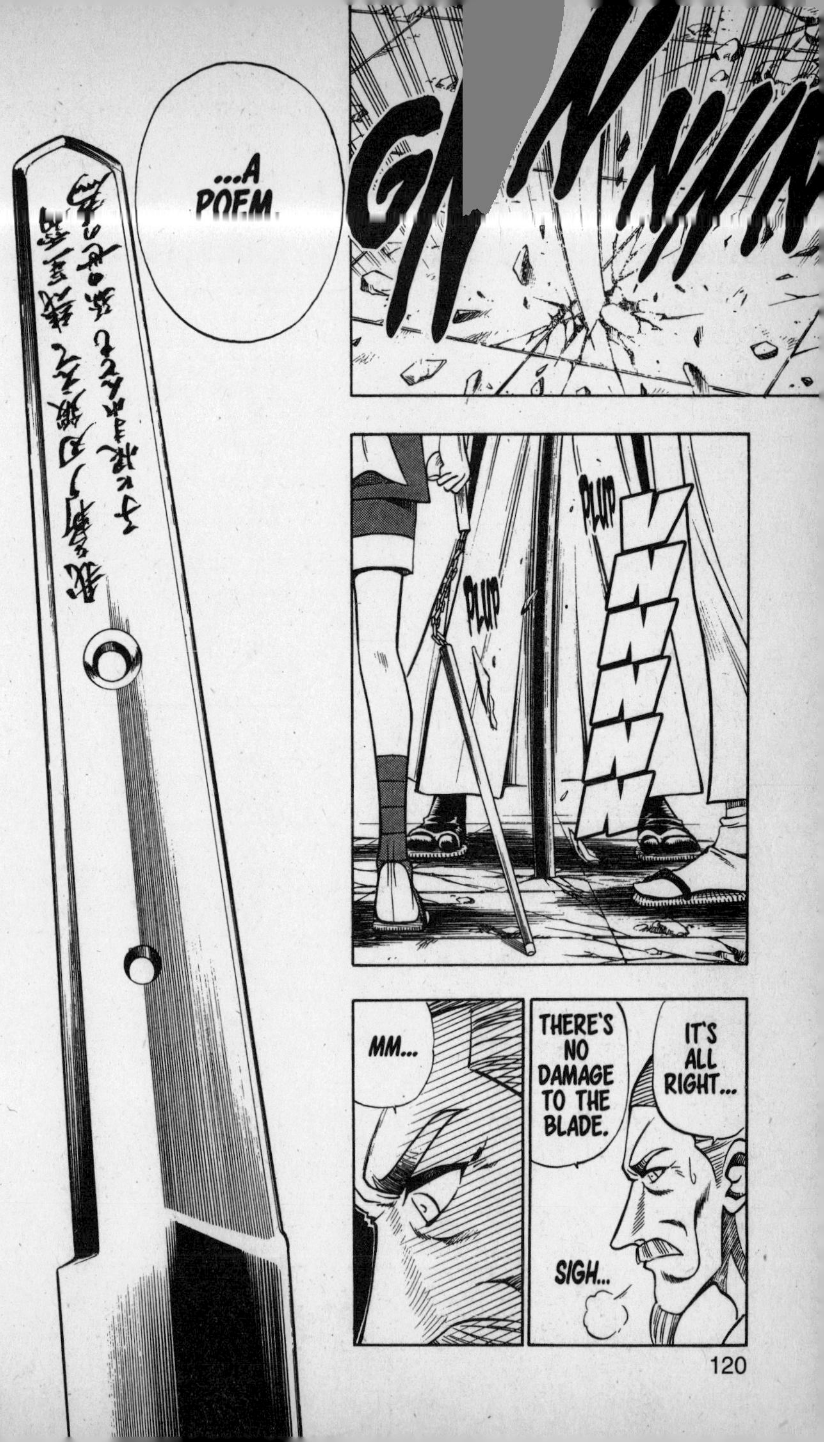
GNNNN
PLUP
PLUP
NNNNNN
IT'S ALL RIGHT...
THERE'S NO DAMAGE TO THE BLADE.
SIGH...
MM...
...A POEM.

READ THIS WAY

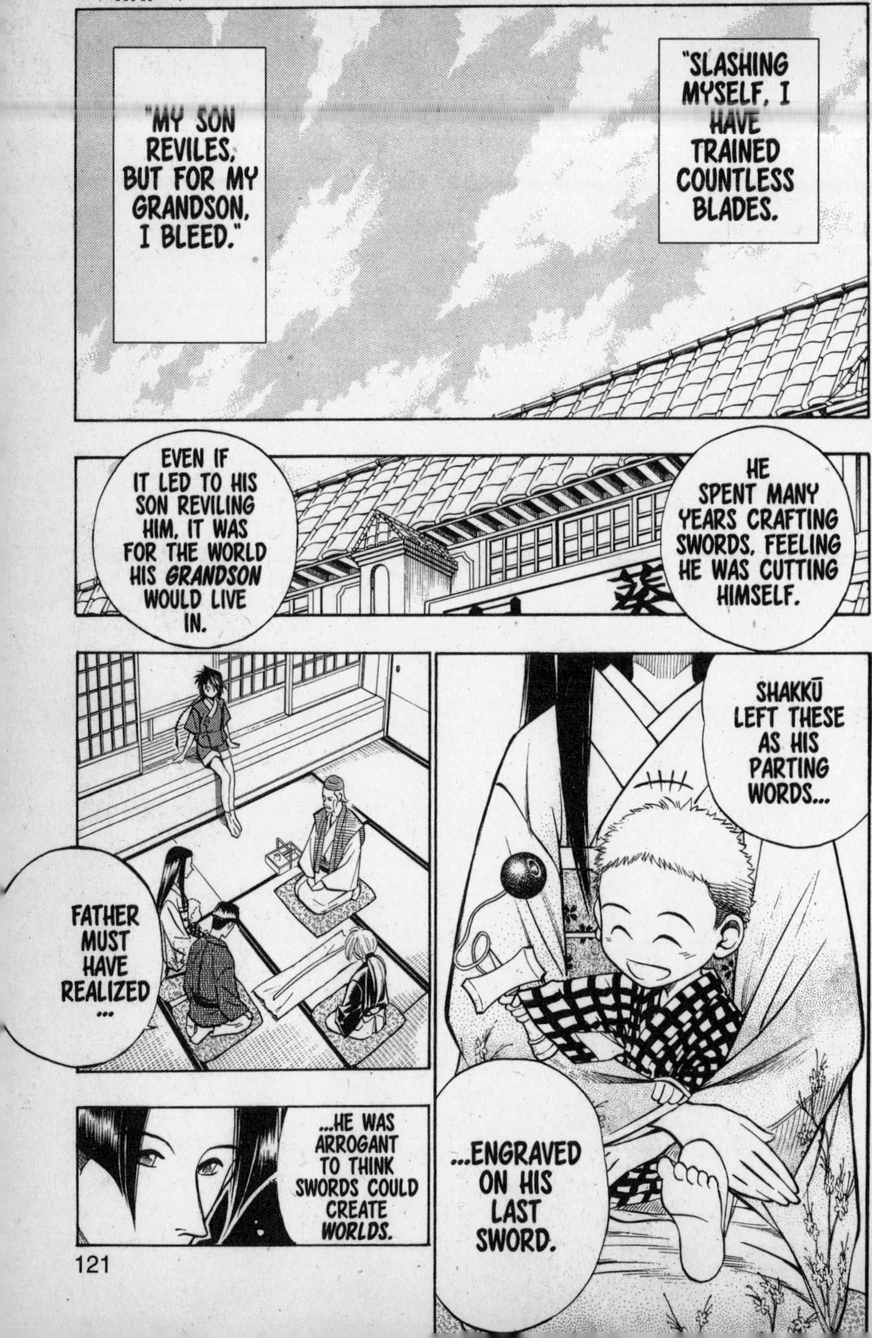

"SLASHING MYSELF, I HAVE TRAINED COUNTLESS BLADES.
"MY SON REVILES, BUT FOR MY GRANDSON, I BLEED."
HE SPENT MANY YEARS CRAFTING SWORDS, FEELING HE WAS CUTTING HIMSELF.
EVEN IF IT LED TO HIS SON REVILING HIM, IT WAS FOR THE WORLD HIS *GRANDSON* WOULD LIVE IN.
SHAKKŪ LEFT THESE AS HIS PARTING WORDS...
...ENGRAVED ON HIS LAST SWORD.
FATHER MUST HAVE REALIZED...
...HE WAS ARROGANT TO THINK SWORDS COULD CREATE *WORLDS*.

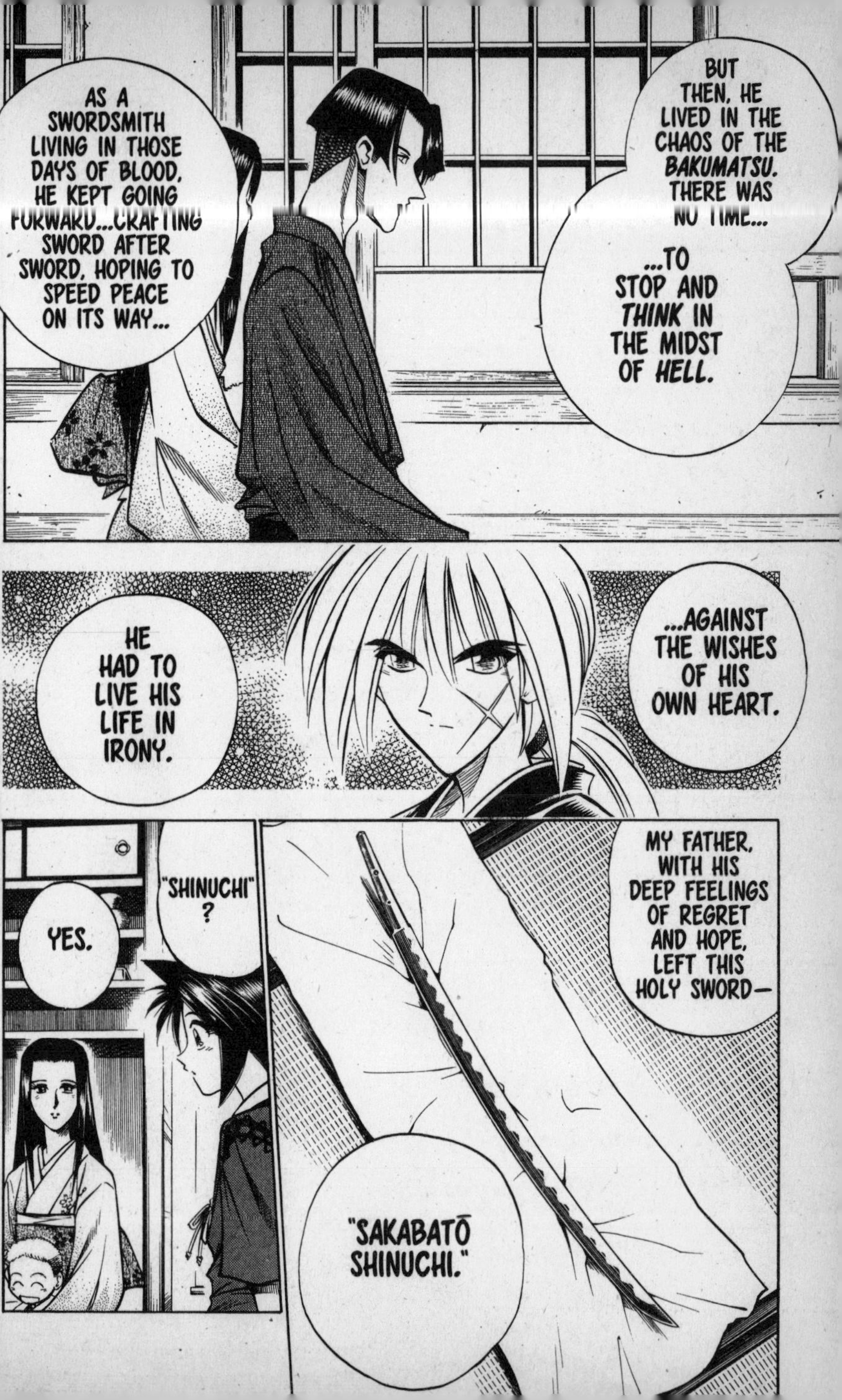
BUT THEN, HE LIVED IN THE CHAOS OF THE *BAKUMATSU*. THERE WAS NO TIME...
...TO STOP AND *THINK* IN THE MIDST OF *HELL*.
AS A SWORDSMITH LIVING IN THOSE DAYS OF BLOOD, HE KEPT GOING FORWARD...CRAFTING SWORD AFTER SWORD, HOPING TO SPEED PEACE ON ITS WAY...
...AGAINST THE WISHES OF HIS OWN HEART.
HE HAD TO LIVE HIS LIFE IN IRONY.
MY FATHER, WITH HIS DEEP FEELINGS OF REGRET AND HOPE, LEFT THIS HOLY SWORD—
"SAKABATŌ SHINUCHI."
"SHINUCHI"?
YES.

READ THIS WAY

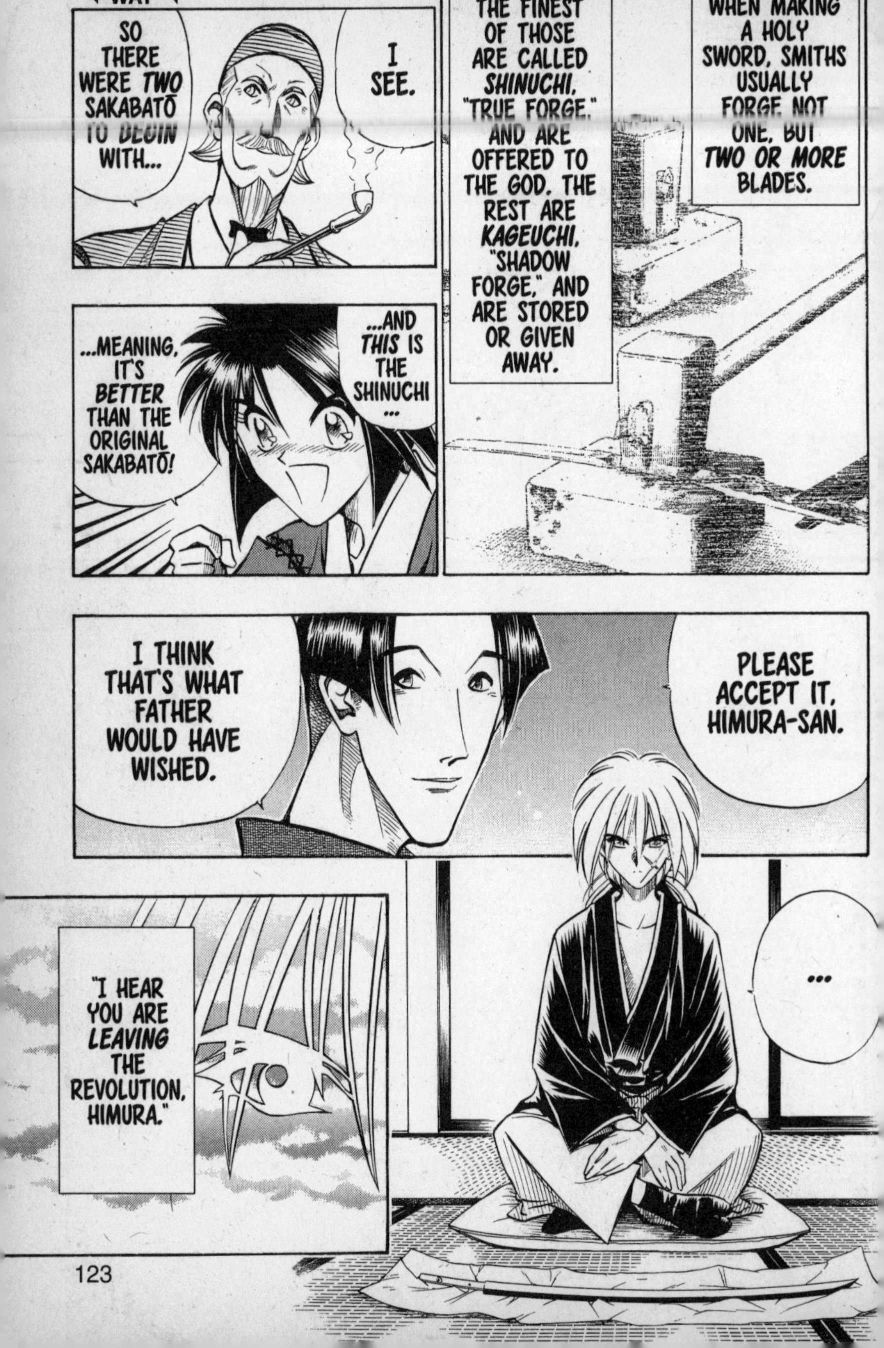

WHEN MAKING A HOLY SWORD, SMITHS USUALLY FORGE NOT ONE, BUT *TWO OR MORE* BLADES.
THE FINEST OF THOSE ARE CALLED *SHINUCHI*, "TRUE FORGE," AND ARE OFFERED TO THE GOD. THE REST ARE *KAGEUCHI*, "SHADOW FORGE," AND ARE STORED OR GIVEN AWAY.
I SEE.
SO THERE WERE *TWO* SAKABATŌ TO *BEGIN* WITH...
...AND *THIS* IS THE SHINUCHI...
...MEANING, IT'S *BETTER* THAN THE ORIGINAL SAKABATŌ!
PLEASE ACCEPT IT, HIMURA-SAN.
I THINK THAT'S WHAT FATHER WOULD HAVE WISHED.
...
"I HEAR YOU ARE *LEAVING* THE REVOLUTION, HIMURA."

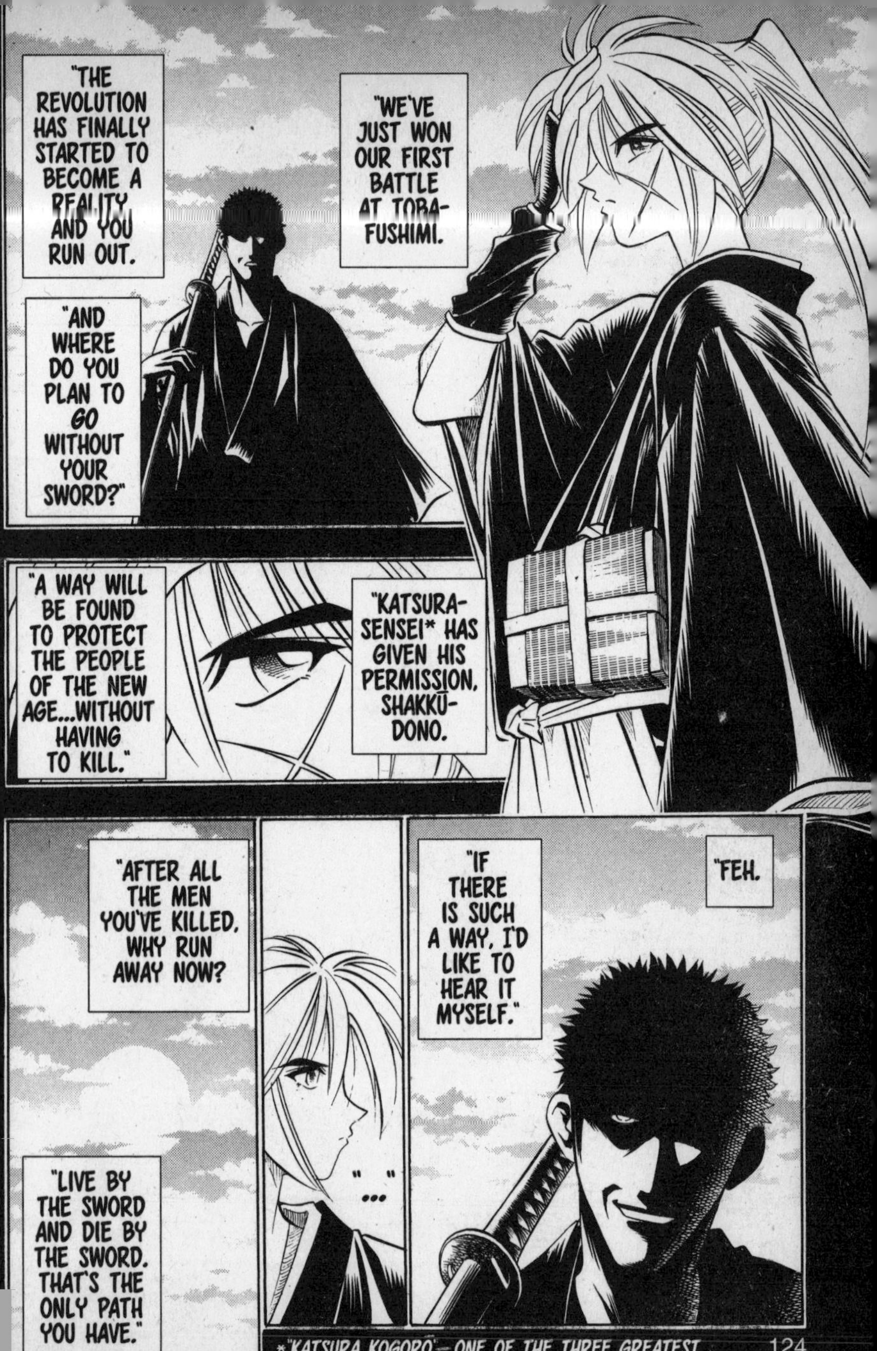
"WE'VE JUST WON OUR FIRST BATTLE AT TOBA-FUSHIMI.
"THE REVOLUTION HAS FINALLY STARTED TO BECOME A REALITY AND YOU RUN OUT.
"AND WHERE DO YOU PLAN TO GO WITHOUT YOUR SWORD?"
"KATSURA-SENSEI* HAS GIVEN HIS PERMISSION, SHAKKŪ-DONO.
"A WAY WILL BE FOUND TO PROTECT THE PEOPLE OF THE NEW AGE...WITHOUT HAVING TO KILL."
"FEH.
"IF THERE IS SUCH A WAY, I'D LIKE TO HEAR IT MYSELF."
"..."
"AFTER ALL THE MEN YOU'VE KILLED, WHY RUN AWAY NOW?
"LIVE BY THE SWORD AND DIE BY THE SWORD. THAT'S THE ONLY PATH YOU HAVE."

*"KATSURA KOGORO"—ONE OF THE THREE GREATEST PATRIOTS, AND HEAD OF THE CHŌSHŪ REVOLUTIONISTS.

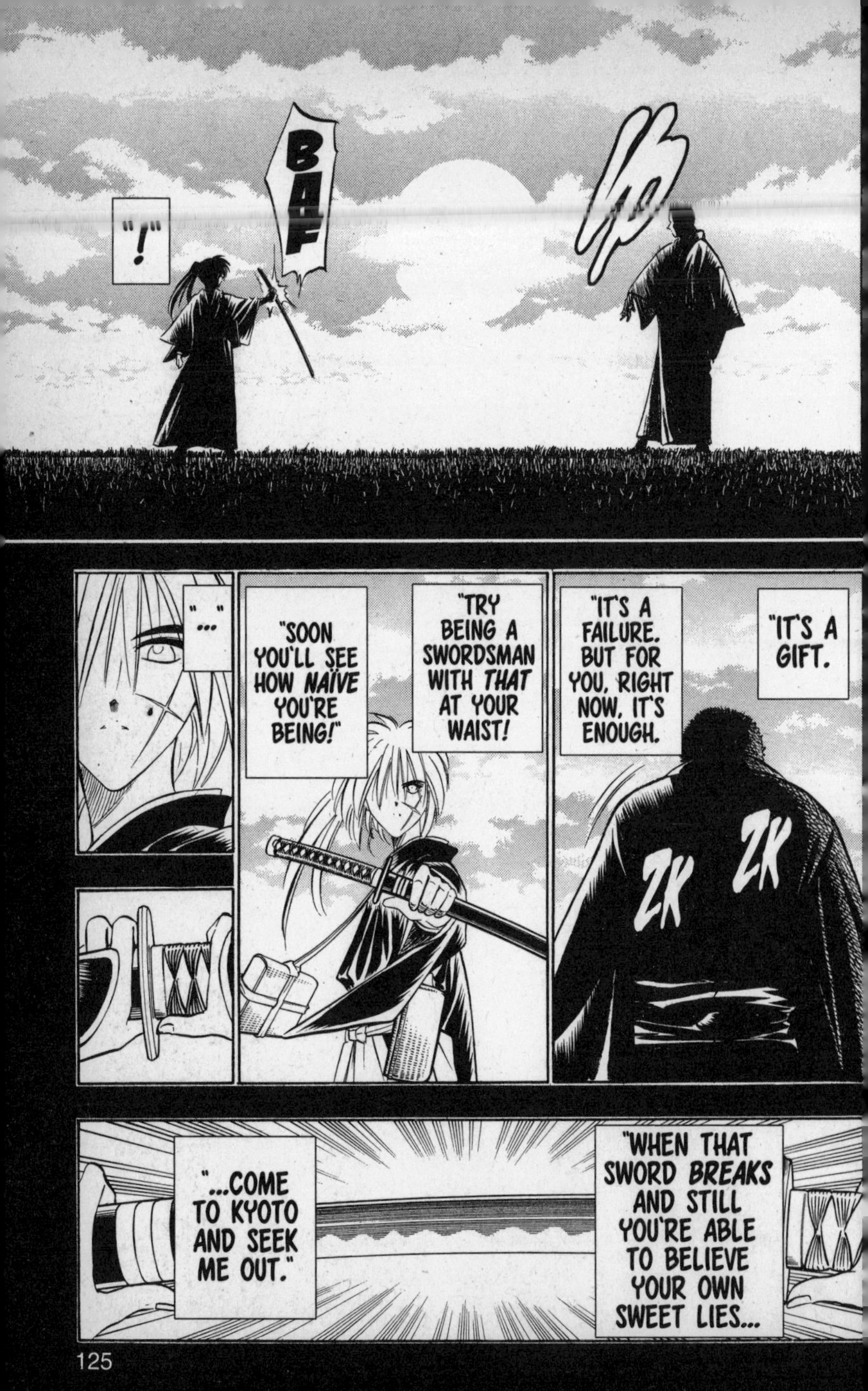
BAF
"!"
"IT'S A GIFT.
"IT'S A FAILURE. BUT FOR YOU, RIGHT NOW, IT'S ENOUGH.
ZK
ZK
"TRY BEING A SWORDSMAN WITH *THAT* AT YOUR WAIST!
"SOON YOU'LL SEE HOW *NAÏVE* YOU'RE BEING!"
"..."
"WHEN THAT SWORD *BREAKS* AND STILL YOU'RE ABLE TO BELIEVE YOUR OWN SWEET LIES...
"...COME TO KYOTO AND SEEK ME OUT."

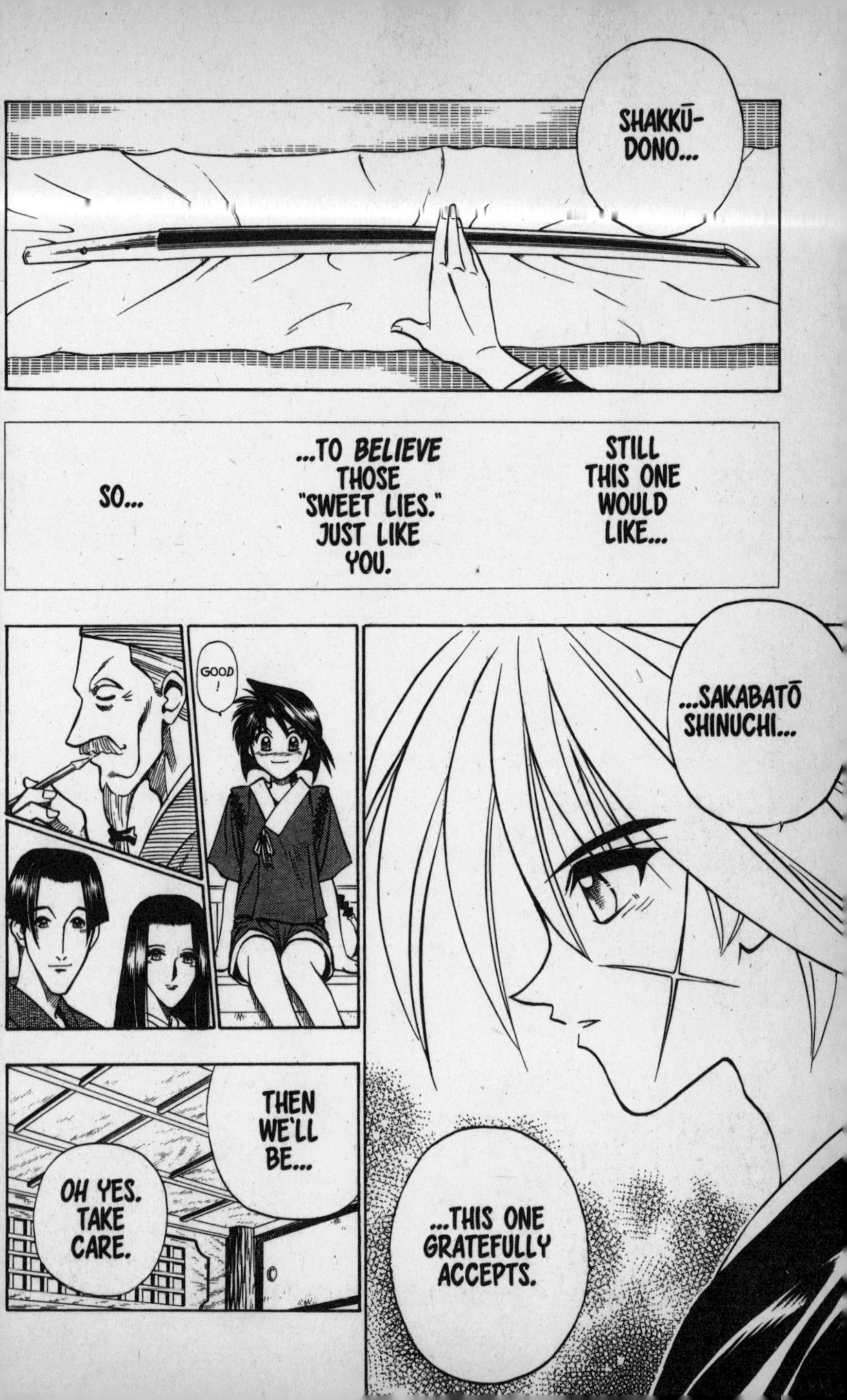

SHAKKŪ-DONO...
STILL THIS ONE WOULD LIKE...
...TO *BELIEVE* THOSE "SWEET LIES." JUST LIKE YOU.
SO...
...SAKABATŌ SHINUCHI...
...THIS ONE GRATEFULLY ACCEPTS.
GOOD!
THEN WE'LL BE...
OH YES. TAKE CARE.

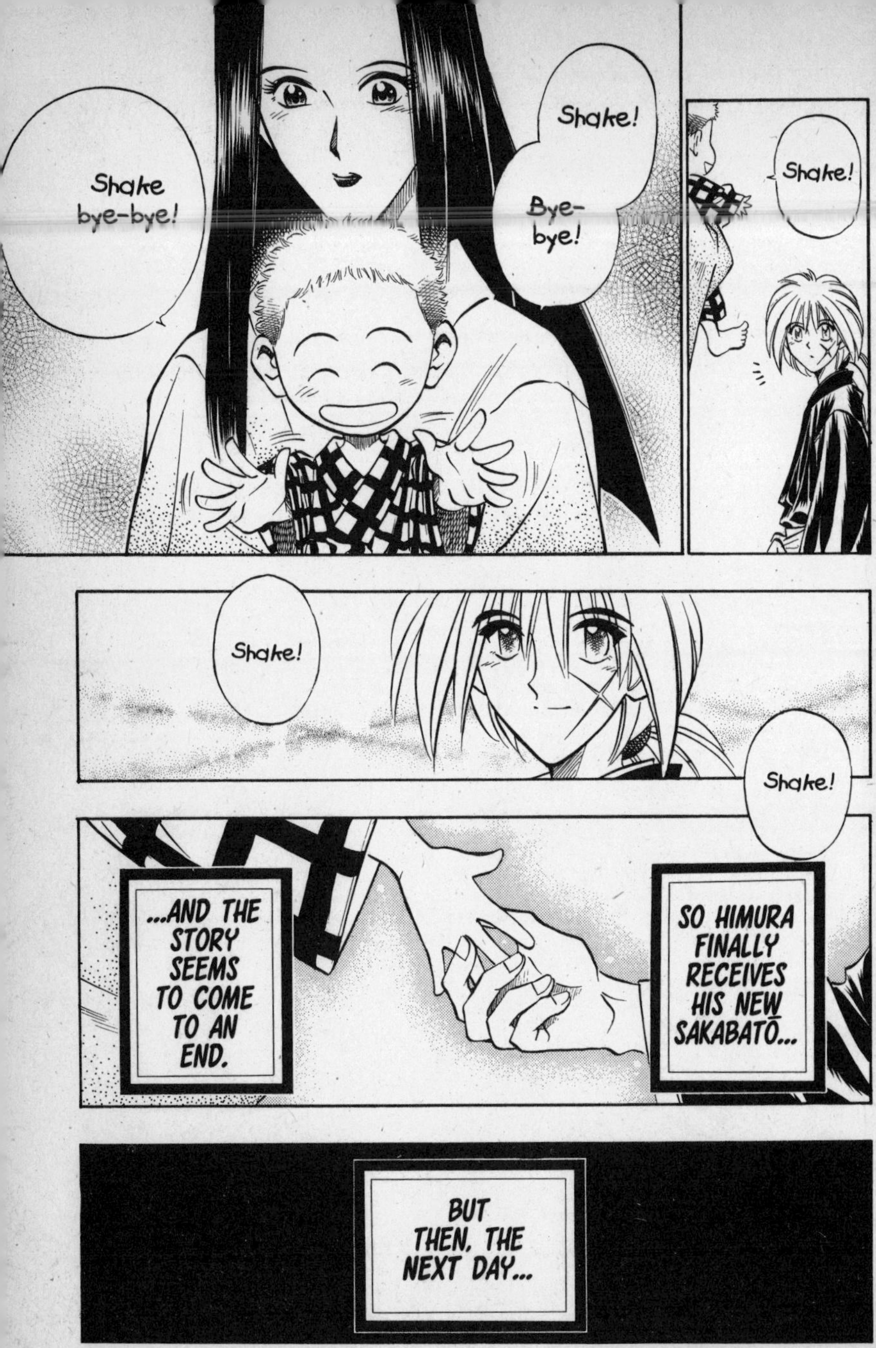
Shake!
Shake!
Bye-bye!
Shake bye-bye!
Shake!
Shake!
SO HIMURA FINALLY RECEIVES HIS NEW SAKABATŌ...
...AND THE STORY SEEMS TO COME TO AN END.
BUT THEN, THE NEXT DAY...

The Secret Life of Characters (30)
—Seikū's Family—

Let's see—the family was created with lots of different things in mind but, honestly, I no longer remember too many of them. The murderous end-of-year schedule's made my memory pretty flaky....

As a character who has no history with the revolution, Iori symbolizes peace; Seikū demonstrates the selfishness that fathers can sometimes show; and his wife... uh... holds it all together? (Hey, now.) That's it. Yeah.

The bit about the "holy sword" and the "Sakabatō Shinuchi" is something researched by a novelist friend studying swords, so it's actually true.

I do plan to bring back Seikū's family in the middle or after the Kyoto Arc, in a story revolving around—not Kenshin!—but Yahiko.

The model in terms of design for Iori was a fairly famous women's manga involving babies; Seikū was made up on-the-spot, as was his wife. "Sakabatō Shinuchi" was originally just a wooden sheath, but it didn't look right, so I went ahead and added those white-paper-streamer-things you see all the time in shrines.

Iori was popular with female readers because he's so cute—especially during the sling-part, where he was hung up on the tree by Chō. Seikū kind of ended up looking like Kanryū—so that didn't turn out quite right—but, with the wife, I also started out by saying "she's not quite right," and ended up by saying "she's a really good character." In thinking about it, this is the first female character I've done who shows her entire forehead; I think I found that refreshing. The Shinuchi wouldn't fit Kenshin's fighting style if kept within a wooden sheath—he uses the metal sheaths for fighting—so I changed it back to metal. Of course, the assistants then complained that the wooden one was much easier to draw.

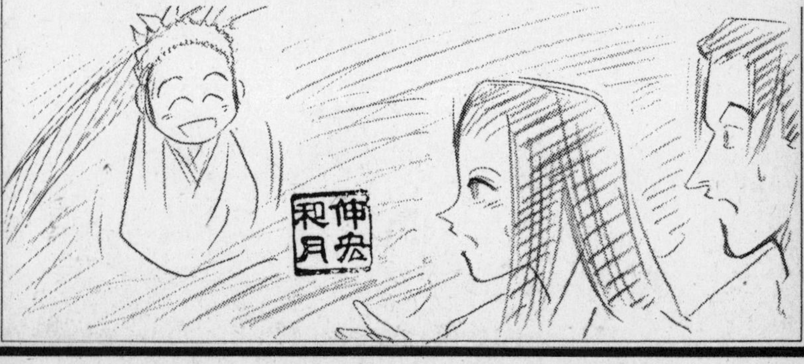
伸宏
和月

Act 82
Where the Strings Meet

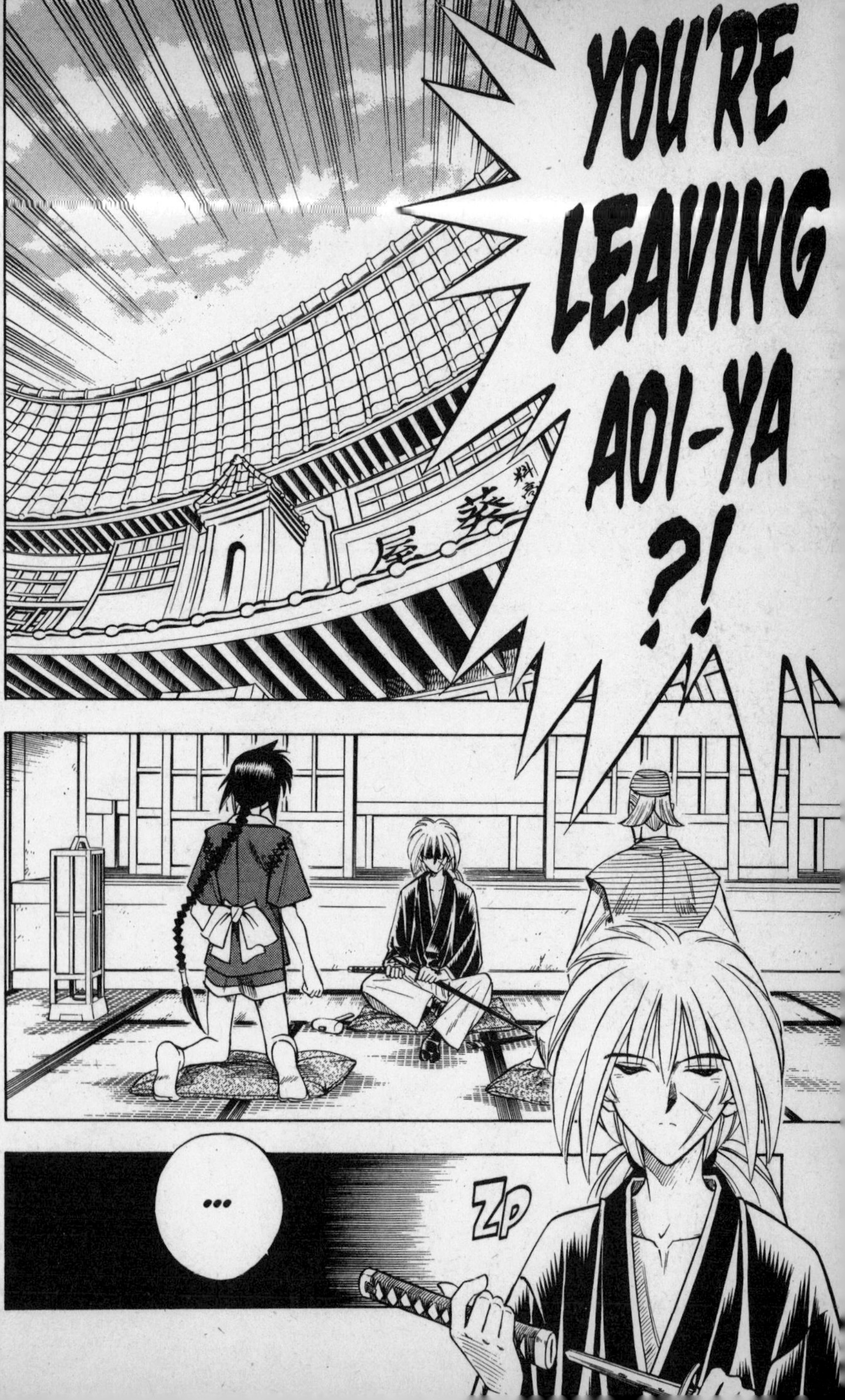
YOU'RE LEAVING AOI-YA ?!
料亭
葵屋
...
ZP

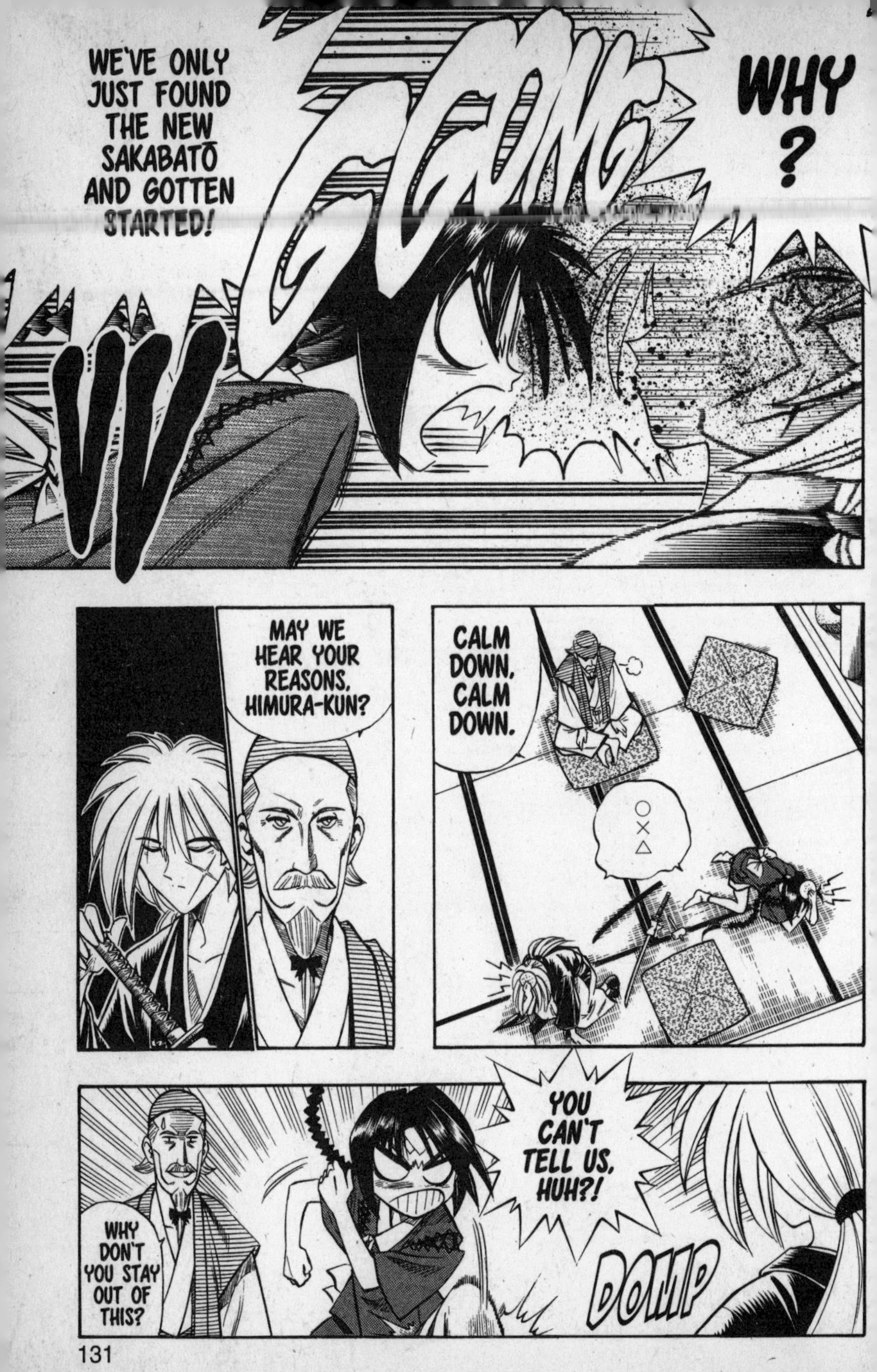
WHY ?
WE'VE ONLY JUST FOUND THE NEW SAKABATŌ AND GOTTEN STARTED!
CALM DOWN, CALM DOWN.
○×△
MAY WE HEAR YOUR REASONS, HIMURA-KUN?
DOMP
YOU CAN'T TELL US, HUH?!
WHY DON'T YOU STAY OUT OF THIS?

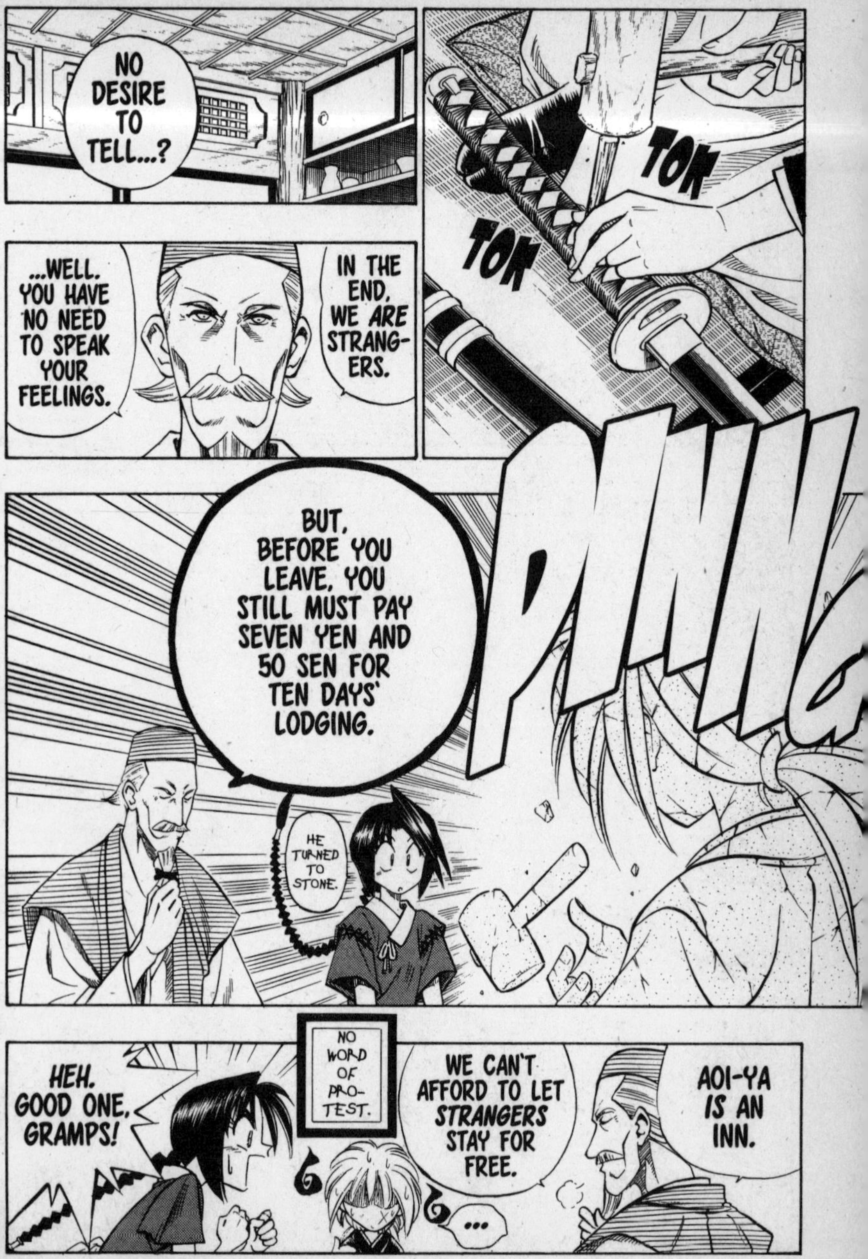
TOK
TOK
NO DESIRE TO TELL...?
IN THE END, WE *ARE* STRANGERS.
...WELL. YOU HAVE NO NEED TO SPEAK YOUR FEELINGS.
PINNG
BUT, BEFORE YOU LEAVE, YOU STILL MUST PAY SEVEN YEN AND 50 SEN FOR TEN DAYS' LODGING.
HE TURNED TO STONE.
AOI-YA *IS* AN INN.
WE CAN'T AFFORD TO LET *STRANGERS* STAY FOR FREE.
NO WORD OF PRO-TEST.
...
HEH. GOOD ONE, GRAMPS!

READ THIS WAY

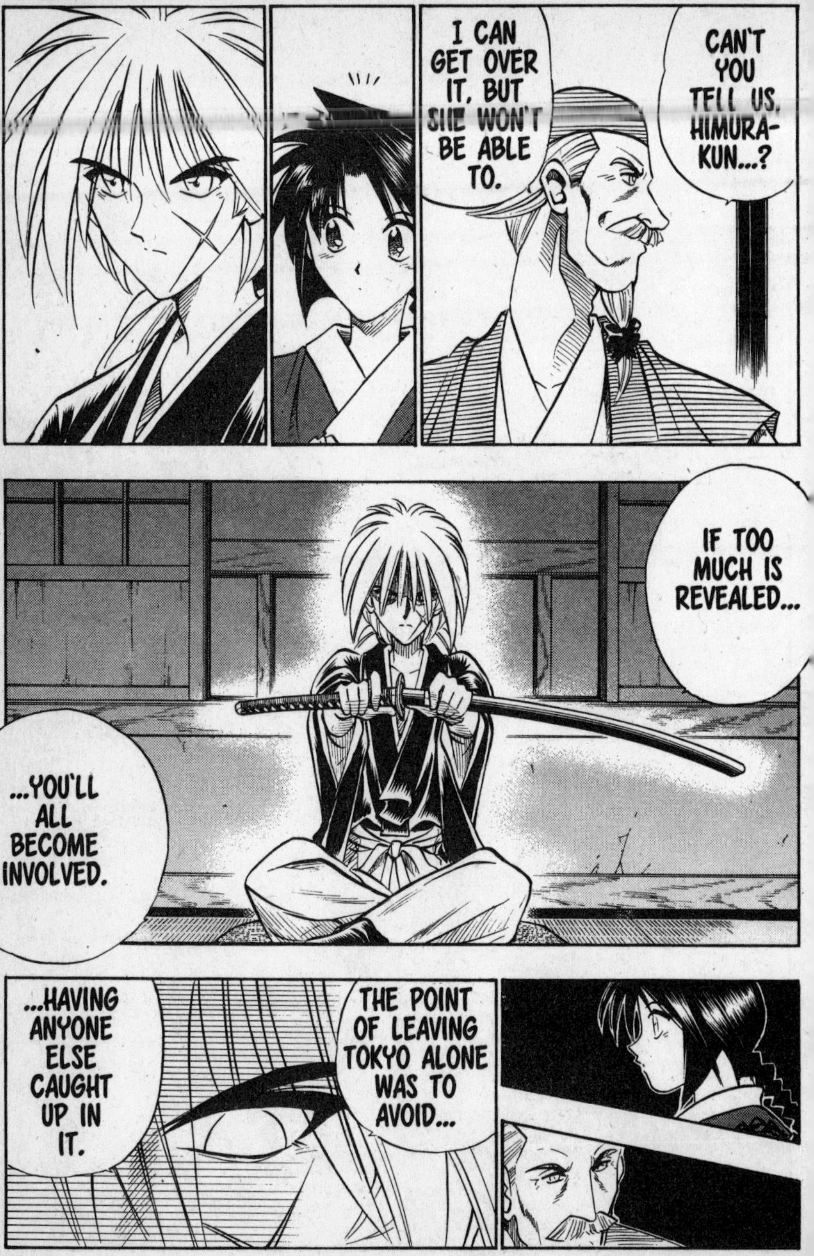

CAN'T YOU TELL US, HIMURA-KUN...?
I CAN GET OVER IT, BUT SHE WON'T BE ABLE TO.
IF TOO MUCH IS REVEALED...
...YOU'LL ALL BECOME INVOLVED.
THE POINT OF LEAVING TOKYO ALONE WAS TO AVOID...
...HAVING ANYONE ELSE CAUGHT UP IN IT.

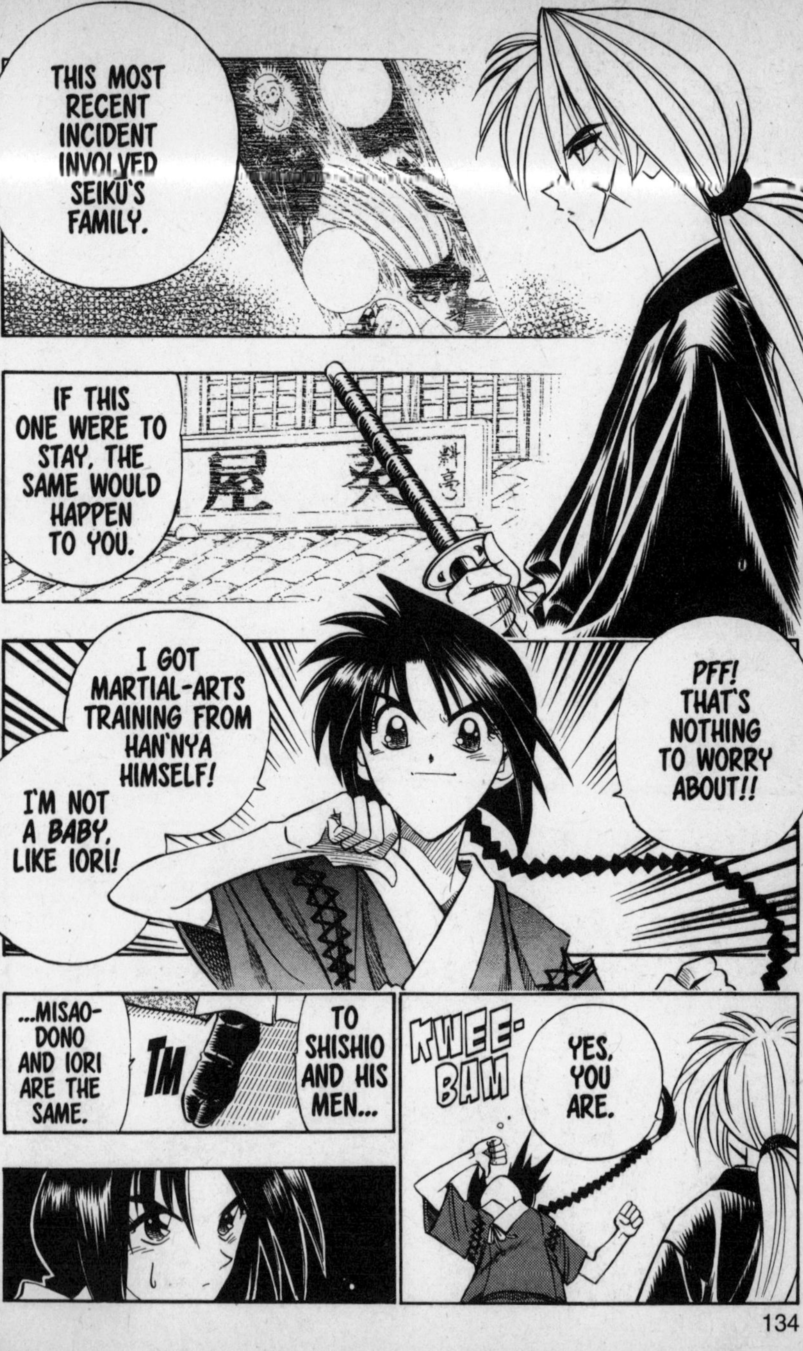
THIS MOST RECENT INCIDENT INVOLVED SEIKU'S FAMILY.
IF THIS ONE WERE TO STAY, THE SAME WOULD HAPPEN TO YOU.
PFF! THAT'S NOTHING TO WORRY ABOUT!!
I GOT MARTIAL-ARTS TRAINING FROM HAN'NYA HIMSELF!
I'M NOT A BABY, LIKE IORI!
KWEE-BAM
YES, YOU ARE.
TO SHISHIO AND HIS MEN...
TM
...MISAO-DONO AND IORI ARE THE SAME.

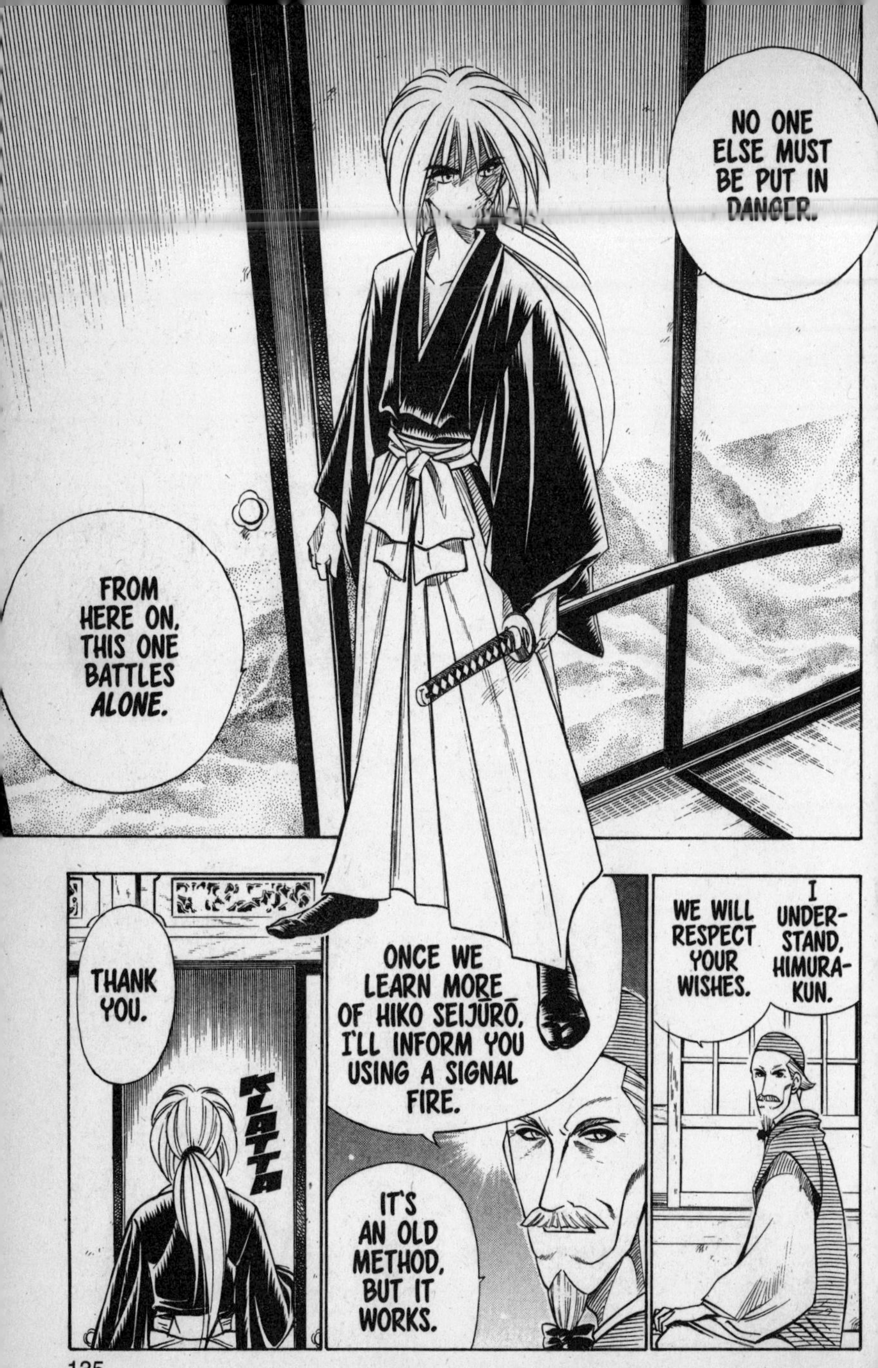
NO ONE ELSE MUST BE PUT IN DANGER.
FROM HERE ON, THIS ONE BATTLES ALONE.
I UNDER-STAND, HIMURA-KUN.
WE WILL RESPECT YOUR WISHES.
ONCE WE LEARN MORE OF HIKO SEIJŪRŌ, I'LL INFORM YOU USING A SIGNAL FIRE.
IT'S AN OLD METHOD, BUT IT WORKS.
THANK YOU.
KLATTA

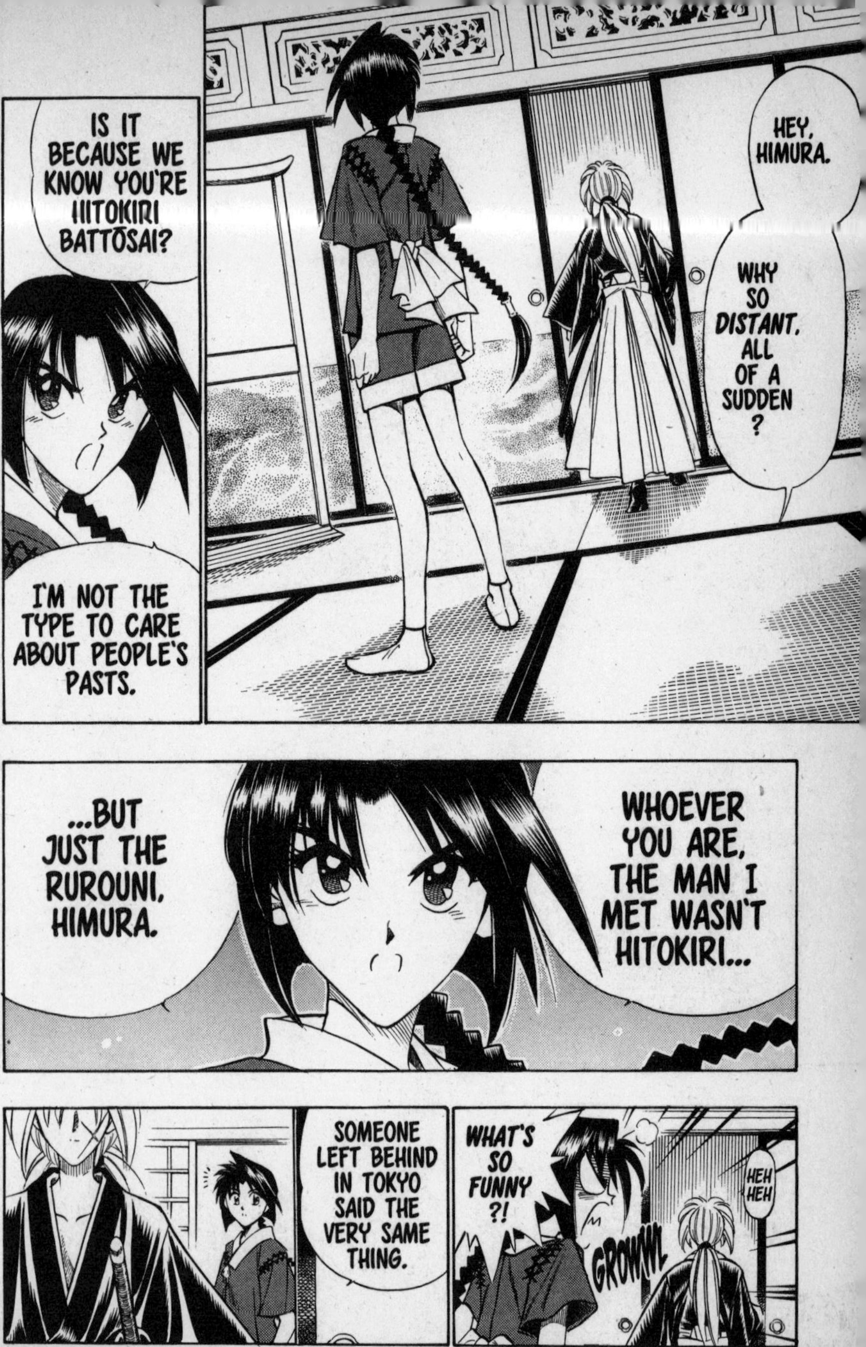
HEY, HIMURA.
WHY SO DISTANT, ALL OF A SUDDEN?
IS IT BECAUSE WE KNOW YOU'RE HITOKIRI BATTŌSAI?
I'M NOT THE TYPE TO CARE ABOUT PEOPLE'S PASTS.
WHOEVER YOU ARE, THE MAN I MET WASN'T HITOKIRI...
...BUT JUST THE RUROUNI, HIMURA.
HEH HEH
WHAT'S SO FUNNY?!
GROWWL
SOMEONE LEFT BEHIND IN TOKYO SAID THE VERY SAME THING.

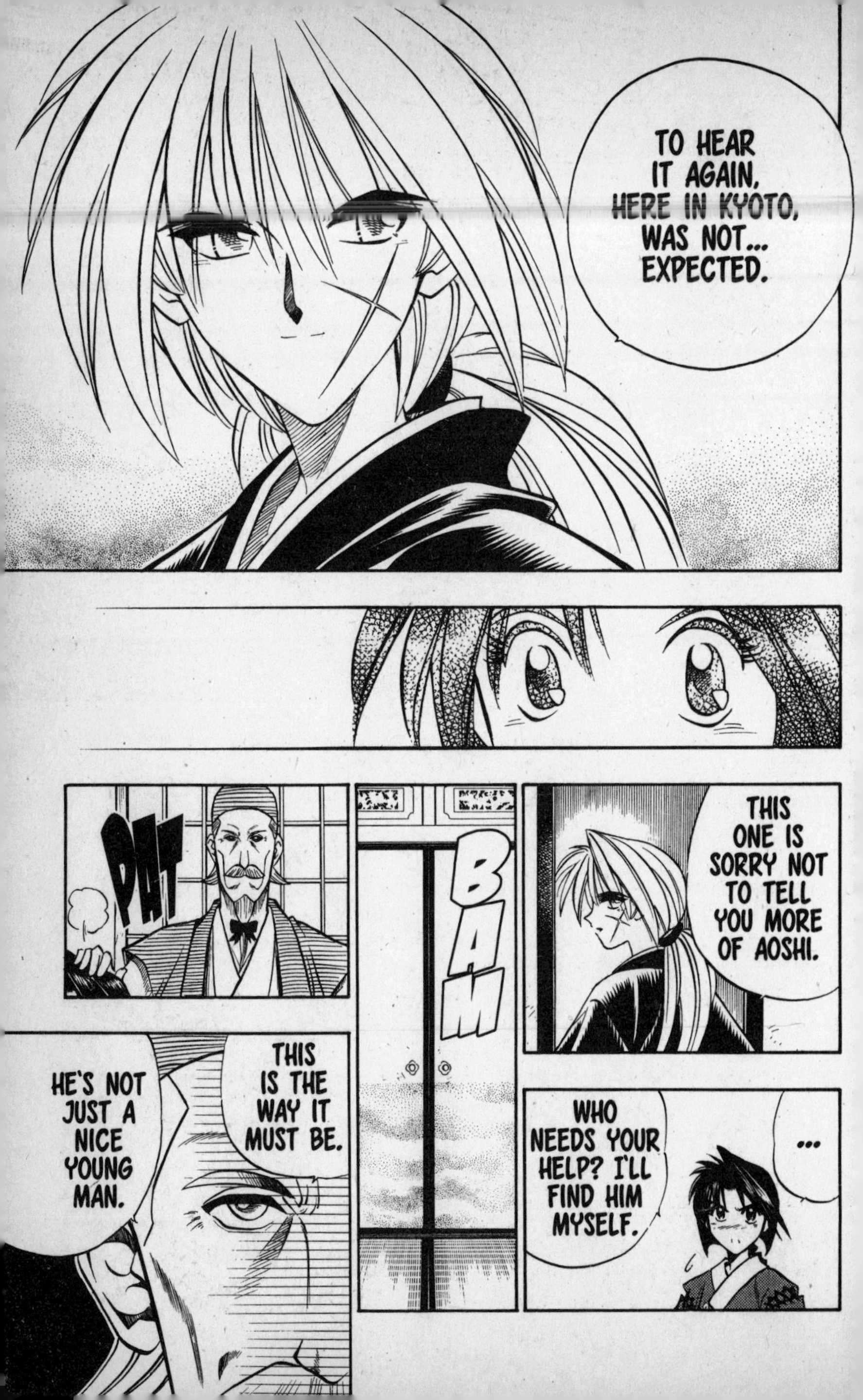
TO HEAR IT AGAIN, HERE IN KYOTO, WAS NOT... EXPECTED.
THIS ONE IS SORRY NOT TO TELL YOU MORE OF AOSHI.
...
WHO NEEDS YOUR HELP? I'LL FIND HIM MYSELF.
BAM
PAT
THIS IS THE WAY IT MUST BE.
HE'S NOT JUST A NICE YOUNG MAN.

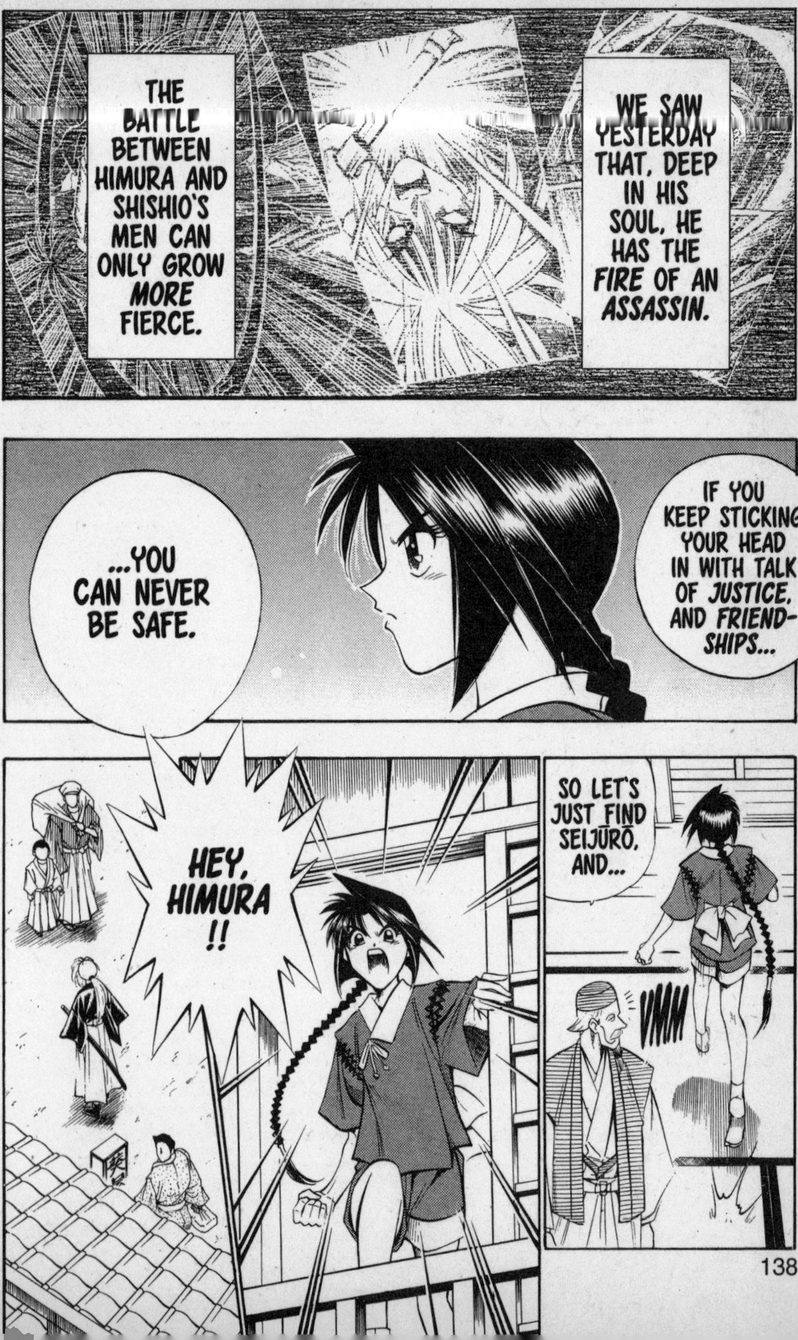

WE SAW YESTERDAY THAT, DEEP IN HIS SOUL, HE HAS THE FIRE OF AN ASSASSIN.
THE BATTLE BETWEEN HIMURA AND SHISHIO'S MEN CAN ONLY GROW MORE FIERCE.
IF YOU KEEP STICKING YOUR HEAD IN WITH TALK OF JUSTICE, AND FRIEND-SHIPS...
...YOU CAN NEVER BE SAFE.
SO LET'S JUST FIND SEIJŪRŌ, AND...
VMM
HEY, HIMURA !!

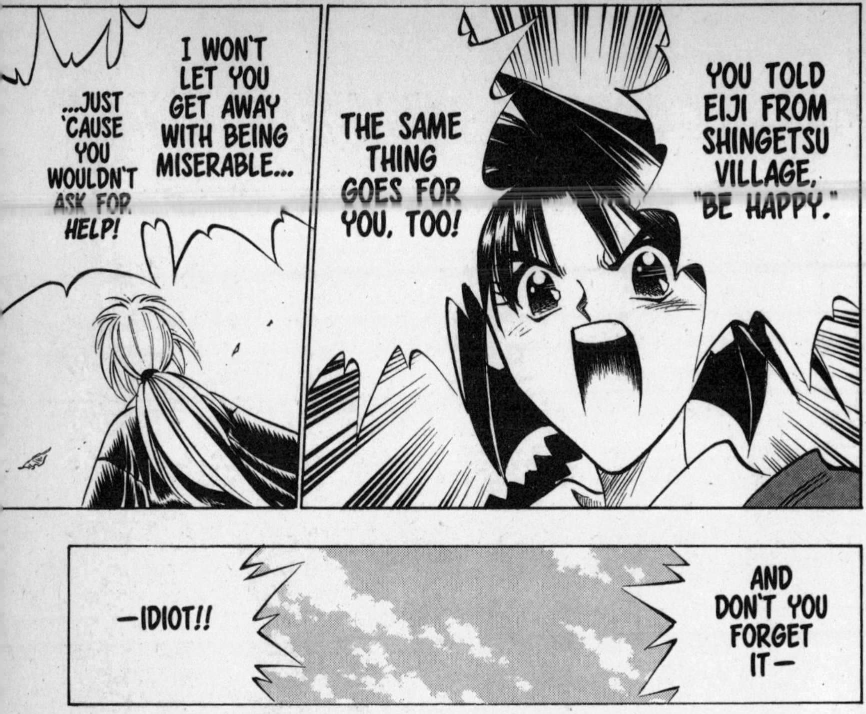
YOU TOLD EIJI FROM SHINGETSU VILLAGE, "BE HAPPY."
THE SAME THING GOES FOR YOU, TOO!
I WON'T LET YOU GET AWAY WITH BEING MISERABLE...
...JUST 'CAUSE YOU WOULDN'T ASK FOR HELP!
AND DON'T YOU FORGET IT—
—IDIOT!!

Seems I've been apologizing a lot lately, so this time I'll tell a stupid story about games, instead. I bought "Samurai Spirits: Zankurō Musōken," and it's good, but to be honest, I can't really get into it. It's more hardcore Japanese style than "Shin · Samurai Spirits," and I do like new characters such as Headhunter Basara, but here's the thing....

The huge gap between the abilities of different characters... the cruel, evil combos that go on unnecessarily... and, most of all, the incredible strength of the CPU! In Level 1 "Swordsman" mode, if you let down your guard for a minute, you're finished! I can only think it's an attempt to weed out the no-good players like Watsuki... I'm really disappointed, since I do like the "Samurai Spirits" games. I'm keeping my hopes up for the "Samurai Spirits" RPG, and for the fourth version of the game. Right now, what I'm hooked on is "Vampire Hunter." Straight out, it's awesome, especially the ability to set levels to allow beginners to enjoy the game. Arcade games aside, I think home-platform games should all be made that way. Watsuki's current character of choice is Morrigan (heh). Until lately, I haven't been the female-character type—and that "dynamite body" of hers doesn't really do it for me—but, somehow, she's still my favorite. I especially like the face she makes when she takes a knock-over hit. I've been thinking I should start checking out 3-D fighting games soon, but Watsuki guesses maybe he'll keep messing around in the 2-D world a while longer.

和月伸宏

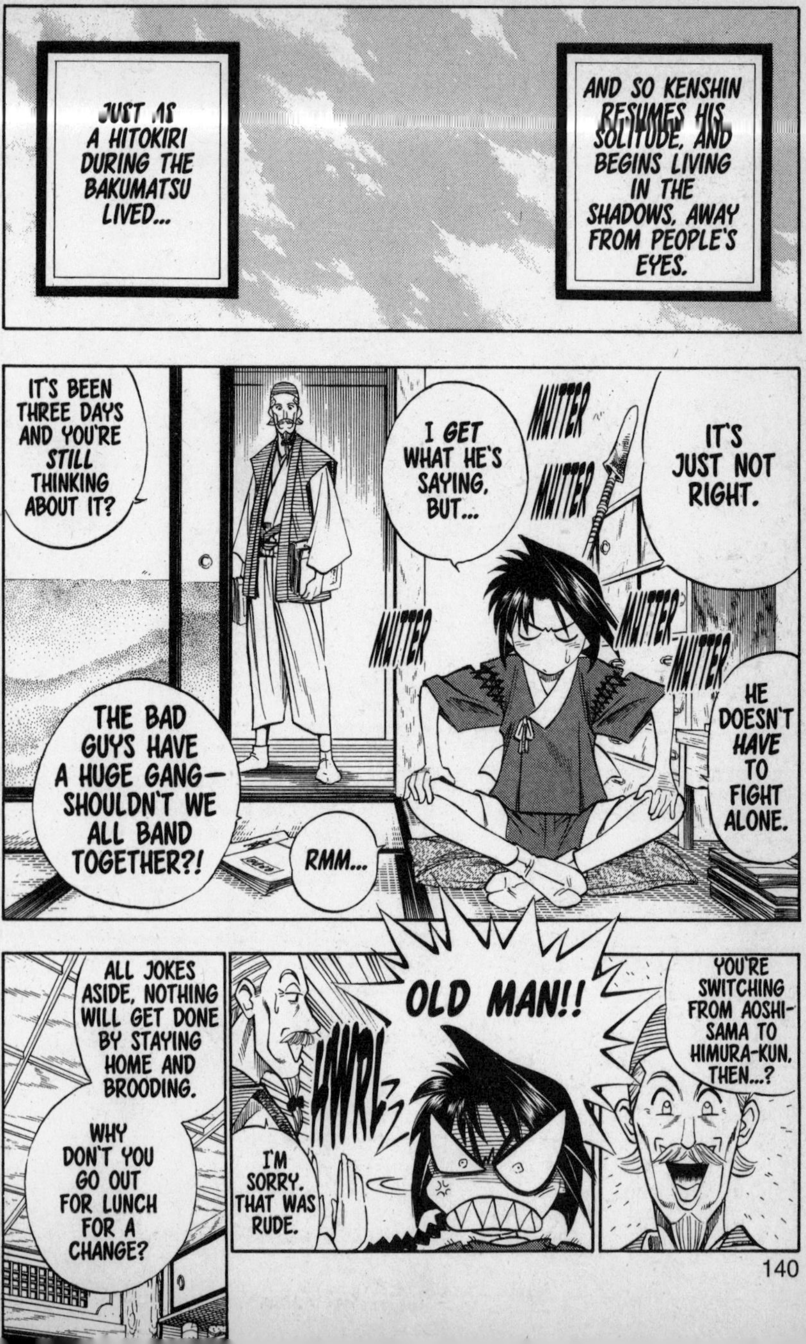
AND SO KENSHIN RESUMES HIS SOLITUDE, AND BEGINS LIVING IN THE SHADOWS, AWAY FROM PEOPLE'S EYES.
JUST AS A HITOKIRI DURING THE BAKUMATSU LIVED...
IT'S JUST NOT RIGHT.
HE DOESN'T HAVE TO FIGHT ALONE.
MUTTER
MUTTER
MUTTER
MUTTER
I GET WHAT HE'S SAYING, BUT...
THE BAD GUYS HAVE A HUGE GANG— SHOULDN'T WE ALL BAND TOGETHER?!
MUTTER
RMM...
IT'S BEEN THREE DAYS AND YOU'RE STILL THINKING ABOUT IT?
YOU'RE SWITCHING FROM AOSHI-SAMA TO HIMURA-KUN, THEN...?
OLD MAN!!
HWRL
I'M SORRY. THAT WAS RUDE.
ALL JOKES ASIDE, NOTHING WILL GET DONE BY STAYING HOME AND BROODING.
WHY DON'T YOU GO OUT FOR LUNCH FOR A CHANGE?

READ THIS WAY

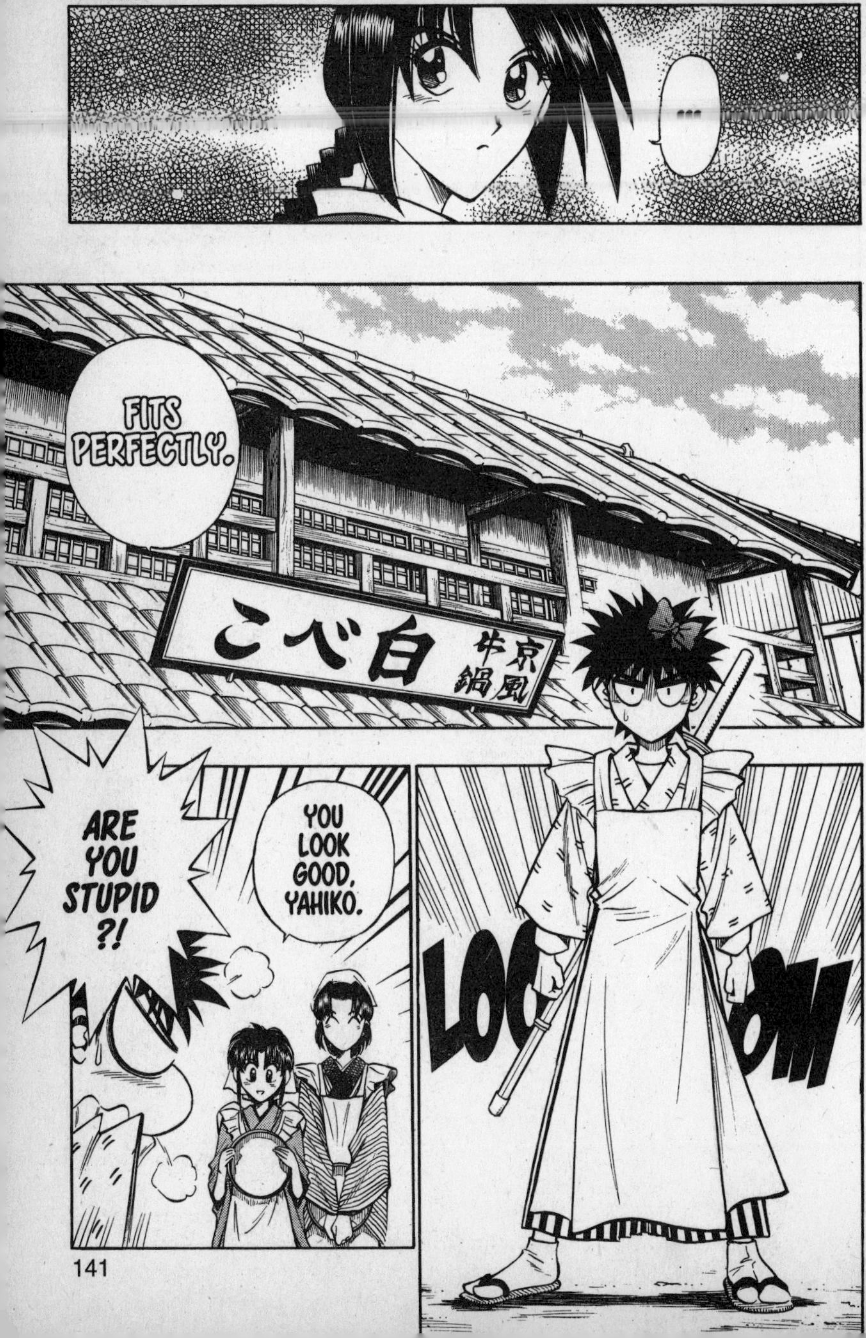
...
FITS PERFECTLY.
白べこ
京風
牛鍋
YOU LOOK GOOD, YAHIKO.
ARE YOU STUPID?!

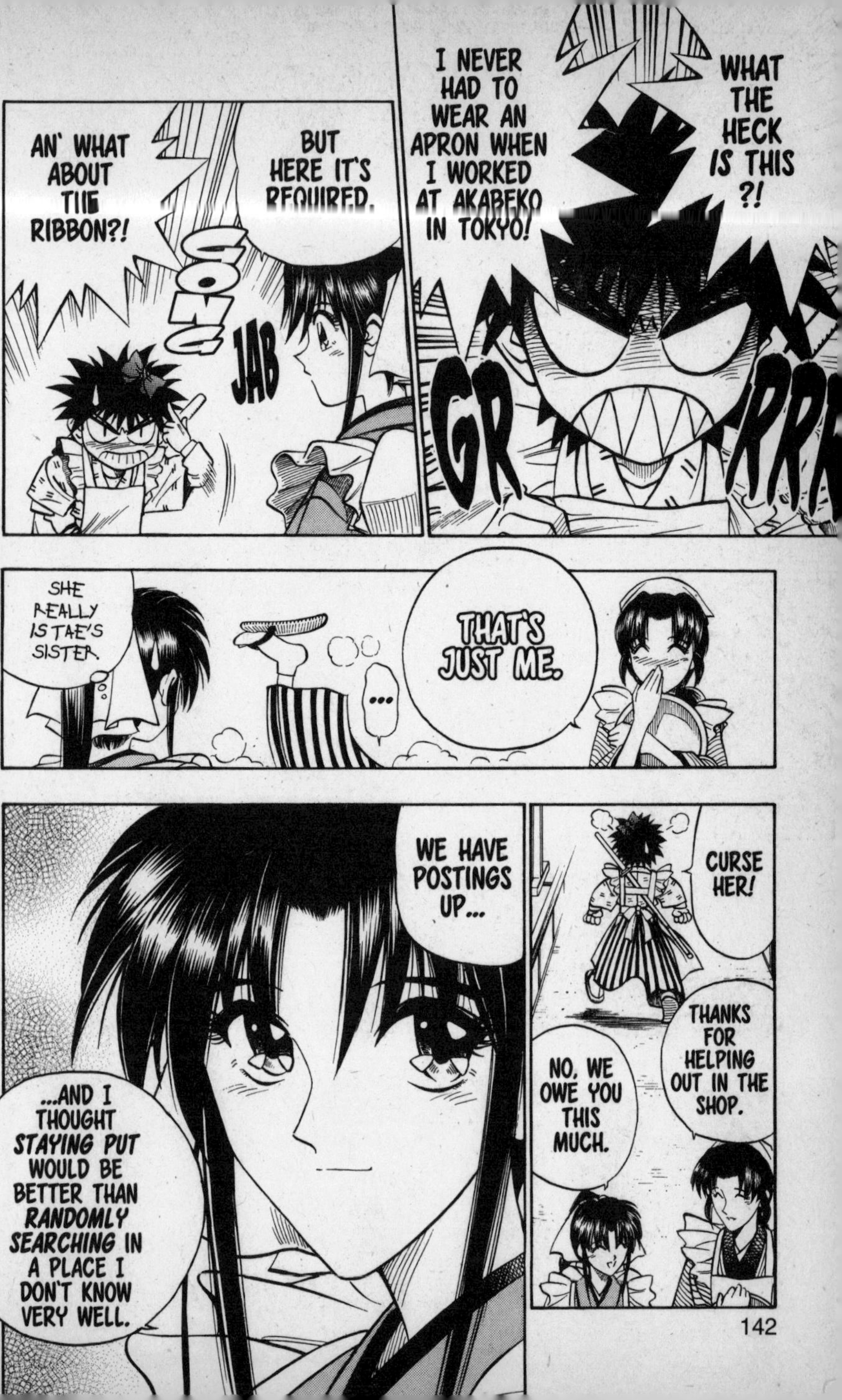
WHAT THE HECK IS THIS?!
I NEVER HAD TO WEAR AN APRON WHEN I WORKED AT AKABEKO IN TOKYO!
GRRRR
BUT HERE IT'S REQUIRED.
AN' WHAT ABOUT THE RIBBON?!
GONG
JAB
THAT'S JUST ME.
...
SHE REALLY IS TAE'S SISTER.
CURSE HER!
THANKS FOR HELPING OUT IN THE SHOP.
NO, WE OWE YOU THIS MUCH.
WE HAVE POSTINGS UP...
...AND I THOUGHT *STAYING PUT* WOULD BE BETTER THAN *RANDOMLY SEARCHING* IN A PLACE I DON'T KNOW VERY WELL.

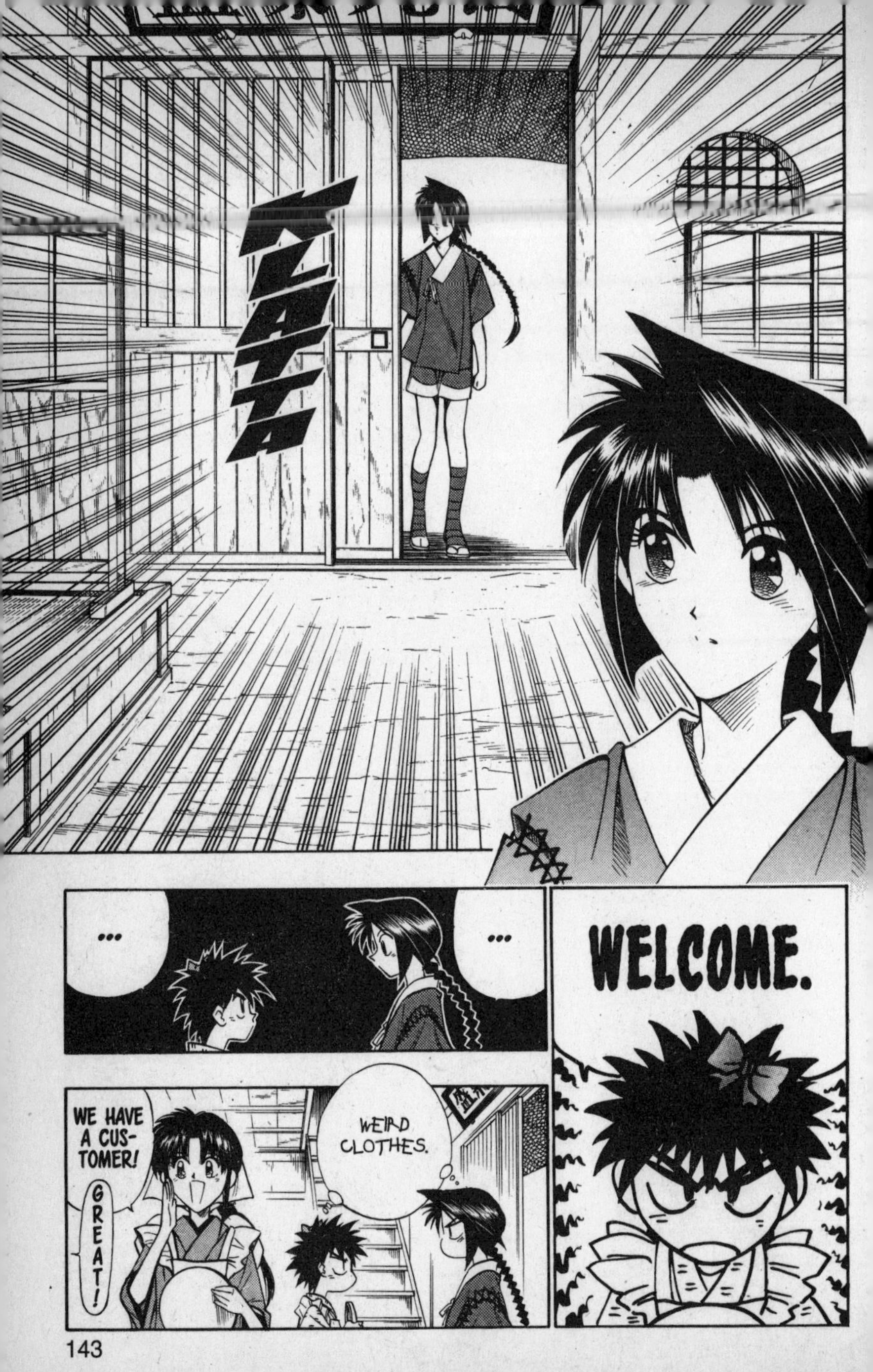
WELCOME.
...
...
WEIRD CLOTHES.
WE HAVE A CUS-TOMER!
GREAT!

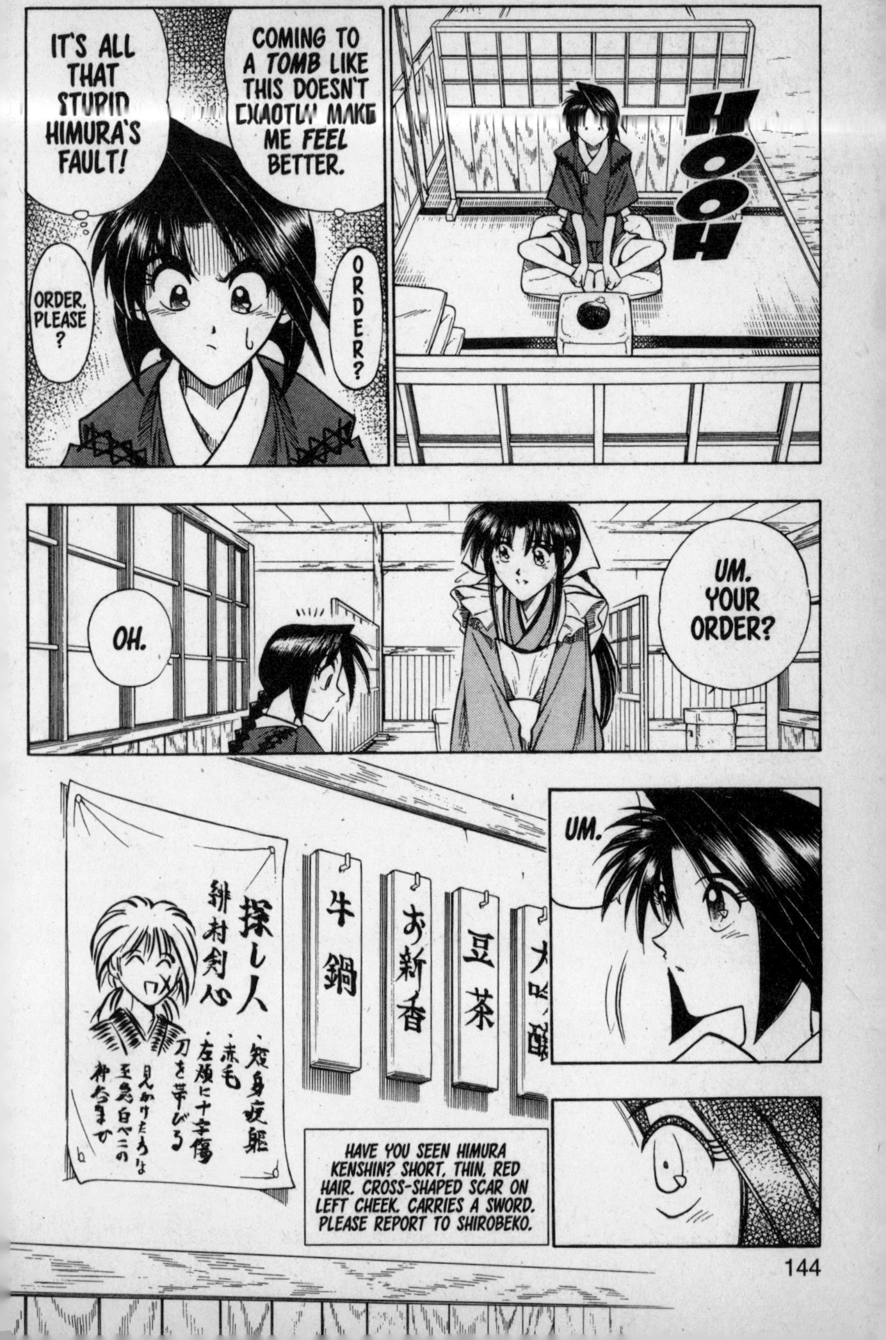
HOOOH
COMING TO A TOMB LIKE THIS DOESN'T EXACTLY MAKE ME FEEL BETTER.
IT'S ALL THAT STUPID HIMURA'S FAULT!
ORDER?
ORDER, PLEASE?
UM. YOUR ORDER?
OH.
UM.
豆茶
お新香
牛鍋
探し人
緋村剣心
・短身痩躯
・赤毛
・左頬に十字傷
刀を帯びる
見かけたら至急白べこの神谷まで
HAVE YOU SEEN HIMURA KENSHIN? SHORT, THIN, RED HAIR. CROSS-SHAPED SCAR ON LEFT CHEEK. CARRIES A SWORD. PLEASE REPORT TO SHIROBEKO.

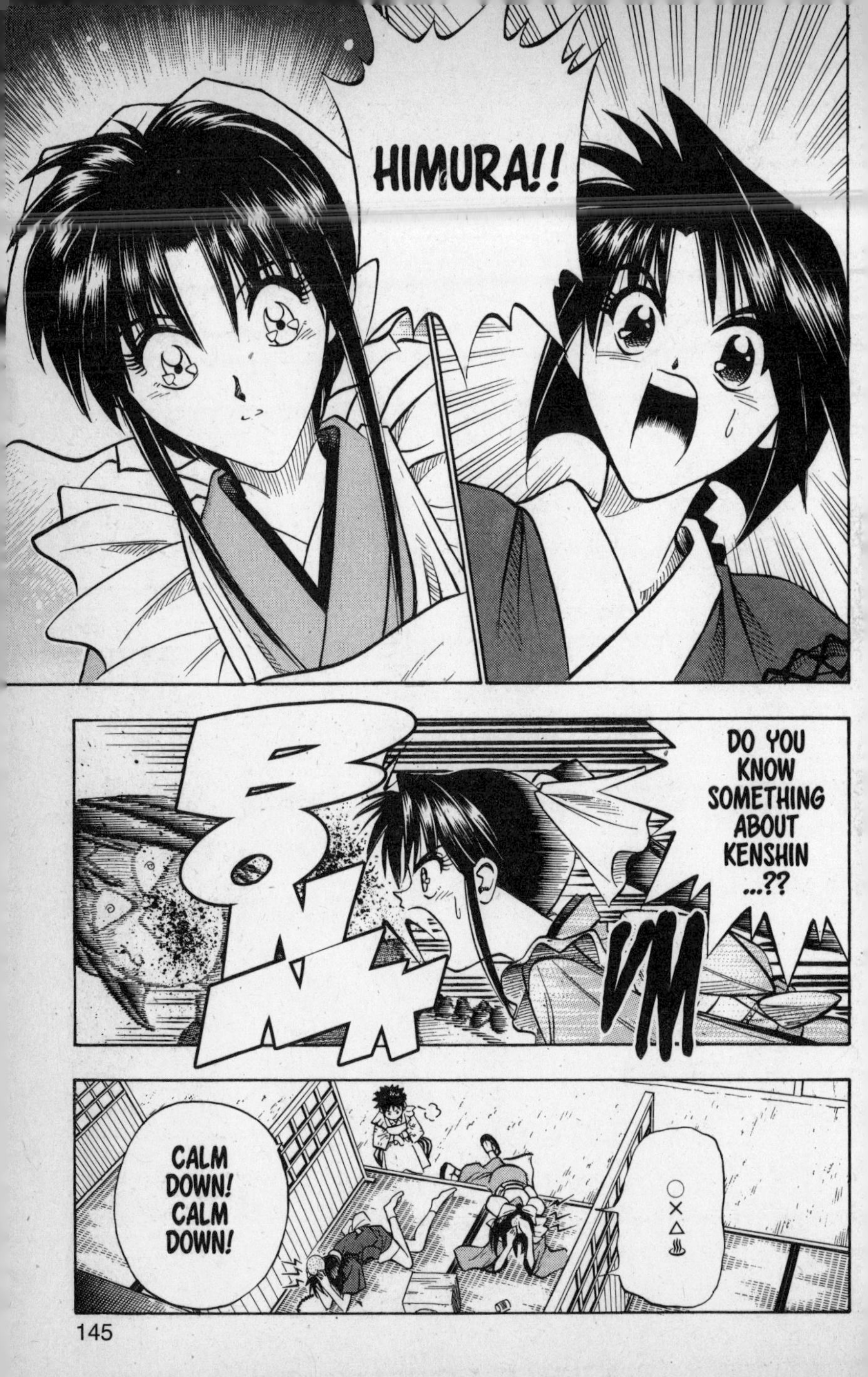
HIMURA!!
DO YOU KNOW SOMETHING ABOUT KENSHIN ...??
○×△♨
CALM DOWN! CALM DOWN!

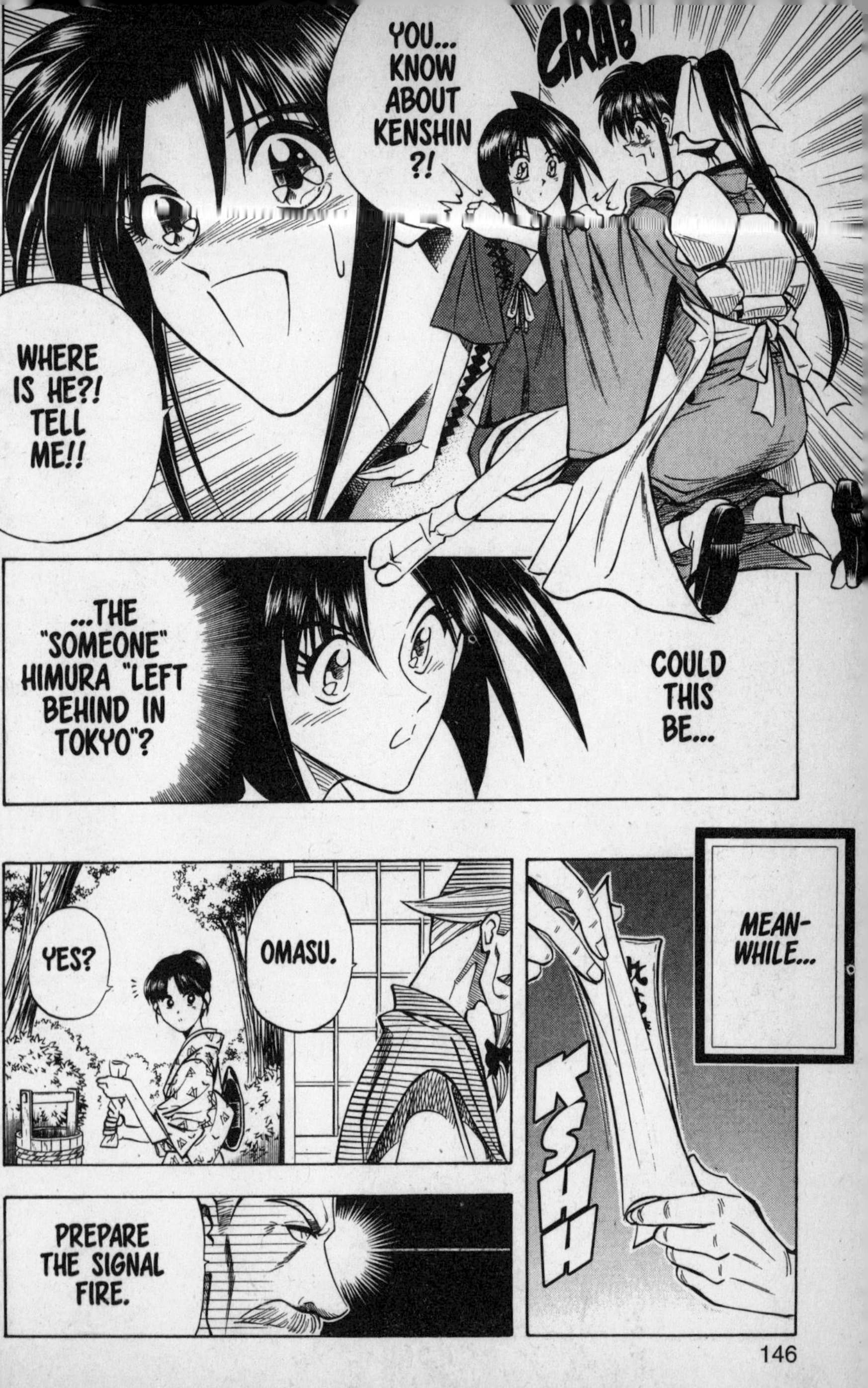
GRAB
YOU... KNOW ABOUT KENSHIN?!
WHERE IS HE?! TELL ME!!
COULD THIS BE...
...THE "SOMEONE" HIMURA "LEFT BEHIND IN TOKYO"?
MEAN-WHILE...
KSHH
OMASU.
YES?
PREPARE THE SIGNAL FIRE.

READ THIS WAY

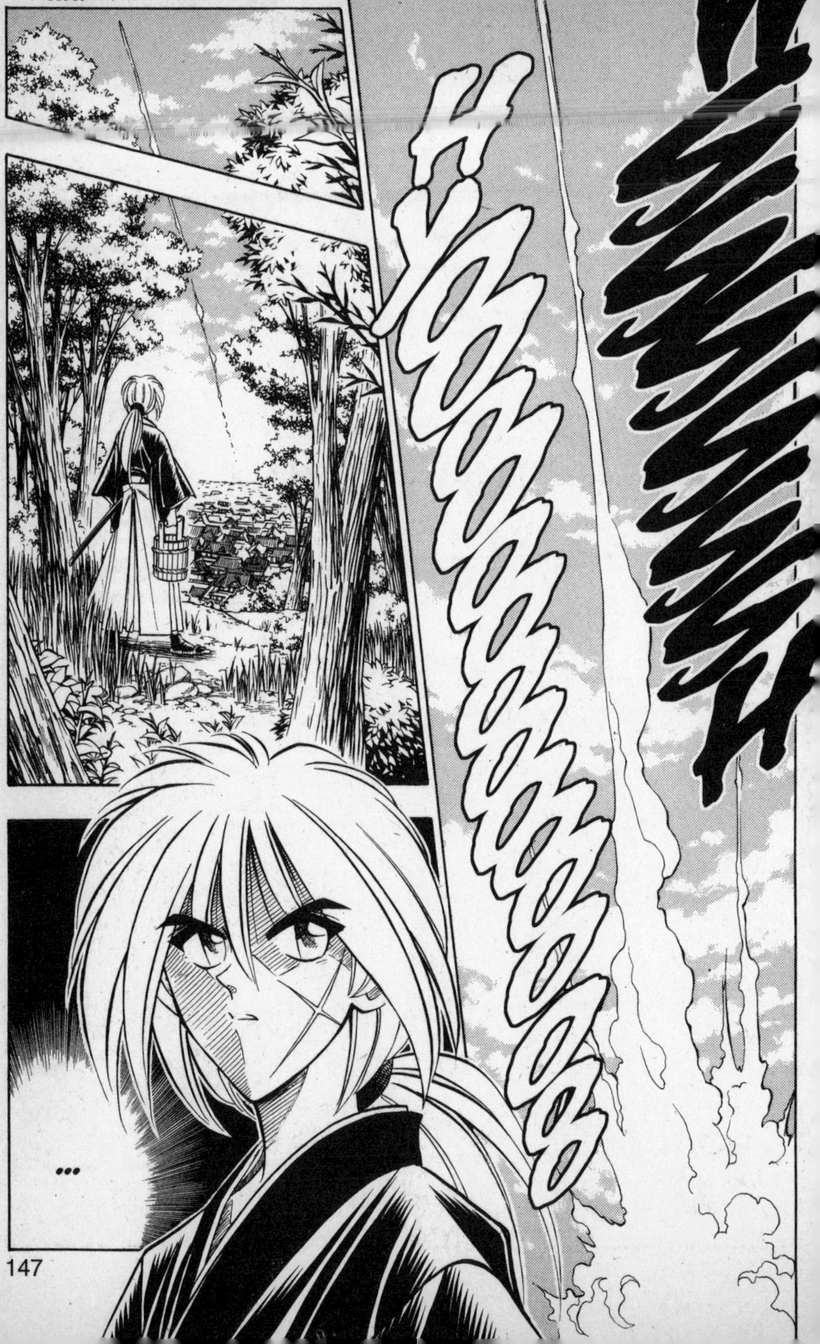
...

Rurouni Kenshin

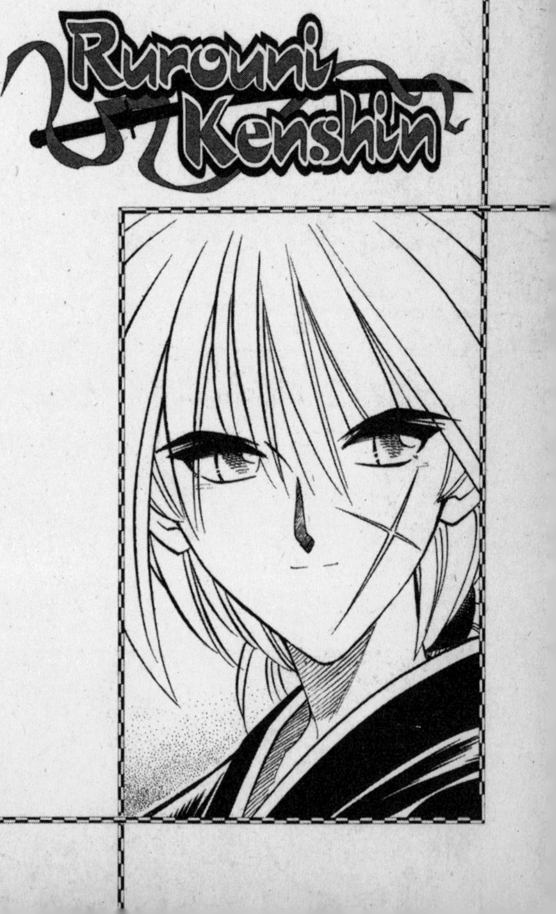

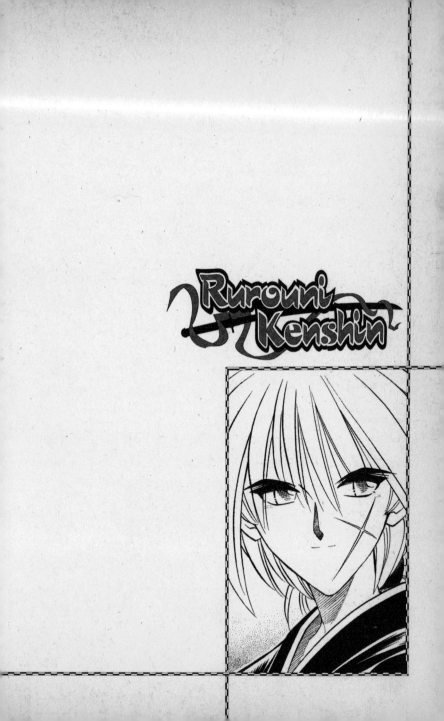

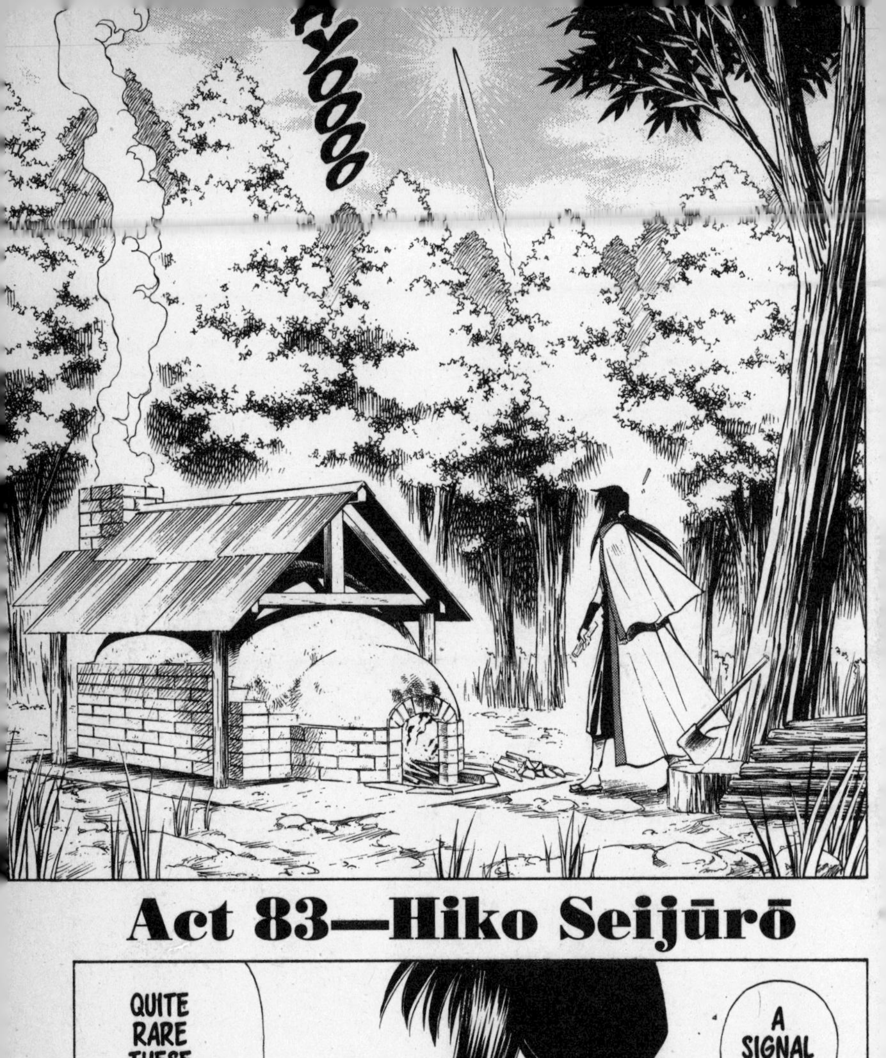

Act 83—Hiko Seijūrō

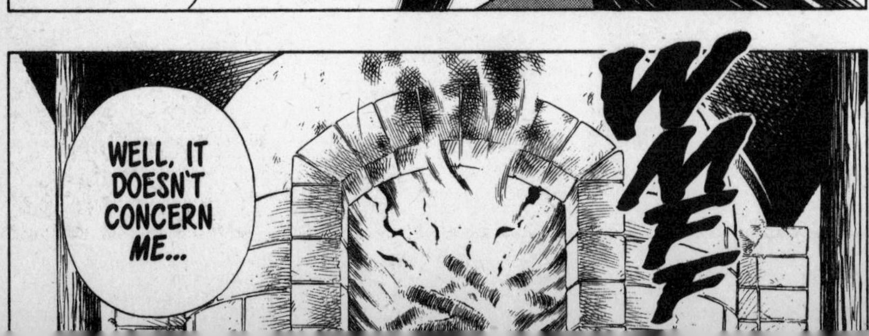
A SIGNAL FIRE.
QUITE RARE THESE DAYS.
WELL, IT DOESN'T CONCERN ME...

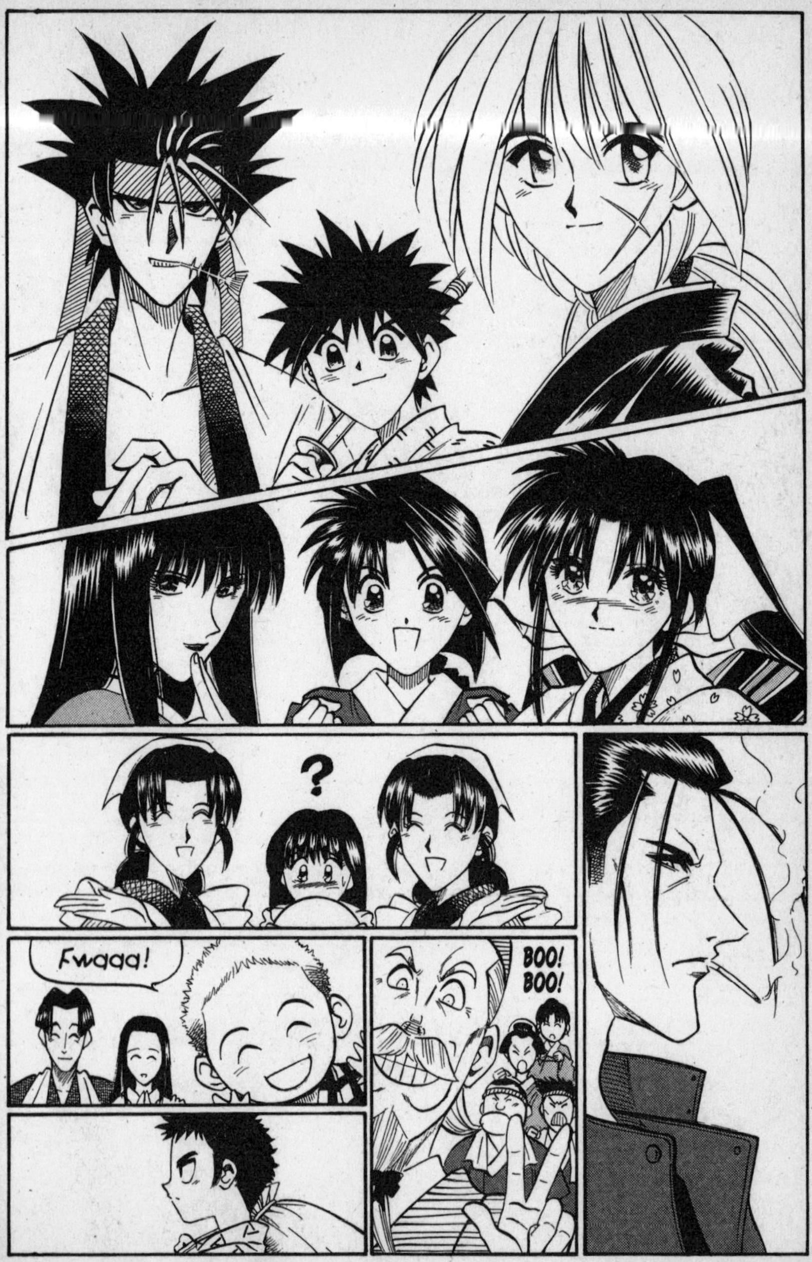
?
BOO! BOO!
Fwaaa!

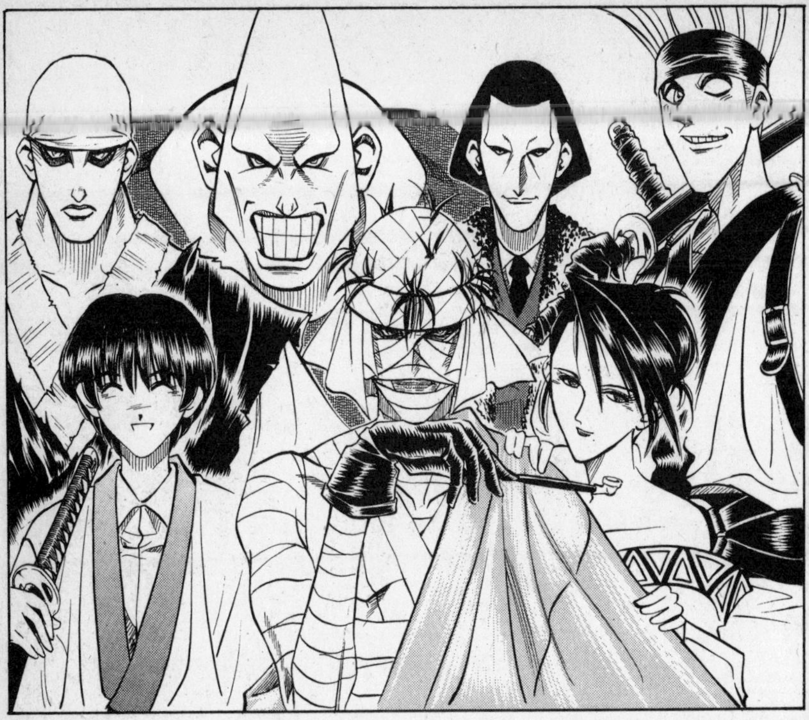

Act 83
Hiko Seijūrō

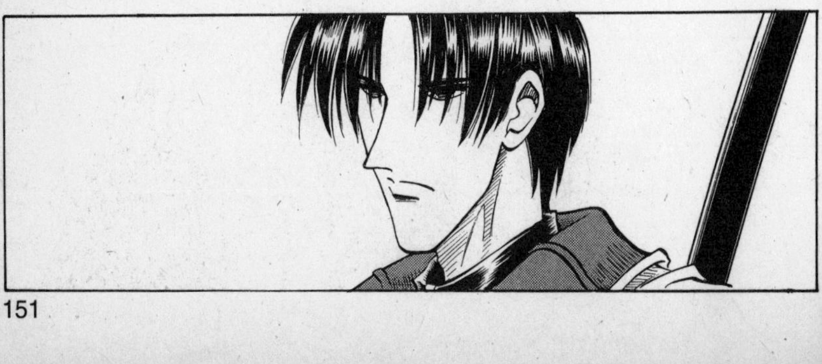

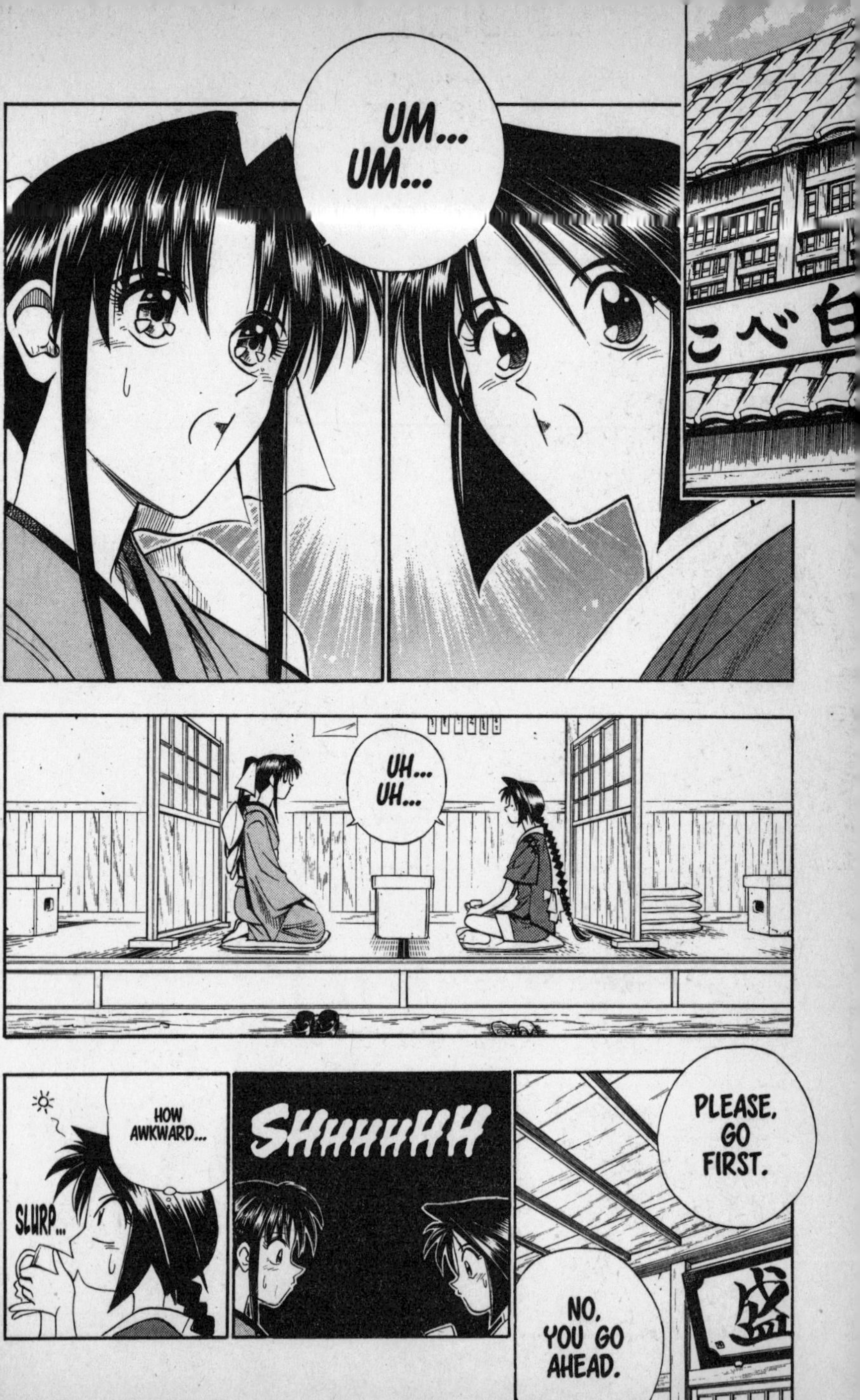
白べこ
UM... UM...
UH... UH...
PLEASE, GO FIRST.
NO, YOU GO AHEAD.
盛
SHHHHHH
HOW AWKWARD...
SLURP...

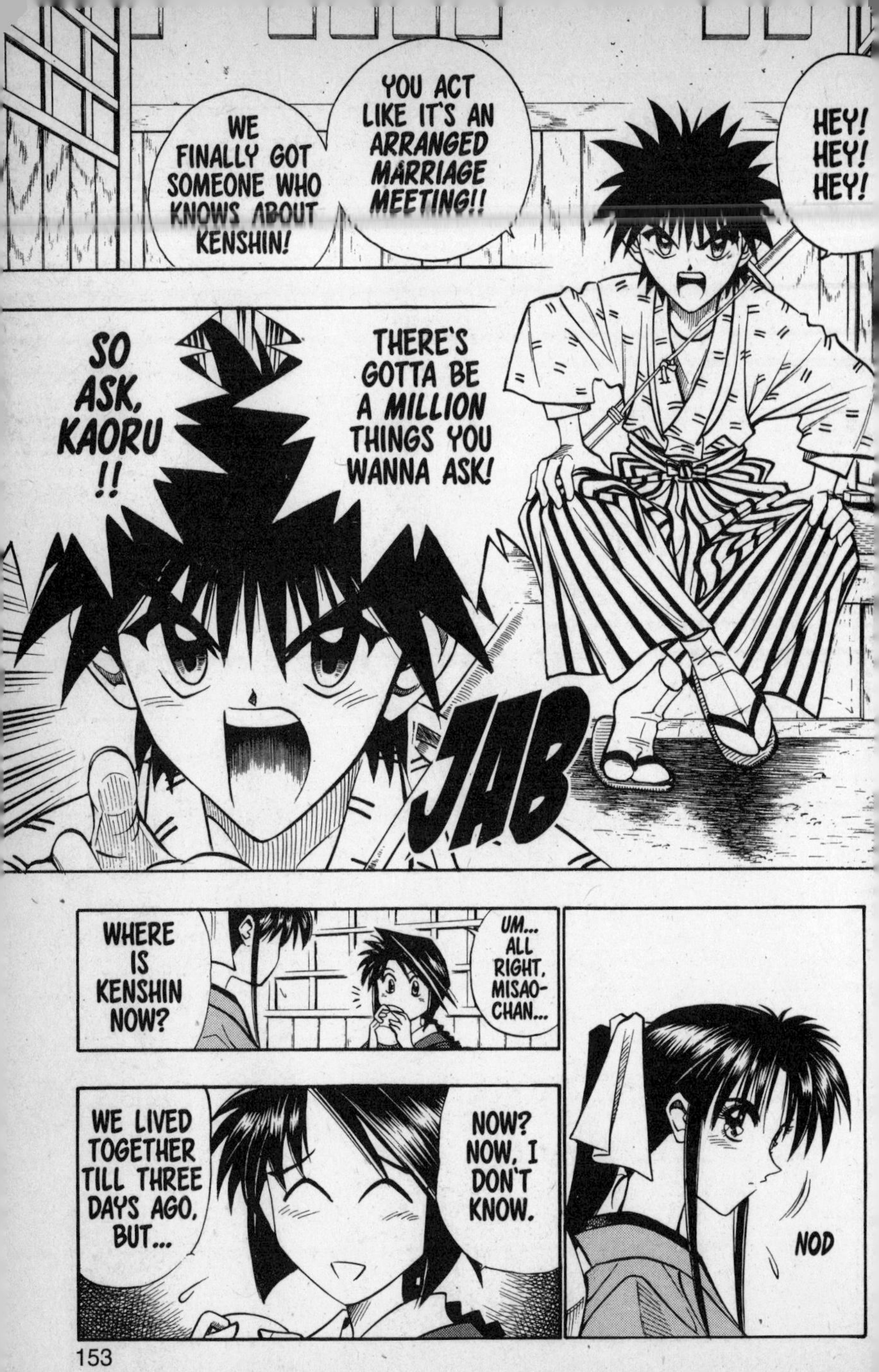
HEY! HEY! HEY!
YOU ACT LIKE IT'S AN ARRANGED MARRIAGE MEETING!!
WE FINALLY GOT SOMEONE WHO KNOWS ABOUT KENSHIN!
THERE'S GOTTA BE A MILLION THINGS YOU WANNA ASK!
SO ASK, KAORU!!
JAB
NOD
UM... ALL RIGHT, MISAO-CHAN...
WHERE IS KENSHIN NOW?
NOW? NOW, I DON'T KNOW.
WE LIVED TOGETHER TILL THREE DAYS AGO, BUT...

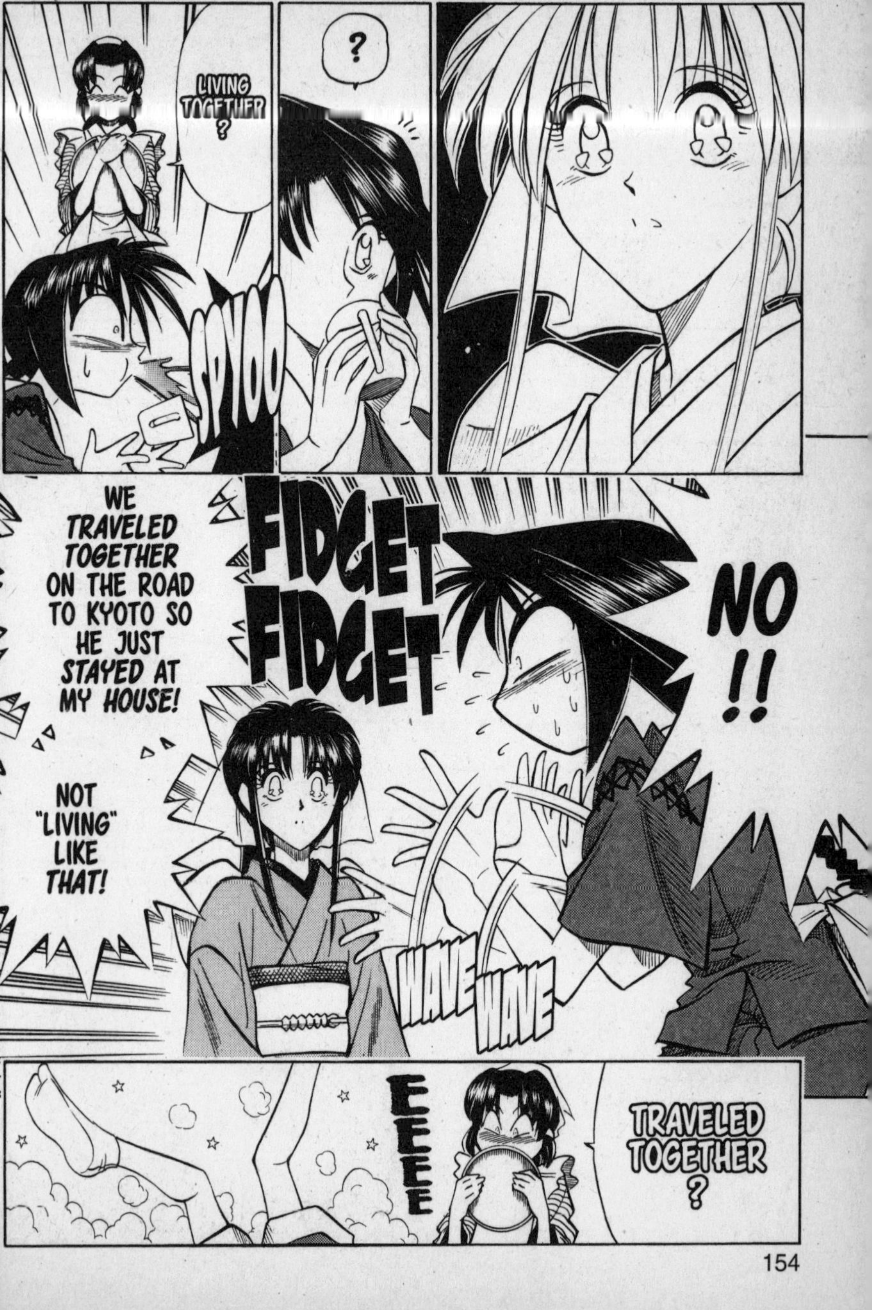
?
LIVING TOGETHER ?
SPYOO
NO !!
FIDGET FIDGET
WE TRAVELED TOGETHER ON THE ROAD TO KYOTO SO HE JUST STAYED AT MY HOUSE!
NOT "LIVING" LIKE THAT!
WAVE WAVE
TRAVELED TOGETHER ?
EEEEE

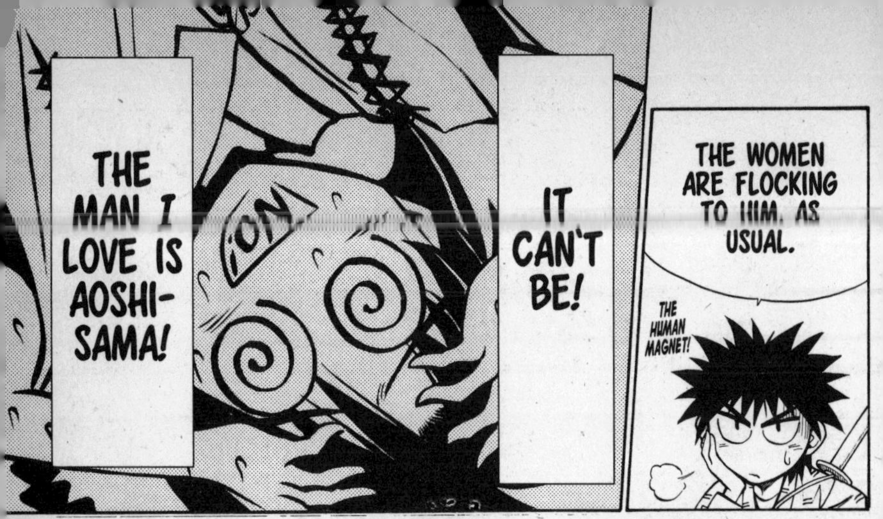
THE WOMEN ARE FLOCKING TO HIM, AS USUAL.
THE HUMAN MAGNET!
IT CAN'T BE!
THE MAN I LOVE IS AOSHI-SAMA!

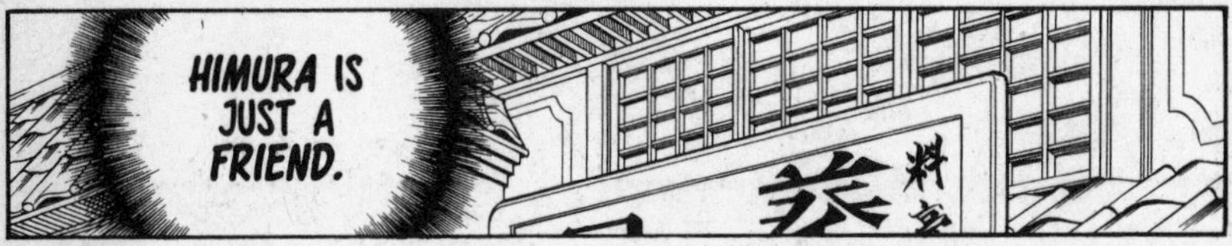
HIMURA IS JUST A FRIEND.

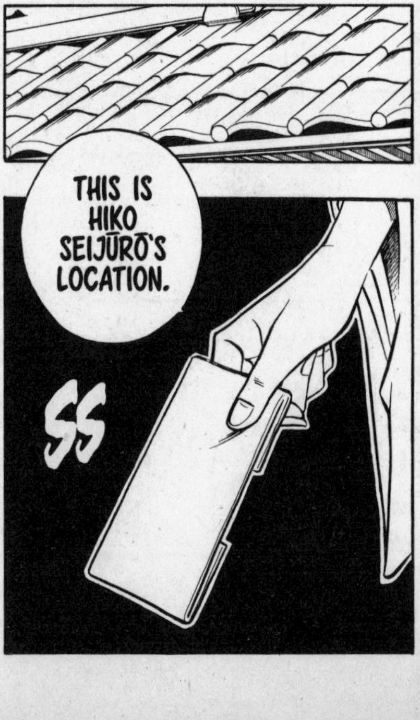
THIS IS HIKO SEIJŪRŌ'S LOCATION.
SS

In a "Secret Life of Characters" section, I wrote that I got lots of complaint letters about Misao and Saitō—and then received support letters in response. I got more back when I was whining in Volume 5 (though there were negatives mixed in—saying stuff like, "Quit whining and write something interesting" or "If you can't uphold your own standards, why not quit?").

When so many people cared about me when I whined, I felt a little happier... and, at the same time, felt accountable to those people in my work. The worsening of my "murderous" schedule, and the increased number of fan letters has created a huge lag between the time each letter arrives and when it's read, but with that as my incentive, I'll work hard on "RuroKen." See you next volume!

伸宏和月

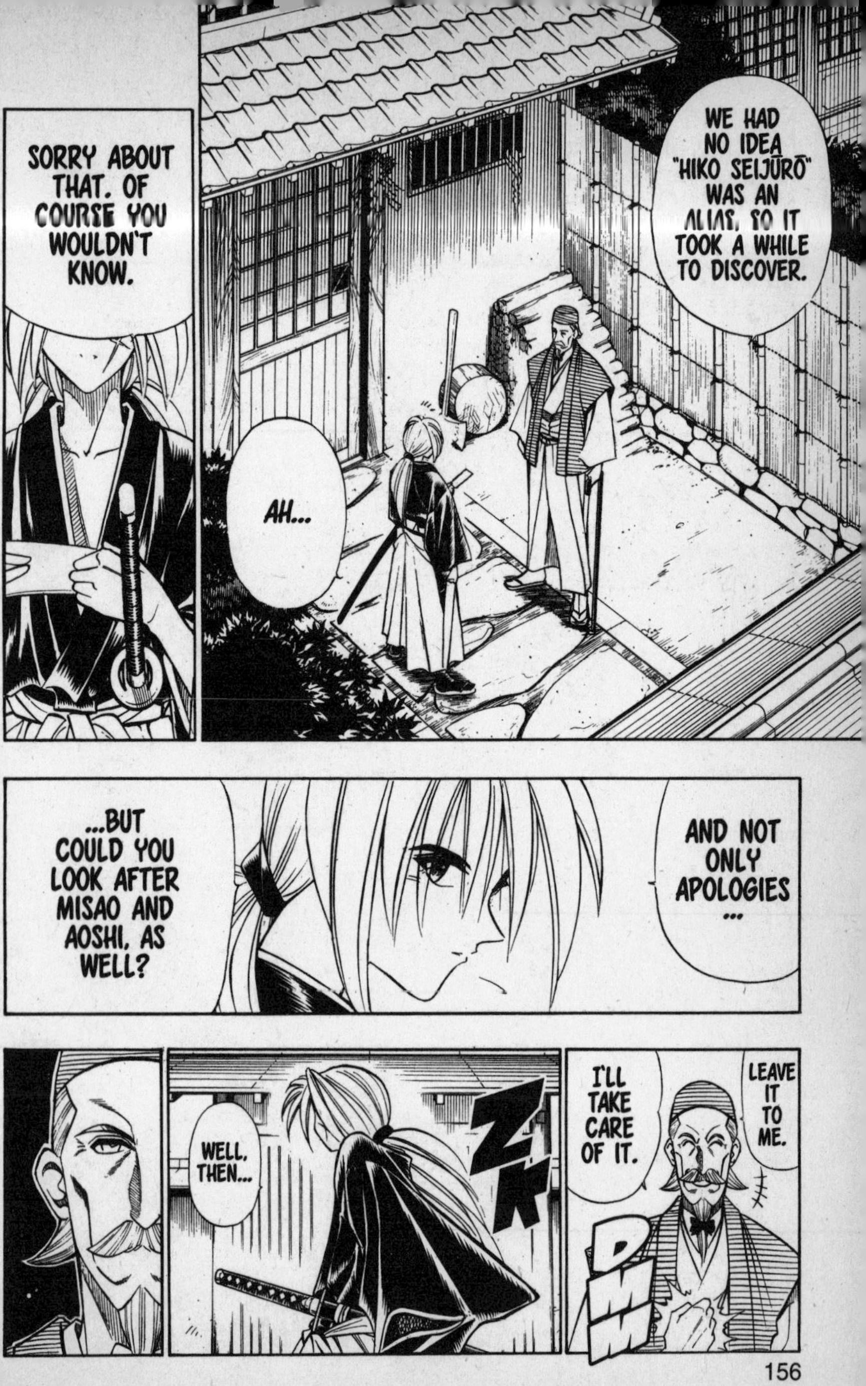
WE HAD NO IDEA "HIKO SEIJŪRŌ" WAS AN ALIAS, SO IT TOOK A WHILE TO DISCOVER.
AH...
SORRY ABOUT THAT. OF COURSE YOU WOULDN'T KNOW.
AND NOT ONLY APOLOGIES...
...BUT COULD YOU LOOK AFTER MISAO AND AOSHI, AS WELL?
LEAVE IT TO ME.
I'LL TAKE CARE OF IT.
DMM
ZK
WELL, THEN...

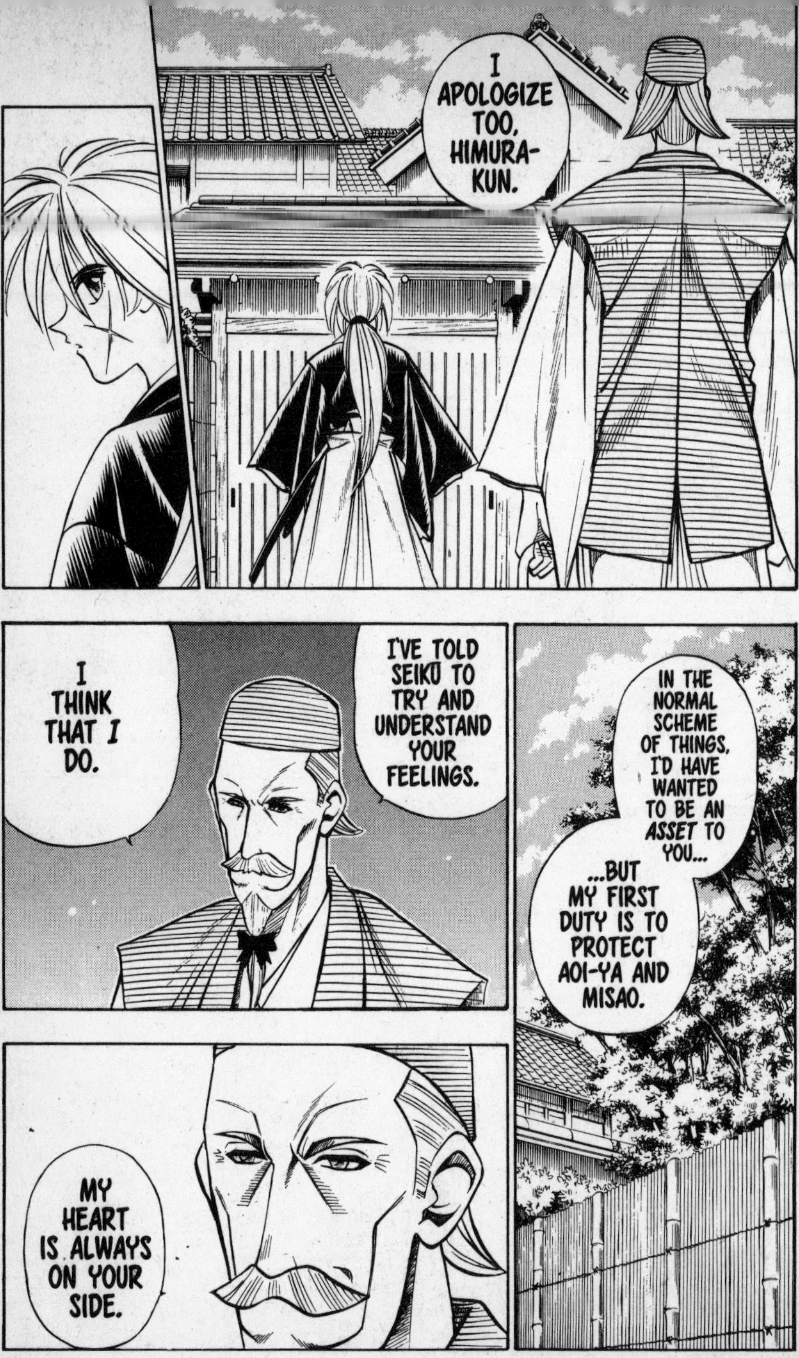
I APOLOGIZE TOO, HIMURA-KUN.
IN THE NORMAL SCHEME OF THINGS, I'D HAVE WANTED TO BE AN *ASSET* TO YOU...
...BUT MY FIRST DUTY IS TO PROTECT AOI-YA AND MISAO.
I'VE TOLD SEIKŪ TO TRY AND UNDERSTAND YOUR FEELINGS.
I THINK THAT *I* DO.
MY HEART IS ALWAYS ON YOUR SIDE.

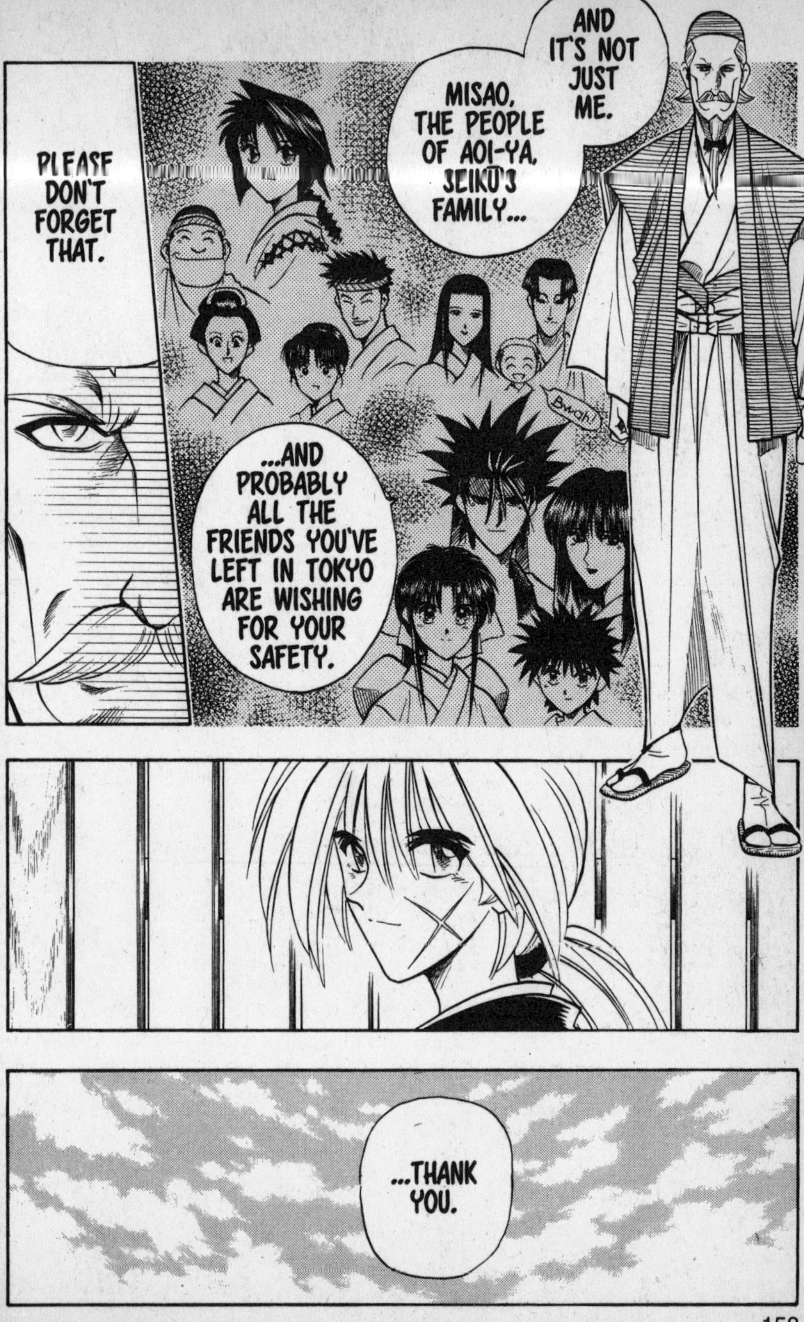
AND IT'S NOT JUST ME.
MISAO, THE PEOPLE OF AOI-YA, SEIKU'S FAMILY...
Bwah!
...AND PROBABLY ALL THE FRIENDS YOU'VE LEFT IN TOKYO ARE WISHING FOR YOUR SAFETY.
PLEASE DON'T FORGET THAT.
...THANK YOU.

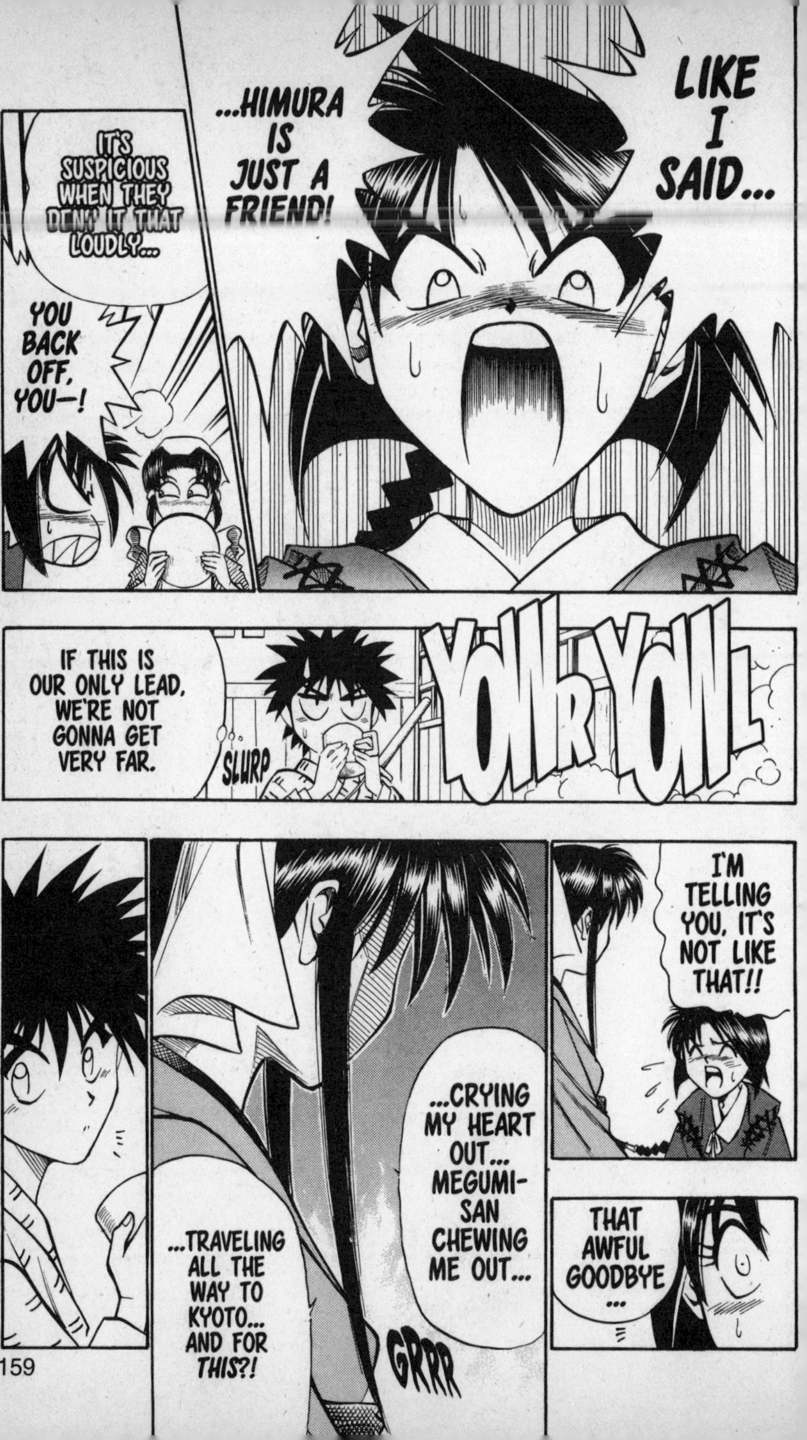
LIKE I SAID...
...HIMURA IS JUST A FRIEND!
IT'S SUSPICIOUS WHEN THEY DENY IT THAT LOUDLY...
YOU BACK OFF, YOU—!
YOWL YOWL
IF THIS IS OUR ONLY LEAD, WE'RE NOT GONNA GET VERY FAR.
SLURP
I'M TELLING YOU, IT'S NOT LIKE THAT!!
THAT AWFUL GOODBYE ...
...CRYING MY HEART OUT... MEGUMI-SAN CHEWING ME OUT...
...TRAVELING ALL THE WAY TO KYOTO... AND FOR THIS?!
GRRR

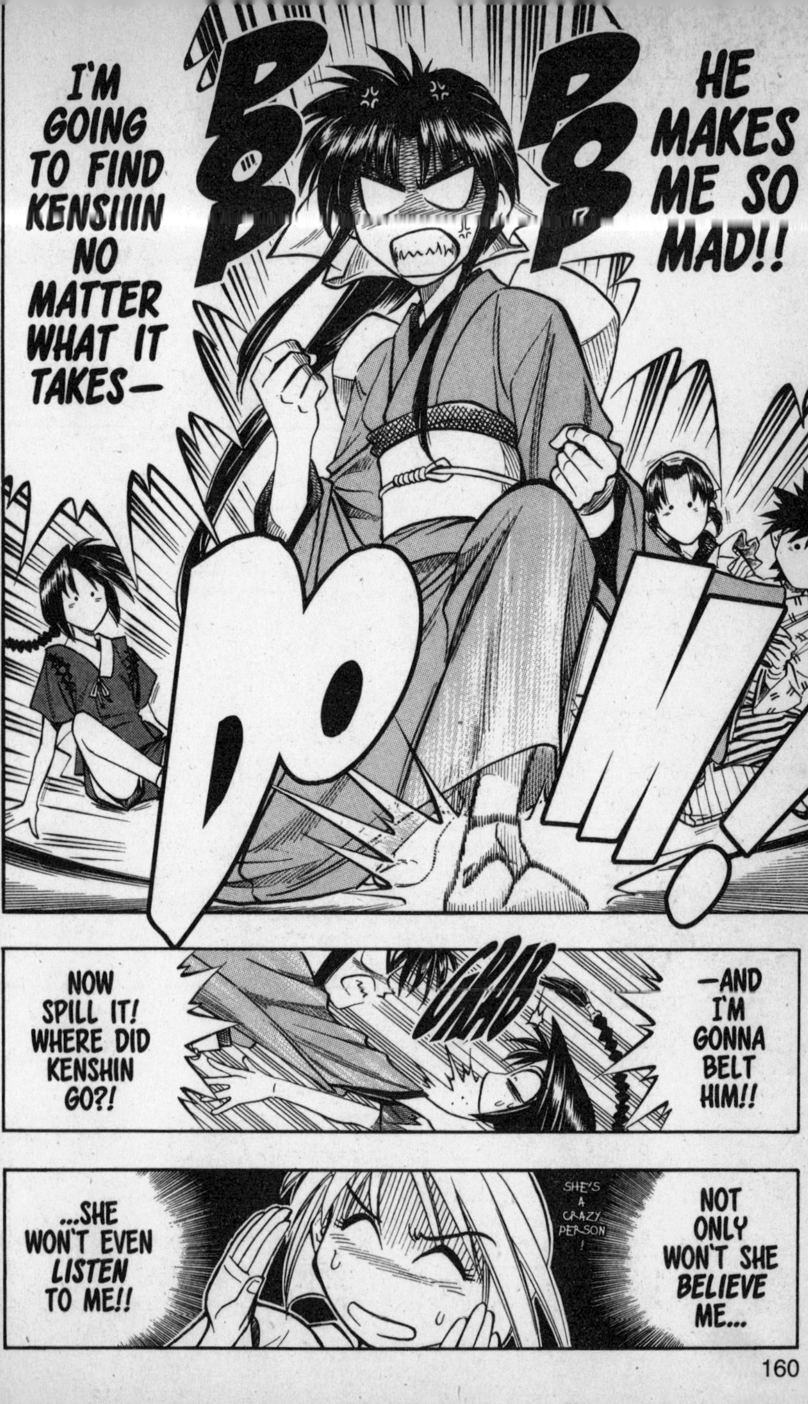
HE MAKES ME SO MAD!!
I'M GOING TO FIND KENSIIIN NO MATTER WHAT IT TAKES—
—AND I'M GONNA BELT HIM!!
GRAB
NOW SPILL IT! WHERE DID KENSHIN GO?!
NOT ONLY WON'T SHE BELIEVE ME...
SHE'S A CRAZY PERSON!
...SHE WON'T EVEN LISTEN TO ME!!

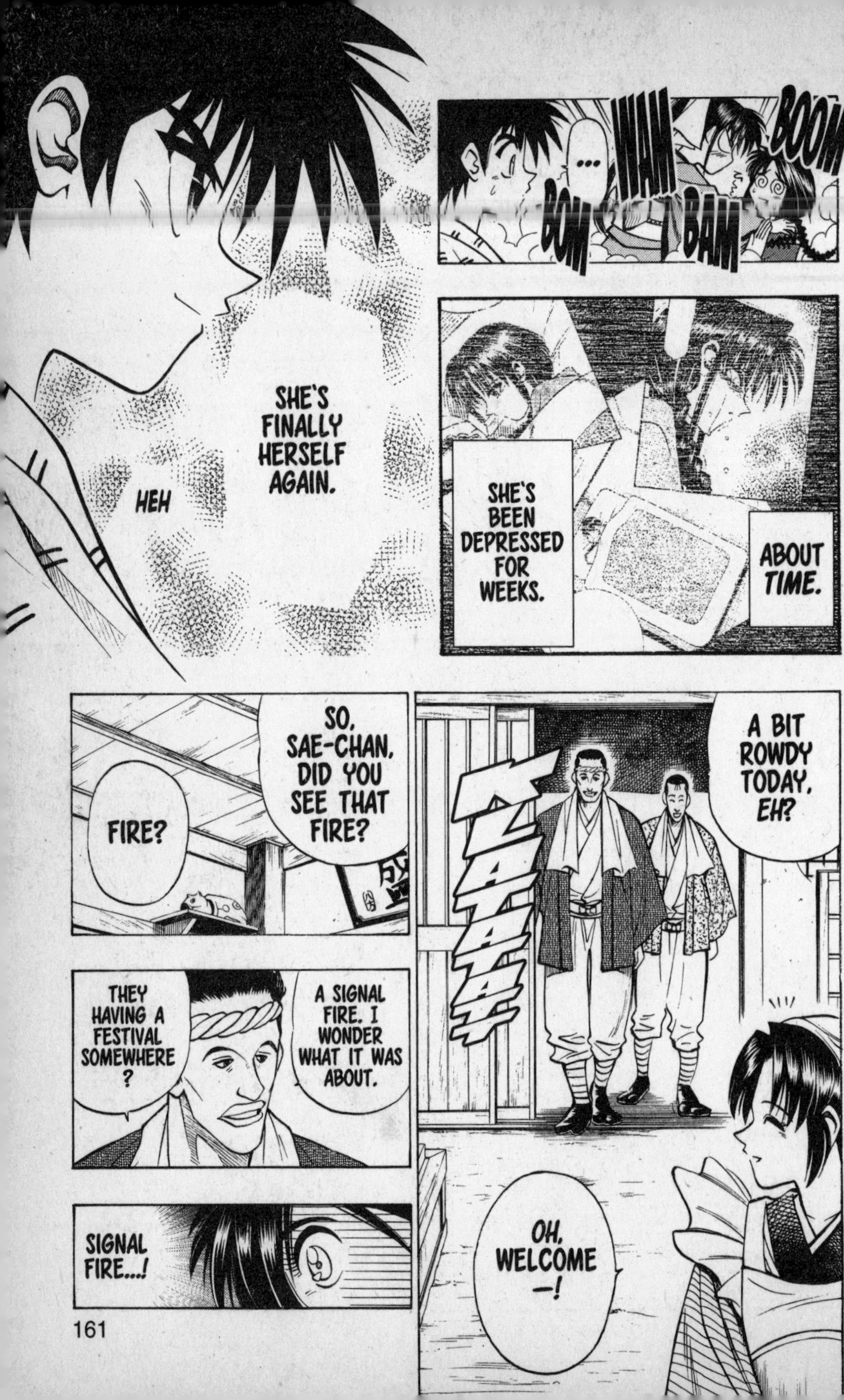
BOOM
WHAM
BAM
BOM
...
ABOUT TIME.
SHE'S BEEN DEPRESSED FOR WEEKS.
SHE'S FINALLY HERSELF AGAIN.
HEH
A BIT ROWDY TODAY, EH?
OH, WELCOME—!
SO, SAE-CHAN, DID YOU SEE THAT FIRE?
FIRE?
A SIGNAL FIRE. I WONDER WHAT IT WAS ABOUT.
THEY HAVING A FESTIVAL SOMEWHERE?
SIGNAL FIRE...!

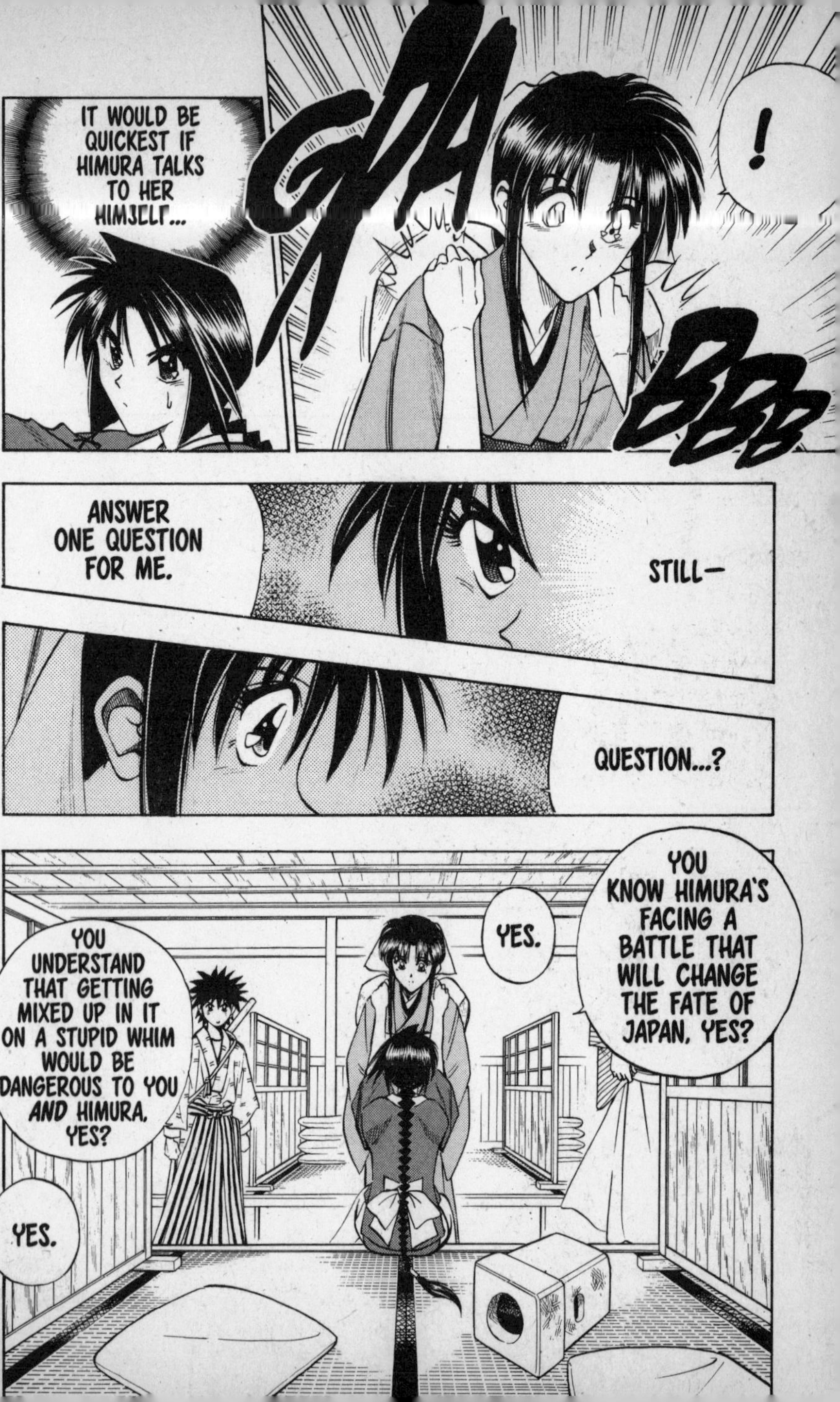
!
GA
IT WOULD BE QUICKEST IF HIMURA TALKS TO HER HIMSELF...
STILL—
ANSWER ONE QUESTION FOR ME.
QUESTION...?
YOU KNOW HIMURA'S FACING A BATTLE THAT WILL CHANGE THE FATE OF JAPAN, YES?
YES.
YOU UNDERSTAND THAT GETTING MIXED UP IN IT ON A STUPID WHIM WOULD BE DANGEROUS TO YOU *AND* HIMURA, YES?
YES.

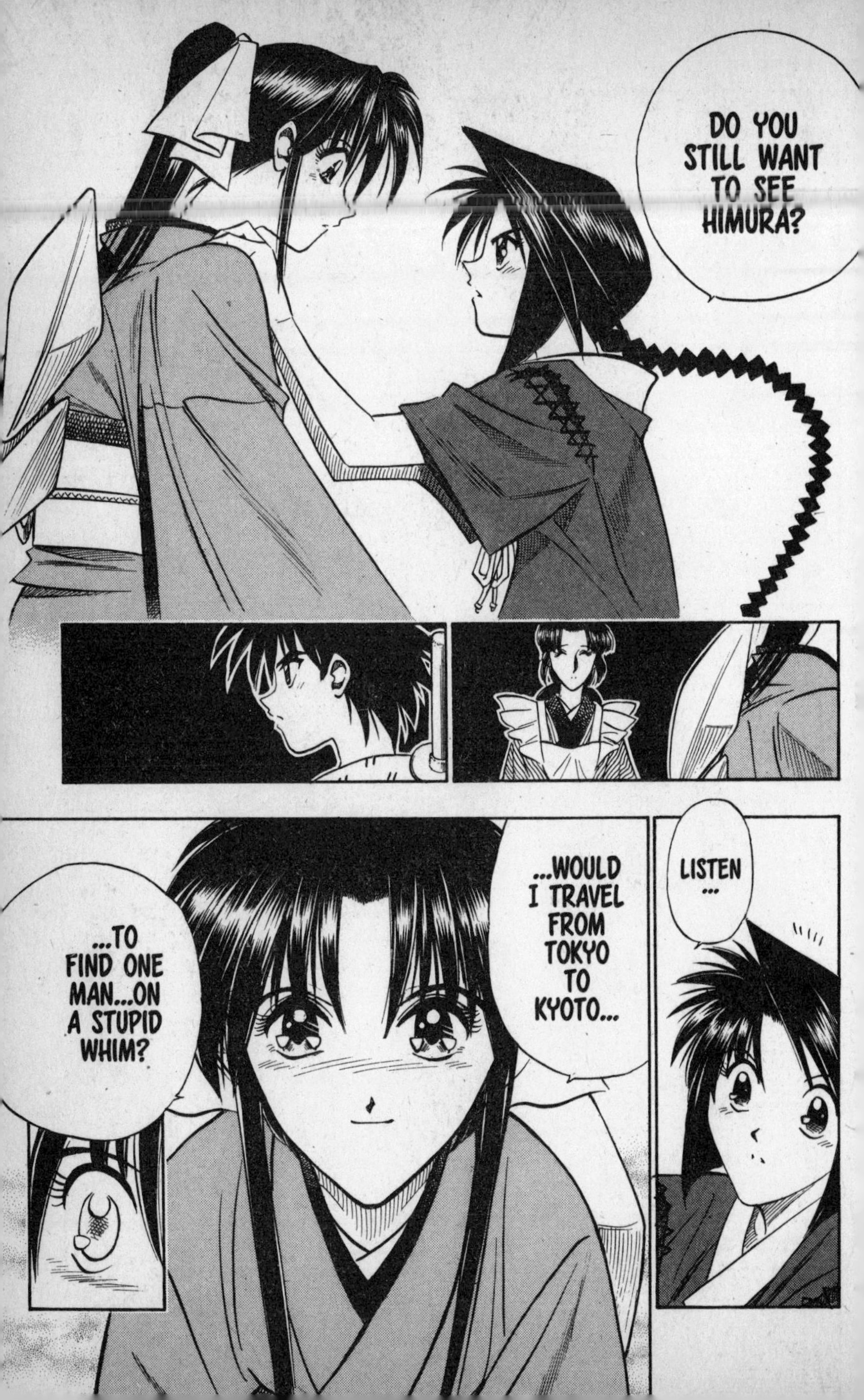
DO YOU STILL WANT TO SEE HIMURA?
LISTEN ...
...WOULD I TRAVEL FROM TOKYO TO KYOTO...
...TO FIND ONE MAN...ON A STUPID WHIM?

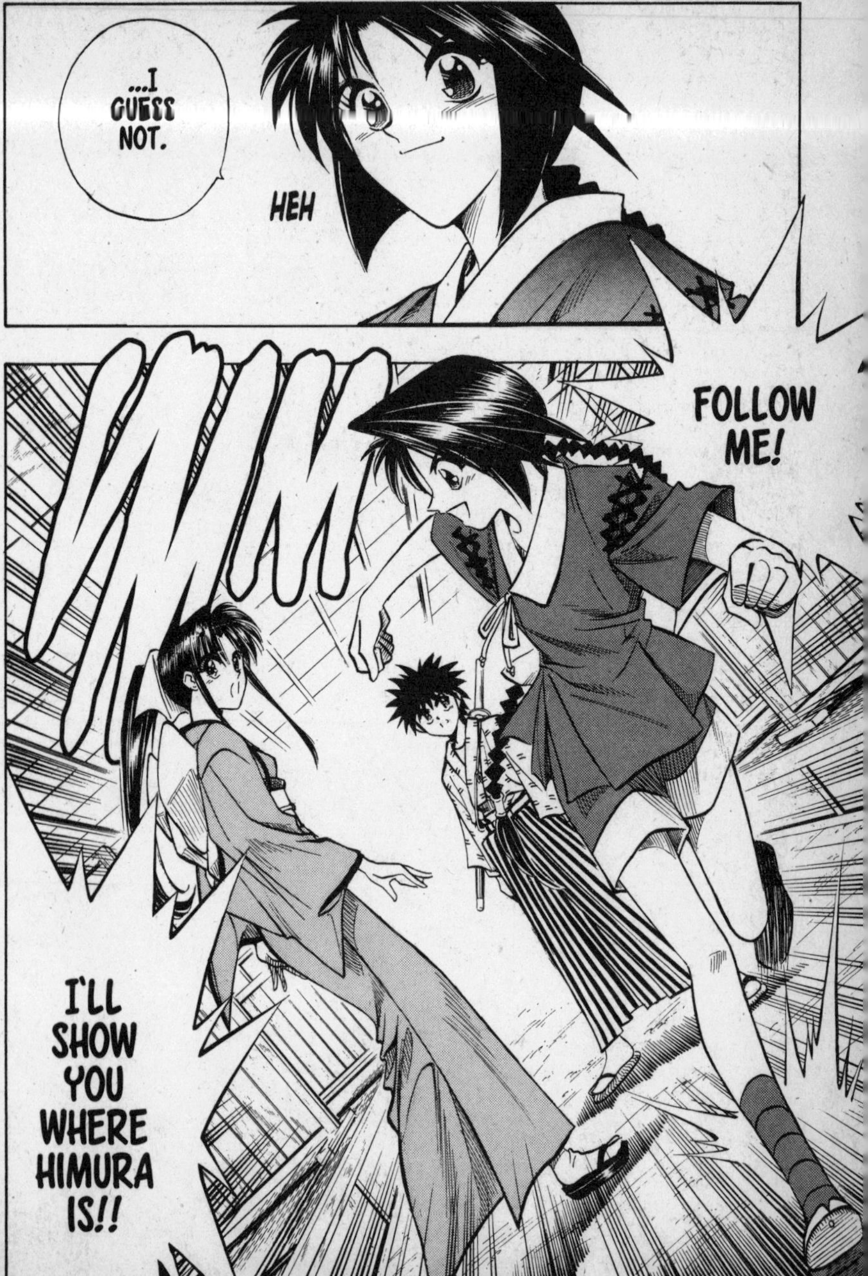
...I GUESS NOT.
HEH
FOLLOW ME!
I'LL SHOW YOU WHERE HIMURA IS!!

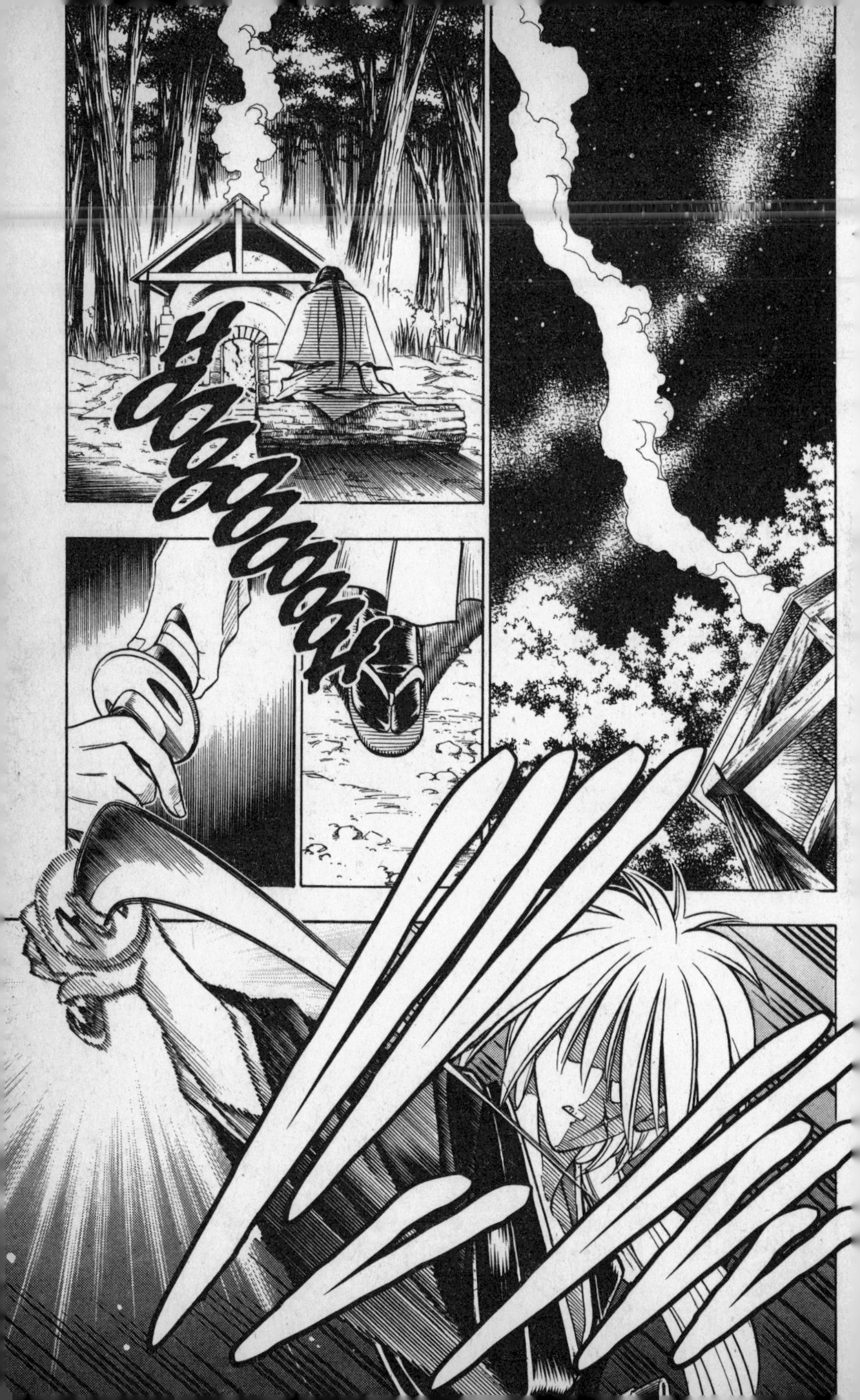

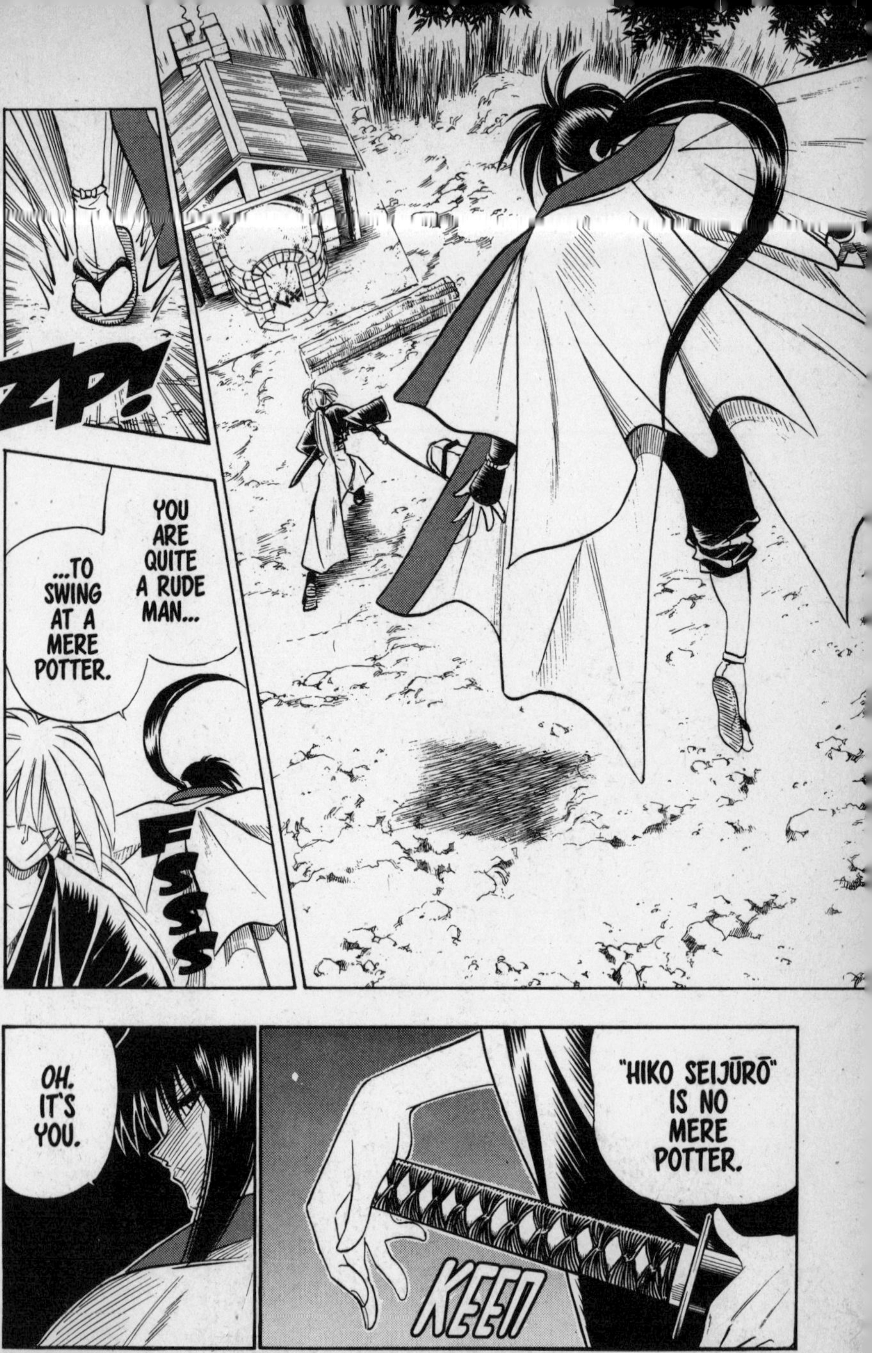

ZIP!
YOU ARE QUITE A RUDE MAN...
...TO SWING AT A MERE POTTER.
FSSS
"HIKO SEIJŪRŌ" IS NO MERE POTTER.
KEEN
OH. IT'S YOU.

READ THIS WAY

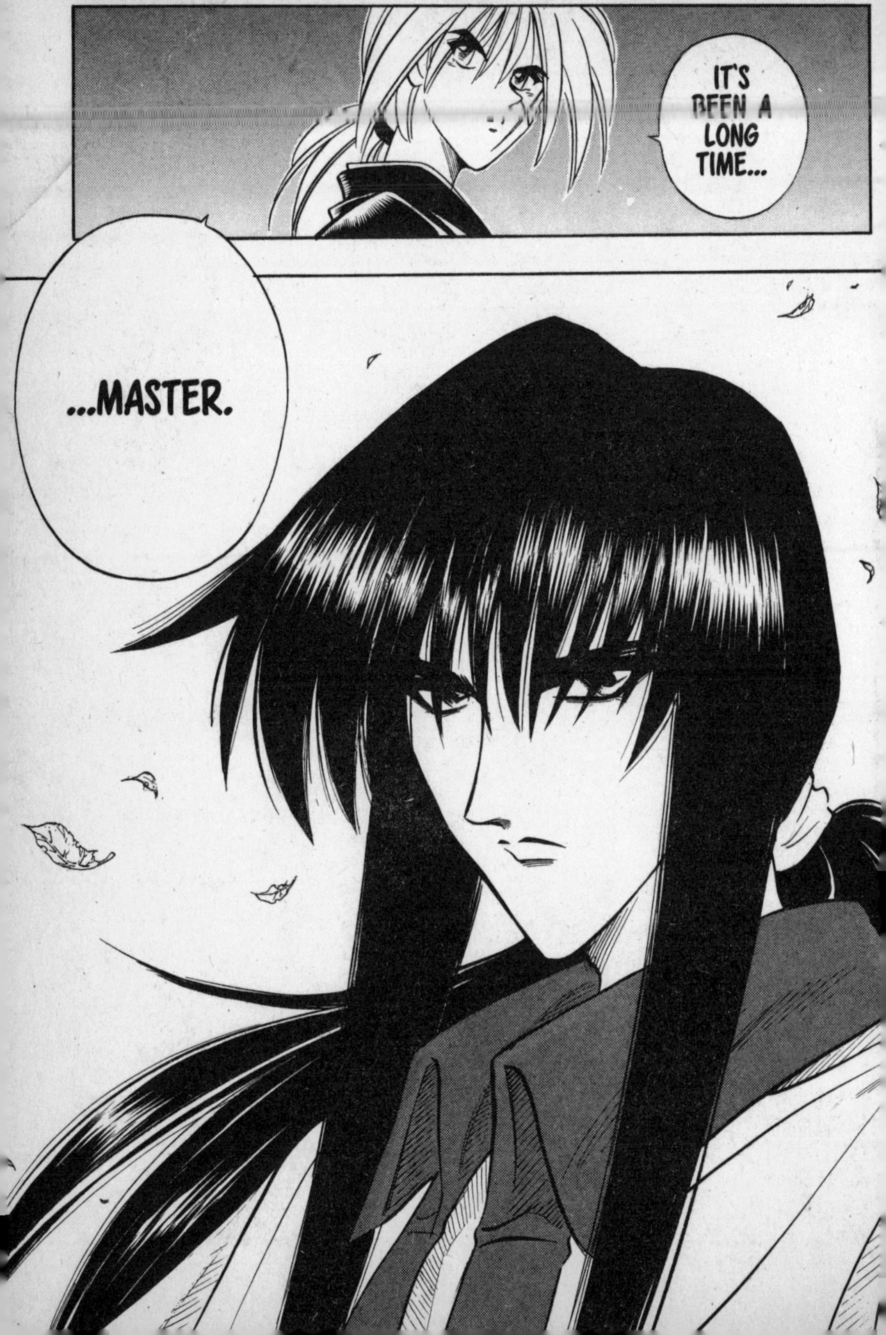
IT'S BEEN A LONG TIME...
...MASTER.

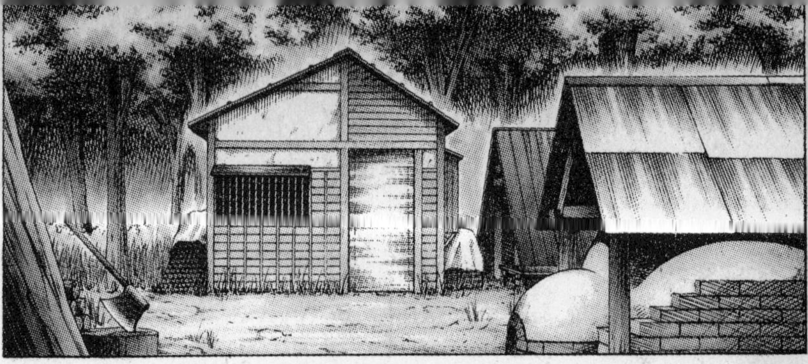

Act 84—The Mitsurugi Apprenticeship

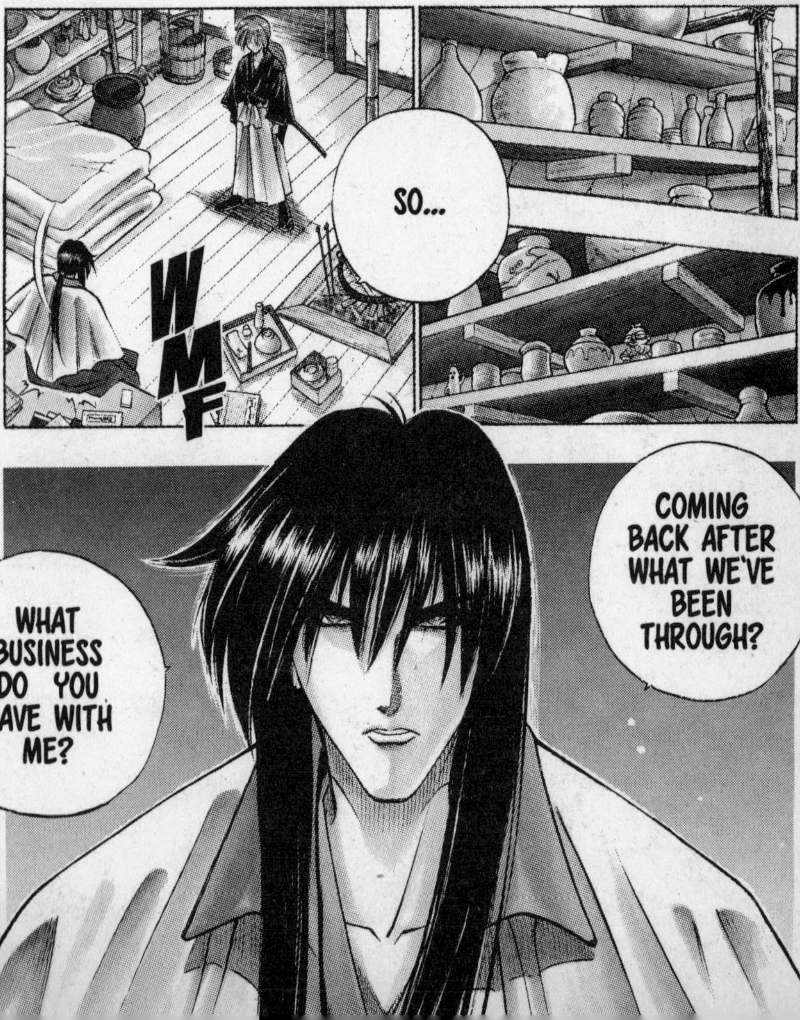
SO...
WMF
COMING BACK AFTER WHAT WE'VE BEEN THROUGH?
WHAT BUSINESS DO YOU HAVE WITH ME?

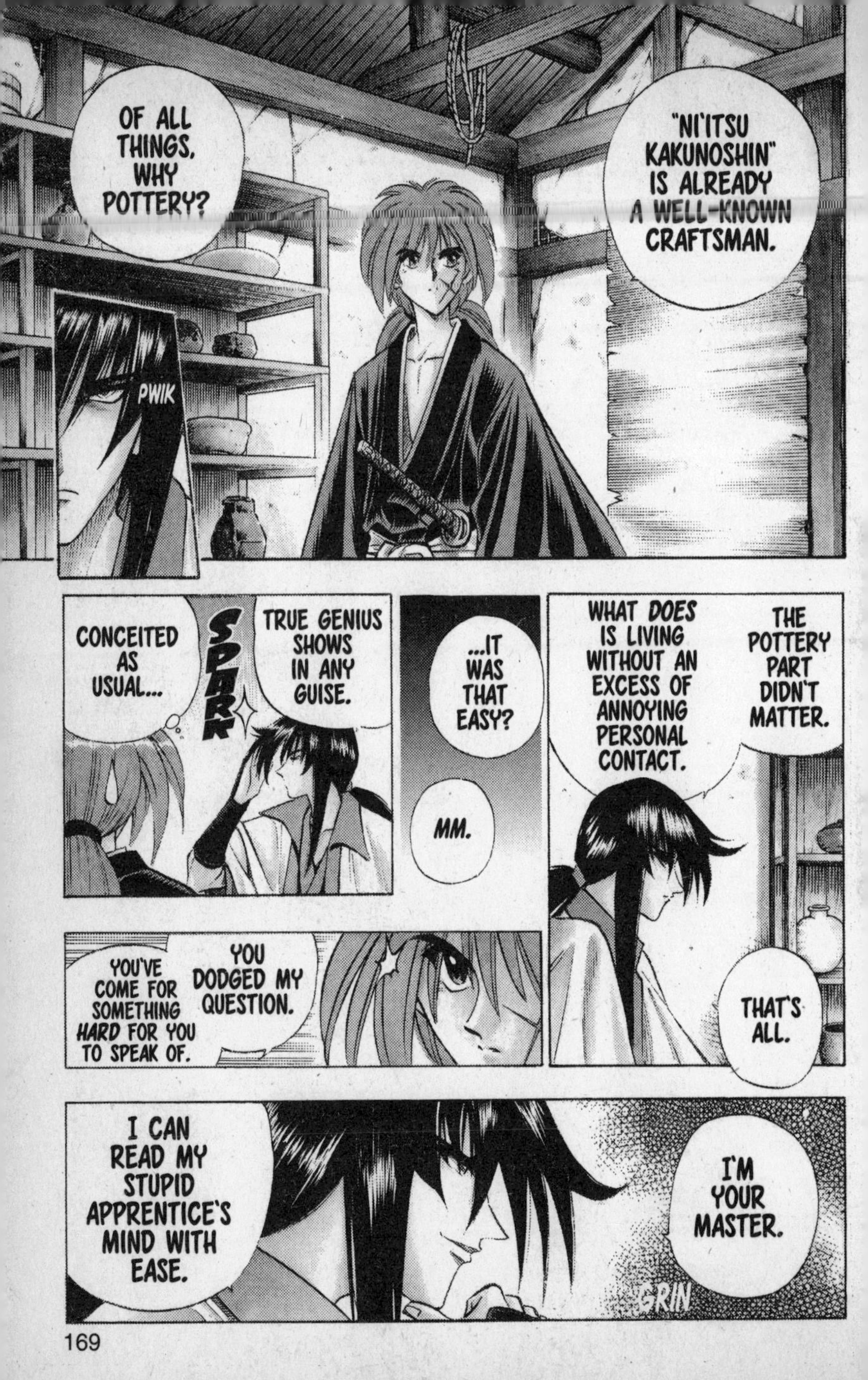
"NI'ITSU KAKUNOSHIN" IS ALREADY A WELL-KNOWN CRAFTSMAN.
OF ALL THINGS, WHY POTTERY?
PWIK
THE POTTERY PART DIDN'T MATTER.
WHAT *DOES* IS LIVING WITHOUT AN EXCESS OF ANNOYING PERSONAL CONTACT.
THAT'S ALL.
...IT WAS THAT EASY?
MM.
TRUE GENIUS SHOWS IN ANY GUISE.
SPARK
CONCEITED AS USUAL...
YOU DODGED MY QUESTION.
YOU'VE COME FOR SOMETHING *HARD* FOR YOU TO SPEAK OF.
I'M YOUR MASTER.
I CAN READ MY STUPID APPRENTICE'S MIND WITH EASE.
GRIN

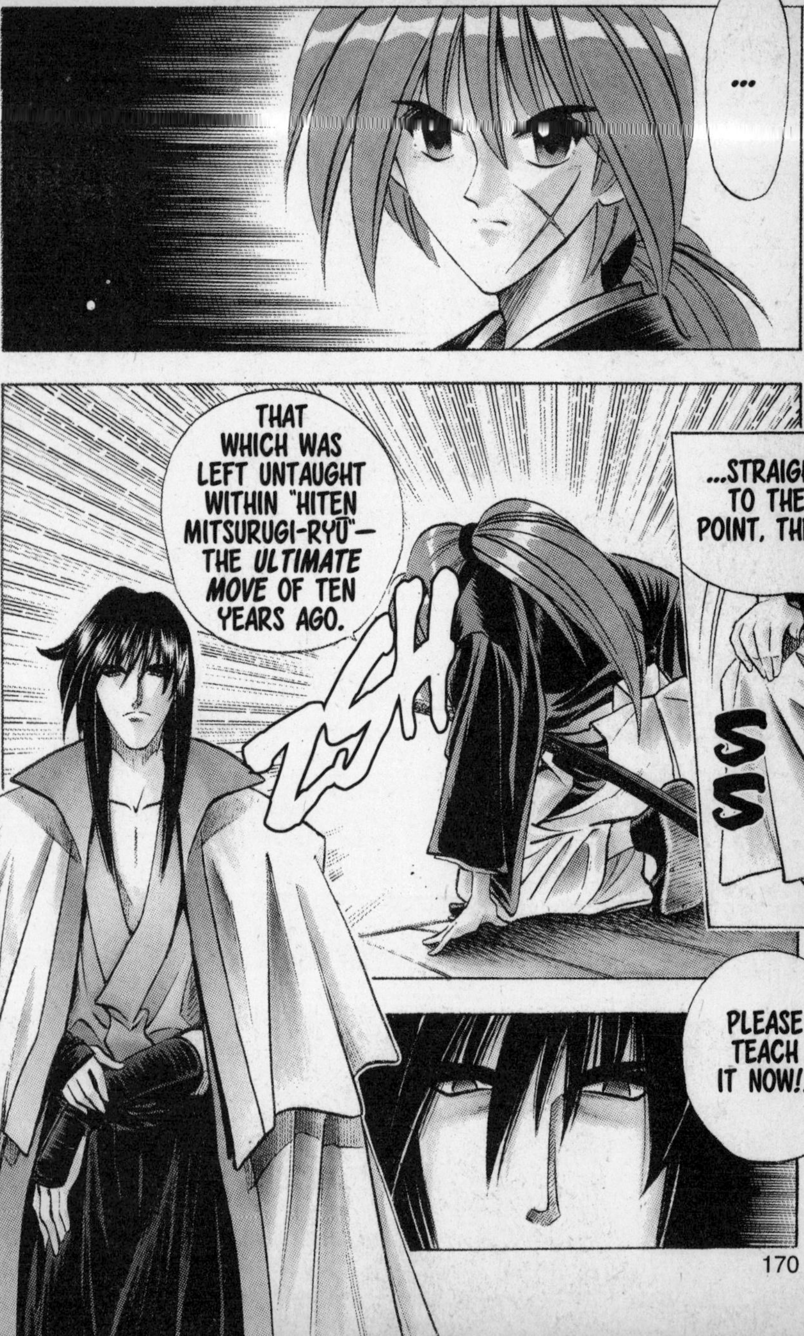
...
...STRAIGHT TO THE POINT, THEN.
SS
THAT WHICH WAS LEFT UNTAUGHT WITHIN "HITEN MITSURUGI-RYŪ"— THE *ULTIMATE MOVE* OF TEN YEARS AGO.
ZSH
PLEASE TEACH IT NOW!!

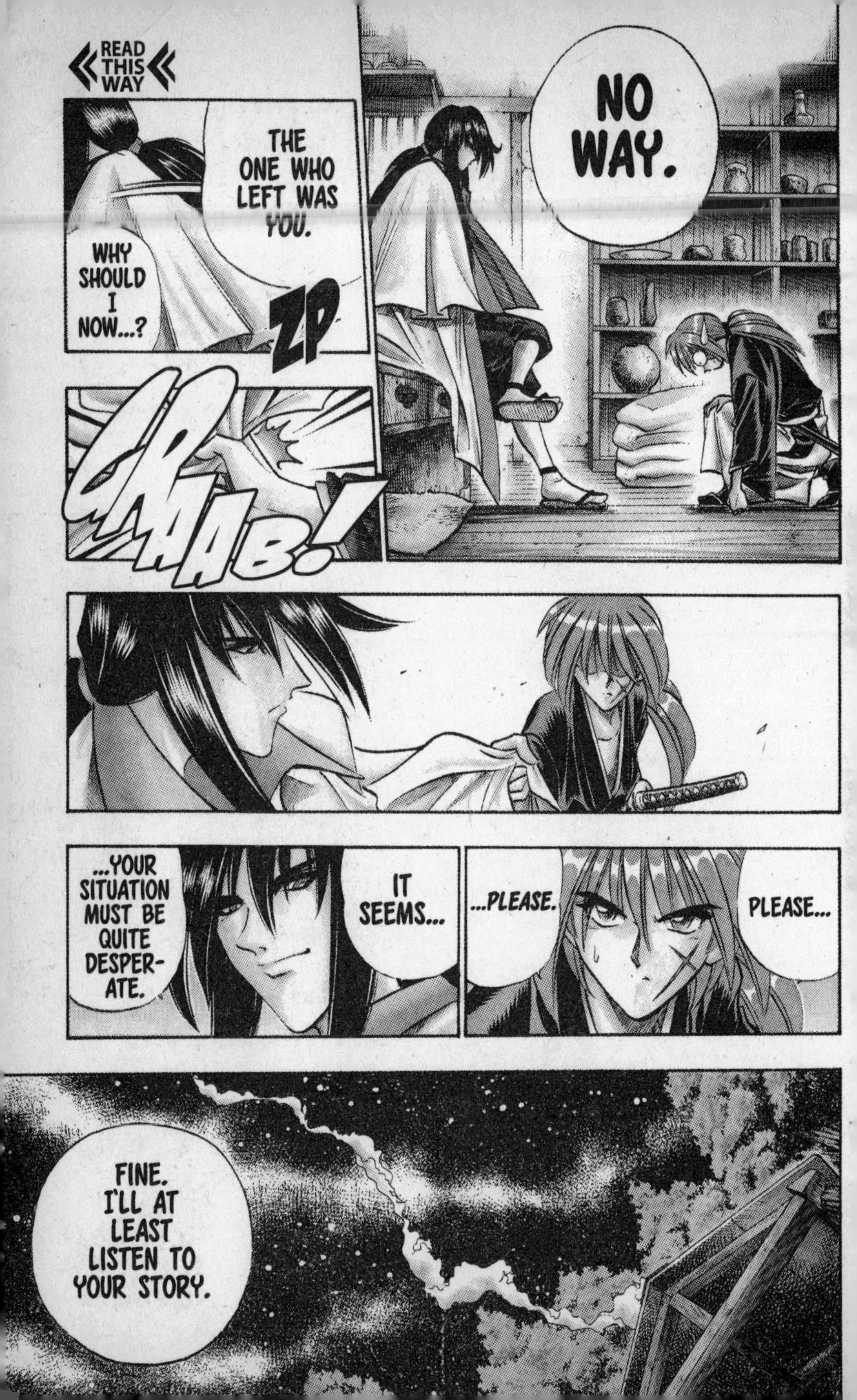
READ THIS WAY
NO WAY.
THE ONE WHO LEFT WAS YOU.
WHY SHOULD I NOW...?
ZP
GRAAB!
PLEASE...
...PLEASE.
IT SEEMS...
...YOUR SITUATION MUST BE QUITE DESPERATE.
FINE. I'LL AT LEAST LISTEN TO YOUR STORY.

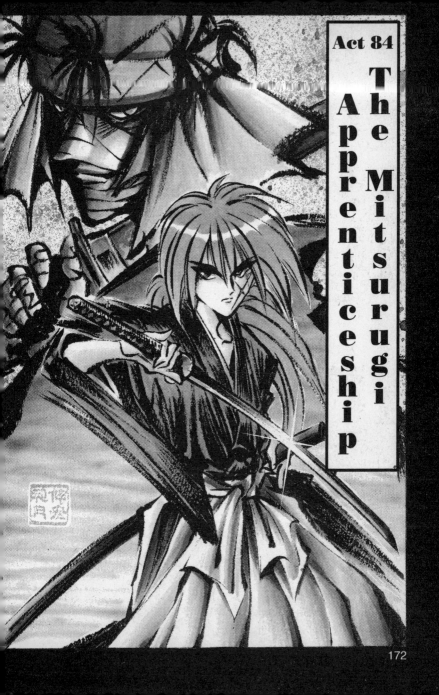

Act 84

The Mitsurugi Apprenticeship

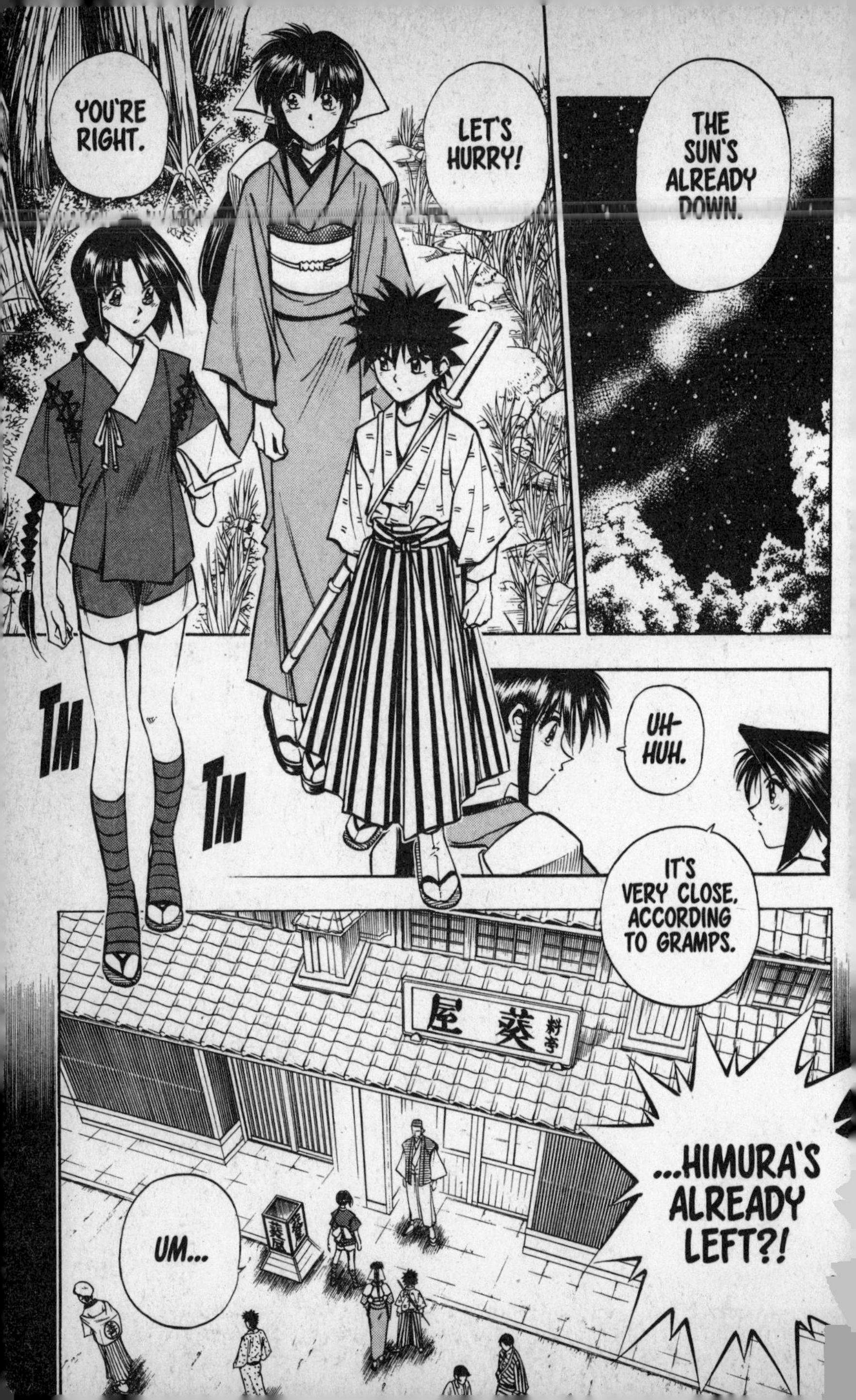
THE SUN'S ALREADY DOWN.
LET'S HURRY!
YOU'RE RIGHT.
TM
TM
UH-HUH.
IT'S VERY CLOSE, ACCORDING TO GRAMPS.
...HIMURA'S ALREADY LEFT?!
UM...

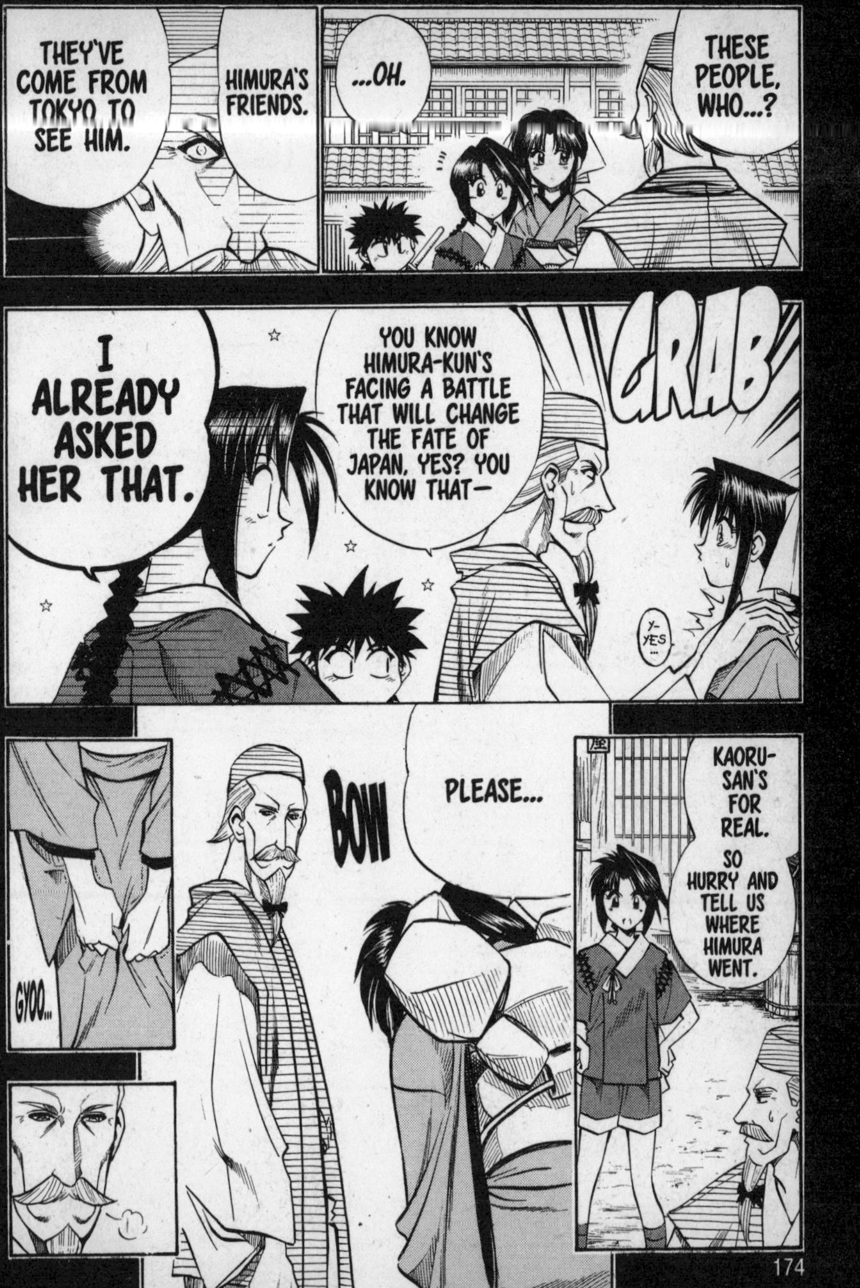
THESE PEOPLE, WHO...?
...OH.
HIMURA'S FRIENDS.
THEY'VE COME FROM TOKYO TO SEE HIM.
GRAB
YOU KNOW HIMURA-KUN'S FACING A BATTLE THAT WILL CHANGE THE FATE OF JAPAN, YES? YOU KNOW THAT—
Y-YES...
I ALREADY ASKED HER THAT.
KAORU-SAN'S FOR REAL.
SO HURRY AND TELL US WHERE HIMURA WENT.
PLEASE...
BOW
GYOO...

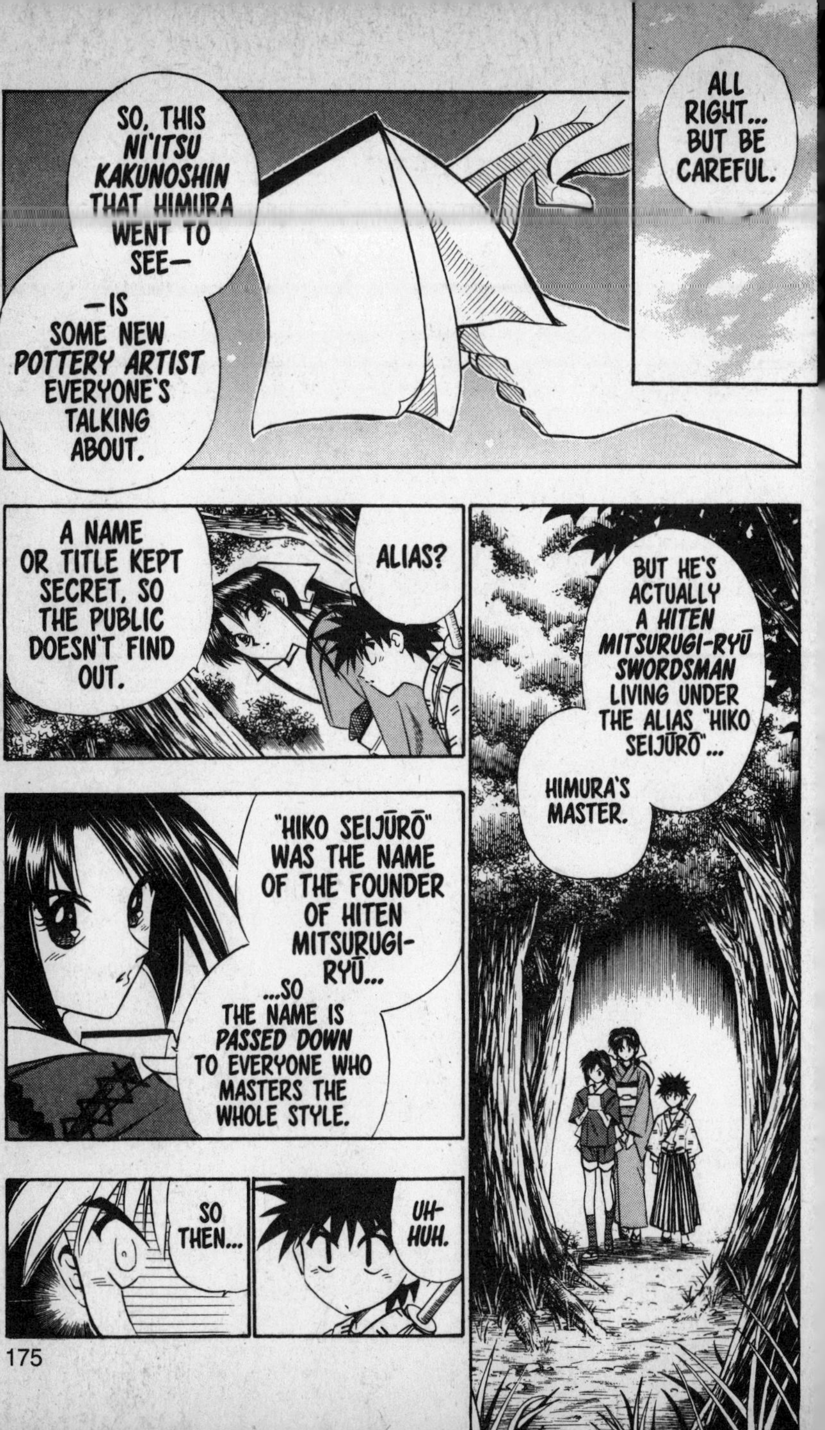
ALL RIGHT... BUT BE CAREFUL.
SO, THIS NI'ITSU KAKUNOSHIN THAT HIMURA WENT TO SEE—
—IS SOME NEW POTTERY ARTIST EVERYONE'S TALKING ABOUT.
BUT HE'S ACTUALLY A HITEN MITSURUGI-RYŪ SWORDSMAN LIVING UNDER THE ALIAS "HIKO SEIJŪRŌ"...
HIMURA'S MASTER.
ALIAS?
A NAME OR TITLE KEPT SECRET, SO THE PUBLIC DOESN'T FIND OUT.
"HIKO SEIJŪRŌ" WAS THE NAME OF THE FOUNDER OF HITEN MITSURUGI-RYŪ...
...SO THE NAME IS PASSED DOWN TO EVERYONE WHO MASTERS THE WHOLE STYLE.
UH-HUH.
SO THEN...

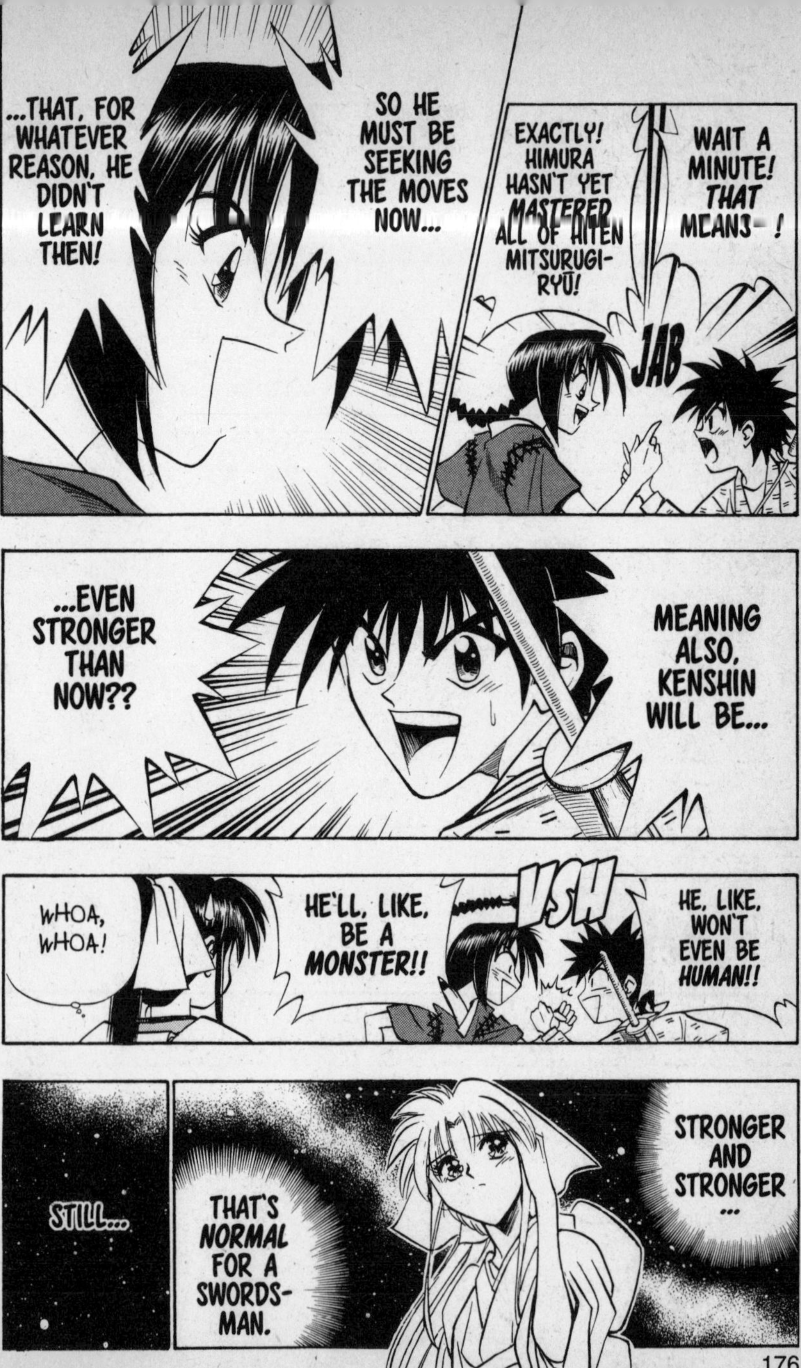
WAIT A MINUTE! *THAT* MEANS— !
EXACTLY! HIMURA HASN'T YET *MASTERED* ALL OF HITEN MITSURUGI-RYŪ!
JAB
SO HE MUST BE SEEKING THE MOVES NOW...
...THAT, FOR WHATEVER REASON, HE DIDN'T LEARN THEN!
MEANING ALSO, KENSHIN WILL BE...
...EVEN STRONGER THAN NOW??
HE, LIKE, WON'T EVEN BE *HUMAN!!*
VSH
HE'LL, LIKE, BE A *MONSTER!!*
WHOA, WHOA!
STRONGER AND STRONGER ...
THAT'S *NORMAL* FOR A SWORDS-MAN.
STILL...

READ THIS WAY

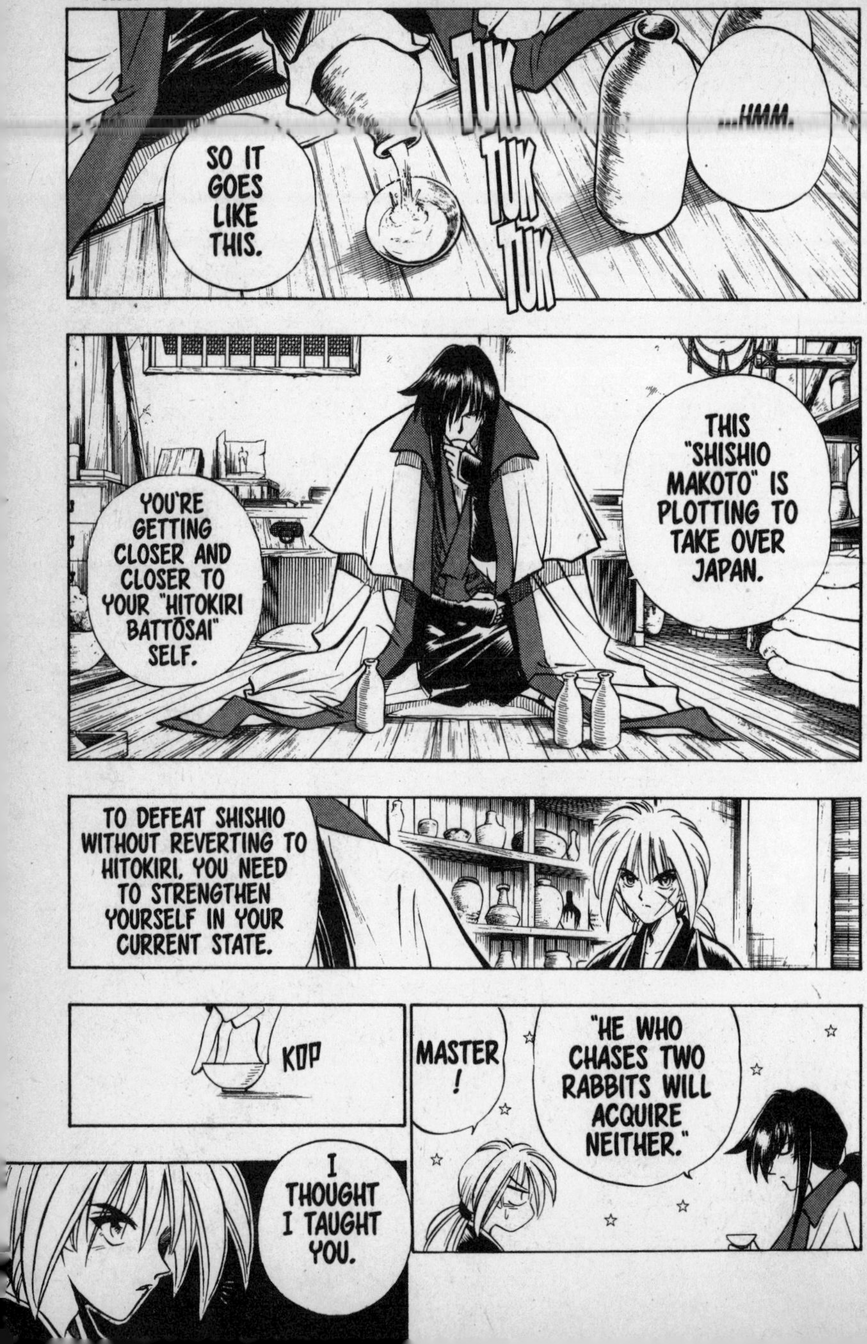

...HMM.
TUK TUK TUK
SO IT GOES LIKE THIS.
THIS "SHISHIO MAKOTO" IS PLOTTING TO TAKE OVER JAPAN.
YOU'RE GETTING CLOSER AND CLOSER TO YOUR "HITOKIRI BATTŌSAI" SELF.
TO DEFEAT SHISHIO WITHOUT REVERTING TO HITOKIRI, YOU NEED TO STRENGTHEN YOURSELF IN YOUR CURRENT STATE.
"HE WHO CHASES TWO RABBITS WILL ACQUIRE NEITHER."
MASTER!
KOP
I THOUGHT I TAUGHT YOU.

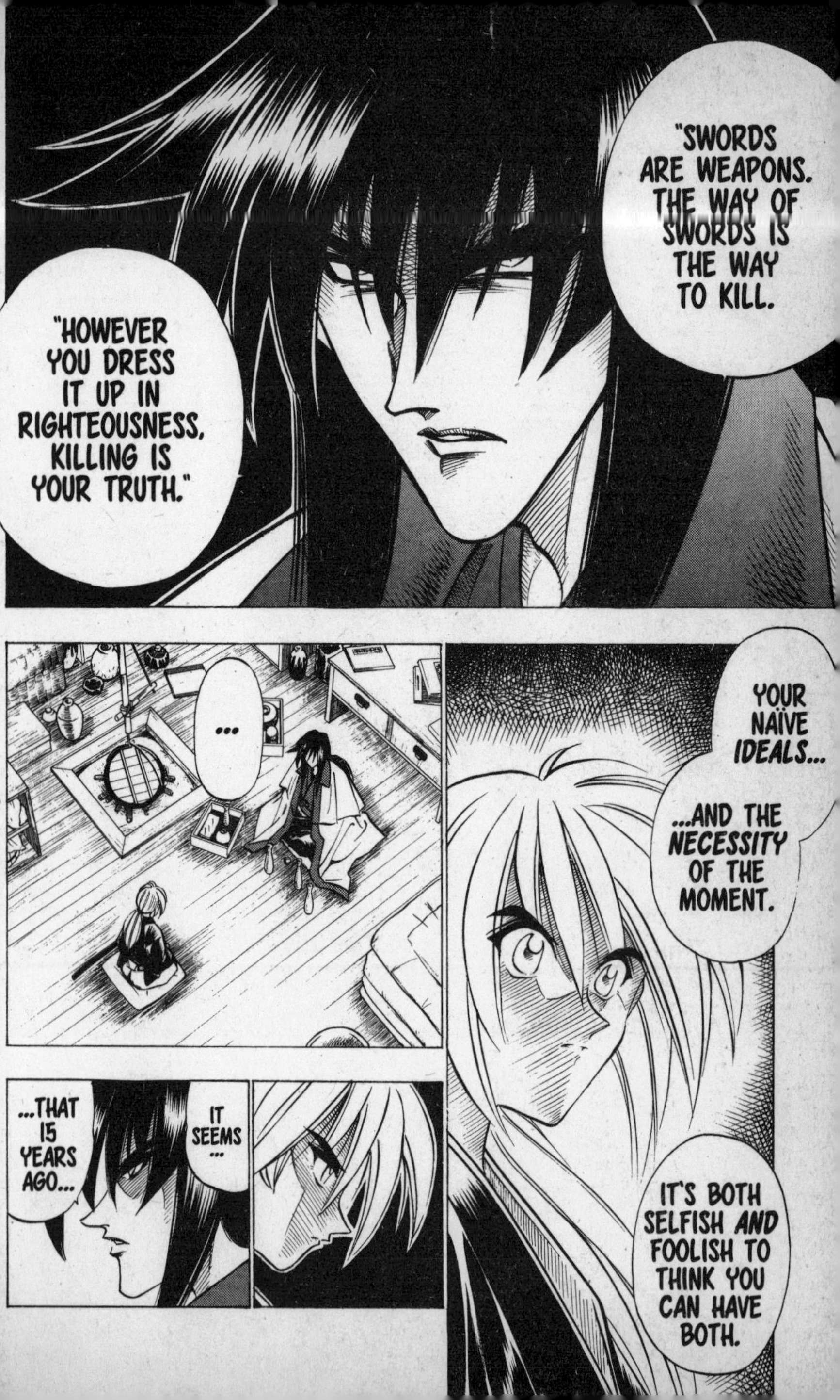
"SWORDS ARE WEAPONS. THE WAY OF SWORDS IS THE WAY TO KILL.
"HOWEVER YOU DRESS IT UP IN RIGHTEOUSNESS, KILLING IS YOUR TRUTH."
YOUR NAÏVE *IDEALS*...
...AND THE *NECESSITY* OF THE MOMENT.
IT'S BOTH SELFISH *AND* FOOLISH TO THINK YOU CAN HAVE BOTH.
...
IT SEEMS...
...THAT 15 YEARS AGO...

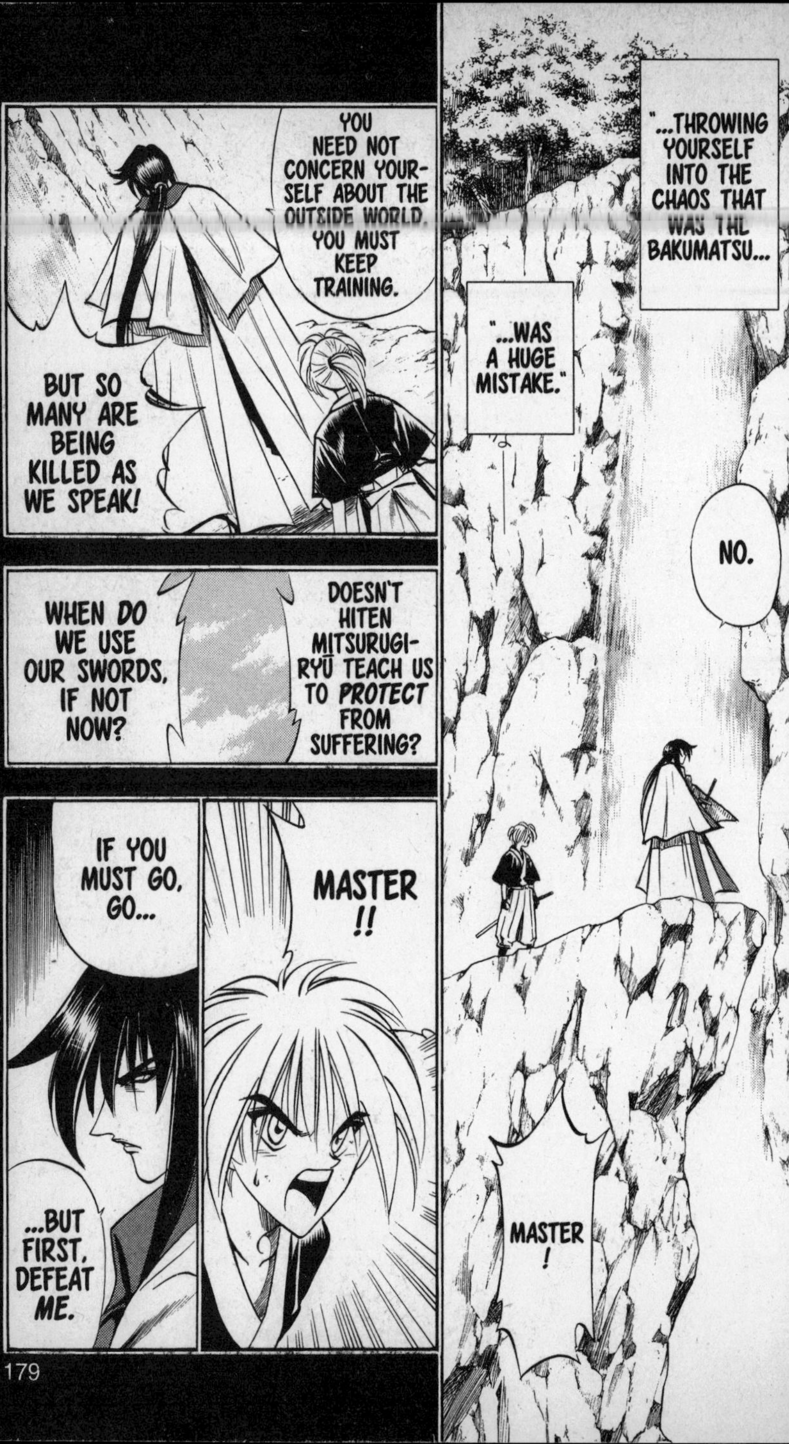
"...THROWING YOURSELF INTO THE CHAOS THAT WAS THE BAKUMATSU...
"...WAS A HUGE MISTAKE."
NO.
MASTER!
YOU NEED NOT CONCERN YOURSELF ABOUT THE OUTSIDE WORLD. YOU MUST KEEP TRAINING.
BUT SO MANY ARE BEING KILLED AS WE SPEAK!
DOESN'T HITEN MITSURUGI-RYŪ TEACH US TO *PROTECT* FROM SUFFERING?
WHEN *DO* WE USE OUR SWORDS, IF NOT NOW?
MASTER!!
IF YOU MUST GO, GO...
...BUT FIRST, DEFEAT *ME*.

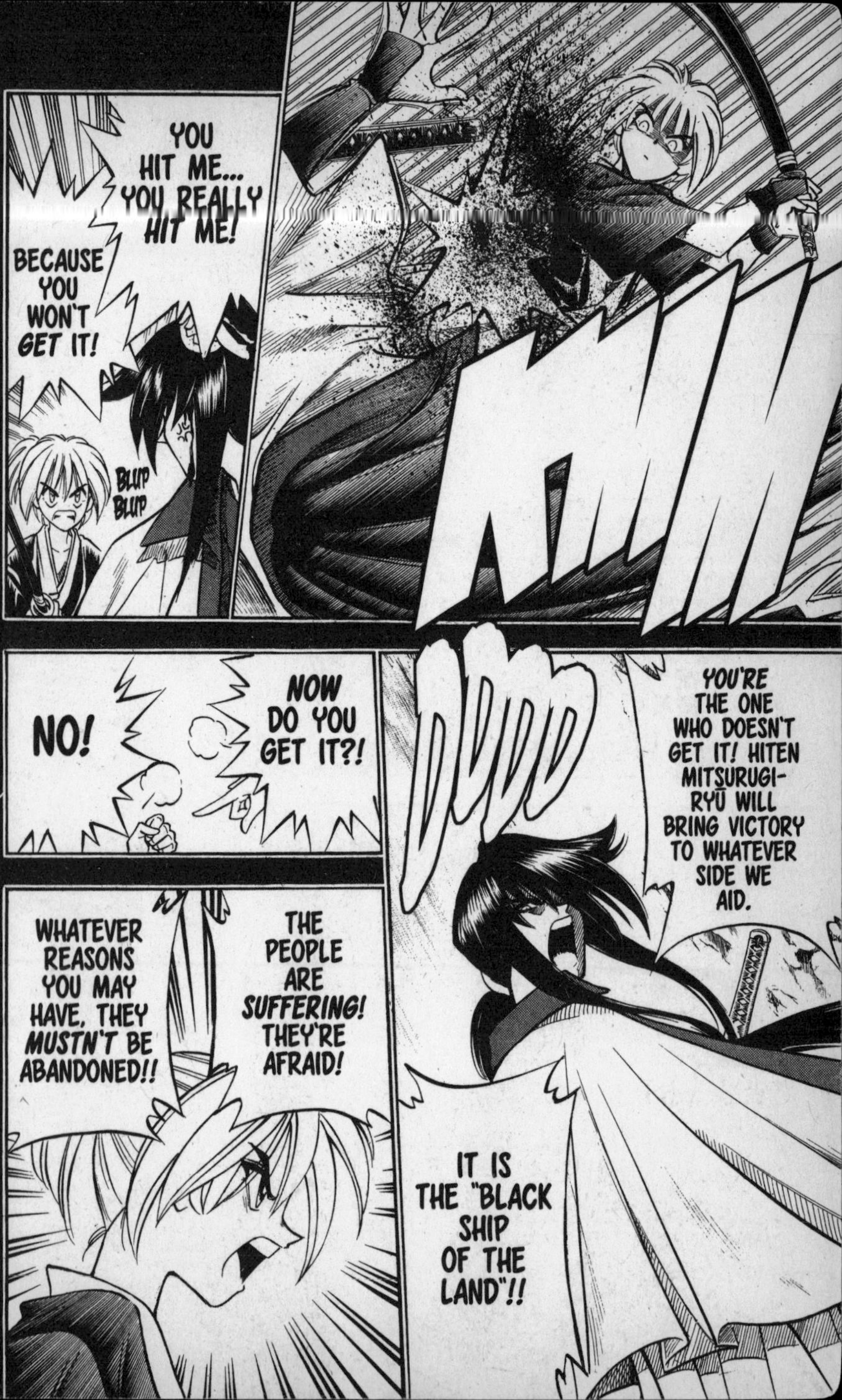
YOU HIT ME... YOU REALLY HIT ME!
BECAUSE YOU WON'T GET IT!
BLUP BLUP
YOU'RE THE ONE WHO DOESN'T GET IT! HITEN MITSURUGI-RYŪ WILL BRING VICTORY TO WHATEVER SIDE WE AID.
IT IS THE "BLACK SHIP OF THE LAND"!!
NOW DO YOU GET IT?!
NO!
THE PEOPLE ARE SUFFERING! THEY'RE AFRAID!
WHATEVER REASONS YOU MAY HAVE, THEY MUSTN'T BE ABANDONED!!

READ THIS WAY

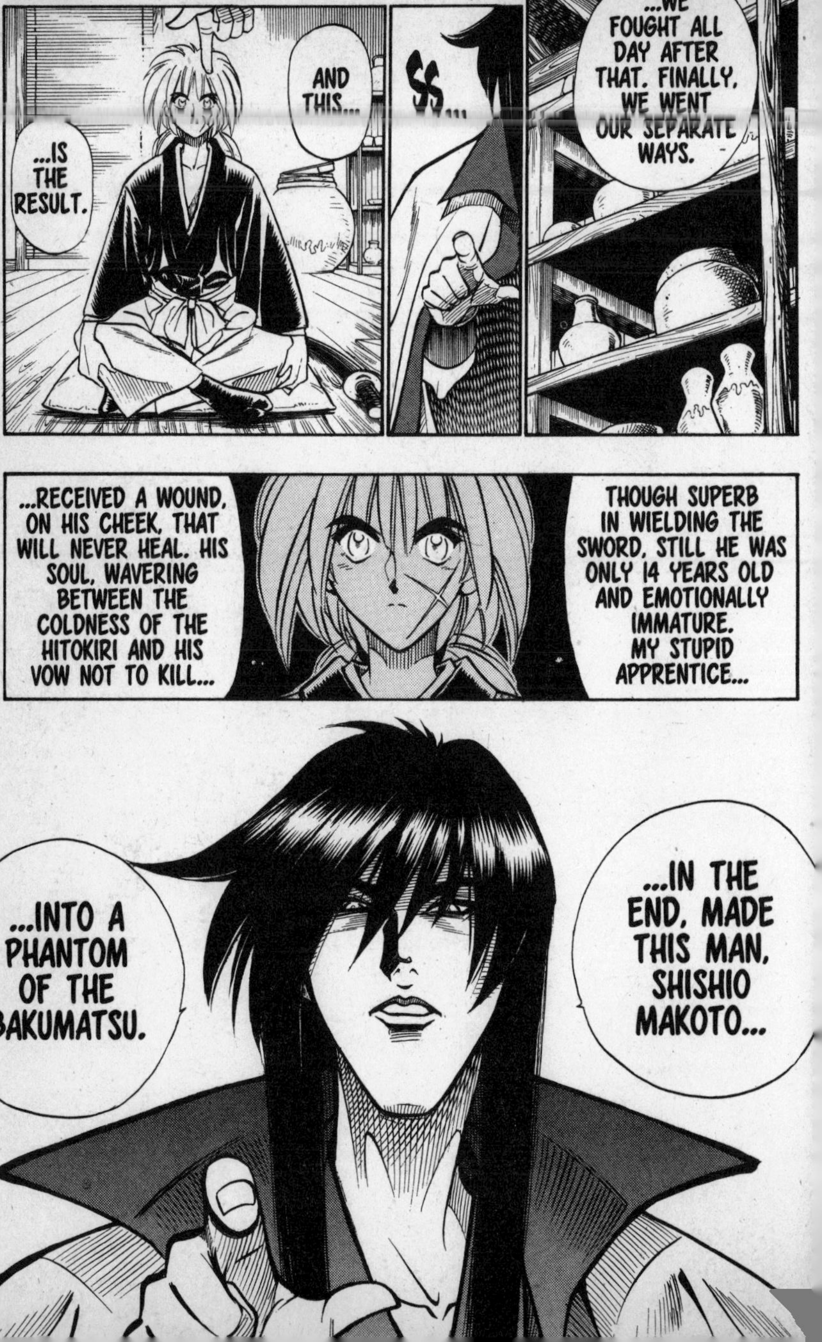
...WE FOUGHT ALL DAY AFTER THAT. FINALLY, WE WENT OUR SEPARATE WAYS.
SS...
AND THIS...
...IS THE RESULT.
THOUGH SUPERB IN WIELDING THE SWORD, STILL HE WAS ONLY 14 YEARS OLD AND EMOTIONALLY IMMATURE. MY STUPID APPRENTICE...
...RECEIVED A WOUND, ON HIS CHEEK, THAT WILL NEVER HEAL. HIS SOUL, WAVERING BETWEEN THE COLDNESS OF THE HITOKIRI AND HIS VOW NOT TO KILL...
...IN THE END, MADE THIS MAN, SHISHIO MAKOTO...
...INTO A PHANTOM OF THE BAKUMATSU.

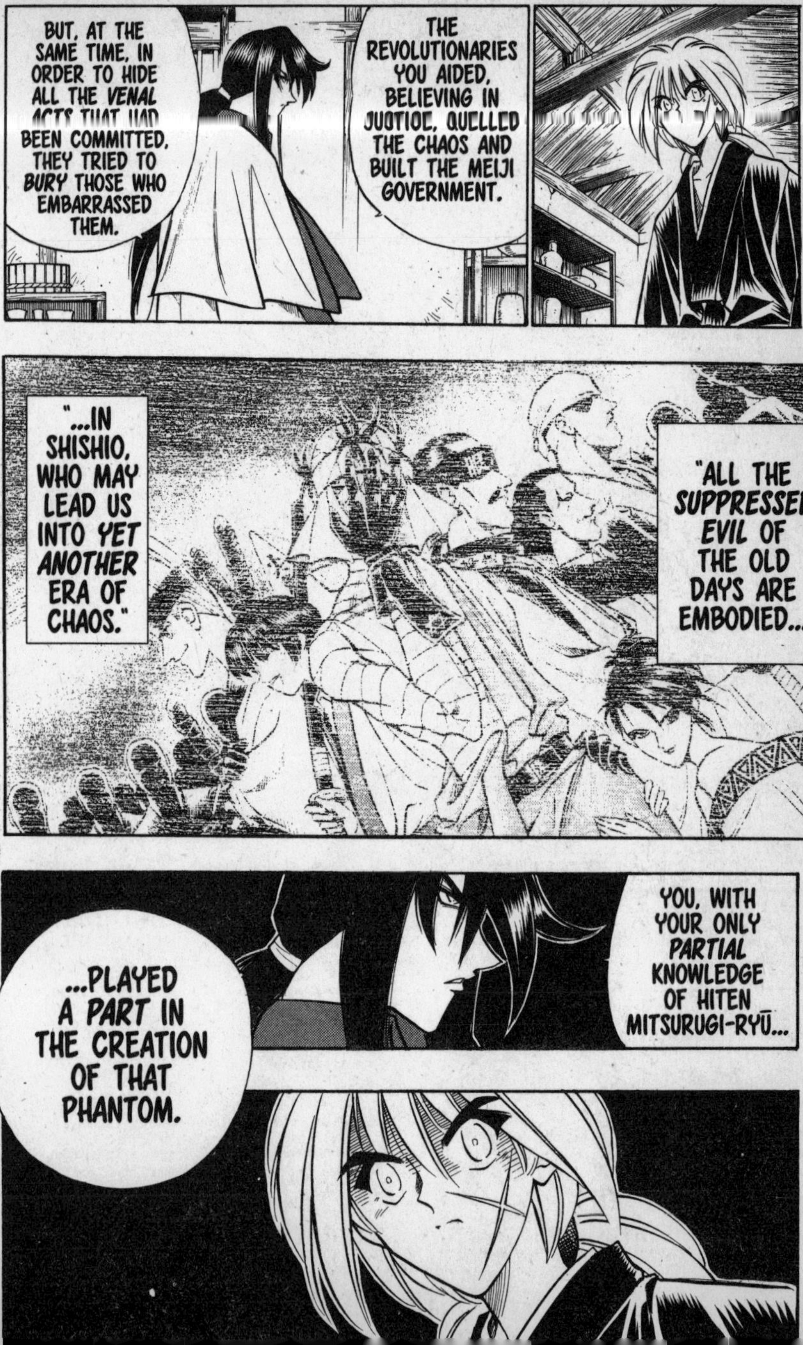
THE REVOLUTIONARIES YOU AIDED, BELIEVING IN JUSTICE, QUELLED THE CHAOS AND BUILT THE MEIJI GOVERNMENT.
BUT, AT THE SAME TIME, IN ORDER TO HIDE ALL THE VENAL ACTS THAT HAD BEEN COMMITTED, THEY TRIED TO BURY THOSE WHO EMBARRASSED THEM.
"ALL THE SUPPRESSED EVIL OF THE OLD DAYS ARE EMBODIED...
"...IN SHISHIO, WHO MAY LEAD US INTO YET ANOTHER ERA OF CHAOS."
YOU, WITH YOUR ONLY PARTIAL KNOWLEDGE OF HITEN MITSURUGI-RYŪ...
...PLAYED A PART IN THE CREATION OF THAT PHANTOM.

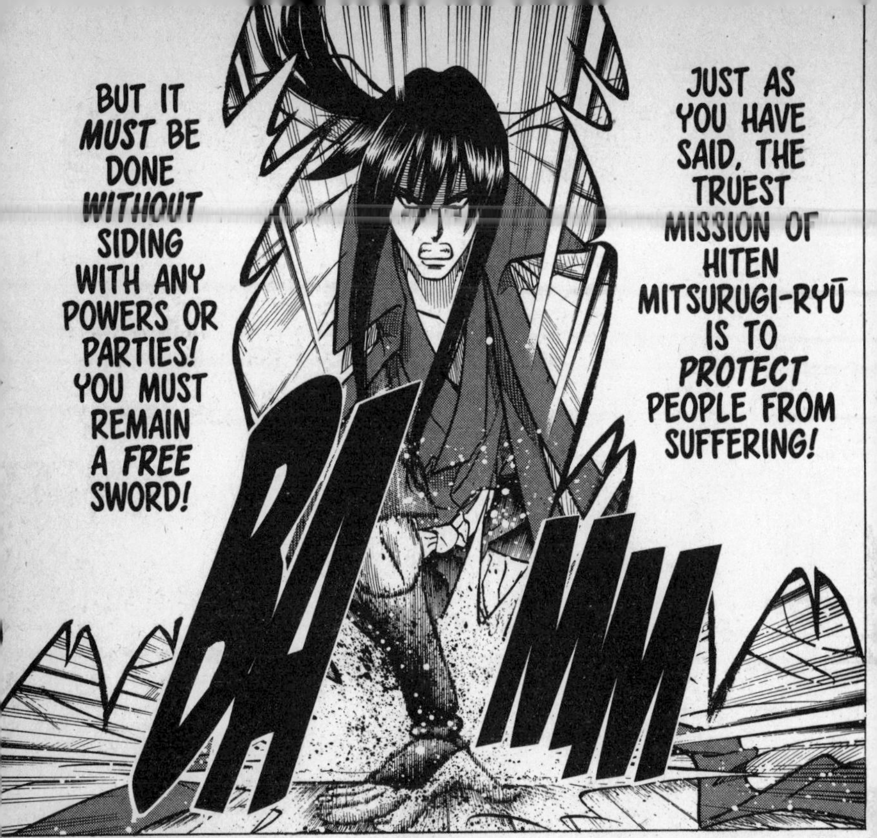
JUST AS YOU HAVE SAID, THE TRUEST MISSION OF HITEN MITSURUGI-RYŪ IS TO *PROTECT* PEOPLE FROM SUFFERING!
BUT IT *MUST* BE DONE *WITHOUT* SIDING WITH ANY POWERS OR PARTIES! YOU MUST REMAIN A *FREE* SWORD!

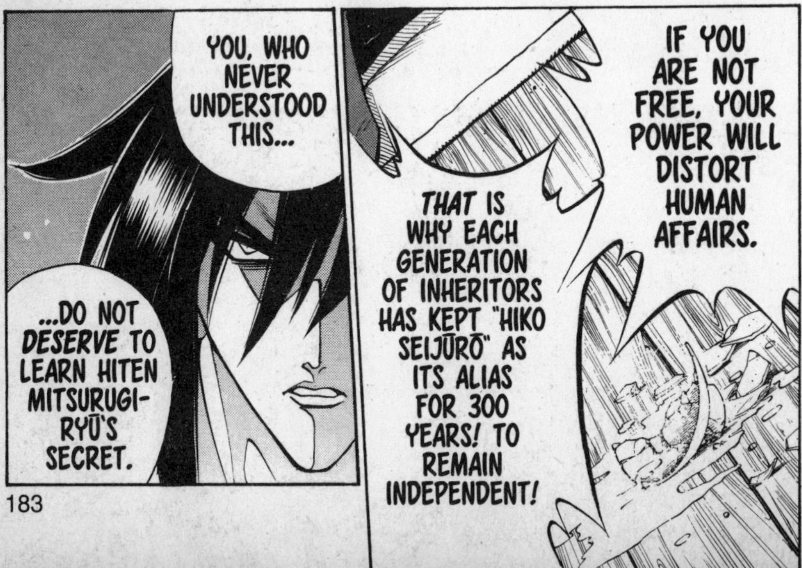
IF YOU ARE NOT FREE, YOUR POWER WILL DISTORT HUMAN AFFAIRS.
THAT IS WHY EACH GENERATION OF INHERITORS HAS KEPT "HIKO SEIJŪRŌ" AS ITS ALIAS FOR 300 YEARS! TO REMAIN INDEPENDENT!
YOU, WHO NEVER UNDERSTOOD THIS...
...DO NOT *DESERVE* TO LEARN HITEN MITSURUGI-RYŪ'S SECRET.

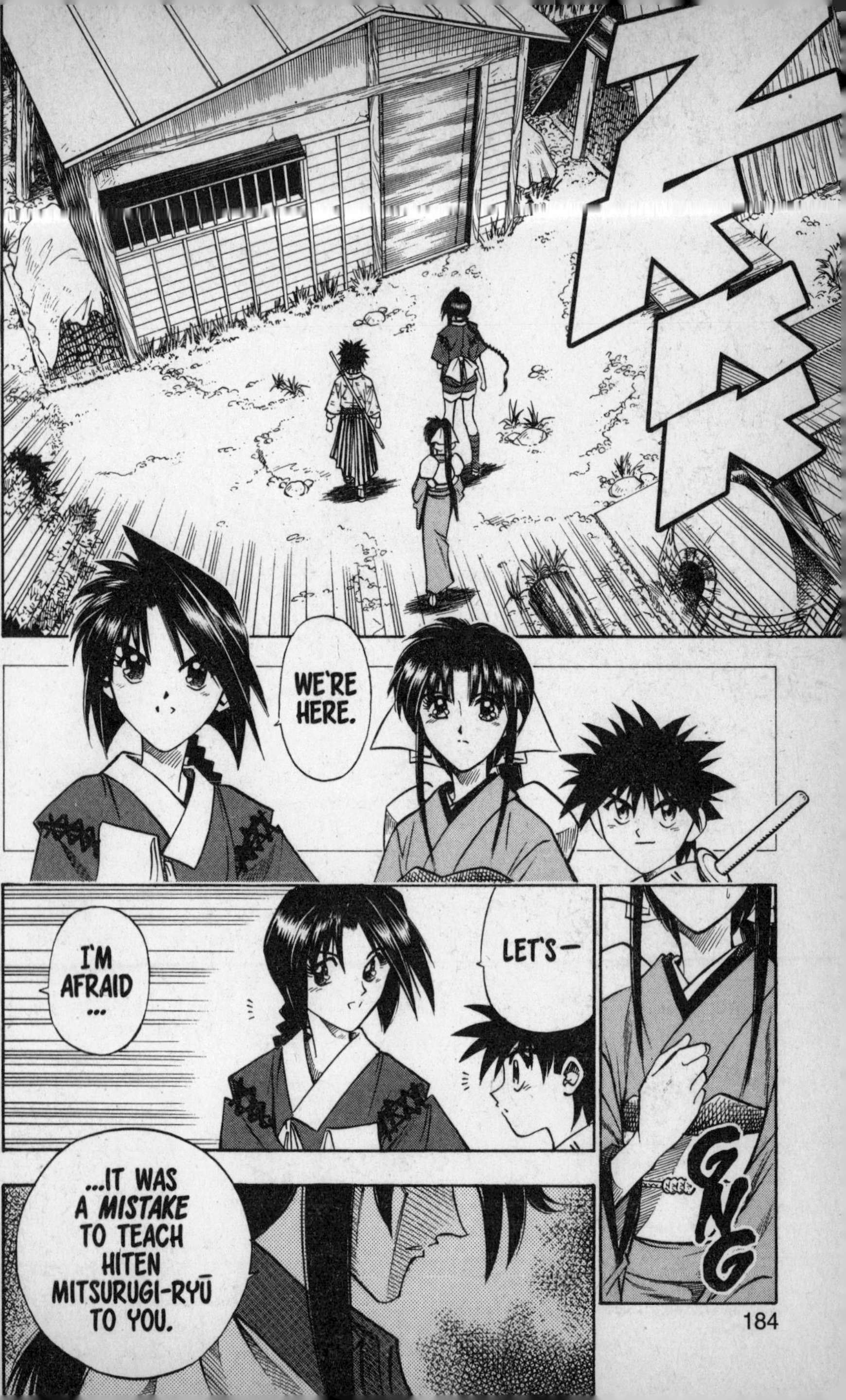
WE'RE HERE.
LET'S—
I'M AFRAID ...
...IT WAS A *MISTAKE* TO TEACH HITEN MITSURUGI-RYŪ TO YOU.

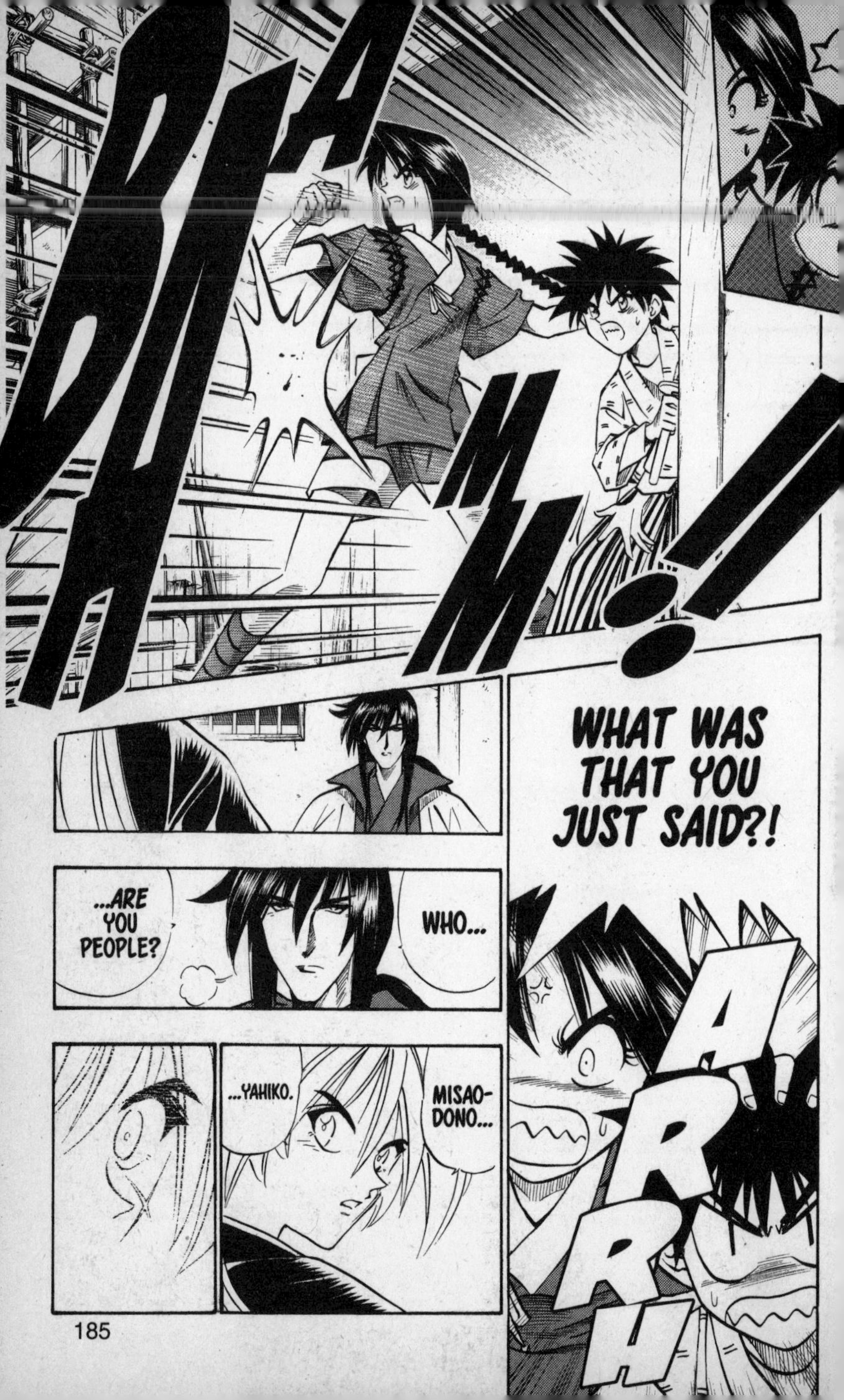
WHAT WAS THAT YOU JUST SAID?!
ARRH
WHO...
...ARE YOU PEOPLE?
MISAO-DONO...
...YAHIKO.

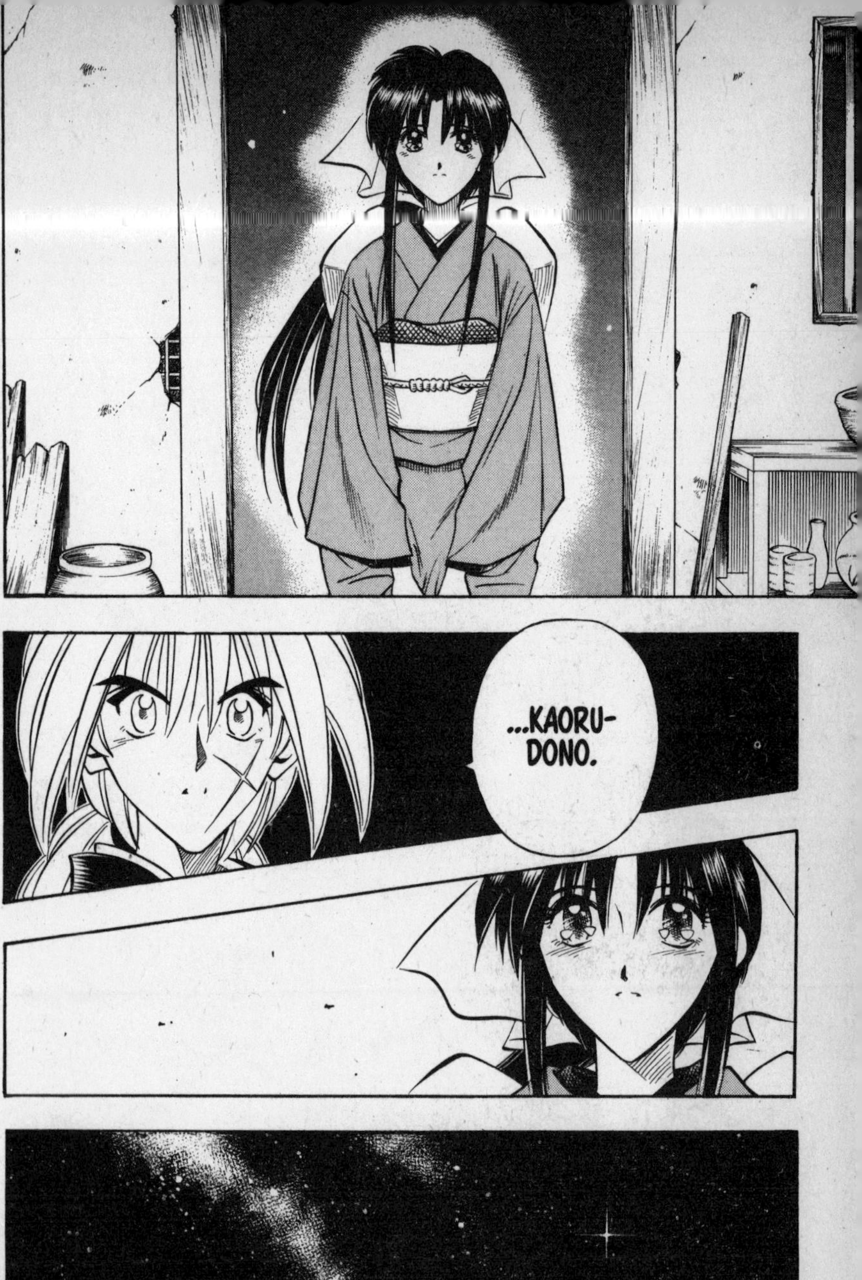
...KAORU-DONO.

To Be Continued in Volume 11: Overture to Destruction

Rurouni Kenshin

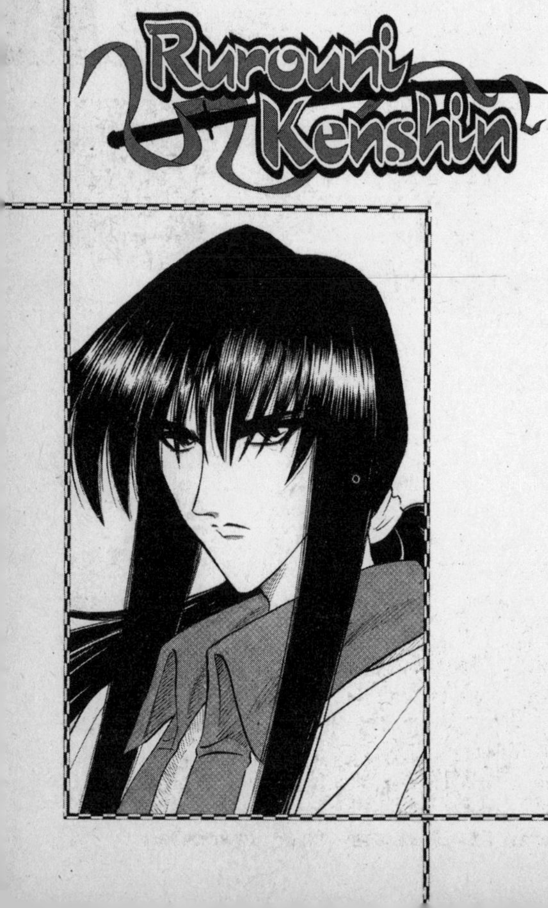

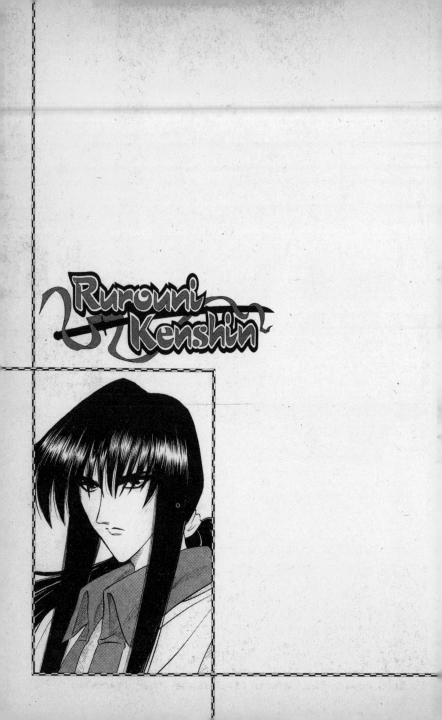

GLOSSARY of the RESTORATION

A brief guide to select Japanese terms used in **Rurouni Kenshin**. *Note that, both here and within the story itself, all names are Japanese style—i.e., last or "family" name first, with personal or "given" name following. This is both because* **Kenshin** *is a "period" story, as well as to decrease confusion—if we were to take the example of Kenshin's* sakabatô *and "reverse" the format of the historically established assassin-name "Hitokiri Battôsai," for example, it would make little sense to then call him "Battôsai Himura."*

Hiten Mitsurugi-ryû
Kenshin's sword technique, used more for defense than offense. An "ancient style that pits one against many," it requires exceptional speed and agility to master.

hitokiri
An assassin. Famous swordsmen of the period were sometimes thus known to adopt "professional" names—**Kawakami Gensai**, for example, was also known as "Hitokiri Gensai."

Ishin Shishi
Loyalist or pro-Imperialist **patriots** who fought to restore the Emperor to his ancient seat of power

Juppongatana
Written with the characters for "ten" and "swords," Shishio's **Juppongatana** are literally that—the ten "swords" or generals he plans to use in his overthrow of Japan

Kamiya Kasshin-ryû
Sword-arts or **kenjutsu** school established by Kaoru's father, who rejected the ethics of **Satsujin-ken** for **Katsujin-ken**

katana
Traditional Japanese longsword (curved, single-edge, worn cutting-edge up) of the samurai. Used primarily for slashing; can be wielded either one- or two-handed.

Katsujin-ken
"Swords that give life"; the sword-arts style developed over ten years by Kaoru's father and founding principle of **Kamiya Kasshin-ryû**

Bakumatsu
Final, chaotic days of the Tokugawa regime

-chan
Honorific. Can be used either as a diminutive (e.g., with a small child—"Little Hanako or Kentarô"), or with those who are grown, to indicate affection ("My dear...").

dojo
Martial arts training hall

-dono
Honorific. Even more respectful than **–san**; the effect in modern-day Japanese conversation would be along the lines of "Milord So-and-So." As used by Kenshin, it indicates both respect and humility.

Edo
Capital city of the **Tokugawa Bakufu**; renamed **Tokyo** ("Eastern Capital") after the Meiji Restoration

"Gojaru!"
Rendered in the English version as "shake, shake," in Japanese one thing Baby Iori says over and over is "gojaru"—his version of "degozaru," the polite, humble verb that is Kenshin's trademark. Thus, when Iori in the Japanese version says "gojaru," what he's really saying is: "Kenshin!"

Himura Battôsai
Swordsman of legendary skills and former assassin (*hitokiri*) of the **Ishin Shishi**

Himura Kenshin
Kenshin's "real" name, revealed to Kaoru only at her urging

sakabatô
Reversed-edge sword (the dull edge on the side the sharp should be, and vice-versa); carried by Kenshin as a symbol of his resolution never to kill again

-sama
Honorific. Even more respectful than **-dono**. Used to show extreme respect—and when used in reference to Shishio—extreme fear.

-san
Honorific. Carries the meaning of "Mr.," "Ms.," "Miss," etc., but used more extensively in Japanese than its English equivalent (note that even an enemy may be addressed as "-san").

Satsujin-ken
"Swords that give death"; a style of swordsmanship rejected by Kaoru's father

Shinsengumi
"True to the old ways and risking their lives to preserve the old shôgunate system," the popular view of the **Shinsengumi** ("newly elected group") was that of swordsmen as charismatic as they were skilled. Of note: Thanks to the popularity of the NHK drama of the same name, several historical sites in Japan are reportedly enjoying record attendance levels of late.

shôgun
Feudal military ruler of Japan

shôgunate
See **Tokugawa Bakufu**

Tokugawa Bakufu
Military feudal government which dominated Japan from 1603 to 1867

Tokyo
The renaming of "**Edo**" to "**Tokyo**" is a marker of the start of the **Meiji Restoration**

Wolves of Mibu
Nickname for the **Shinsengumi**, so called because of the town (Mibu) where they were first stationed

Kawakami Gensai
Real-life, historical inspiration for the character of **Himura Kenshin**

kenjutsu
The art of fencing; sword arts; kendô

-kun
Honorific. Used in the modern day among male students, or those who grew up together, but another usage—the one you're more likely to find in Rurouni Kenshin—is the "superior-to-inferior" form, intended as a way to emphasize a difference in status or rank, as well as to indicate familiarity or affection.

kunoichi
Female ninja. In that they are not referred to as simply "onmitsu" (ninja), their special name suggests their relative scarcity.

loyalists
Those who supported the return of the Emperor to power; **Ishin Shishi**

Meiji Restoration
1853-1868; culminated in the collapse of the **Tokugawa Bakufu** and the restoration of imperial rule. So called after Emperor Meiji, whose chosen name was written with the characters for "culture and enlightenment."

patriots
Another term for **Ishin Shishi**... and when used by Sano, not a flattering one

rurouni
Wanderer, vagabond

ryûshôsen
Sometimes translated as "Soaring Dragon Flash," the **ryûshôsen** of Kenshin's Hiten Mitsurugi school is one of his special moves, and is also known as "Dragon Flight"

ryûkansen
Also translatable as "Winding Dragon Flash," Kenshin's Hiten Mitsurugi school special move ryûkansen is given in here as "Dragon Spiral Strike"

IN THE NEXT VOLUME...

Kaoru finally manages to find Kenshin in Kyoto—at the home of his former Hiten Mitsurugi master, Hiko Seijûrô! As other, dangerous forces start coming together in Kyoto, Kenshin takes on the role of pupil once more, and resumes his Hiten Mitsurugi training—this time, hopefully, to the end. With the arrivals of both Shinomori Aoshi and Saitô Hajime, the truth of the mad Shishio's plan for Japan is beginning to unveil....

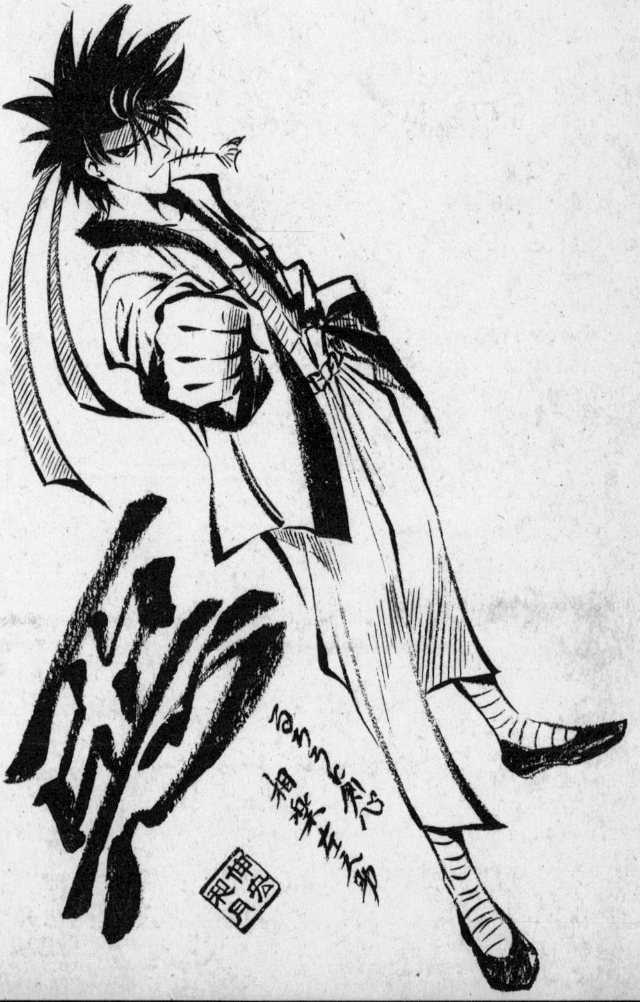

Available in February 2005